D0205935

NUCLEAR WEAPONS AND LAW

NUCLEAR WEAPONS AND LAW

Edited by
ARTHUR SELWYN MILLER
and
MARTIN FEINRIDER

Contributions in Legal Studies, Number 31

GREENWOOD PRESS
Westport, Connecticut • London, England

Library of Congress Cataloging in Publication Data
Main entry under title:

Nuclear weapons and law.

(Contributions in legal studies, ISSN 0147-1074 ;
no. 31)
   Includes bibliographical references and index.
   1. Nuclear weapons (International law)   2. United
States—Constitutional law.   I. Miller, Arthur Selwyn,
1917-   . II. Feinrider, Martin.   III. Series.
JX5133.A7N83 1984   341.6'3   84-4482
ISBN 0-313-24206-2 (lib. bdg.)

Library of Congress Catalog Card Number: 84-4482
ISBN: 0-313-24206-2
ISSN: 0147-1074

First published in 1984

Greenwood Press
A division of Congressional Information Service, Inc.
88 Post Road West
Westport, Connecticut 06881

Printed in the United States of America

10   9   8   7   6   5   4   3   2   1

Contents

Preface

A volume such as this could not be compiled without the aid and support provided by several individuals and organizations. Accordingly, we take this opportunity to express our most profound appreciation to all who have contributed to this effort.

Ovid C. Lewis, Professor of Law and Dean of Nova University Center for the Study of Law, provided the inspiration for this volume and, through his support of the Conference on Nuclear Weapons and Law and the work of the *Nova Law Journal,* made our work possible. The staff of Nova Law Center, in particular faculty secretaries Lillian Sartell and Anita Pinser, and word processor operator Jesse Monteagudo, gave us the means to accomplish our tasks and were always there when needed. We thank them, knowing that any expression of appreciation could not match the value of their work to this book.

Among the articles printed here are pieces reprinted with permission from four law journals: *Nova Law Journal*; *McGill Law Journal*; *Brooklyn Journal of International Law*; and, *New York Law School Journal of International and Comparative Law.* We gratefully acknowledge copyright permission provided to us by these journals, and express our appreciation for the dedicated work done by all the student editors and staffs that worked on these nuclear weapons symposium issues. In particular, we would like to thank the following law journal editors: at Nova, Gary Sherman, Shoshanna Ehrlich, and Mary Ava Bobko; at McGill, Stephen J. Toope; at Brooklyn, Veronica Perry and Helen Ostenberg; and, at New York Law School, Anita Zigman.

The American Society of International Law provided financial, moral, and intellectual support for the Conference on Nuclear Weapons and Law held at Nova Law Center on February 5, 1983. Out of the Conference, which was a regional meeting of the Society, grew several of the articles printed here. For this we are indebted, particularly to the Society's Administrative Director, Judy Hall.

We received special inspiration for this volume from the work of Elliott L. (Lee) Meyrowitz and the Lawyers' Committee on Nuclear Policy.

Meyrowitz, as vice-chair of the Committee, has probably done more than anyone else in the United States to provoke thought and scholarship on the question of nuclear illegality, and we thank him.

For invaluable assistance in tracking down and obtaining the wide assortment of obscure materials we needed for our own research and for the footnoting of others' articles, we thank the staff of the Nova Law Center Law Library, in particular Patricia Harris and Nicki Singleton, and the Library's Director, Professor Carol Roehrenbeck.

We are also deeply appreciative of the work put into this book by Ed Petkevis, a second-year law student and Goodwin Research Fellow at Nova Law Center. As research assistant to Professor Feinrider for the 1983-84 academic year, he worked countless hours on the manuscripts and notes that appear herein, always doing a first-rate job, and we warmly acknowledge his contribution.

And, finally, and perhaps most importantly of all, we acknowledge our moral and intellectual debt to the millions of so-called ordinary citizens in the United States and all over the world, including the Soviet Union, who have variously taken to the streets, written their governmental leaders, argued with their neighbors, taught their children, pleaded for sanity, and in countless other ways prompted members of the legal profession to turn their special talents to the question of nuclear illegality.

Arthur S. Miller
Martin Feinrider

Introduction:
On the Relevance of Law
to Nuclear Weapons

Arthur Selwyn Miller and Martin Feinrider

Since the first primitive atomic bombs all but obliterated Hiroshima and Nagasaki in 1945, few lawyers have questioned the doctrine that a nation-state at war may employ such weapons in its absolute discretion. The time has come—indeed, it is long past due—to examine this doctrine critically under the precepts of both international and constitutional law. This volume is the first effort to present a rounded critique of the conventional wisdom about the legality of nuclear weapons.

In large part, the several essays published here are forays into legal *terra incognita*. Those who question the legality of the manufacture, storage, deployment, and possible—some say likely—use of nuclear bombs, are responding to Albert Einstein's oft-quoted challenge: "The unleashed power of the atom has changed everything save our modes of thinking, and we thus drift toward unparalleled catastrophe." Even those who doubt that law can have much, if any, efficacy in dealing with nuclear weapons agree with the others, and inferentially with Einstein, that change must come in "our modes of thinking" if the human race is to survive.

It is, of course, quite easy to dispute the idea that law has anything meaningful to say about the nuclear peril. The immediate objection, noted in some of the essays in this volume, is that there is no precedent for law controlling such terrible weapons without the explicit consent of the states possessing them. There is no existing law on the subject, they say. (Some of the authors argue that there *is* law on the subject, particularly those writing in the international law field who cite the principles of law recognized by nations, the U.N. Charter, the Geneva Conventions of 1949 on the law of war, and other treaties.) The argument about lack of precedent, which common lawyers see as basic to the very idea of law, is only seemingly valid. In the last analysis, *stare decisis,* taken to its illogical conclusion, merely says that nothing should ever be done for the first time. The history of law is to the contrary; it is one of growth, of the adaptation of legal precepts and principles to new factual situations, and of the creation of new principles as required. Just as at Nuremberg, when the Allied powers had to face the defense argument of the Nazi war criminals that there was no law under which they could be brought to the bar of justice, so it is with the nuclear question. If, as Robert J. Jackson, America's prosecutor at Nuremberg, said, no law existed to punish the Nazis, then it was time to make some law.

So it is here: It is time to use the law we now have to make some law about nuclear weapons, law in both an interdictory and an instrumental sense. Governmental officers the world over should be made to see, and in seeing to act appropriately, that the madness of the nuclear arms race is a crime against all humanity, against civilization itself. The very existence of nuclear arms presents the greatest peril faced by *Homo sapiens* in known history. Surely legal thought is not so impoverished as to force the conclusion that law is impotent in such circumstances. People the world over are becoming more and more exasperated with the governmental leaders' inability or refusal to take measures adequate to deal with the growing threat. International and constitutional lawyers who cannot or do not effect law ensuring survival will fare no better in the popular judgment. Strangely, it appears to us, the global citizenry seems to understand that which government leaders and military strategists desperately avoid acknowledging: there will be no such thing as a limited nuclear war. Sooner or later, such a conflict would escalate into an all-out nuclear conflagration. The meaning, if that came about, is that the living, should there be any, would surely envy the dead.

While no doubt law has limits as a principle of social order, by no means must it be completely ineffective. Law can join with other, and possibly more efficacious forms of social control to help influence or possibly direct the future. Those who care about the fate of the earth and of the species upon it—and only saints and fools do not—will do well to ponder the question of what means of social control can best be employed to halt the nuclear madness. That is what the contributors to this volume undertake to do.

Law has always been more than merely a set of interdictory rules. Instead of a body of fixed, pre-existing principles inhabiting a heaven of legal concepts, law is goal-seeking, purposive, a type of human activity that exists for an identifiable end: the betterment of the human condition. That has not always been recognized. For example, the French social critic Bertrand de Jouvenel missed the mark when, believing that "nomocracy is the supremacy of law; telocracy is the supremacy of purpose," he maintained that "[i]ndividual security is assured if the citizens are not exposed to arbitrary acts of the government, but only to the application of the law, which they know." True enough, protection against arbitrary governmental acts is essential; but that is itself a purposive statement. It can and should be read affirmatively as well as negatively. In other words, limiting government arbitrariness, whether as policeman or nuclear warmaker, can affirmatively promote human values; faithfully obeying rules that permit unconscionable but non-arbitrary government behavior, on the other hand, serves no useful end.

Rules have always been more *a posteriori* than *a priori,* while basic concepts such as fundamental human rights are essentially durable in nature, tending toward being timeless. Between the two are the mundane day-to-day operative principles of functioning legal systems, which, however, usually have a remarkably short existence; as embodied in positive law, they essentially legitimize accommodations and compromises made in society. They have always been, in theory, subject to change, and indeed often did change as societal conditions were altered. History teaches us, though, that when law becomes so immutable that it is just enforced "rules" set in stone, incapable of adjusting to new and often dangerous realities, or "principles" uncritically invoked as shibboleths, the society which that law seeks to organize is surely doomed.

Extraordinary conditions call for extraordinary actions. Though we cannot escape the past, the future is no mere predetermined extension of what occurred in yesteryear. We can affect our own future, maybe.

The cultivation and proliferation of nuclear weapons has led not only Americans but all of humankind into a fearsome trap. The proposition, therefore, that law has an enduring relevance to the problem of nuclear weapons should be obvious. Sooner or later, in some form or another, law must be brought to bear upon the ultimate peril, or that peril will surely be realized. That is the reason for publication of this volume. Even though, as Andre Glucksmann has pointed out, reciprocal terror characterized Western culture long before nuclear weapons were even thought of, the existence of these weapons has created an entirely new situation, an entirely new level of reciprocal terror. Civilization itself is in danger.

The meaning is—at least, should be—clear: time-honored principles of governmental behavior must be re-examined. Political leaders no longer can ensure the survival of the state, or of the populace, should nuclear war break out. Accordingly, nuclear weapons must be eliminated. Just as Western liberal democracies have limited the state as ultimate repository of the police power, the state must be limited in its behavior as the ultimate repository of nuclear war-making power.

This book has three parts. One deals with international law applicable to nuclear weapons; a second is concerned with the (American) constitutional law dimension; and the third inquires briefly into the medical and environmental aspects of the mounting peril. As should be expected from the nature of such a novel and controversial subject matter, there is considerable disagreement among the authors. The unifying thread is a deepseated concern that humankind may well be on the edge of the abyss.

Agreement, of course, is not the question. Rather, it is how to advance the debate upon the propriety of nuclear weapons in the world today. That question, as Samuel Johnson remarked in a different context, is one that should concentrate any person's mind "wonderfully." Lawyers and political scientists join in the endeavor to confront the nuclear problem as relative late-comers. Already in the field are groups of scientists and of physicians: the Union of Concerned Scientists and Physicians for Social Responsibility being examples. These groups, and others, have done much to pave the way for creative thinking about applicable legal norms. The scientists are fully aware of what nuclear bombs can do, the destruction they can wreak; and the physicians know full well that prevention is indicated because medical treatment of the victims of nuclear war is simply not possible.

The law, as Chief Justice Earl Warren once said, "floats in a sea of ethics." Nuclear warfare is an ethical, a moral problem, the resolution of which can and should be translated into legal principles. Professor Ronald Dworkin has maintained that "our constitutional system rests on a particular moral theory, namely, that men have moral rights against the state." That they do. And if international law is taken to be, as it should, the nascent constitutional framework for the world community, then those moral rights run not only against the state (singular) but also against states (plural). The risks raised by nuclear weapons are not of the type that any responsible government, of whatever ideology, places on its citizens or on the citizens of other nations, or that any legal system should allow to be so placed.

International law provides a reasonably familiar, if as yet nondeterminative context within which to discuss the question of nuclear weapon illegality. Marked, as always, for its lack of an institutionalized enforcement mechanism, international law, as revealed by the essays in Part I, finds itself locked in a dialectical relationship with deterrence theory, that self-justifying reciprocal paranoia that makes this volume possible and necessary. Though recognizing the absence of a specific conventional prohibition of nuclear weapons, most of the international law contributors have little difficulty drawing upon treaties and international custom to stake out a normative field that brings us, rather persuasively, to the conclusion that most uses of nuclear weapons are illegal and that seemingly even the mere possession of nuclear weapons is not justifiable. This normative aspect appears, however, to be the easier part of the task.

Several of the contributors remind us, clearly without joy, that mere moral injunction is of little use when stacked up against the weapons of the United States and the Soviet Union, and against the all-too-often justifiable fear each superpower has of the other. They suggest that *realpolitik* and state practice reveal the impotence of the international community in the face of an insistent bipolar reality, an impotence they believe likely to continue even if substantial agreement on nuclear illegality were reached among nations. Whether we like it or not, they argue, a multipolar world is not yet sufficiently developed to enforce its law on states absent their consent. The fundamental contradiction of international law, that states are the creators of the law as well as its subjects, thus provides the theme for Part I: are nuclear weapons illegal under international law?; and, if they are illegal, so what?

In contrast to the freedom claimed by the nuclear-equipped superpowers under the international law concept of state sovereignty, the concept of constitutionalism has historically meant that governments were to be limited in what they could do. In the United States, the Bill of Rights and the Civil War amendments are the primary examples of such limits on official power. There is, of course, nothing expressly stated in the Constitution about nuclear weapons—nor, indeed, about weapons of any type. Choice of what tools to use in war has always been peculiarly a prerogative of Congress and the Executive working together.

The advent of nuclear bombs has so changed the milieu in which constitutional institutions operate that what has been taken for granted since the beginnings must be rethought. Are there limits, if not in the Constitution itself, then in the notions of constitutionalism that bear directly upon the nuclear peril? That is the question explored by the several essays in Part II. Quite obviously, the authors differ, both in conclusions and in approach. Some considered the question to be a mere technical legal problem, one that is easily and quickly answered. Others take a broader approach. The wide differences of opinion that are set forth in these essays are the first attempt to explore the constitutional aspects of nuclear weaponry. They should be read as tentative probes into a constitutional no-man's land. Although each essay stands by itself, they were all originally reactions to the views of the senior editor of this volume, as he presented them in the *Nova Law Journal* and at the Conference on Nuclear Weapons and Law held at Nova University Center for the Study of Law on February 5, 1983.

Finally, in Part III, we turn to an environmental expert and a physician to ensure we don't forget that law must be for the living. Faced with the dire consequences they describe as the certain result of nuclear warfare, we, authors and readers alike, ought to pledge renewed effort to the struggle to end the nuclear nightmare. A deterrence justification for American and Soviet nuclear stockpiles is nothing more than circular logic so clearly insane that even its proponents shudder to think of a world perpetually trapped in it.

No one likes nuclear weapons, thinks they better the human existence, or should be used. Can't we get rid of them?; and, can't law be of some help?

Part I
Nuclear Weapons and International Law

1.
Nuclear Weapons and International Law*

Richard B. Bilder**

We would all like nuclear weapons to disappear tomorrow. Most people agree that these weapons are abominable and that no rational society should allow the threat of nuclear holocaust to continue. As international lawyers, we could sit down today and draft the text of a treaty prohibiting the development, possession, deployment, or use of nuclear weapons, providing for the destruction of existing stockpiles, and establishing an international tribunal to impose criminal penalties on individuals, including government officials, violating these rules. If every nation agreed to and complied with this treaty, our problem would be solved.

We all know this isn't likely to happen. The nuclear genie is out of the bottle. There are already over 50,000 of those weapons, knowledge of how to build them will never disappear, and the weapons are continually becoming easier and cheaper to make. Thus, for the foreseeable future, every nation will have to face the prospect that some other state or group may acquire such weapons and be prepared to use them. Public officials are adverse to risks and few of them will be willing to expose their country to nuclear blackmail or destruction. Confronted with this threat—or even the threat of overwhelming attack by conventional arms—many governments will see little choice but to seek a deterrent capability, either through acquiring nuclear weapons itself or alliance with another nation which has them.

The principal means available to nations to defuse and de-escalate this very difficult and dangerous situation is to try to reach international agreements and other normative arrangements providing for the mutual control, reduction, or elimination of nuclear weapons. But in our present international system, international rules, institutions, and arrangements are

---

* This essay is based on remarks delivered at the Conference on Nuclear Weapons and Law held at Nova University Center for the Study of Law on February 5, 1983.
** Professor of Law, University of Wisconsin School of Law.

creatures of the will of states. Unless nations see proposed agreements as in their national interest, they will not accept them. Thus, no matter how moral, sensible, or necessary particular arms control arrangements may seem to those outside government, there will be little chance of governments accepting them unless the proposals seem to officials to meet the national security considerations which constrain their policy decisions.

Our task then is both to come up with good arms control ideas which meet government perceptions of national security and deterrence needs, and also, just as important, to help establish a more favorable climate of international relations and official and public opinion in which government perceptions of national security requirements become less demanding and more flexible.

What has been accomplished thus far?

At the least, there is now an almost universal consensus that general nuclear war would constitute a global catastrophe, threatening the survival of civilization and perhaps of all humanity. Few people defend the possession or use of nuclear weapons on any grounds other than deterrence. There is wide agreement that, to the extent national security permits, everything possible must be done to control these weapons.

Moreover, nations have reached a number of international agreements which constrain the development, possession, deployment, and use of nuclear weapons in a variety of ways. For example:

—International law, as embodied in the U.N. Charter, now prohibits the aggressive threat or use of force by one state against another, by any means, including nuclear weapons. This means that the "first use" of nuclear weapons for aggressive, as contrasted with defensive purposes, is already internationally prohibited. Moreover, the Charter establishes a framework and procedure under which the international community can, if it chooses, collectively respond to nuclear or any other form of aggression.

—The Non-Proliferation Treaty and other arrangements establish rules and procedures which have helped to contain or at least delay the further spread of nuclear weapons to nations not now having them.

—We have reached a variety of treaties prohibiting the deployment or use of nuclear weapons in particular areas or environments, such as Antarctica, Latin America, the seabeds outside territorial limits, and outer space. Proposals have been advanced for the establishment of other nuclear-free zones.

—The widely accepted Limited Test Ban Treaty prohibits the testing of nuclear weapons in the atmosphere, underwater, or in outer space. We have negotiated, but not yet made effective, treaties which would limit even underground tests to low levels, and have largely completed the technical drafting of a Comprehensive Test Ban Treaty which would, if completed and accepted, ban all nuclear tests.

—The United States and Soviet Union have negotiated and continue to observe a number of agreements such as SALT I and SALT II, which place at least some limits on the numbers and types of their weapons and attempt to reduce the risks of accidental nuclear war. They are presently engaged in negotiations purportedly aimed at more far-reaching agreements.

Obviously these agreements, by themselves, establish only a partial, patchwork quilt of legal regulation of nuclear weapons. None of them expressly prohibits the possession or use of such weapons by the nuclear nations. Moreover, there are gaps and weaknesses in many of the agreements; for example, important states have failed to join in some of them. Cynics argue that the nuclear states have been willing to accept these agreements only because they place few restrictions on the nuclear states' freedom to develop, deploy, or use their weapons as they believe their national security interests require. Nevertheless, this framework shows a growing international commitment to the norm of nuclear limitation and control and shows that, where national security interests can be met, agreement is possible.

This is the legal state of play viewed by the nuclear powers. But some lawyers take the more far-reaching position that nuclear weapons are now illegal *per se* under international law and that consequently the development, possession, deployment, or use of these weapons is already prohibited. Let me briefly summarize the arguments *pro* and *con* as I understand them.

Those who argue that nuclear weapons are now illegal base their case on a variety of widely accepted treaties and principles of customary international law dealing primarily with the humanitarian laws of war and the protection of human rights. These rules, for example, require combatants to protect civilians and avoid attacking non-military targets, bar the use of weapons likely to inflict indiscriminate and disproportionate damage or cause needless suffering, prohibit genocide, and require governments to respect human life and dignity. The proponents argue that the use of nuclear weapons would inevitably involve massive violations of these fundamental rules of war and of human rights. As further evidence of an international consensus barring such weapons, they point to a number of recent U.N. General Assembly resolutions expressly declaring nuclear weapons illegal and their use criminal. More broadly, they suggest that nuclear weapons should be viewed as inherently illegal since nuclear war is inconsistent with the fundamental values of human dignity and organized society upon which international law itself rests; a rational civilized society cannot accept as legitimate weapons which are likely to destroy it.

Those who disagree with this position argue that, while nations may ultimately agree to prohibit nuclear weapons totally, they have not yet done so. In their view, international law rests solely on state consent; there is no "natural" international law. And to date, the nuclear states have never agreed either explicitly by treaty or implicitly through conduct evidencing customary international law that their possession or use of nuclear weapons—at least for defensive or deterrent purposes—is in itself illegal. On the contrary, existing treaties placing certain restrictions on nuclear weapons explicitly or implicitly recognize that, except as so limited by treaty, the possession and use of nuclear weapons is permitted. Attempts to stretch older treaties dealing with conventional weapons to cover the very different situation created by the recent development of nuclear weapons are not realistic and go beyond what nations agreed to or intended in these treaties. Nor can General Assembly resolutions, which are not legally binding and to which the nuclear states in any event have not agreed, be regarded as establishing rules affecting such states. They argue, in sum, that it is unpersuasive to contend that nuclear weapons are illegal *per se* when all of the nuclear states, which are the principal actors in the international community, reject this position and rely on such weapons for their national security. Thus, the U.S. position, as reflected in its military manuals, apparently continues to be:

> There is at present no rule of international law expressly prohibiting a state from the use of nuclear weapons in warfare. In the absence of any express prohibition, the use of such weapons against enemy combatants or other military objectives is permitted.[1]

In my opinion, the argument that nuclear weapons are now illegal *per se* is very questionable, and I think it is unlikely that any international court would support this position. The arguments the other way seem to me more persuasive. Moreover, as a practical matter, I doubt that the illegality argument will be taken seriously by any of the nuclear powers, directly affect their behavior, or significantly influence or advance arms control negotiations. Indeed, if nuclear weapons are clearly illegal, it is not easy to explain to people why we need to continue working so hard, and with only limited success, to achieve other less far-reaching legal agreements.

But it may be less important to ask whether an international court would accept the argument that nuclear weapons are now illegal than to recognize some very useful functions the argument performs. Certainly, it raises the crucial moral issue of nuclear weapons—the deep and pervasive inconsistency between these weapons and all that civilized society has long struggled for in terms of humanitarian ideals, individual human dignity, a rational world order, and indeed human survival. It reinforces and serves as a rallying point for the growing normative consensus and pressure against the weapons' legitimacy. It forcefully demonstrates the relevance of the traditional humanitarian laws of war to nuclear weapons and shows that there *are* existing norms at least *limiting* the ways in which such weapons can legitimately be used. Thus, so long as the illegality argument supplements rather than diverts our efforts to develop new agreements and approaches, it can certainly help to develop broader public awareness of the issue of the legitimacy of such weapons and help to shape a moral consensus against them.

In any event, however one comes out on the present illegality issue, it is clear that many additional measures will be needed if we are to make progress in stopping the arms race, stabilizing deterrence, and reducing proliferation. Our agenda might include:

—firm commitments to continue adherence to SALT I and II limits;

—serious START and European weapons negotiations;

—ratification of the Threshold Test Ban Treaty;

—completion and ratification of the Comprehensive Test Ban Treaty;

—an agreement barring anti-satellite systems and the development of weapons in outer space;

—a no-first-use agreement;

—further agreements to avoid the risks of accidental war or to prevent a limited nuclear exchange from escalating;

—further agreements to reduce nuclear proliferation and to establish additional nuclear free zones; and,

—agreements prohibiting enhanced radiation or radiological weapons.

But, unfortunately, at the moment, we don't seem to be getting very far toward achieving such agreements.

Why haven't we been able to make more progress? What are the obstacles?

One problem is that it isn't clear that either the United States or the Soviet Union is serious about controlling nuclear weapons. Each may still believe that it can "win" an arms race or even an eventual nuclear confrontation. Some U.S. strategists seem to think that superior U.S. economic resources will permit us ultimately to wear down the Soviets, forcing them to accept a position of nuclear inferiority. The Soviets believe that, if they are patient, anti-nuclear public sentiment in the West will create political pressures for a slackening of its nuclear arms efforts, leaving the Soviets, free of such pressures, with superiority. A variety of pressures in each country—such as the relentless desire of the military for more and better arms, economic interests of armaments industries and workers, automatic deference to the assumed expertise of the nuclear strategy bureaucracy, fascination with high technology, a fear by politicians and officials of being seen as too "soft" or of taking risks with national security—all create a powerful inertia impeding efforts to halt the nuclear arms race. The "bargaining chip" theory—that the other side won't seriously negotiate arms control unless you demonstrate that you are prepared to match or exceed their level of armament—further fuels the fire. Long and discouraging experience with

U.S.-Soviet arms control negotiations led recent Nobel Laureate Alva Myrdal to label them a sham—a "game of disarmament."

Another problem is each nation's worry that the other may somehow turn out to have "won"—or at least seem to have "won"—a particular arms control negotiation. This is hardly surprising since, given the complexities of nuclear weapons and the uncertainties and imponderables of nuclear deterrence theory, it is very hard to say how one can measure the ultimate balance of any agreement. This has led to continuing debates as to who's ahead now, the comparative vulnerabilities and deterrent effect of different kinds of weapons used for different purposes in different situations, how the other side is likely to perceive or react to different arms control configurations, and so forth. Each government is afraid to take responsibility for an agreement which involves so much uncertainty and which political opponents or the public may later say was a mistake. The tendency on each side will be to play it safe by demanding clearly favorable terms, which, of course, will be unlikely to be acceptable to the other side.

A third problem is that the United States and the Soviet Union—and other nations involved in arms control negotiations—don't trust each other. Each is afraid that the other might cheat. On the U.S. side, the concern that "You can't trust the Russians" results in an insistence on ever more stringent verification measures to ensure compliance. But, at least in a number of arms control contexts, it is very difficult to devise practical verification techniques which can make it *absolutely* certain that the other side won't cheat. And demands for certain kinds of verification measures, such as on-site inspection, may involve intrusions into other societies which are politically unacceptable. Thus, the difficulty of agreeing on mutually acceptable verification measures has often proved an insuperable obstacle on which arms control negotiations have foundered.

How can we overcome these obstacles? What kinds of conditions are necessary to achieve more effective nuclear arms control and what can we do to foster these conditions?

Certainly, international lawyers have a special responsibility in this regard. We understand how norms help to control government behavior. We are experts in the process of international agreement and cooperation and can help government to find ways of better structuring arms control agreements and resolving negotiating problems. We can help explain many of the issues to the public. But much that needs to be done transcends issues of law.

First, we have to keep the arms control process going. Even if particular agreements are unattainable at present, nations have to continue talking, trying to work out at least the framework and technical details of measures that might one day be possible. If we keep nibbling away, we will be in a position to seize opportunities when they come.

Second, we have to continue building a widespread global consensus, among people everywhere, that nuclear weapons are immoral and illegitimate. The non-nuclear states, in the U.N. and other international forums, should continue to condemn these weapons and demand their prohibition. Professional, religious, and other groups must keep hammering at the point that these weapons are wrong. If enough governments and peoples say that these weapons are wrong, it will be increasingly difficult for the governments of nuclear states to continue to defend their legitimacy.

Third, people in the nuclear states themselves must really want nuclear arms control. Certainly the easiest and least risky course for most governments is simply to continue to acquire weapons. Unless there is strong public pressure and support for arms control, governments are unlikely to undertake the risks and work of seeking and reaching agreements.

This means broader efforts to educate the public and to mobilize politically in support of arms control objectives. But the American and Soviet peoples are clearly ambivalent; many of them are uncomfortable with nuclear weapons, but most of them want deterrence and nuclear security. So we have to find ways to persuade the broad mass of people in these states that nuclear wars aren't ''winnable,'' that continuing the arms race is a prescription for disaster, and that it's worth running the risks and cost of arms control agreements to avoid the greater risks of nuclear holocaust. And we have to find ways to translate such beliefs into effective political action so as to ensure that people who understand these things are running our governments.

Certainly, public awareness and political action have increased dramatically in the United States and Western Europe in the last few years. But we must recognize that this has not occurred in the Soviet Union and is not likely to occur in other authoritarian societies. The Russian people are probably as frightened and tired of living with the bomb as we are, but the chances of their exerting effective pressure on their leaders seem remote. Certainly this makes our task more difficult.

Fourth, we have to try to decrease U.S.-Soviet tensions and build at least some degree of mutual confidence. So long as each country continues to consider and treat the other as the ultimate enemy, it is difficult to see either country taking significant risks for arms control. If each nation really believes that the other is determined to destroy it, what choice does it have but to try to build more and better weapons? Perhaps, as George Kennan suggests, both we and the Russians have to ask ourselves what our differences really are and whether there is any conflict of interest or ideology between us that can possibly be worth our mutual destruction.

Serious arms control negotiations, particularly on no-first-use, are certainly one very good way to try to de-escalate this sense of mutual threat. The Russian and Warsaw Pact governments have recently come forward with a variety of proposals, including a commitment to no-first use. Perhaps these are only a trick. But if the United States is really interested in arms control and diminishing tensions, it should consider these initiatives seriously.

Fifth, we have to think more realistically about risk, trust, and verification. Are the risks of one side "winning" a negotiation or cheating as serious or crucial as governments say? If each country has sufficient forces to destroy the other, does the fact that one ends up with somewhat more weapons really make a difference? If each side has at least some ways of verifying compliance, is it really likely that the other will try to cheat? As international lawyers, we know that there are many reasons why nations are likely to keep their agreements, and that fear of being caught cheating is not necessarily the most important.

Certainly we should try to devise verification arrangements which can overcome distrust and meet nations' concerns regarding compliance. Perhaps an international verification agency could help. Reasonably adequate and sufficient techniques will often be possible, but no verification technique can guarantee compliance. We should not allow nations to use over-stringent verification demands as an excuse. Arms control agreements will inevitably involve some risks, both for us and the Soviets—but, considering the alternative, they may be well worth taking.

Sixth, we have to realize that the problem of nuclear war can't be divorced from the problem of war and conflict more generally. If nuclear weapons are available, nations will be tempted to use them to deter or repel conventional as well as nuclear attack; NATO's nuclear deterrent policy against a Soviet conventional attack in Europe is an example. So our concern with nuclear war must not divert us from continuing urgently to search for ways to control all types of conflict. In particular, we have to give much more serious and urgent attention, and commit more of every kind of resource, to dealing with pervasive global problems that give rise to war—nationalism, ideological differences, economic inequality, injustice, and the denial of human rights. We have to think of what a world without nuclear weapons would be like and make sure that it would, in fact, be a better and safer world.

Finally, we have to ask, as Jonathan Schell and others have, whether a world of nation-states can really have much hope of solving the nuclear dilemma and avoiding nuclear destruction—whether, in a world of nuclear weapons, nationalism and the present international system are simply incompatible with human survival. Surely many of us would like to go back to the Baruch plan and complete international control of the atom—but we probably can't any longer "get there from here." Perhaps, if the chips were down and we really thought it was necessary to avoid a nuclear holocaust, we would be willing to give up quite a lot—in terms of nationalistic prejudices, economic privileges, special political status—to attain a world in which we could live in peace and without fear. We ought, as Louis Sohn, Dick Falk, and others suggest, to begin working out how we could possibly achieve such a world.

Will we be able to achieve agreements effectively controlling or prohibiting nuclear weapons? It is not easy, at this moment, to be optimistic, but it is also certainly too soon to give up. What seems likely is that humanity will be living with the bomb for some time to come. And if effective arms control isn't achieved—and yet we somehow avoid a holocaust—we may face a future in which international lawyers may be dealing with some strange questions. For example, if limited nuclear wars really become likely, might it make sense for nations to agree to more explicit Hague-type rules of war trying at least to limit their consequences? Or, as the dangers of nuclear war continue to mount, nations may be prepared to try even more far-out ways of maintaining deterrence and providing assurance against a first strike—hostage arrangements, doomsday devices, prohibitions on civil defense or on shelters or safe-havens for high military and government officials, or an independent deterrent force under international or perhaps even nongovernmental authority. If nuclear war becomes thinkable, even the most bizarre schemes for trying to avoid it may also become thinkable.

A world in which nuclear arms control has failed and arms races and proliferation continue indefinitely will be a grim and dangerous world at best. We must somehow bring nations to their senses and make sure that our children never have to live in such an absurd world.

NOTE

1. United States Naval Instructions, art. 613 (1955): *see also* Dept. of the Army, Law of Land Warfare 18 (FM 27-10, 1956).

2.
Nuclear Weapons, Global Values and International Law*

Dinesh Khosla**

Professor Bilder has clearly identified the legal arguments on both sides of this issue.[1] Like most legal debate, there is logic in those arguments, and, depending upon the role that one assumes and the values and interests one wishes to serve, both sides appear equally convincing. As a teacher of international law, it was extremely hard for me to avoid the temptation of writing a paper debating the legality of the issue, but I take a slightly different approach here.

I have pointed out, in an earlier paper,[2] the pragmatic character of the decision taken by the International Court of Justice in the Nuclear Test Cases.[3] Cautious pragmatism, I had argued, was a natural outcome of the court's desire not to lose its legitimacy in the eyes of those powerful nations with nuclear capabilities and on whose support the very life of the court may depend. A decision to the contrary, declaring the French nuclear tests illegal, would certainly not have been respected by the French. Further, I believe, through their steadfast and publically maintained silence throughout the history of the case, the other nuclear states, including the United States and Soviet Union, had sent clear signals to the court about what they wanted the outcome to be. It may sound as if I am suggesting the court was a puppet of the big powers. I am not. All I am suggesting is the near impossibility for the International Court of Justice, or any court, for that matter—international or national—reaching a decision that it has reason to believe will not be followed either in content or spirit by the concerned actors. Equality as an underlying principle of American constitutional structure, for example, was not translated and interpreted in a way respectful of black aspirations for humane treatment until recently. How could it have been otherwise without at least some indication of its acceptance by the people in the rest of the social milieu? It is the same kind

* This essay is based on remarks delivered at the Conference on Nuclear Weapons and Law held at Nova University Center for the Study of Law on February 5, 1983.

** Associate Professor, City University of New York Law School at Queens College.

of dilemma that the International Court of Justice was faced with while dealing with the Nuclear Test Cases. I, therefore, agree with Professor Bilder and others who argue that it is unlikely that any international court will support the view that nuclear weapons are illegal, unless and until those nations that now possess them are willing to move away from the impulse to have them.

That acceptance does not, however, lead me to accept that the use of nuclear weapons is legal. To accept this would mean that a law cannot exist without a code or without the authoritative blessings of an institution endowed with the responsibility of creating or interpreting it. If we were to accept that position, what would then happen to custom or the expectations of the community that form the basis of every socially acceptable or aspirationally legitimate law? To take that position would also imply denying value to all the relevant declarations and treaties, such as the Treaty Banning Nuclear Tests in the Atmosphere, in Outer Space and Under Water (1963), the Treaty on The Non-Proliferation of Nuclear Weapons (1970), General Assembly Resolution 2032 (XX) on the Urgent Need for Suspension of Nuclear and Thermonuclear Tests (1965), etc. It would mean discarding them as insufficient indicators of the preferences and values of the majority of international actors. Some may argue that some of these declarations in the United Nations, and other agency forums, are not law but at best good faith efforts to sow seeds for the legal plant which might eventually bear non-nuclear flowers. That argument would be convincing provided one believes in the non-binding nature of General Assembly resolutions and declarations of other United Nations forums and views these treaties as having only a very limited scope. I do not necessarily share that view as it seems to disrespect fundamental principles of democracy, and views these treaties in a very narrow sense. Further, to accept Professor Bilder's view, that the power elites in an ideologically divided world have no choice but to seek a deterrent capability through nuclear weapons, would amount to accepting that it is a world of nations belonging to camps run and managed by the superpowers exclusively for their own ends. It would not only amount to denying the interests of over one hundred nations who belong to the camp of non-aligned nations but also to disenfranchising them in the constitutive process of international law. Further, it would amount to granting the power to make international law to national elites of those societies which have nuclear capabilities, at an enormous cost to the millions of citizens of those societies now engaged in anti-nuclear social movements. One may pause and ask, since when have the processes of disenfranchising societies and peoples been accepted as legitimate and morally justifiable?

There is yet another way of looking at the entire picture. A relatively more responsive and responsibility-oriented impulse would argue that law, whether concretized or in its conception stages, should not be divorced from its broad moral and social contours and that we should not leave the decision-making process in fewer hands—hands that are likely to make such laws that are subservient to the needs of the present power distribution in the global arena. That subservience to a given social structure or global order might not be perceived as unacceptable if the social structure and global order were just, which I don't believe it is, and, if it served the broadly shared common needs of the global population, which I also believe it does not. Thus, efforts at narrow definitions of legality seem to me to be a trivial exercise. This is true in particular in a situation where we claim to recognize political and social necessities and to respect moral and ethical needs of people and of global society.

Having made that statement, I would next ask a simple question. Do nuclear weapons serve any legitimate social and political function; do they help us to define moral principles on which to build a global society of peace and international brotherhood? If the answer to these questions is yes, then one might be able to pronounce favorably on the status of nuclear weapons and declare them as legitimate for our needs.

It is argued by some scholars and political leaders that the most important function nuclear weapons or any weapons systems serve is deterrence—that is, helping keep the aggressors in their proper place, whatever that place may be. Needless to say, this line of argument supports the preservation of the sovereign state system (a very legitimate function) and is very hard to rebut because of the nationalist interests and the interests of survival. I do not rebut the argument because it is a very important element of the given structure of power relationships in the global arena. But, let me raise a few questions aimed at rescuing the state from being drowned in the sea of survivalist mentality. Let us consider a few issues that might help us compel the state to reintegrate, in its functioning and in its very existence, the very moral and philosophical reasons that justify its existence without necessarily sacrificing the needs of deterrence. Deterrence for what, and at what cost? Could it be achieved by conventional weapons which may be relatively more compatible with the necessity and proportionality tests of the laws of war? How moral or legal is it to achieve that deterrence by holding the population of the perceived aggressor as hostage or letting them do that to our own population? How acceptable is it to live with a constant threat of nuclear annihilation, either by accident or by design? How compatible is deterrence strategy with the fundamental principles of human dignity, human rights, and human development to which we claim to be so committed? To what extent is the environment of psychological fear of mass indiscriminate destruction of human and ecological systems detrimental to our very being and to the development of a humane, compassionate, and rational society? To what extent has that fear contributed to our carelessness and the neglect of the values respectful of human life, and with what political and social consequences?

Let me raise yet another question. What about our unstated, yet implied and most cherished promise to mankind that thou shall not live in fear so that you may maximize the human potential of your creativity? Further, even if my notions about the existence of a state of constant fear were to be discarded as unscientific or pseudopsychological hysteria, or, if we were to be convinced that human beings have enormous abilities to internalize or avoid fear and thus to continue to function as normal beings, one might still ask a further question. Should we, and if yes, how can we get around the means and ends debate, the fundamental debate with which we all have to struggle, all the time, in a civilization where division between self and roles creates an enormous dilemma for each of us? And, finally, even assuming that deterrence theory is valid in the non-utopian reality within which we live, what about the risk of nuclear accident and its consequences within our own territory? One may ponder and ask, haven't we in our excessive preoccupation with deterrence and increased reliance on weapons of mass destruction of both human and ecological systems, created an environment wherein the fear of our protectors, our own state system, our own government, our own leaders, has become equal to, if not more important than the fear of our adversaries? To sum up, haven't we become our own worst enemies, and if yes, hasn't the state lost the very moral and philosophical rationale for its existence by taking the course to nuclear weapons? Suddenly, in the face of these questions, the debate on the legality of nuclear weapons seems to me to be meaningless. I believe that if we start asking some of these questions of ourselves, we might get a broader and clearer picture—perhaps a picture of a world not sitting on the atom bomb.

There is yet another issue that has surfaced several times during the debate on nuclear legality. What is the role of international law and lawyers on the issue of nuclear weapons? I swing from one extreme to the other in my process of understanding our role as a lawyer. Sometimes I speak with great cynicism and sometimes I speak with the great hope that we can change the world. I don't have any answer; I haven't found the synthesis. But, I completely agree with Professor Bilder when he says that much that needs to be done transcends issues of law. The fundamental problems that we face as a civilization are the fundamental problems of taking responsibility and assuming the risks that are involved therein, and the fundamental problems of building trust in a world turned against itself. We live in a world in which approximately two billion humans starve while we spend billions for deterrence. How ironic! We can't fight hunger and disease, but we can fight each other and destroy each other forty times over! These two fundamental problems of taking responsibility and assuming risk are not only the problems of the international actors in their relationships with each other, but of human society as a whole. It may not be wrong to say that taking responsibility and building trust are the operative principles of the utopian world, which is not yet in existence. But, history is replete with examples where people have taken responsibility and risks and have succeeded in creating an enormous amount of trust. I do not know what consequences there would be if only we were willing to take the risk of unilateral disarmament.

There are no quick fixes or prescriptions for resolving these problems. One possible source of strength for resolving these two fundamental problems may be found in the clearly observable trend of growing global consensus around values of human and environmental rights and the increasing awareness of the delicate nature of global economic interdependence. This growing consensus and awareness among the ultimate participants and beneficiaries of the international constitutive process cuts across most, if not all, of the man-made and man-perceived boundaries—the boundaries of state, ideology, race, and religion. Maybe we can take the clue from that. This trend indicates to me the beginnings of the realization of the idea of the universe as a family, an idea spelled out thousands of years ago by an Indian philosopher and dreamer. In this trend lie the seeds of hope. Of course, it will require that we, as international lawyers, start re-evaluating our notions and our commitments to the idea of the state and eventually to the very rationale for nuclear weapons.

NOTES

1. *See* Bilder, Nuclear Weapons and International Law *in* Nuclear Weapons and Law (A. S. Miller & M. Feinrider eds. 1984).

2. Khosla, Nuclear Test Cases: Judicial Valour v. Judicial Discretion, 18 Indian J. Int'l L. 322 (1978).

3. The Nuclear Tests Cases (Australia & New Zealand v. France) I.C.J. [1974].

3.
The Laws of War and Nuclear Weapons*

Elliott L. Meyrowitz**

With the bombing of Hiroshima and Nagasaki, the world witnessed the use of a weapon unprecedented in its destructive power.[1] The development and eventual use of those atomic bombs irrevocably changed the nature and objective of war.[2] Since 1945, humanity has lived on the edge of a precipice, with human history literally hanging in the balance. Indeed, today's nuclear weapons arsenals have the distinct potential for annihilating a substantial portion of the earth's population, devastating and contaminating vast areas of the earth's surface and producing unpredictable and uncontrollable biological and environmental consequences — all of which could occur within a matter of minutes.[3]

In this "nuclear age," more than any other time in history, the civilian population has become directly and indirectly the primary object of destruction.[4] While the effects of war have always fallen to some degree upon civilians, it is the magnitude of the destruction of the civilian population during a nuclear war that overwhelms the senses.[5] Yet, the indiscriminately destruc-

---

* Reprinted, with permission, from the *Brooklyn Journal of International Law,* Volume 9, Number 2 (1983).

** Adjunct Professor of Law, Benjamin N. Cardozo School of Law of Yeshiva University; Vice-Chairperson, Lawyers' Committee on Nuclear Policy. An earlier version of this article was presented at the 1981 Annual Meeting of the American Society of International Law.

1. For a comprehensive account of the destructive impact of atomic weaponry, *see* COMMITTEE FOR THE COMPILATION OF MATERIALS ON DAMAGE CAUSED BY THE ATOMIC BOMBS IN HIROSHIMA AND NAGASAKI, HIROSHIMA AND NAGASAKI: THE PHYSICAL, MEDICAL AND SOCIAL EFFECTS OF THE ATOMIC BOMBINGS (1981).

2. During the nineteenth century, there developed a school of thought which believed that the increasing destructiveness of weapons would bring an end to war. The paradox is that quite the opposite has occurred. On this point, *see* Roling, *Arms Control, Disarmament and Small Countries,* 31 IMPACT 97 (1981) and Smith, *Modern Weapons and Modern War,* THE Y.B. OF WORLD AFFAIRS 224-25 (1955); *See also* M. WALZER, JUST AND UNJUST WARS (1977).

3. For an excellent assessment of the possible human and ecological consequences of nuclear war, *see* ROYAL SWEDISH ACADEMY OF SCIENCES, *Nuclear War: The Aftermath,* 11 AMBIO 76 (1982).

4. For a discussion whether the protection of civilians is consistent with "total war", *see* Roling, *The Significance of the Laws of War,* CURRENT PROBLEMS OF INTERNATIONAL LAW: ESSAYS ON U.N. LAW AND ON THE LAW OF ARMED CONFLICT 142-44 (A. Cassese ed. 1975). *See also* J. MOORE, INTERNATIONAL LAW AND SOME CURRENT ILLUSIONS AND OTHER ESSAYS 1-15 (1924).

5. For an analysis of the effects of a full range of nuclear attacks, *see* OFFICE OF

tive nature of nuclear weapons flies in the face of the traditional function of the laws of war, which is to set limits on the conduct of war.[6] This traditional function has been controversial because of the readiness and willingness of military and political leaders to use weapons and tactics that are militarily decisive regardless of legal consequences. It is this tension between legal restraint and military necessity that has reached its outer limit with the advent of the nuclear age. Consequently, now, when frequent predictions of nuclear war are being made, it is time to consider whether the contemplated uses of nuclear weapons are consistent with international law.[7]

THE LEGAL SILENCE

Since 1945, the legitimacy of nuclear weapons as an instrument of statecraft has not been questioned in a serious way by the American legal community.[8] In recent years, this momentous topic has received virtually no attention. In some respects, this neglect is ironic. Only a few years after the bombing of Hiroshima and Nagasaki, the American legal community played a very important role in the legal developments at Nuremberg.[9]

TECHNOLOGICAL ASSESSMENT OF THE CONGRESS OF THE UNITED STATES, THE EFFECTS OF NUCLEAR WAR. For an analysis of the environmental impact of nuclear weapons, see, STOCKHOLM INTERNATIONAL PEACE RESEARCH INSTITUTE, WEAPONS OF MASS DESTRUCTION AND THE ENVIRONMENT 2-30 (1977).

6. M. GREENSPAN, THE MODERN LAW OF LAND WARFARE 371 (1959).

7. For recent studies on this question, see Falk, Meyrowitz, & Sanderson, Nuclear Weapons and International Law, 20 I.J.I.L. 541 (1980); Weston, Nuclear Weapons Versus International Law: A Contextual Reassessment, 28 McGILL L.J. 542 (1983)(Forthcoming); M. GRAUBARD, THE INTERNATIONAL LAW OF ARMED CONFLICT: IMPLICATIONS FOR THE CONCEPT OF ASSURED DESTRUCTION (1982).

8. Among early exceptions, see G. SCHWARZENBERGER, THE LEGALITY OF NUCLEAR WEAPONS (1958); N. SINGH, NUCLEAR WEAPONS AND INTERNATIONAL LAW (1959); Brownlie, Some Legal Aspects of the Use of Nuclear Weapons, 14 INT'L & COMP. L.Q. 437 (1965); Meyrowitz, Les Juristes Devant L'Harme Nucleaire, 67 REVUE GÉNÉRALE DE DROIT INTERNATIONAL PUBLIC 820 (1963). For discussions of the legality of nuclear weapons, see Bright, Nuclear Weapons as a Lawful Means of Warfare, 30 MIL. L. REV. 1 (1965); McDougal & Feliciano, International Coercion and World Public Order: The General Principles of the Law of War, 67 YALE L. J. 771 (1958); O'Brien, The Meaning of Military Necessity in International Law, 1 Y. B. WORLD POLITY 109 (1957); O'Brien, Some Problems of the Law of War in Limited Nuclear War, 14 MIL. L. REV. 1 (1961); McDougal & Schlei, The Hydrogen Bomb Tests and Perspective, 64 YALE L. J. 649, 689-90 (1955). For a discussion of the Soviet views on international law and nuclear weapons, see Maggs, The Soviet Viewpoint on Nuclear Weapons and International Law, 29 LAW & CONTEMP. PROBS. 956, 957-60 (1964).

9. For a listing of American lawyers who participated in the war-crime trials and a discussion of the views of the American legal community on the Nuremberg Trials, see

From the beginning, however, almost nothing was done to incorporate into the laws of war an authoritative prohibition on the use of nuclear weapons. How do we explain this reticence? A partial explanation can be found in the events immediately following the bombing of Hiroshima and Nagasaki.

The use of atomic bombs is conventionally understood to have spared the Allies from carrying out an invasion of the Japanese homeland, where the cost in lives would have been quite heavy.[10] This perception initially dulled any substantive debate over the legal implications of this "life-saving" weapon. Only later did revisionist assessments cast doubt upon whether the atomic attacks were ordered primarily for the achievement of the main war goals or whether there had been more geopolitical motivations, principally the intimidation of the Soviet Union.[11]

The legal silence during the post-1945 period was further augmented when a consensus developed in the United States that the possession of nuclear weapons was the most important counterweight to the Soviet Union. Consequently, American strategic doctrine was rapidly built around deterring the Soviet Union by threatening the use of atomic weapons. As a result,

---

W. Bosch, Judgment on Nuremberg 130-44 (1970).

10. This potential loss in lives has been estimated at one million. On the military decision to drop the atomic bombs on Japan, see H. Feis, Japan Subdued: The Atomic Bomb and the End of the War in the Pacific (1961). For a legal analysis, see Paust, *The Nuclear Decision in World War II—Truman's Ending and Avoidance of War*, 8 Int'l Law. 160 (1974).

For a contrary point of view as to the military necessity for the use of atomic bombs, see Roling supra note 4. Roling concludes that "it is a myth that the Japanese surrendered because of the atomic bombs." *Id.* at 143. He further concludes that "As a judge in the I.M.T.F.E. I have seen all the records of the sessions of the Japanese Imperial Council and other governmental councils during the war, and it is clear that Japan was prepared to capitulate before the atomic bombs were dropped, on the sole condition that the imperial system would be maintained and that the emperor might keep his position." *Id.* at 143-44. In support of the Roling position, see E. Castren, The Present Law of War & Neutrality 204-05 (1954).

11. Gar Alperovitz has, for example, argued that America's primary motivation for dropping the atomic bombs on Hiroshima and Nagasaki had more to do with demonstrating to the Russians the awesome power of the weapon (thereby deterring the spread of Soviet influence) than it did with bringing the war to a speedy end. See G. Alperovitz, Atomic Diplomacy: Hiroshima and Potsdam (1965). Kai Erikson makes the following significant observation: "The attacks on Hiroshima and Nagasaki were not 'combat' in any of the ways that word is normally used. Nor were they primarily attempts to destroy military targets, for the two cities had been chosen not despite, but because they had a high density of civilian housing. Whether the intended audience was Russian or Japanese or a combination of both, then, the attacks were to be a show, a display, a demonstration." Erikson, *A Final Accounting of the Death and Destruction*, N. Y. Times, Aug. 9, 1981, § 7 (Book Review), at 24.

legal questions generated by the use of atomic weapons were never really confronted. It appears to be the consensus of the legal community, then and now, that any questions as to the legality of nuclear weapons should be subordinated to considerations of military necessity and national security.[12]

Moreover, the opinion has grown within the American legal community that many of the traditional principles of the laws of war were invalidated during World War II because of the practice of the Allies, especially in relation to the strategic bombing of civilians.[13] Thus, by implication, any serious inquiry into the legal status of nuclear weapons under international law would seem futile. This belief stands in stark contrast to the legal developments at Nuremberg that not only reaffirmed the applicability of the traditional rules of war to modern warfare, but, in fact, strengthened them by making governmental leaders individually responsible for the policies they formulated and executed.

Many individuals, both inside and outside the legal community, have also come to believe that the "balance of terror" has actually maintained peace — that *but for* nuclear weapons, World War III would almost certainly have occurred. Besides, it is claimed, there was no way to get the "genie" back in the bottle; once nuclear weapons were invented, it was best to adjust to this reality rather than to pretend that pre-nuclear realities could be achieved by legal fiat.

Notwithstanding the reasons for this legal silence, efforts by the legal community to question the normative order, with respect to the legality of nuclear weapons, would not only strengthen governmental and non-governmental disarmament initiatives, but would also reinforce the conclusion of the scientific, medical and religious communities. It is a legal perspective which can give full social expression to the facts and concepts formulated by the scientists, doctors and religious leaders. In fact, the scientific evidence developed by physicians and scientists with respect to the effects and consequences of nuclear weapons establishes the foundation for such a legal analysis. Thus, the issue of nuclear weapons is of far too great importance

---

12. *See* 2 L. OPPENHEIM, INTERNATIONAL LAW, 351-52 (H. Lauterpacht 7th ed. 1952); *See also* Kunz, *The Chaotic Status of the Laws of War and the Urgent Necessity for Their Revision*, 45 A.J.I.L. 37 (1951); J. STONE, LEGAL CONTROLS OF INTERNATIONAL CONFLICT 344 (1954).

13. G. SCHWARZENBERGER, *supra* note 8, at 48.

to be solely the preserve of government leaders, foreign policy experts, or military professionals. The legal community must be involved in answering the question as to whether there are any rational or moral grounds for the use of nuclear weapons. The inclusion of a legal analysis in answering a question of such historic importance will help create an atmosphere affirming the validity of democratic standards and processes to issues of national security.

THE LAWS OF LAND WARFARE

The claim for the legality of nuclear weapons rests on the tolerance afforded by the international system for national claims that are not already the subject of an international prohibition. This traditional international legal view holds that a State can do whatever it is not strictly forbidden from doing and that "the rules of law binding upon states emanate from their own free will as expressed in conventions or by usages generally accepted as expressing principles of law."[14] Consistent with this theory of obligation in international law, which requires that any prohibition on international conduct be based on the express or implied consent of the State, is article 613 of the United States Naval Instructions of 1955. This article represents the American position that "there is at present no rule of international law expressly prohibiting states from the use of nuclear weapons in warfare. In the absence of any express prohibition, the use of such weapons against enemy combatants and other military objectives is permitted."[15]

Traditional restraints in the laws of war are, however, not limited to those given explicit voice solely through treaties. The famous "Martens Clause" of the Preamble to the fourth Hague Convention of 1907, concerning the Laws and Customs of War on Land, introduced a very general legal yardstick intended exactly for those situations in which no specific international convention existed to prohibit a particular type of weapon or tactic.

---

14. S.S. Lotus (Fr. v. Turk.), 1927, P.C.I.J., Ser. A, No. 10, p. 18 (Judgment of Sept. 7).

15. R. TUCKER, LAW AND NEUTRALITY AT SEA 410 app. : Law of Naval Warfare, Sept. 1955 (XLX Naval War College 1957). See also DEPARTMENT OF THE ARMY, FM 27-10 THE LAW OF LAND WARFARE 18 (1956); DEPARTMENT OF THE AIR FORCE, AFP 110-31 INTERNATIONAL LAW: THE CONDUCT OF ARMED CONFLICT AND AIR OPERATIONS 6-5 (1976). For the most unequivocal exposition of the legitimacy of nuclear weapons, see McDougal & Schlei, The Hydrogen Bomb Test in Perspective, 64 YALE L. J. 649, 689-90 (1955).

The Convention mandated:

> Until a more suitable code of laws of war can be drawn up, the high contracting parties deem it expedient to declare that, in cases not covered by the rules adopted by them, the inhabitants and the belligerents remain under the protection and governance of the general usages established among civilized peoples, from the laws of humanity and from the dictates of the public conscience.[16]

It seems evident, then, that the legality of nuclear weapons cannot be judged simply by the existence or lack of existence of a treaty rule specifically prohibiting or restricting their use. Instead, the legality of nuclear weapons must be judged in light of the varied sources of international law — i.e., generalized treaty prohibitions (e.g., on indiscriminate or cruel weaponry), custom and usage reflected in the practices and policies of States, general principles of law recognized by civilized nations, and the elementary and fundamental dictates of humanity.[17] Of particular relevance to this inquiry are international treaties and conventions that limit the use of force during wartime; the fundamental distinctions between combatant and noncombatant and between military and nonmilitary targets, which provide the main foundation upon which the laws of war have been built; and the principles of humanity,[18] including a prohibition on weapons and tactics that are cruel in their effects and cause unnecessary suffering.

The laws of war have traditionally occupied an important

---

16. Convention (No. IV) Respecting the Laws and Customs of War on Land, The Hague, Oct. 18, 1907, 36 Stat. 2277, T.S. No. 539, 1 Bevans 631 [hereinafter cited as Hague Regulations]; for a discussion of the Martens Clause, *see* Fried, *The Electronic Battlefield and the Dictates of the Public Conscience*, REVUE BELGE DE DROIT INTERNATIONAL 431, 451-52 (1972). In 1945, the Nuremberg Tribunal was confronted with a similar problem — the absence of prior definitions of crimes against peace. In response to this situation, the Nuremberg judgment concluded:

> The law of war is to be found not only in treaties, but in customs and practices of states, which gradually obtained universal recognition, and from the general principles of justice applied by jurists and practiced by military courts. The law is not static, but by continued adoption follows the needs of a changing world . . . .

22 INTERNATIONAL MILITARY TRIBUNAL, TRIAL OF THE MAJOR WAR CRIMINALS BEFORE INTERNATIONAL TRIBUNALS, 1947-1949, 464. *See generally* 41 A.J.I.L. (1947).

17. *See* Statute of the International Court of Justice, June 26, 1945, art. 38, 59 Stat. 1055, T.S. 993, 3 Bevans 1179.

18. L. OPPENHEIM, *supra* note 12, at 347-48.

place in the development of international law.[19] During the nineteenth century, the horrors associated with technological developments in military weaponry inspired the codification and development of the laws of war in the form of the Hague Conventions of 1899 and 1907.[20] Those conventions stressed the prohibition of inhumane warfare and the protection of civilians and neutral states. Notwithstanding the various developments in weapons technology and military strategy in the years since the Hague Conventions of 1899 and 1907, the most recent position of governments unanimously confirms the basic guidelines and restraints of the classical international law of war.[21]

Historically, principles of humanity that limit the permissible means by which belligerents injure each other have been among the more important sources of the international laws of war. Since the Declaration of St. Petersburg in 1868,[22] the principles of humanity have been asserted as a constraint upon military necessity. The Declaration of St. Petersburg embodied what may be the most basic principle of the laws of war — namely, that the right of a nation-state to injure a belligerent is not unlimited.

Nuclear Weapons vs. Other Prohibited Weapons

The Declaration of St. Petersburg was the result of a conference of European military officers who met to take action on a new type of bullet that expanded on entry into the body, causing painful wounds which were difficult to treat medically. The conferees reached an agreement forbidding the use of "any projectile of a weight below 400 grams which is either explosive or charged with fulminating or inflammable substance,"[23] and adopted more general principles which have had a lasting effect upon the development of the laws of war.[24] The Preamble to the

---

19. Kunz, *supra* note 12, at 37.

20. *See generally* CARNEGIE ENDOWMENT FOR INTERNATIONAL PEACE, REPORTS TO THE HAGUE CONFERENCES OF 1899 AND 1907 (J.B. Scott ed. 1917).

21. *See* Diplomatic Conference on Reaffirmation and Development of International Humanitarian Law Applicable in Armed Conflict: Protocols I and II to the Geneva Convention, June 8, 1977, 16 I.L.M. 1391 [hereinafter cited as Protocols to the Geneva Convention].

22. Declaration Renouncing the Use In Time of War of Explosive Projectiles Under 400 Grammes Weight, Dec. 11, 1868, 138 Parry's T.S. 297 [hereinafter cited as Declaration of St. Petersburg].

23. Declaration of St. Petersburg, *supra* note 22, at 298.

24. *See infra* text accompanying note 25.

Declaration of St. Petersburg specifically prohibits, as contrary to the laws of humanity, the use of weapons that cause unnecessary and excessive suffering. It states:

> Considering that the progress of civilization should have the effect of alleviating as much as possible the calamities of war;
>
> That the only legitimate object which States should endeavor to accomplish during war is to weaken the military forces of the enemy;
>
> That this object would be exceeded by the employment of arms which uselessly aggravate the sufferings of disabled men, or render their death inevitable;
>
> That the employment of such arms would therefore be contrary to the laws of humanity.[25]

Hence, the Declaration of St. Petersburg stands for the principles that the necessities of war cannot override the laws of war, that wartime "sovereignty" is not absolute, and that warfare is governed by "the laws of humanity," which are valid even without the express consent of governments.

Subsequently, the principles established in the Declaration of St. Petersburg were embodied in article 22 of the Regulations annexed to the fourth Hague Convention of 1907.[26] Article 22 confirmed the basic principle of the laws of war that "the right of belligerents to adopt means of injuring the enemy is not unlimited."[27] Given the development of weapons of mass destruction in this century, article 22, as a general formulation subject to certain ambiguities, remains valid even today. If this principle were applied literally, nuclear weapons and strategy would be illegal under international law because their manifest effect almost certainly causes unnecessary and excessive human suffering, an extreme instance contrary to the limitations of the declaration. It is obvious that the use of nuclear weapons in populated areas would result in the indiscriminate slaughter of civilians.[28] Even if nuclear weapons were targeted only on an enemy's strategic nuclear forces, massive civilian deaths would be an inevitable by-product. As the experiences of Hiroshima and

---

25. Declaration of St. Petersburg, *supra* note 22, at 298.
26. Hague Regulations, *supra* note 16.
27. *Id.*
28. A similar conclusion is the basis for the legal analysis of C. BUILDER & M. GRAUBARD, *supra* note 7.

Nagasaki amply demonstrate, the effects of nuclear weapons, because of their very awesome nature, cannot be limited to military targets. In view of the total and indiscriminate destruction resulting from the use of nuclear weapons and the residual genetic effects of radioactive fallout, it would seem unreasonable to conclude that the use of nuclear weapons involves only the limited application of proportionate force required to weaken an enemy.

The sweeping Declaration of St. Petersburg prohibition on weapons causing unnecessary and excessive suffering was also embodied in article 23(e) of the Hague Regulations of 1907.[29] This provision unequivocally prohibits the use of "arms, projectiles or material calculated to cause unnecessary suffering."[30]

The principles established in the Declaration of St. Petersburg regarding unnecessary suffering and aggravated injury are also the basis for the prohibition against the use of poison or poisoned weapons found in article 23(a) of the Regulations annexed to the Hague Convention. This prohibition is one of the most time-honored rules of the laws of war. In terms of the nuclear weapons debate, a strong case can be made that the introduction of radiation or radioactive fallout into the body would produce symptoms indistinguishable from, and in some respects more serious than, those induced by poison.[31] Uranium, a central element in a nuclear weapon, is highly toxic. Furthermore, a nuclear explosion releases a variety of other toxic chemicals, including some whose toxicity endures for thousands of years.[32] The release of these substances in the course of a nuclear explosion establishes *prima facie* that nuclear weapons are poisonous weapons. As one commentator has concluded, "[I]f the use of a poison on an arrow made it a 'poisoned weapon,' the use of uranium in a nuclear weapon would appear to render the latter 'poisoned' in the same sense."[33] Hence, because nuclear weapons

29. Hague Regulations, *supra* note 16.

30. *Id.*

31. Poison is defined as a substance having an inherent deleterious property which renders it, when taken into the system, capable of destroying life; a substance which, on being applied to the human body, internally or externally, is capable of destroying the action of the vital functions, or of placing the solids and fluids in such a state as to prevent the continuance of life. BLACK'S LAW DICTIONARY 1041 (rev. 5th ed. 1979).

32. *See generally* Feld, *The Mechanics of Fallout*, in THE FINAL EPIDEMIC 110-16 (R. Adams & S. Cullen eds. 1981); UNITED STATES DEPARTMENT OF DEFENSE, THE EFFECTS OF NUCLEAR WEAPONS (S. Glasstone ed. 1962).

33. G. SCHWARZENBERGER, *supra* note 8, at 27.

cause radioactive fallout that contaminates people, property and the environment, the effect of such contamination seems sufficiently analogous to the effect of a poison or poisoned weapon. Thus, nuclear weapons should fall within the prohibition of article 23(a).[34]

Furthermore, the effect of a radioactive fallout can be considered the functional equivalent of the effects resulting from the use of poison gas and/or bacteriological weapons. Some international conventions, such as the Hague Declaration Respecting Asphyxiating Gases of 1899[35] and the Geneva Gas Protocol of 1925,[36] have such universal recognition and adherence as to be considered binding upon the international community. The generality of these prohibitions appears to encompass the production, possession, threat, or use of *any* poisonous substances or emissions, as well as bacteriological agents, as weapons of war. These weapons are recognized by the international community as being so odious as to be unequivocally illegal. The Hague Declaration of 1899[37] specifically prohibits "the use of projectiles, the sole object of which is the diffusion of asphyxiating or deleterious gases."[38]

Eventually, in the Geneva Gas Protocol of 1925,[39] not only was the use of poisoned gas prohibited, but bacteriological weapons were also deemed illegal. The Protocol states:

The undersigned Plenipotentiaries, in the name of their respective Governments:

Whereas the use in war of asphyxiating, poisonous or other gases, and of all analogous liquids, materials or devices, has been justly condemned by the general opinion of the civilized world; and

---

34. M. GREENSPAN, *supra* note 6, at 372-73.

35. Declaration Respecting the Prohibition of the Use of Projectiles Diffusing Asphyxiating Gases, The Hague, July 29, 1899. 187 Parry's T.S. 453 [hereinafter Hague Declaration Respecting Asphyxiating Gases].

36. Protocol for the Prohibition of the Use in War of Asphyxiating, Poisonous or Other Gases, and of Bacteriological Methods of Warfare, June 17, 1925, 26 U.S.T. 571, T.I.A.S. 8061, 94 L.N.T.S. 65 [hereinafter Geneva Gas Protocol]. Insofar as bacteriological warfare is concerned, the Geneva Protocol of 1925 was supplemented and improved on by the Convention on the Prohibition of the Development, Production and Stockpiling of Bacteriological (Biological) and Toxic Weapons, April 10, 1972, 26 U.S.T. 585, T.I.A.S. 8062.

37. Hague Declaration Respecting Asphyxiating Gases, *supra* note 35.

38. *Id.* at 453.

39. Geneva Gas Protocol, *supra* note 36.

Whereas the prohibition of such use has been declared in Treaties to which the majority of Powers of the world are Parties; and

To the end that this prohibition shall be universally accepted as part of International Law, binding alike the conscience and practice of nations;

Declare:

That the High Contracting Parties, so far as they are not already Parties to Treaties prohibiting such use, accept this prohibition, agree to extend this prohibition to the use of bacteriological methods of warfare and agree to be bound as between themselves according to the terms of this declaration.

The High Contracting Parties will exert every effort to induce other States to accede to the present Protocol.[40]

This Protocol is so comprehensive that any weapon whose effects are similar to that of poison gas or bacteriological warfare would seem to be subject to its prohibition. Since a weapon's characteristics and overall impact determine whether it is prohibited, the effects of radioactive contamination would appear to make nuclear weapons illegal under the Protocol. Here again, a strong case exists for the proposition that human exposure to radiation or radioactive fallout produces symptoms and effects indistinguishable from, and in some respects more serious than those of poison — including delayed disease and genetic distortion.[41]

The Geneva Gas Protocol also prohibits bacteriological warfare.[42] Although nuclear explosions do not directly produce bacteria, fungi or other living organisms, they are in certain fundamental ways similar to bacteriological weapons. Nuclear explosions alter the chemical structure of humans, plants, and animals, in addition to having long-term genetic effects. Bacteriological weapons and nuclear weapons share an unprecedented temporal longevity, affect a vast geographic area, and have un-

---

40. *Id.*

41. On the delayed medical effects of nuclear weapons, *see* Ohkita, *Delayed Medical Effects of Hiroshima and Nagasaki*, in LAST AID: THE MEDICAL DIMENSIONS OF NUCLEAR WAR 93-107 (E. Chirran et al. eds. 1982).

42. Bacteriological warfare has been defined as the use of bacteria, fungi, viruses, rickettsias, and toxic agents upon living organisms to produce death or disease in men, animals and plants. P.M.S. BLACKETT, MILITARY AND POLITICAL CONSEQUENCES OF ATOMIC ENERGY, 63 (1948), *quoted in* N. SINGH, *supra* note 8, at 165.

predictable and uncontrollable macrobiological effects, such as increasing the rate of cancer within communities. Certainly, both bacteriological and nuclear weapons are potentially uncontrollable agents of mass destruction with an unprecedented capability to destroy the physical integrity of the planet and to threaten our existence as a species. Thus, if the conscience of the international community finds the scale of potential effects produced by the use of biological weapons inherently objectionable, it should follow that this prohibition against their use should be extended to include nuclear weapons. Indeed, it is difficult to grasp the legal or moral basis for condemning one type of weaponry but tolerating the other, since the scale and scope of destruction is analogous for these two varieties of weaponry.

Protection of Civilians During War

The protection of civilians and neutrals and the distinction between combatant and noncombatant are elementary principles of the laws of war. John Bassett Moore concluded:

> Among the elementary principles which the development of modern rule of warfare, running through several centuries, has been designed to establish and to confirm, the principle most fundamental in character, the observance of which the detailed regulations have largely been designed to assure, is the distinction between combatants and non-combatants against injuries not incidental to military operations against combatants.[43]

That the protection of civilians is at the very heart of the laws of war was also evident in the Declaration of St. Petersburg, which stipulated that the "only legitimate object which states should endeavor to accomplish during war is to weaken the military forces of the enemy."[44] As long as a civilian population does not participate actively in combat, it is shielded from direct attack. An essential element in the commitment to protect civilians in the course of warfare is the recognized principle that weapons must be employed selectively.[45] Without the element of discrimination between military and nonmilitary targets, the fundamental distinction between combatants and noncombatants becomes meaningless.

---

43. 6 THE COLLECTED PAPERS OF JOHN BASSETT MOORE 153 (1944).
44. Declaration of St. Petersburg, *supra* note 24, at 297.
45. Almond, *Law of Armed Conflict: Some of the Shared Policies*, 9 CASE W. RES. J. INT'L L. 175, 181-90.

The protection of and respect for the civilian population was the major premise of the 1923 Hague Draft Rules on Aerial Warfare.[46] Specifically, article 24(3) of those rules established that only military targets could be bombed, and then, only if this could be done without indiscriminate bombardment of civilians.[47] Although these Draft Rules were never translated into a treaty, they provide some evidence that customary international law recognizes that attacks upon military targets which cause indiscriminate suffering to a civilian population should be prohibited. It should also be recalled in this connection that general international law embraces the principle that the object of war cannot be the complete and total destruction of an enemy. These earlier ideas have been carried forward in explicit terms in the 1977 Geneva Protocol on Humanitarian Law Applicable in Armed Conflict.[48]

In addition, the Hague Draft Rules sought to prohibit aerial bombardment of a civilian population undertaken with the clear objective of terrorizing it to win the war. Publicist Hersch Lauterpacht supported this principle when he argued that "destruction of a civilian population as an avowed or obvious object" of warfare is forbidden because inherent in this prohibition is "the last vestige of the claim that war can be legally regulated at all."[49] Thus, although the Hague Draft Rules lack binding force as customary international law, reasonably construed, they protect the civilian population from being a lawful military target regardless of the means used or the justification provided.

In opposition to Lauterpacht, some commentators maintain that the very nature of modern war, the era of "total war," makes it impossible to preserve the noncombatants' traditional immunity from attack.[50] They argue that technological advances in military weaponry, such as long-range artillery, air warfare, and missiles, have made the enemy hinterlands "accessible as a target of attack."[51] Additionally, they contend that the idea of a military objective was so greatly expanded by Allied military

---

46. *The Hague Rules of Aerial Warfare*, 17 A.J.I.L. 245 (Supp. 1923).

47. *Id.* at 250.

48. Protocols to the Geneva Convention, *supra* note 20.

49. Lauterpacht, *The Problem of the Revision of the Law of War*, 29 Brit. Y.B. Int'l L. 360, 369 (1952).

50. Baxter, *The Role of the Law in Modern War*, Proceedings of the American Society of International Law 90-98 (1953); *see also* Nurick, *The Distinction Between Combatant and Noncombatant in the Law of War*, 39 A.J.I.L. 680 (1945).

51. G. Schwarzenberger, The Legality of Nuclear Weapons 18-20 (1958).

tactics during World War II that "the immunity of the civilian population from international attack is reaching a vanishing point."[52] As a result, it can be said that the classification of non-combatants has become far narrower, if it can be said to exist at all.

Obviously, the international legal order erected in the period prior to World War II proved insufficient to limit the use of conventional weapons and tactics, much less the use of atomic weapons against Japan. Technological innovation rapidly outstripped the capability of the international legal system to respond, and belligerent States seemed disinclined during the course of hostilities to inhibit their freedom of action in any way. This relationship between the development and use of a weapons system in the conduct of war and the unwillingness of States to forego military advantages has been characteristic of war in the twentieth century.[53]

Nevertheless, it must be remembered that the use of atomic weapons against Nagasaki and Hiroshima in 1945 resulted in an indiscriminate slaughter of civilians. In order to recognize its terrifying extent, one need only consider the number of *immediate* deaths — at least 140,000 at Hiroshima and 70,000 at Nagasaki — caused by these low-yield atomic weapons.[54] More important, the evident intention behind using these weapons against cities was not primarily to destroy Japan's capability to wage war, but to undermine the morale and will of the Japanese people and government.[55] Today, the use of strategic nuclear weapons in populated areas would result in the indiscriminate and massive destruction of the civilian population, even if the specific doctrine of use fully incorporated counterforce targeting

---

52. *Id.* at 20.

53. *See generally*, Howard, *Tempermenta Belli: Can War Be Controlled*, in Restraints on War 1 (M. Howard ed. 1979).

54. Both of these weapons were less than 20,000 kt in explosive strength. Smaller totals (70,000 for Hiroshima, 40,000 for Nagasaki) are often given in estimates based on those killed immediately; the higher figures in the text include bomb-related fatalities in the ensuing weeks; they seem likely to be more accurate. In addition, another 130,000 inhabitants of the two Japanese cities died during the next five years, and deaths whose cause can be traced back to the atomic explosions of more than 35 years ago are still being reported. For a full account of the damage, *see* The Committee for the Compilation of Materials on Damage Caused by the Atomic Bombs in Hiroshima and Nagasaki, Hiroshima and nagasaki: The Physical, Medical and Social Effects of the Atomic Bombing, *supra* note 1.

55. *See* Roling, *supra* note 4; *see also* E. Castren, *supra* note 10.

of military objectives.[56] If the stated threat and potential objective of nuclear weapons is the destruction of the enemy State — which is the central premise of assured destruction — then the terrorization of the civilian population is an inevitable by-product,[57] and a partial annihilation or extermination of that population would likely result if nuclear weapons were used. In view of the capacity of such weapons to terrorize and destroy a civilian population, recognition of the legality of nuclear weapons would virtually eliminate the entire effort to constrain this mode of combat — at least in large-scale warfare — by means of the laws of war.[58] One commentator has concluded:

> [T]he admission of a right to resort to the creation of terror among the civilian population, as being a legitimate object *per se*, would *inevitably* mean the actual and formal end of the law of warfare. For that reason, so long as the assumption is allowed to subsist that there is a law of war, the prohibition of a weapon of terror not incidental to lawful operations must be regarded as an absolute rule of law.[59]

Protecting Neutral States

The uncontrollable, unpredictable and pervasive nature of the effects of nuclear weapons is also likely to wreak havoc and destruction among the populations of neutral States outside the theater of war which would be affected by nuclear weapons as if the States were located in the combat zone. One jurist has argued:

> If the radio-active fallout can be carried by wind hundreds of miles in an unpredictable direction, the region of nuclear war-

---

56. The point is not that nuclear weapons are inherently incapable of being used primarily against a military target, as on a battlefield, or to block an advancing army proceeding through mountainous terrain, or in the course of a naval engagement; it is that the characteristics of this weaponry, even if its use is directed exclusively against military targets, are such that it should be independently prohibited under any reasonable interpretations of international law. For an analysis of the projected civilian deaths that would result from the use of small battlefield nuclear weapons in Germany, *see* Arkin, von Hippel & Levi, *The Consequences of Limited Nuclear War in East and West Germany*, 11 AMBIO, 163-73 (1982).

57. It is well recognized that the bombardment of civilians with the purpose of spreading fear, havoc or terror in order to break the morale and will to resist of the civilian population is unlawful under the laws of war. *See* CASTREN, *supra* note 10, at 200.

58. To this effect, *see* M. WALZER, *supra* note 2; *see also* M. GREENSPAN, *supra* note 6.

59. Lauterpacht, *supra* note 49, at 369.

fare cannot be confined with any precision to the belligerent territories, and the air and sea which go with them. With the unpredictable and indiscriminate effects of nuclear bombardment, particularly of the 20-megaton or higher capacity bombs, the theatre of war along with its vast area of damaging effects can spread to any part of the globe, affecting neutral States and permanently neutralized territories. If the German invasion of Belgium was condemned as a violation of international law in the Second World War and declared a war crime, it is submitted that the use of nuclear weapons in circumstances in which the user knows that it is bound to injure neutral States, must be considered as a violation of international law and, if it involves the killing of innocent neutrals, a clear war crime.[60]

Hence, in order to endow the principles of neutrality with contemporary validity, it must be recognized that any contemplated large-scale use of nuclear weapons, with the attendant uncontrollable effects, is almost certain to have a direct impact upon neutral States. As such, their use would seem contrary to the basic intent of the laws of war and the dictates of humanity. To conclude otherwise would be to abandon the traditional laws of neutrality, as well as their essential distinction between belligerent and nonbelligerent States.[61] If, because of the acceptance of the legitimacy of nuclear weapons, legal efforts to protect civilians and neutrals are abandoned, then we will indeed have witnessed the "formal end of the law of warfare" — and the triumph of the law of nuclear terror.

Efforts to restrict the character and conduct of hostilities are also affected by the self-defense doctrine. Under the framework of the Kellog-Briand Pact[62] and the United Nations Charter,[63] resort to war for purposes of self-defense or collective defense remains lawful. This right, however, is not unlimited. Actions taken in self-defense or as reprisals for an alleged breach of international law must be proportionate to the quantum of

---

60. N. SINGH, *supra* note 8, at 106.

61. It has been argued, of course, that the prohibition of all non-defensive force, together with the provisions on collective security in the United Nations Charter makes neutrality obsolete as a legal concept. However, the Charter's framework on such matters seems only sporadically applicable to international conflict, thereby making the pre-Charter international law of war, including neutral rights and duties, still useful as a form of second-order legality. The bearing of rights of neutrals on the potential claims of states affected by the use of nuclear weapons should therefore be examined.

62. Treaty for the Renunciation of War, 46 Stat. 2343, 94 L.N.T.S. 57.

63. U.N. CHARTER, art. 51.

force used by the aggressor. In practice, the defending side has enjoyed unchallenged discretion to use whatever military capabilities were at its disposal, provided only that it did not resort to weaponry and tactics that were unconditionally prohibited, e.g., bacteriological/biological warfare and torture.

Traditional international law survives to confirm that the right to injure an aggressor is not unlimited. In the absence of an unconditional prohibition against the use of nuclear weapons, it would appear that such weapons could be deployed restrictively in self-defense if the aggressor initiated their use. However, the right to self-defense is available only to the individual State attacked and must be limited to legal methods of warfare and to damage that does not exceed the boundaries of the aggressor State.[64] Most uses of nuclear weapons, moreover, are likely to have a direct and immediate adverse impact upon States not party to the conflict. Moreover, if nuclear and bacteriological weapons are functionally equivalent due to the pervasiveness and indiscriminate character of their effects, it would seem to follow that since a State cannot use bacteriological weapons in self-defense, it also cannot use nuclear weapons in self-defense.

Integral to United States national security policy is discretionary recourse to the first use of nuclear weapons in response to conventional attacks upon vital interests. The United States retains this option, especially in relation to the defense of Western Europe against a possible Soviet attack. Here again, if the right of self-defense is expanded to authorize the use of prohibited weapons of mass destruction in alleged deference to the exigencies of the nuclear age, then the laws of war seem to have become virtually meaningless. Nuclear weapons will have abolished the laws of war by a *fait accompli*.[65]

Arguments exist that a variety of international legal norms supports the prohibition of the use and threat of use of nuclear weapons, and that the law of war as a whole is jeopardized to the extent that nuclear weaponry is legitimized. These contentions are reinforced by evaluating nuclear weapons and strategy within the context of the Nuremberg Principles. Specifically, the use or threat of use of nuclear weapons seems, by Nuremberg standards, to be a crime against peace and a crime against hu-

---

64. *See* D. Bowett, Self-Defense in International Law (1958).
65. To this effect, *see* M. Walzer, *supra* note 2.

manity for which individual military and political leaders could and should be held accountable.[66]

American leaders in the immediate postwar era supported the assimilation of the principles established by the Nuremberg and Tokyo War Crimes Trials into the permanent corpus of international law. President Truman, in an address to the United Nations General Assembly, affirmed the Nuremberg Principles and asserted that they pointed to "the path along which [international] agreement might be sought, with hope of success."[67] Accordingly, the United States delegation introduced a draft resolution before the General Assembly to render the Nuremberg Principles binding as international law. The resolution, which "affirm[ed] the Principles of International Law recognized by the Charter of the Nuremberg Tribunal" was adopted unanimously by the General Assembly on December 11, 1946.[68]

Nuclear Deterrence Theory

This author previously pointed out that, since the beginning of this century, the traditional distinction between combatants

---

66. The text of Principle VI of the Nuremberg Principles, as formulated by the International Law Commission in 1950, is reprinted in CRIMES OF WAR 108 (R. Falk, G. Kolko & R. Lifton eds. 1971). The text of Principle VI states:

The crimes hereinafter set out are punishable as crimes under international law:

a. Crimes against peace:

(i) Planning, preparation, initiation or waging of a war of aggression, or a war in violation of international treaties, agreements, or assurances;

(ii) Participation in a common plan or conspiracy for the accomplishment of any of the acts mentioned under (i).

b. War Crimes:

Violations of the laws or customs of war which include, but are not limited to, murder, ill-treatment or deportation to slave labour or for any other purpose of civilian population of or in occupied territory, murder or ill-treatment of prisoners of war or persons on the seas, killing of hostages, plunder of public or private property, wanton destruction of cities, towns or villages, or devastation not justified by military necessity.

c. Crimes against humanity:

Murder, extermination, enslavement, deportation and other inhuman acts done against any civilian population, or persecutions on political, racial or religious grounds, when such acts are done or such persecutions are carried on in execution of, or in connection with any crime against peace or any war crime.

67. The first Secretary General of the United Nations, Trygve Lie, asserted that "[i]n the interest of peace and in order to protect mankind against future wars, it will be of decisive significance to have the principles which were applied in the Nuremberg Trials . . . made a permanent part of the body of international law as quickly as possible." *Quoted in* 2 THE LAW OF WAR 1028 (L. Friedman ed. 1972).

68. G.A. Res. 95, U.N. Doc. A/64/Add. 1, at 188 (1946).

and noncombatants has been eroded by technological developments in weaponry and by doctrinal developments pertaining to war goals and the character of military necessity. The military practice of seeking to break the will of a nation by attacking its industrial war-making base and, ultimately, its civilian population, has been the basis for the concept of "total war," extended in the nuclear era to encompass the theory and practice of deterrence. The atomic bomb, used in the closing days of World War II, constituted not only a technological revolution in military weaponry, but also a logical culmination of this evolving concept of carrying warfare into the enemy heartland.

Even if one accepts the claim that deterrence doctrines have prevented widespread conflict, the basis of that claim, the threat of mass destruction, seems legally and morally bankrupt. If threats to inflict mass destruction alone assure the survival of the United States, then perhaps we should reassess our notions of survival. In some sense, strategic deterrence threatens every person in the world, directly and indirectly. Indeed, the world is held hostage by a military strategy whose inevitable consequence can only be the decimation of the world's population. Article 6(c) of the Nuremberg Principles in part defines crimes against humanity as the "extermination of a civilian population, before or during a war." It seems clear that the use or threat of use of nuclear weapons under the doctrine of deterrence or, worse yet, as an instrument of geopolitics, is inconsistent with this prohibition.

It is claimed that under the doctrine of deterrence, the world has been at peace; true, there have been no nuclear wars. The peace, however, has been tenuous and fragile. There have been several notable occasions in which the United States has seriously contemplated using nuclear weapons.[69] Moreover, this "peace" allegedly provided by nuclear weapons has been limited largely to the industrial circumference of the North. Wars of various sizes, types and duration have flourished continuously in the Third World. The role of nuclear weapons in making the South "safe" for warfare should not be underestimated.

Limited Nuclear War and Counterforce

Furthermore, limited nuclear war and counterforce doc-

---

69. Barnet, *Ultimate Terrorism*, 43 THE PROGRESSIVE 14 (1979).

trines are premised upon a dangerous conception that may well be an illusion, i.e., that a nuclear war short of a full-scale war is both winnable and containable. It has been estimated that twenty million people would be killed even in a nuclear exchange in which only strategic forces and key military targets were attacked.[70] For the decision-makers who formulated the doctrines of limited nuclear war and counterforce, these costs are perhaps acceptable when compared with the far higher costs of a full-scale nuclear war or of backing down in a geopolitical crisis. The aura of rationality or reasonableness attached to such calculations, however, does not establish their moral or legal validity. It seems most foolhardy to rely on the assertions of "experts" that a limited nuclear war could, in all probability, be kept from escalating to a full-scale nuclear war. The argument for surgical nuclear strikes — as being "efficient" because they destroy only military targets while sparing cities and civilians — is deceptive. Once the threshold is crossed, an escalatory spiral is likely to be initiated. It seems improbable that either side will conduct a nuclear war as if governed by the Marquis of Queensberry's rules of conduct. Once nuclear war is initiated, the pressures to prevail, or at least to avoid defeat, will be such that "rational" constraints are likely to give way. What was almost "unthinkable" in the past has now been packaged in a more intellectually acceptable form. However, even if limited nuclear war is feasible as a project for governments, it remains morally, legally and biologically unacceptable.

If the development of these strategic options and implementing capabilities is designed to maintain the peace, then we are certainly facing an era of peace based on a fragile foundation. The insistence on a limited nuclear war option increases dramatically the prospect that nuclear weapons will be used in a crisis situation. Equally, the assertion that limited nuclear war can be kept from escalating into an all-out nuclear exchange is open to serious dispute. Even aside from the danger of escala-

---

70. A recent congressional study entitled THE EFFECT OF NUCLEAR WAR, *supra* note 5, prepared by the Office of Technology Assessment of the Senate Foreign Relations Committee, estimated that in an all-out nuclear war between the United States and the U.S.S.R. over 300 million people would be killed in the initial exchange. The report also concluded that the survivors of this conflict would be forced to live under conditions "equivalent to the Middle Ages," but no mention is made of the impact of an all-out nuclear exchange on the rest of the world. However, it is expected that cancer deaths in the millions could be expected for 40 years after a nuclear war. *See also Effects of Nuclear War*, 34 J. FED'N AM. SCIENTISTS (1981).

tion. Thus, the contention that nuclear weapons — however limited their use — constitute an acceptable mode of warfare seems to be an endorsement of a modern variant of barbarism. Any nuclear exchange, whether limited or massive, has the potential for killing, wounding, maiming and terrorizing large numbers of civilians devastating vast areas of land and producing long-term environmental and biological consequences[71] clearly contrary to the spirit, if not the letter, of the Nuremberg Principles.

International Conventions

The Convention on the Prevention and Punishment of the Crime of Genocide[72] (hereinafter referred to as the Genocide Convention), although not ratified by several important countries including the United States, also has some bearing on our inquiry. Article I declares genocide to be a crime under international law.[73] Article II defines genocide as killing or causing serious bodily or mental harm to members of a national, ethnic, racial, or religious group; conditions of life calculated physically to destroy the group in whole or in part; imposing measures to prevent births within the group; or forcibly transferring children from one group to another.[74] In light of the destructive power of nuclear weapons and their known radioactive effects, it seems clear that any large-scale use of nuclear weapons would meet most, if not all, of the criteria defining genocide in article II.

The Genocide Convention was adopted mainly in response to attempts to exterminate the Jewish population of Europe and Russia during World War II.[75] The deaths that would result from an all-out nuclear exchange between the United States and the Soviet Union are estimated, probably conservatively, at more than 300 million.[76] These figures do not reflect the indirect harm to the populations of nations not involved in the conflict, nor the long-term medical, economic and cultural effects upon the populations that experience the nuclear exchange. The indiscriminate human slaughter resulting from a major nuclear war

---

71. *See, e.g., Effects of Nuclear War*, 34 J. FED'N AM. SCIENTISTS.

72. Convention on the Prevention and Punishment of the Crime of Genocide, 78 U.N.T.S. 277 (1948).

73. *Id.*

74. *Id.*

75. M. McDOUGAL, H. LASSWELL & L. CHEN, HUMAN RIGHTS AND WORLD PUBLIC ORDER 355 (1980).

76. *See generally,* THE EFFECTS OF NUCLEAR WAR, *supra* note 5.

could make pale by comparison even the awesome genocidal policies carried out by Hitler's Germany during World War II. Hence, any substantial use of nuclear weapons would produce consequences clearly contrary to the spirit, and probably to the letter, of the Convention.[77]

The four Geneva Conventions of 1949[78] offer a further yardstick by which to measure the legality of nuclear weapons under customary international law. These Conventions not only reaffirm the fundamental distinction between combatant and noncombatant and the prohibition against unnecessary and aggravated suffering, but they also reflect the continuing validity of the applicability of principles of humanity to the laws of war. In fact, the primary objective of the Conventions is to assure that "disinterested aid [is] given without discrimination to all victims of war who, on account of their wounds, capture or shipwreck, cease to be enemies but become suffering and defenseless human beings."[79]

These Conventions enumerate various categories of people who are to be protected by these treaties. Convention I protects the wounded and sick in the field, for example, medical personnel engaged in the search for, or the collection, transport or treatment of wounded, and auxiliary medical personnel such as orderlies, nurses, stretcher-bearers and the staffs of voluntary medical societies.[80] The Maritime Convention (II) provides similar protection for religious, medical and hospital personnel of

---

77. This conclusion has admittedly avoided the distinction between different categories of nuclear weapons (strategic and tactical) and different targeting concepts (counterforce and countervalue) because these categories are too fuzzy and subjective to be the basis of meaningful legal guidelines. Nevertheless, current nuclear weapons policy has sought to reconcile nuclear weapons with the traditional limits of the laws of war by emphasizing military strategies and weapons which produce "minimum" collateral civilian damage. For the analysis of the projected civilian deaths resulting from the use of less than 100-200 kiloton or 1-2 kiloton weapons (10-20 million and 1-10 million) in two limited nuclear war scenarios, see Arkin, Von Hippel & Levi, The Consequences of Limited Nuclear War in East and West Germany, supra note 56.

78. Convention for the Amelioration of the Condition of the Wounded and Sick in the Armed Forces in the Field, 6 U.S.T. 3114, T.I.A.S. No. 3362, 75 U.N.T.S. 31 (Convention I); Convention for the Amelioration of the Wounded, Sick and Shipwrecked Members of Armed Forces at Sea (Convention II), 6 U.S.T. 3217, T.I.A.S. No. 3363, 75 U.N.T.S. 85; Convention Relative to the Treatment of Prisoners of War (Convention III), 6 U.S.T. 3316, T.I.A.S. No. 3364, 75 U.N.T.S. 135; Convention Relative to the Protection of Civilian Persons in Time of War (Convention IV), 6 U.S.T. 3516, T.I.A.S. No. 3365, 75 U.N.T.S. 287.

79. See THE GENEVA CONVENTION OF AUGUST 12, 1949, (1950).

80. See supra note 78, Convention I, arts. 24-26.

hospital ships.[81] The Prisoner of War Convention (III), in addition to protecting medical personnel, protects chaplains.[82] The Civilian Convention (IV) prohibits the coercion, intimidation, terrorizing or extermination of civilians in the hands of an occupying power of which they are not nationals.[83]

Even though technological advances have made the aim of nuclear weapons more accurate, it does not necessarily follow that they are more "discriminate." The nature and effect of nuclear weapons is such that they are inherently incapable of being limited, with any degree of certainty, to a specific military target. Given that an overwhelming majority of weapons in the American nuclear arsenal, particularly the limited and theater nuclear weapons, exceed many times over the destructive power of the weapon used at Hiroshima,[84] and given the targets that the American military planners consider "military objectives,"[85]

---

81. *See supra* note 78, Convention II, art. 36.

82. *See supra* note 78, Convention III, art. 33.

83. *See supra* note 78, Convention IV, arts. 31-32.

84. For a listing of the delivery systems and warheads currently employed by the U.S. and the U.S.S.R., *see* Forsberg, *A Bilateral Nuclear-Weapon Freeze*, 247 SCIENTIFIC AMERICAN 52, 54-55 (1982).

85. The U.S. Department of Defense has listed the following three categories of targets (population targets, military targets and economic/industrial targets) as examples of targets which would be attacked by nuclear weapons. This list is cited in *How a Nuclear War Might be Fought*, 11 AMBIO 76, 94-99.

1. Soviet nuclear forces
     Intercontinental and intermediate-range ballistic missiles, together with
     their launch facilities and launch command centers
     Nuclear weapons storage sites
     Airfields supporting nuclear-capable aircraft
     Bases for submarines firing nuclear missiles
2. Conventional military forces
     Casernes
     Supply depots
     Marshalling points
     Conventional air fields
     Ammunition storage facilities
     Tank and vehicle storage yards
3. Military and political leadership
     Command posts
     Key communication facilities
4. Economic and industrial targets
     a. War-supporting industry
        Ammunition factories
        Tank and armored personnel carrier factories
        Petroleum refineries
        Railway yards and repair facilities
     b. Industry contributing to economic recovery

it is quite difficult to conceive of a use of nuclear weapons that would not produce extensive destruction of areas populated by civilians that would spare hospitals, the sick and wounded in those hospitals, churches and other protected places, such as prisoner of war camps. Consequently, by their very nature, nuclear weapons make it *impossible* to carry out the humanitarian obligations enumerated in the Geneva Conventions.

The Geneva Conventions of 1949 were amplified by the 1977 Protocols (I and II) on Humanitarian Law Applicable in Armed Conflict.[86] These Protocols represent the culmination of efforts taken since 1907 to state in a unified and coherent way the basic laws of armed conflict governing the selection and use of weapons and methods of warfare.[87] Although avoiding explicit reference to nuclear weapons and strategy,[88] Protocol I espouses principles designed primarily to protect the civilian population, which, if reasonably construed, support the conclusion of nuclear illegality.[89]

Coal
Basic steel
Basic aluminum
Cement
Electric power

86. Protocols to the Geneva Convention, *supra* note 21.

87. *Id.*

88. *See* Aldrich, *Establishing Legal Norms Through Multilateral Negotiations—The Laws of War*, 11 Int'l Law. 107 (1977); *see also* Aldrich, *New Life for Laws of War*, 75 Am. J. Int'l L. 764 (1981).

89. Those principles are:

Article 35—Basic rules

1. In any armed conflict, the right of the Parties to the conflict to choose methods or means of warfare is not unlimited.
2. It is prohibited to employ weapons, projectiles and material and methods of warfare of a nature to cause superfluous injury or unnecessary suffering.
3. It is prohibited to employ methods or means of warfare which are intended, or may be expected, to cause wide-spread, long-term and severe damage to the natural environment.

Article 48—Basic rule

In order to ensure respect for and protection of the civilian population and civilian objects, the Parties to the conflict shall at all times distinguish between the civilian population and combatants and between civilian objects and military objectives and accordingly shall direct their operations only against military objectives.

Article 51—Protection of the civilian population

1. The civilian population and individual civilians shall enjoy general protection against dangers arising from military operations. To give effect to this pro-

The most important declaration on the legal status of nu-

tection, the following rules, which are additional to other applicable rules of international law, shall be observed in all circumstances.

2. The civilian population as such, as well as individual civilians, shall not be the object of attack. Acts or threats of violence the primary purpose of which is to spread terror among the civilian population are prohibited.

3. Civilians shall enjoy the protection afforded by this Section, unless and for such time as they take a direct part in hostilities.

4. Indiscriminate attacks are prohibited. Indiscriminate attacks are:

(a) those which are not directed at a specific military objective;

(b) those which employ a method or means of combat which cannot be directed at a specific military objective; or

(c) those which employ a method or means of combat the effects of which cannot be limited as required by this Protocol:

and consequently, in each such case, are of a nature to strike military objectives and civilian objects without distinction.

5. Among others, the following types of attacks are to be considered as indiscriminate:

(a) an attack by bombardment by any methods or means which treats as a single military objective a number of clearly separated and distinct military objectives located in a city, town, village or other area containing a similar concentration of civilians or civilian objects; and

(b) an attack which may be expected to cause incidental loss of civilian life, injury to civilians, damage to civilian objects, or a combination thereof, which would be excessive in relation to the concrete and direct military advantage anticipated.

6. Attacks against the civilian population or civilians by way of reprisals are prohibited.

7. The presence or movements of the civilian population or individual civilians shall not be used to render certain points or areas immune from military operations, in particular in attempts to shield military objectives from attacks or to shield, favour or impede military operations. The Parties to the conflict shall not direct the movement of the civilian population or individual civilians in order to attempt to shield military objectives from attacks or to shield military operations.

8. Any violation of these prohibitions shall not release the Parties to the conflict from their legal obligations with respect to the civilian population and civilians, including the obligation to take the precautionary measures provided for in Article 57.

Article 52—General protection of civilian objects

1. Civilian objects shall not be the object of attack or of reprisals. Civilian objects are all objects which are not military objectives as defined in paragraph 2.

2. Attacks shall be limited strictly to military objectives. In so far as objects are concerned, military objectives are limited to those objects which by their nature, location, purpose or use make an effective contribution to military action and whose total or partial destruction, capture or neutralization, in the circumstances ruling at the time, offers a definite military advantage.

3. In case of doubt whether an object which is normally dedicated to civilian purposes, such as a place of worship, a house or other dwelling or a school, is being used to make an effective contribution to military action, it shall be presumed not to be so used.

clear weapons is United Nations General Assembly Resolution

Article 53—Protection of cultural objects and of places of worship

Without prejudice to the provisions of the Hague Convention for the Protection of Cultural Property in the Event of Armed Conflict of 14 May 1954, and of other relevant international instruments, it is prohibited:
(a) to commit any acts of hostility directed against the historic monuments, works of art or places of worship which constitute the cultural or spiritual heritage of peoples;
(b) to use such objects in support of the military effort;
(c) to make such objects the object of reprisals.

Article 54—Protection of objects indispensable to the survival of the civilian population

1. Starvation of civilians as a method of warfare is prohibited.
2. It is prohibited to attack, destroy, remove or render useless objects indispensable to the survival of the civilian population, such as foodstuffs, agricultural areas for the production of foodstuffs, crops, livestock, drinking water installations and supplies and irrigation works, for the specific purpose of denying them for their sustenance value to the civilian population or to the adverse Party, whatever the motive, whether in order to starve out civilians, or cause them to move away, or for any other motive.

Article 55—Protection of the natural environment

1. Care shall be taken in warfare to protect the natural environment against widespread, long-term and severe damage. This protection includes a prohibition of the use of methods or means of warfare which are intended or may be expected to cause such damage to the natural environment and thereby to prejudice the health or survival or the population.
2. Attacks against the natural environment by ways of reprisals are prohibited.

Article 56—Protection of works and installations containing dangerous forces

1. Works or installations containing dangerous forces, namely dams, dykes and nuclear electrical generating stations, shall not be made the object of attack, even where these objects are military objectives, if such attack may cause the release of dangerous forces and consequent severe losses among the civilian population. Other military objectives located at or in the vicinity of these works or installations shall not be made the object of attack if such attack may cause the release of dangerous forces from the works or installations and consequent severe losses among the civilian population.

See 16 I.L.M. 1408-15.

On September 8, 1977, George H. Aldrich, Deputy Legal Advisor of the Department of State and U.S. Representative to the 4th Session of the Geneva Diplomatic Conference on Reaffirmation and Development of International Law Applicable in Armed Conflicts submitted a report to the Secretary of State concerning the U.S. views on the applicability of the Protocols to nuclear warfare. He said:

During the course of the Conference there was no consideration of the issues raised by the use of nuclear weapons. Although there are several articles that could see to raise questions with respect to the use of nuclear weapons, most clearly, article 55 on the protection of the natural environment, it was the understanding of the United States Delegation throughout the Conference that the rules to be developed were designed with a view to conventional weapons and their effects and that the new rules established by the Protocol were not intended to have any effects on, and do not regulate or prohibit the use of

1653 (XVI),[90] which declared that "any state using nuclear and

---

nuclear weapons. We made this understanding several times during the Conference, and it was also stated explicitly by the British and French delegations. It was not contradicted by any delegation so far as we are aware. Despite this clear record, however, the United States may wish to make a formal statement of understanding on this subject, given its importance, at the times of signature and of ratification.

DIG. U.S. PRAC. IN INT'L L. 919 (1977).

Eventually, on December 10, 1977, the United States signed Protocol I subject to the following understanding:

It is the understanding of the United States of America that the rules established by this Protocol were not intended to have any effect on and do not regulate or prohibit the use of nuclear weapons.

Id. at 920.

However, given that the Protocols codify existing general principles of the laws of war, there is still a question whether the intention of the United States, as enunciated, is decisive for subsequent interpretations of a treaty of this nature. The plain meaning of the text is usually taken as the principal guide for treaty interpretation, and there is no hint of any intention to exclude; to the contrary, as nuclear weapons seem to be the most obvious concern of Articles 35 and 36. If governments stipulate the exclusion of nuclear weapons in their instruments of ratification, then the situation becomes more complicated, although again the legal result is not self-evident. If such an understanding is regarded as incompatible with the essential purposes of the treaty, then the understanding might be viewed as an incompatible reservation that invalidates the ratification rather than achieves its purposes of excluding nuclear weapons from the coverage of the treaty itself. *See* Reservations to the Convention on Genocide, 1951 I.C.J. 15, (Advisory Opinion).

Moreover, given that the 1977 Protocols codify principles that are already part of customary international law and given that such rules are considered applicable to a legal evaluation of nuclear weapons, the position of the United States that the 1977 Protocols are inapplicable to nuclear weapons is untenable. Indeed, a recent study by the Rand Corporation, *see* GRAYBARD *supra* note 7, on the legal implications of nuclear weapons uses the norms of the 1977 Protocols in evaluating nuclear weapons.

Finally, the United States position that nuclear warfare is not regulated by the humanitarian law of armed conflict is a highly questionable legal position in light of the United States position that it would use nuclear weapons in conventional war settings. *See* Note, *The United States' Nuclear First Strike Position: A Legal Appraisal of Its Ramifications*, 7 CAL. WESTERN INT'L L.J. 508, 508-512 (1977); for a discussion of the use of conventional weapons and nuclear weapons at the same time in future armed conflicts, *see* DEPARTMENT OF THE ARMY, OPERATIONS: AIRLAND BATTLE 2000, FM 100-5 (1982). While these Protocols do contain a series of new prohibitions, specifically articles 54, 55 and 56, it is important to recognize that articles 35 (1) and (2), 48, 51, 52 and 53 codify principles that have long been a part of customary international law and are applicable to evaluating the legal status of nuclear weapons: "(1) protection of the civilian population and property, (2) attacks only against military targets, and (3) precautions that the first two requirements are met."

90. G.A. Res. 1653, 15 U.N. GAOR Supp. (No. 17) at 4, U.N. Doc. A/5100 (1961). Declaration on the Prohibition of the Use of Nuclear and Thermo-nuclear Weapons (55 to 20 with 26 abstentions) (hereinafter cited as "G.A. Res. 1653"). This Resolution was reaffirmed in subsequent resolutions in 1978 and 1980 by larger margins. *See*, Non-use of Nuclear Weapons and Prevention of Nuclear War, G.A. Res. 33/71-B, 33 U.N. GAOR Supp. (No. 45) at 48, U.N. Doc. 2/33/45 (1978); G.A. Res. 35/152-0, 35 U.N. GAOR Supp.

thermo-nuclear weapons is to be considered as violating the Charter of the United Nations, as acting contrary to the laws of humanity, and as committing a crime against mankind and civilization."[91] This resolution also offered a legal interpretation of the status of nuclear weapons. The resolution cautioned, for example,

(b) The use of nuclear and thermo-nuclear weapons would exceed even the scope of war and cause indiscriminate suffering and destruction to mankind and civilization and, as such, is contrary to the rules of international law and to the laws of humanity;

(c) The use of nuclear and thermo-nuclear weapons is a war directed not against an enemy or enemies alone, but also against mankind in general, since the peoples of the world not involved in such a war will be subjected to all the evils generated by the use of such weapons;

(d) Any State using nuclear and thermo-nuclear weapons is to be considered as violating the Charter of the United Nations, as acting contrary to the laws of humanity and as committing a crime against mankind and civilization.[92]

In December 1966, the General Assembly adopted Resolution 2162A (XXI), which directed the Secretary General to assess the effects of the use of nuclear weapons.[93] This report concluded:

There is one inescapable and basic fact. It is that the nuclear armories which are in being already contain large megaton weapons every one of which has a destructive power greater than that of all the conventional explosive that has ever been used in warfare since the day gunpowder was discovered. Were such weapons ever to be used in numbers, hundreds of millions of people might be killed, and civilization as we know it, as well as organized community life, would inevitably come to an end in the countries involved in the conflict. Many of those who survived the immediate destruction as well as others in countries outside the area of conflict, would be exposed to widely-spreading radio-active contamination, and would suffer from long-term effects of irradiation and transmit, to their offspring,

(No. 48) at 69, U.N. Doc. A/35/48 (1980).
   91. G.A. Res. 1653, *supra* note 90.
   92. *Id.*
   93. G.A. Res. 2162A, U.N. GAOR Supp. (No. 16), U.N. Doc. A/6316 (1966).

a genetic burden which would become manifest in the disabilities of later generations.[94]

Even though General Assembly resolutions are not legally binding, they do have a significant value in that they are evidence of a consensus which considers the threat of use or use of nuclear weapons as a contradiction to the fundamental humanitarian principles upon which the international laws of war are founded. Indeed, implicit to this consensus is the recognition that global "survivability" is so elemental that a prohibition on the threat of use, or use of nuclear weapons can be reasonably inferred from the existing laws of war.

CONCLUSION

This survey of traditional international law has shown that treaty rules and standards, principles of international customary law and the demands of public conscience have been historically useful in developing and codifying the laws of war, often in response to the challenge of new weaponry. In view of the relevance of the principles of humanity to the formulation of the laws of war, an express prohibition on the use of nuclear weapons seems almost unnecessary, at least on the level of legal analysis, because of the relative clarity and bearing of conventional and customary international law.[95] If the traditional limiting goals of the laws of war are to be realized to any serious degree, then it would seem necessary to conclude that any use, or threat of use of nuclear weapons violates international law. To conclude differently would be to ignore the barbaric character of nuclear warfare. If the laws of war embody minimum ideas of decency, were we to exempt nuclear weaponry from such regulatory prohibition, we would be abandoning even this minimum effort.

However, can it not be said that nuclear weapons have been legitimated by the authoritative practice of the nuclear powers? To call such practice "authoritative" is to beg the central question, as well as to avoid the issue of whether general interna-

94. Report of the Secretary General on the Effects of the Possible Use of Nuclear Weapons and on the Security and Economic Implications for States of the Acquisition and Further Development of These Weapons at 5, U.N. Doc. A/6858.

95. Nevertheless, an international convention specifically prohibiting the threat of or use of nuclear weapons can only serve to reaffirm and strengthen the existing body of law.

tional law places absolute or unconditional boundaries on what political actors can legitimately do, regardless of the embodiment of international legal principles in positive law. If nuclear terrorism is exempted from scrutiny, any judgment on lesser-included varieties of terroristic activity, however grisly, becomes morally suspect. It would establish a double standard in which nuclear powers stand outside law and morality, but other actors would not. Why should others accept such a claim, except for what it is — an expression of naked force? Thus, coherence of the entire structure of international law with respect to warfare depends on condemning nuclear weapons as illegal.

The specter of war which may include the use of nuclear weapons has produced the need for a fundamental re-evaluation of the nature and objectives of war in the nuclear age. The use of nuclear weapons pursuant to a doctrine of mutual assured destruction or limited nuclear war or counterforce would have unpredictable and uncontrollable human and environmental consequences. Moreover, the development of nuclear doctrines has been complimented by technological innovations in weaponry which have the potential for producing extensive and indiscriminate suffering for combatants and noncombatants alike.

Certainly, nuclear war is qualitatively distinguishable from a conventional war. Never has a conventional war had the potential for destroying the biological identity — possibly even the existence — of the human race, or the economic and ecological viability of the planet. Indeed, the genetic and environmental effects alone that would result from the use of nuclear weapons provide a compelling moral and humanitarian argument against their legality. The analogy of the effects of a nuclear weapon to a poison, a poison gas or a bacteriological weapon; the indiscriminate nature of the effects of nuclear weapons on civilians and combatants; and the unnecessary and disproportionate suffering resulting from nuclear weapons and their consequent fallout — each of these is sufficient reason to prohibit the use, or threat of use of nuclear weapons under existing international law. Together these arguments provide overwhelming support for the conclusion that any threat or use of nuclear weapons is contrary to the dictates of international law.

Despite the clarity of the fundamental precepts of international law regarding nuclear weapons, there is an influential school of thought that claims that in an era of "total war," even the most fundamental rules can be disregarded in the name of military necessity. Ironically, this view of international law was urged in another context by some of the Nuremberg defendants and indignantly rejected by the International Tribunal. The Tribunal's judgment warns that this "Nazi conception" of total war would destroy the validity of international law altogether.[96] Ultimately, the legitimacy of such a view would exculpate Auschwitz; therefore, military necessity cannot be allowed to justify barbarism.

Nor is the fact that the laws of war were violated on numerous occasions during World War II by the Allies a sufficient reason to abandon these laws. Rather than ignoring the content of international law, the American legal community needs to restore respect for the limits on state sovereignty set by the laws of war, instead of validating past disrespect and criminality by cynical dismissals of international law.

It is practical, not idealistic, to take international law seriously. We would be more secure as a people, not less, if our governmental leaders were to try to conform national policy to the minimal obligations of international law. To assume the legality of a weapon with the distinct capability to terrorize and to destroy an entire civilian population would make meaningless the entire effort to limit combat through the law. Global "survivability" is so fundamental that the prohibition against nuclear weapons can be reasonably inferred from the existing laws of war. To conclude differently would be to ignore the barbaric and nefarious character of the use of nuclear weapons. As the laws of war embody the minimum demands of decency, exempting nuclear weapons from the regulatory prohibition would mean abandoning even this minimum standard.

While it is true that international law has not been as effective as it should be in regulating decisive state acts, the strength of the laws of war as constraints upon the war-making behavior of government cannot be measured by the extent of adherence on the part of governments alone. The assimilation and acceptance of these constraints on warfare by soldiers and citizens may influence the choice of tactics and policies at official levels of decision and eventually build support for nuclear disarmament initiatives and less militarized conceptions of national security. Fragile as the laws of war may be, they must be supported, espe-

---

96. For the text of the Final Judgment *see* 1 INT'L MILITARY TRIBUNAL, TRIAL OF THE MAJOR WAR CRIMINALS 171 (1947).

cially in the present setting in which the risks to humanity and civilization seem so great.

Consequently, it is essential that the legal community put the issue of the legality of nuclear weapons on the national agenda. To that end, the American legal community should indicate to its political leaders the importance of this issue by urging the formulation and adoption of a treaty prohibiting the first-use of nuclear weapons, a treaty prohibiting further production of nuclear weapons, and an international convention prohibiting the threat of use or use of nuclear weapons. While such treaties alone are not sufficient to prevent nuclear war, they would represent a symbolic first step in the more difficult process of nuclear disarmament. Such treaties would force unwilling governments to take the issue of abolition of nuclear weapons more seriously, as these treaties would represent a global consensus that nuclear weapons are not morally or legally tolerable.

In order to forestall an overwhelming tragedy, eliminating the possibility of nuclear war must be the highest priority for the American legal community. The demand for an effective international legal structure no longer seems quixotic — it is an absolute requirement of global survivability. Just as the rule of law within domestic society provides a civilized alternative to violence, there can be no more appropriate goal for the American legal community than the abolition of nuclear weapons.

4.

Nuclear Weapons and the Law: Enhancing Strategic Stability*

John Norton Moore**

No one can contemplate a nuclear exchange with anything but horror and a determination to make certain that it never occurs. Indeed, enhancing strategic stability and reducing the risk of war is the single most important task facing mankind. Accordingly, it is altogether proper that international lawyers and all other citizens should concern themselves, as Professor Weston and Professor Meyrowitz have eloquently argued, with issues of nuclear weapons and arms control. More importantly, however, all such efforts, including those suggested by Professor Meyrowitz,[1] must be judged by their contribution on the merits to enhancing stability and reducing the risk of war.

I might add in that connection that it does seem to me a little anomalous, thirty years after the height of the legal realist period, that the heart of the intellectual discussion so far today should be whether lawyers should take a stand in dealing with normative issues. That should be taken for granted. Rather, the heart of the intellectual discussion and our moral obligation in dealing with these issues is to deal with them on the merits and by the standard of what in fact reduces the risk of war and the kind of Armageddon that all of us want to avoid. Let me also add that I believe that all of us in these debates have an obligation to take seriously and listen seriously to the arguments of those on both sides of the discussion. It is all too easy, in dealing with an issue as emotional as this, to label those presenting imaginative new proposals as simply naïve dreamers on the one hand, or to say that those that have serious questions about the efficacy of such proposals are simply defenders of the status quo or of the horrors of nuclear weapons. Moreover, because of the special nature of this issue, it seems to me there is also a special moral obligation to candor, scholarly rigor and avoidance of polemics in presenting or appraising such issues. Since I owe that obligation of candor to you as an audience, and to Professor

---

* Reprinted, with permission from the *Brooklyn Journal of International Law,* Volume 9, Number 2 (1983).

** Walter L. Brown Professor of Law and Director, Center For Law and National Security, University of Virginia School of Law.

1. *See* Meyrowitz, *The Law of War and Nuclear Weapons,* 9 Brooklyn J. Int'l L. 227 (1983).

Meyrowitz, I am sorry to report that I believe his paper is seriously flawed.

Essentially, the problem is two-fold. First, in his conclusion that the use of nuclear weapons is illegal per se under present international law, he is making an inaccurate statement, and more troubling, he relies on an essentially polemical statement of the law to argue his case.[2] Second, Professor Meyrowitz errs when he recommends that all use of nuclear weapons should be made illegal per se, and that treaties should be adopted prohibiting the first use of nuclear weapons, further production of such weapons, and all other use of such weapons. Paradoxically, despite the intuitive reaction to such suggestions, it is my conviction that they would in fact decrease strategic stability and increase the risk of war. More troubling, Professor Meyrowitz seems to deal with the fundamental policy issues of arms control and strategic stability without discussing the real context or the real issues posed by these problems, and avoids recommending a series of arms control measures that may in fact be capable of reducing the risk of war. I will briefly address each of these criticisms in turn.

Initially, there is the question of an accurate description of the law. It is illegal under article 2(4) of the United Nations Charter to seek to achieve political objectives by the use of force, whether the attack is commenced with conventional or nuclear weapons. In addition, all agree that some uses of nuclear weapons, like some uses of conventional weapons, are clearly illegal. For example, a deliberate attack upon a civilian target without a military objective or such a targeting that results in casualties disproportionate to the military objective at stake may be illegal.[3] It is not accepted, however, that all use of nuclear weapons is illegal per se. I think we can state accurately that there is controversy on that issue but that most commentators would not accept the per se illegality of such weapons. I would have no difficulty with Professor Meyrowitz's paper if it had reached that conclusion. Some nations have argued such illegality and have sought to create the fire break on the use of nuclear weapons with an illegality ban per se. But most nations, particularly those which in fact possess the nuclear weapons—and these are the nations whose behavior we have to control—do not accept

---

2. *Id.* at 255-58.
3. *Id.* at 258.

the lawfulness of any such per se ban. France does not accept a per se ban on the use of nuclear weapons; the United States does not accept it; the United Kingdom does not accept it; China does not accept it; and it is unclear today whether the Soviet Union accepts it, although it is clear that from time to time the Soviet Union has worked toward this end in light of its clear conventional superiority in Europe.

In addition to this reality, let me indicate some other problems in the Meyrowitz paper regarding its attempts to present accurately the state of the law.

First, in citing General Assembly Resolution 1653[4] of 1961, Professor Meyrowitz does not tell us of the general rule in international law that General Assembly resolutions taken alone, without further evidence of state practice and state acceptance, in areas outside a variety of administrative matters, do not by themselves create international law. They can be evidence of international law; they can, in areas of popular consensus, perhaps reflect that consensus or even aid in creating it, but a resolution adopted by a margin of fifty-five to twenty or twenty-six does not, by any stretch of the imagination, create binding international law. Additionally, Professor Meyrowitz does not tell us that after being passed, there was a debate on General Assembly Resolution 2444[5] in 1968 in which, as an exchange for deleting a paragraph on nuclear weapons, there was a clear understanding among all participants that the basic principles of the laws of war do apply to nuclear weapons and that they were not per se illegal.

Professor Meyrowitz also does not tell us that during a committee meeting in 1977 dealing with the recent Protocols to the Geneva Conventions, the United States, France, the United Kingdom and the Soviet Union all took the view that the committee was an inappropriate forum to deal with nuclear weapons and that such weapons were not covered by the Protocols. Incidently, he also failed to tell us of the views of Professor Henri Meyrowitz—unrelated, I understand, but bearing the same name—a prominent French international law scholar, who reaches a diametrically different conclusion on the applicability of the Protocols. He fails to point out that there is some inconsistency between a total illegality of the use of nuclear weapons

---

4. G.A. Res. 1653, 15 U.N. GAOR Supp. (No. 17) at 4, U.N. Doc. A/5100 (1961).

5. G.A. Res. 2444, 23 U.N. GAOR Supp. (No. 18) at 50, U.N. Doc. A/7218 (1968).

and a whole set of arms control negotiations that do not deal with that issue. They deal with the SALT issues of controlling strategic arms, nonproliferation, and the like. One would have thought that if the issue were simply illegality, it would be approached in an agreement precisely as biological weapons were approached, that is, with a prohibition of manufacture, use of any kind and stockpiling, for example. Most intriguing to me as an international law craftsman, I suppose, is that Professor Meyrowitz applies a rigid principle of textualism from the Vienna Convention on the Law of Treaties and the 1977 Protocol to demonstrate his point, and yet he has the loosest interpretation of what is bacteriological warfare that I have heard. If you can textually, under the principles of treaty interpretation of the Vienna Convention, bring nuclear weapons under the bacteriological ban, then it seems to me that I have not fully understood the Vienna Convention.

Second, let's move to the question of whether making nuclear weapons illegal per se is a useful prescription. That is, would such a proposal on the merits aid the effort to reduce the risk of nuclear exchange or would it work to increase it? In this connection let us keep in mind the starting point that any offensive attack, whether carried out by nuclear weapons or conventional weapons, is illegal, and that some uses of nuclear weapons may also be illegal even in a clear defensive war. The real issue in the per se ban is whether all uses of nuclear weapons in defense against an armed attack should be made illegal. I have at least two problems with that proposal. To declare the use of nuclear weapons illegal against an ongoing nuclear attack would, it seems to me, increase the risk of such an attack, undermine deterrence and, in any event, be inherently incredible. For example, let's assume for a moment the occurrence of an on-going nuclear attack, first strike, against the United States, in which an enemy submarine located in the mid-Pacific has fired two of its weapons and is in the process of firing its remaining six weapons. Would we argue that the responsive use of a nuclear weapon is illegal in the face of that kind of ongoing nuclear attack? Now I will admit that this is one example that does not go to the heart of the problem of massive exchanges against cities. But if the whole question of a per se prohibition is to hold up, it must do so intellectually, in all the cases.

Another problem I have with a per se ban is that to declare a tactical use of nuclear weapons illegal against an overwhelming conventional attack by, for example, the Soviets in Europe, would substantially decrease deterrence and increase the risk of war. Moreover, if war broke out through conventional means, and the allied powers and NATO began to lose that war, do any of us believe that there would not be an enormous risk of escalation to nuclear weapons in that setting, whether or not there had been a prior nuclear pledge that such weapons were illegal? In fact it seems to me that it is precisely such ambiguity that reduces deterrence, and that in the end, increases the risk of the use of nuclear weapons. This is exactly the point that Professor Eugene Rostow makes: do you want to build your fire break and take your stand on article 2 (4) of the Charter,[6] that it is illegal to attack under international law, a clear attack, let's say, of the Warsaw Pact against the NATO area, or do you want to lessen the potential deterrence of that setting by ambiguously proclaiming in advance that no nuclear weapons can be used in response? The latter would create the kind of situation we had in Korea, after Dean Acheson had, at the Press Club, ruled out any United States involvement in defense of South Korea.

We might also look at the no first use concept. I do not have time to go into that in detail except to say that there is a substantial debate in the arms control literature on that question and there are persuasive arguments to be made that if you were to undermine deterrence, you would reduce stability and increase the risk of actual use of nuclear weapons.

Let me make one final point in conclusion, and in many respects, this for me is the most important point. Rather than focusing our attention at the periphery on a debate that seems to me is likely to add very little, if it does not even detract from strategic stability, we have an obligation as lawyers, again on the merits, to focus on the kinds of proposals that in fact can increase strategic stability. What are some of those proposals? Reductions in strategic and theater nuclear forces by both sides to equal limits through verifiable agreements, an MBFR agreement which reduces the Warsaw Pact conventional force imbalance or strengthens conventional forces in NATO to avoid the necessity of nuclear escalation in threats to vital interests, a comprehensive test ban treaty to degrade the first strike reliability of nu-

---

6. U.N. CHARTER art. 2, para. 4 provides as follows: "All members shall refrain in their international relations from the threat or use of force against the territorial integrity or political independence of any state, or in any manner inconsistent with the Purposes of the United Nations."

clear weapons through time, and strengthened efforts at avoidance of nuclear proliferation. These undertakings would all seem far more promising in enhancing stability and lessening the risk of war than a debate about no use or no first use of nuclear weapons.

5.
Deterrence and a Policy-Oriented Perspective on the Legality of Nuclear Weapons

Harry H. Almond, Jr.*

INTRODUCTION

Major policies are engaged when states prepare themselves for warfare, for their security, and for self-defense. Major policies are engaged, in general, whenever a nation decides that it must resort to the use of force and justify that use before the global community it shares. States in the past have recognized, and in the foreseeable future will continue to recognize, that certain uses of force are permissible, even justifiable on the highest moral principles relating to their survival. The legality of nuclear weapons is accordingly examined in this paper in a policy-oriented perspective.

Law is conceived as part of the authoritative decision flow, and the shaping of law is perceived as a continuing process aimed at policy goals and policy-oriented objectives. Conceived in the policy dimensions, we are enabled to analyze law in terms of policy functions—to avoid the limitations imposed by insisting that law is sufficient because treaties have been drafted, or because the prescriptions, through instruments or international agreements, or otherwise, have been laid down. Moreover, this conception puts particular stress on customary international law, because that law develops both in terms of prescription and application, each, in a sense, synergistically reinforcing and supporting the other function.

The legality of nuclear weapons is most appropriately analyzed against the deployment and use of such weapons to maintain the checks and balancing equilibrium associated with the establishment of deterrence under the major arms control agreements. Such an analysis necessarily compels us

---

* Professor of International Law, National War College, Washington, D.C. This paper is based upon but an enlargement of a presentation made at the Conference on Nuclear Weapons and Law held at Nova University Center for the Study of Law on February 5, 1983. None of the views or statements in this paper should be attributed to the United States Government or any of its agencies, nor to the National War College; the views expressed herein are entirely those of the author.

to examine such weapons not only for deterrence, but, because deterrence depends upon will, credibility, and capabilities, also against what must be done to survive if deterrence fails. Such an examination must extend to the deterrence demanded during warfare, and to the weapons, conventional or nuclear, that might best bring a major war to termination.

The lawyer who examines this subject may be persuaded to pursue differing, perhaps competing alternatives to establish controls. In the one he may seek through global order, including its social and legal processes, to establish the security essential to create a global deterrence against the outbreak of nuclear war. Though this is somewhat ambiguous as a goal, the perception is toward reducing the motivations and incentives to unleash a war for almost any reason. Many who adopt this alternative are adopting the notion that only through human dignity shared among peoples everywhere can we be assured of the security of peoples throughout the globe. When the goal is that of human dignity, warfare and military measures in general then become intolerable.

The other alternative perceives that the use of military measures is perennial—inherent in the competitive processes over power among nation-states—and that to oppose or check the outbreak of major or total wars, the only effective measure is to provide for checks and balancing against war. Of course, both policy goals might be promoted at the same time. But there are tendencies, currently at least, to neglect the attention that should be given to global order processes, and to concentrate on the balancing of nuclear weapons as the fundamental check against nuclear warfare. The balancing process itself is established through arms control agreements and through arms control policy shared among the adversaries, and the process is dependent upon the weapons themselves because it presupposes a checking of weapons, and not disarmament. The goal of general and complete disarmament associated with the McCloy-Zorin Agreed Principles Act of 1961 has been set aside in the practice of states, except for current proposals for the disarmament of chemical weapons, and has not yet resulted in concrete proposals for the elimination of all nuclear weapons.

Ultimately the legality of nuclear and other mass destruction weapons must come from the practice of states. That practice both expresses and exhibits the decision flow that applies state policy. Codification or legislation of the law among states to govern future conflicts is a major step into the unknown, except to the extent that such codification effectively builds upon past trends and upon the conditioning factors that have established the expectations among states concerning their use of weapons or the unleashing of violence in warfare.

The use of the atom bombs in the Second World War did not raise protests—apart from those of individuals—that would have excluded such weapons from future conflicts. Protests since the war have been largely made for polemical or ideological reasons and have been primarily those originating from the Soviet Union in its role as the principal rival of the

United States. The *Shimoda Case* in Japan—the only judicial review of the atomic bombing—did not go beyond the court of record and represents at best one court's view on the matter and no more.[1] Moreover, decisions in such courts and in such cases clearly fail to probe fully the major constitutional or "political" questions as we would expect under our own constitutional practice.

For these reasons, it must be expected that the use of nuclear weapons in future wars will not be perceived as illegal or impermissible, except where that use is inconsistent with international law, or more particularly the law of war. Moreover, it must be the expectation, flowing from the atom bombing in the Second World War, that states and their peoples at that time were able to tolerate such destruction. By the time the weapons were used, the Second World War had produced enormous destruction from conventional weapons and the destruction had been continuing for over four years. Tolerances had already developed with respect to the bombing of major Japanese and European cities. The destruction resulting from those massive conventional attacks was greater than that caused by the atom bombs at Nagasaki and Hiroshima. The targeting of cities as "strategic" and legitimate military targets had been fully established; and, the Nuremberg Tribunal did not address such attacks, nor declare them to be unlawful. Accordingly, reciprocal tolerances, already established, led to an acceptance of the attacks with nuclear weapons.[2]

I.

Strategy, like law, is a policy-oriented decision flow, emerging and changing to take into account the factors that affect a nation's strategic position when opposed to that of its rivals. Strategy has gradually been assimilated as part of a "grand strategy," which is identified in peacetime with national power.[3] This is primarily because no nation now dependent upon the advancing modern technologies can afford to wait, as the United States did in World War II, until a war is well underway, in preparing itself for its own defense.

The interdependence of policies relating to war and peace is described in the works of Carl von Clausewitz, particularly in his book entitled *On War*.[4] Clausewitz' perspectives are policy-oriented. From a policy viewpoint, military measures for the use of force that fall short of a use in warfare may be clarified by turning to the same analysis that Clausewitz used for war itself. Of course, as with military necessity, the resort to the use of force is subject to the legal tests of proportionality, relevance and legitimacy of targets, and the general prohibition against causing unnecessary suffering. But, Clausewitz provides policy content.

Clausewitz fully perceives the use of military measures as a policy instrument. First, he points out the characteristics of strategy—that is, the application and development of strategy as part of a decision flow:

Strategy is the use of the engagement [i.e., of armed combat] for the purpose of war. The strategist must therefore define an aim for the entire operational side of the war that will be in accordance with its purpose. In other words, he will draft the plan of the war, and the aim will determine the series of actions intended to achieve it: he will, in fact, shape the individual campaigns and, within these, decide on the individual engagements. Since most of the matters have to be based on assumptions that may not prove correct, while, other, more detailed orders cannot be determined in advance at all, it follows that the strategist must go on campaign himself. Detailed orders can then be given on the spot, *allowing the general plan to be adjusted to the modifications that are continuously required.* The strategist, in short, must maintain control throughout.[5]

It is clear from this passage that Clausewitz is developing his perception of strategy as an overall decision process, shaped in part by the circumstances in which those decisions must lead to action. The effectiveness of the strategist's decisions depend upon his maintaining control over the application of the decisions. His strategy, in a policy context, involves the formulation phase in which the strategy is conceived as a framework and guideline ("prescription") for action, and its effectiveness is measured by the outcome of action ("application"). As part of this phase the strategist, according to Clausewitz, must participate in the process of carrying out the actions because he is compelled to maintain a working strategy that will be continuously validated by the effectiveness of the actions undertaken. It is evident that he must modify his strategy, though retaining his strategic goals, wherever compelled to do so.

Strategy, for Clausewitz, includes purpose and goals, and these are policy goals. They are not the policy goals of war as such, because war, as an instrument of policy, serves a nation's goals and not simply the "goals of war" (assuming that there are "war goals" apart from rendering an enemy's armed forces incapable of pursuing the war). Hence, Clausewitz proposes certain clarifying propositions to provide us with an understanding of the nature of his policy framework:

If for a start we inquire into the objective of any particular war, which must guide the military action if the political purpose is to be properly served, we find that the object of any war can vary just as much as its political purpose and its actual circumstance. . . . Later, when we are dealing with the subject of war plans, we shall investigate in greater detail what is meant by disarming a country [i.e., as part of a military campaign]. But we should at once distinguish between three things, three broad objectives, which between them cover everything: the armed forces, the country, and the enemy's will. The fighting forces must be destroyed: that is, they must be put in such a condition that they can no longer carry on the fight. Whenever we use the phrase "destruction of the enemy's forces" this alone is what we mean.[6]

This passage from Clausewitz indicates that the goals of war fighting are to destroy the enemy's military forces, or neutralize them so that they cannot continue the fighting. It echoes Chinese thinker Sun Tzu who reached similar conclusions in his work on strategy entitled *The Art of War*.[7] But Clausewitz extends analysis into major objectives. Nations are engaged in war fighting—using military measures as instruments of policy—to reach the "country" of the adversary, to dominate its policies or overcome the opposition created by that country's policies, and therefore to reach the "will" of that nation to maintain such policies.

This policy orientation parallels the rivalry among major states for influence, power, and policy domination. It tends in its logic to lead to positions claiming to revolutionize, replace, and restructure the allocation of authority itself in the system—to see absolute security as the only salvation and hence the insecurity of all other participants as necessary.[8] But while states during the confrontational periods of "peacetime" pursue strategies short of war, they may have recourse to war itself as the addition of "other means" to achieve the nation's grand strategy for dominance.

Clausewitz observed that the "philosophers" were unable to distinguish war from other human interests because the difference lay in human nature—a matter beyond the reach of philosophy. He then pointed out that a unity exists which combines the "contradictory elements" in real life, or of human nature, and declares:

> We might have posited that unity to begin with if it had not been necessary to emphasize the contradictions with all possible clarity and to consider the different elements separately. This unity lies in the concept that war is only a branch of political activity; that it is in no sense autonomous. It is, of course, well known that the only source of war is politics—the intercourse of governments and peoples; but it is apt to be assumed that war suspends that intercourse and replaced it by a wholly different condition, ruled by no law but its own. . . . *We maintain, on the contrary, that war is simply a continuation of political intercourse, with the addition of other means.* We deliberately use the phrase "with the addition of other means" because we also want to make it clear that war in itself does not suspend political intercourse or change it into something entirely different. In essentials that intercourse continues, irrespective of the means it employs. *The main lines along which military events progress, and to which they are restricted, are political lines that continue throughout the war into the subsequent peace.*[9]

As in the legal processes, the application of military measures is identified, at least in part, as an "art." Predictability, certainty, and precision are not expected in these decision processes, and the essence of effective policy is the ability to adapt to changing conditions, to plan for contingencies and unfamiliar situations.

The psychological elements in conducting warfare which Clausewitz notes, and the stress he puts on it, apply equally to the limited uses of force in "peacetime":

> Four elements make up the climate of war: danger, exertions, uncertainty, and chance. If we consider them together, it becomes evident how much fortitude of mind and character are needed to make progress in these impeding elements with safety and success. According to circumstance, reporters and historians of war use such terms as energy, firmness, staunchness, emotional balance, and strength of character. These products of a heroic nature could almost be treated as one and the same force—strength of will—which adjusts itself to circumstances.[10]

Accordingly, the "art" of war evolves from the impact of the unknown, of what Clausewitz describes as "friction." In a most important passage he identifies friction in terms of the conditioning factors that are imposed upon policy and affect it or compel modification:

> Everything in war is very simple, but the simplest thing is difficult. The difficulties accumulate and end by producing a kind of friction that is inconceivable unless one has experienced war. . . . Countless minor incidents—the kind you can never really foresee—combine to lower the general level of performance, so that one always falls far short of the intended goal. Iron will-power can overcome this friction; it pulverizes every obstacle, but of course it wears down the machine as well. . . . Friction is the only concept that more or less corresponds to the factors that distinguish real war from war on paper. The military machine—the army and everything related to it—is basically very simple and therefore easy to manage. But we should bear in mind that none of its components is of one piece: each part is composed of individuals every one of whom retains his potential friction.[11]

Clausewitz introduces here the policy functions that are associated with the business of war fighting, and with the decisions that relate to recourse to war as an instrument of policy. In the more modern sense, Clausewitzian policy would embrace the current, larger context of state relations, where the use of force is not prohibited, but where the expectation associated with the use of force is the effectiveness of that use in limited arenas. But, if the use of force is permissible, and if, in fact, it is the only effective instrument for furthering the policy of states, then states may lawfully have the military capabilities for that purpose. States may also tailor these capabilities to meet the wide range of contingencies in which force is introduced.

The expansion of policy among states has taken place with their growing "interests," and these have been the result of increased mobility and communications. In abstract terms, their power arena has increased, and the power process expands to fill this arena. But more importantly, their perspectives on war have been affected. For example, the term "war" is not used in the Geneva Conventions of 1949, but has been replaced by the more far-reaching term—"armed conflict." The term "force short of war" describes the use of military measures during "peacetime." The Geneva Protocols of 1977, seeking to merge some of these issues, envisage the application of the law of war even to "wars of liberation."

Accordingly, the wider reach of policy toward global interests has led to new perspectives regarding the permissive use of force. The appearance of nuclear weapons has led to perceptions that nuclear weapons—whose existence must now be accepted—will be "used" for deterrence to check against the active use of those weapons by others. More importantly, because deterrence engages perspectives of war fighting or damage limitation if war breaks out, and also engages deterrence of escalation during armed conflict, and so on, the law relating to aggression (*jus ad bellum*—now in Article 2(4) of the U.N. Charter) and the law relating to the conduct of hostilities (*jus in bello*) must be continuously clarified. Clarification of these two interdependent and overlapping elements of law has led to the growing realization among lawyers that controls over nuclear and mass destruction weapons will need to extend beyond those limited to covering some weapons, or beyond those limited to merely placing conditions on their deployment. Underlying this legal analysis is the more formidable policy basis of "control": the recognition that use of nuclear and most mass destruction weapons, as they are coupled with ever-improving delivery systems, would lead to intolerable destruction. This is the fundamental policy base for control in the arms control agreements, put most succinctly by the late Raymond Aron: "The fact is that we are incapable of going beyond the banal proposition that 'thermonuclear war becomes improbable because of the horror it inspires.'"[12]

The same perspective was adopted by former Secretary of Defense James Schlesinger in a recent appearance before a congressional panel: "We must avoid melodrama and mindless emotion. For serious nuclear deterrence we must have serious forces that inspire fear of the consequences of attack. Deterrence rests upon awe."[13]

The legal controls rest upon the realities of the social controls—as just mentioned, upon fear. Such controls may be appropriate to major powers whose primary relationship is identified in competition, and whose primary competitive stock in trade are their military capabilities. These, as noted elsewhere, are part of the communications of confrontation and threat. However, the future of legal controls depends upon the invoking and effective application of community policies—imposing the standards and the perspective of the global community on the use of force. Such an application, in the legal sense, presupposes that we can and will distinguish between permissible and impermissible uses of force. But even this has become part of the rivalry of the two major states, because both are insisting on the legitimacy of their use of force, and hence both must appear beyond themselves to the global community at large.

Further difficulties that need to be explored in this context of control are those associated with the democratic processes, and with the impress of morality and principles of morality. Both of these matters must be explored in another paper. However, the weakness in the democratic approach to future crises is evident in the observations of such writers as Alexis de Tocqueville—recognizing that the democratic process lends itself to allocating the resources of a society with an approximating degree of justice and fairness, but that the process does not lend itself to making decisions and choices in establishing relations with other nations.[14]

The issue of morality is far-reaching for a people like those that inhabit the United States because our fundamental documents and the common law itself are policy oriented toward moral principle—toward justice and fairness, and toward the claims for human dignity. While these are of great importance in assessing the perspectives of the nation, their introduction as law—as the means to control power—is distinctly limited if they are not shared with other nations. While they remain largely the claims of the United States and the West on other nations for meeting the higher standards of conduct that we expect as part of our law, they are not effective control measures over weapons.

The problem of establishing the legality of weapons is difficult enough, under recognized and traditional perspectives relating to law, so that the introduction at too early a stage of moral principle to control what we do with major weaponry, with the unformed expectation that others will do likewise, is extremely risky. Unquestionably, nuclear and mass destruction weapons are barbaric, inhumane, unjust, and immoral. But, unfortunately, so are other weapons. Close attention must be directed to the decision process and controlling that process as it relates to the initiation of conflict or recourse to military measures, because, from past practice, such measures must be anticipated as far as we can see ahead.[15]

To some extent the perspectives of rivals are of great importance. Accordingly, the official doctrine, both military and strategic, should be examined for the basic policies of our rivals. Official doctrine is readily identifiable with the policy of a nation like the Soviet Union. Identified with new weapons, new weapons systems, and, hence, their missions, that doctrine identifies also the policy objectives established with those weapons. Military doctrine, however, necessarily must begin with the recognition that the weapons exist, and, because they exist, the restraints on their use in combat or in making a deliberate choice to engage in combat are limited entirely to whether the policy makers and the commanders perceive their military utility. Perceptions of military utility depend upon the circumstances of combat and are not likely to be affected by treaties or other international instruments either readily denounced, breached, or circumvented by the processes of application and interpretation. These are general perspectives that compel the greatest caution and the greatest care in establishing during peacetime effective and enforceable controls on weapons and weapons systems.

II.

Less clear than the policy implications in deterrence, in the fashioning and use of the strategic instruments of policy, and in law itself, are those that appear in military doctrine. The important texts on military doctrine include the "political" factor, and these texts not only assume the perspectives of the nation and its decision makers, but also tend to shape those perspectives.

A content analysis might show, for example, the policies of the United States and the Soviet Union regarding future wars—both those in which they are involved and other wars. Such an analysis, however, must await future inquiries by others; only a few observations can be made here. A review, even by the legal scholar, of such texts as that of Mahan, Douhet, Gorshkov, and of the overlapping doctrinal elements from Lenin, suggests that while nations have moved toward the use of mass or "democratic" armies, their objectives in warfare have moved toward "total" war. Such a movement is to some extent moderated by expressions of humanity, the latest appearing in the Geneva Protocols of 1977.[16]

States that expect the Geneva Protocols to prevail in their military doctrine, and in the military operations of warfare, will also expect their rivals to fulfill the Protocols' requirements. If the belligerent rivals both were to apply provisions of Protocol I, for example, such as those relating to reprisals, protection of noncombatants, restrictions on attacks on cities and urban areas permitted during World War II, along with the provisions on demilitarized zones and open cities, a long step toward moderation in the interests of humanity will have been achieved. If the belligerent rivals move instead toward "total war," following the trends established in the Second World War, then the belligerent respecting the Protocol's provisions, but facing a rival that does not, would be at a distinct disadvantage. More importantly, if this divergence in perspective prevails in peacetime, the planning, programs, and decisions leading to the preparations for self-defense, will not provide the state that expects to meet the humanitarian objectives and purpose of the Protocols with the appropriate military capabilities or strategies for a "total war." The interaction of peacetime and military strategies and policies is thus of great significance to the security of a nation.

The doctrinal setting of military strategy may be traced in Mahan:

> The history of Sea Power is largely, though by no means solely, a narrative of contests between nations, of mutual rivalries, of violence frequently culminating in war. The profound influence of sea commerce upon the wealth and strength of countries was clearly seen long before the true principles which governed its growth and prosperity were detected. To secure to one's own people a disproportionate share of such benefits, every effort was made to exclude others, either by the peaceful legislative methods of monopoly or

> prohibitory regulations, or, when these failed, by direct violence. . . . There-
> fore the history of sea power . . . is largely a military history.[17]

The same theme was adopted most recently by Gorshkov, Admiral of the Fleet of the Soviet Union, in *The Sea Power of the State,* but his views are presented both in the context of Marxism-Leninism, and in the context of the emerging social order that Gorshkov perceives as the inevitable communist society:

> The role of combat in oceanic directions in the general efforts of the armed forces has greatly increased and in certain conditions these directions may become paramount. At present, a fleet with its strikes from the sea is capable of changing the course and outcome of an armed struggle even in continental theatres of military operations.[18]

While Saul Cohen argues that the Soviet Union need not expand its overseas bases to establish its nuclear threat, he indicates that the magnitude or intensity of the threat is enlarged by such bases, and implies that the domain and scope of the threat, extending beyond that of long-distance missiles, are also intensified.[19] The point of great importance in these doctrinal materials is their argument for more military capabilities, for more effective military instruments, and for utilizing modern technologies. The U.S. Department of Defense Annual Report of 1979 declared in this vein:

> There is increasing evidence that the Soviet bomber and cruise missile force may be overtaking their submarine force as a threat to our fleet and to our forces necessary for the resupply of Europe. They can concentrate aircraft, coordinate attacks with air, surface or submarine launched missiles and use new technology to find our fleet units, jam our defenses and screen their approach.

This would have a serious impact on American deterrence goals to combat massive concentrations of Soviet military arms by high technology, because it would mean that with the acquisition of similar technology, the Soviet Union can with little cost disable or destroy high-value targets such as aircraft carriers or seaports. Moreover, with an increasing range of "interests," the Soviet doctrine must accommodate the need to use military capabilities—including conventional capabilities—to reach those interests:

> To avoid more Cubas and Sinais the Russians will have either to resist the temptation to take on commitments in the Third World (which include encouraging "wars of liberation") or else to acquire the military capacity this sort of policy calls for. This means building aircraft carriers and acquiring staging posts for airborne troops. It will be a bad omen for East-West relations if there are signs that they have chosen this second way out of their dilemma.[20]

But the Soviet Union has moved toward such conventional capabilities, as some observers predicted with concern. The leading Soviet text, by V. D. Sokolovskiy, *Soviet Military Strategy*, indicates that the Soviet Union, to ensure its own security, must face aggressors among the "imperialists"— the United States in particular—with weapons capable of being used in nuclear or conventional wars, or in wars in which both are used. If Soviet thinking is represented by this text, the allegations—also useful for ideological and polemical strategies—include the claim that the United States has long prepared for "preventive" or "pre-emptive" wars. This could suggest that the only alternative is for the Soviet Union to do the same:

> The strategy of "counterforce" primarily stems from the necessity for preventive war and the achievement of surprise. . . . It is believed that as a result of a forceful surprise attack, the enemy might be paralyzed in all respects, and that his fate would be decided in the course of the very first day of the war. . . . [Citing Bernard Brodie, the leading strategist on deterrence, Sokolovskiy continues.] The case for preventive war, in Brodie's opinion, has rested primarily on two premises: first, that in a strategic aerospace war using nuclear weapons, the country that strikes first undoubtedly has crucial advantage, *which with reasonably good planning will almost certainly be a decisive one*; and second, that total war is inevitable.[21]

While doctrine and the opinions of commentators and doctrinists may have differing impacts upon decisions and policy, it is evident that that impact will arise from the effect they have on official planning and policy. Moreover, through an analysis of doctrine it might be possible for both states to determine how their decisions and actions are perceived by each other, and to what extent their policies become a "strategy" promoting rather than inhibiting the development of global order. This, again, is a matter for separate inquiry. But the policy elements, including the impacts upon policies for developing more effective treaty instruments as strategies for achieving global order are of great importance to diplomats and their advisors.[22]

III.

Deterrence is a policy or strategy that may be perceived among states either as an exclusive policy, where, for example, a state believes that through superiority in weapons and in its will to use them it can assure itself that its rivals will not attack it, or as an inclusive policy, where states share a deterrence equilibrium and also share the responsibility for maintaining that equilibrium and making it effective.

With respect to mutual deterrence, Professor Thomas C. Schelling observed some two decades ago that such a strategy for deterrence arises from an interdependence of decisions and communications between rival states, in which, through the development of a common strategy, they establish processes through which both are induced to refrain from using weapons or going to war.[23]

Arms control policy for controlling weapons differs from disarmament policy. The arms control agreement presupposes that the weapons that are to be controlled are the basis for enforcing the agreement and ensuring its effectiveness. The disarmament agreement would eliminate the weapons. It would require control over the research, development, testing, and production of new weapons, so that such weapons could not be quickly produced or used for deception and surprise. However, enforcement of such disarmament agreements depends upon the promises of the parties—i.e., on their mutual undertakings and understandings of self-restraint, and not upon the controlled weapons—and the threat to give up controls—as the means of enforcement. Of course enforcement of disarmament might be based upon the threat to start up with new weapons, but such an enforcement process would clearly lead to instability.

Because disarmament agreements are very difficult to verify without major intrusions into the territory of each of the parties, the possibility of concluding such an agreement is slight. But states maintain arms control and do so both with and without arms control agreements. Such controls may be explicit, if set forth in the agreement itself, or tacit, if permitted to develop by the actions and reactions of parties that are balancing each other out through arms developments. In either case, the arms controls are based on a checks and balancing process, adjusting to asymmetries in weapons capabilities, and through that adjustment expected to accommodate them. Moreover, the controls are premised on the assumption that the weapons will never be used—particularly the nuclear and mass destruction weapons that promise intolerable destruction.

The deterrence equilibrium or arms control process flows from these continuing adjustments—incorrectly identified as an arms race—to the changes in technology and the modernization of weapons. The changing asymmetries of the agreements depend upon both sides sharing the fear that the weapons will be used, but, at the same time, threatening each other to maintain that fear—with the expectation that both will share the will, capabilities and credibility to make the threats effective.

Communication between states is crucial with respect to their relations. Clausewitz has indicated that communication continues—he refers to the process as "politics"—even during wartime. But in the larger policy sense it would be appropriate to refer to the threats, the weapons production, and adjustments in the weapons capabilities, production, procurement, and budgetary policies of nations, as part of the communication process between the rivals. Perhaps such commuinications appear to be relatively crude, and perhaps they lack the closer and more precise communications of free and open discourse. But all of these activities are communications, and each of them leads to reactions or acquiescence on the part of the rival state. Threats are clearly communications, but threats depend for their effectiveness on the will and capability of nations to carry them out. Hence they depend upon national power, and upon prestige and influence in international affairs; under current conditions such communications depend primarily upon weapons and the threat they afford. Under the arms control process, threats are designed as reciprocal to maintain deterrence. The goal for future relations must be to improve communications, stabilize relations, and pursue cooperative in place of competitive endeavors dependent upon military capabilities, through changed attitudes and conduct of the two parties.

The very complex adjustment and communication processes regulated through effective arms control agreements, and the agreements themselves, are effective only as long as there is a commitment to and common interest in keeping the checks and balancing process alive. As mentioned elsewhere, the effectiveness of arms control agreements is also dependent upon major nuclear weapons, because only they have the destructive force to ensure that the weapons will not be used.

Thomas C. Schelling, rightly, puts arms control policy into the decision-making context. The policies for deterrence must then be shared, and analysis would be in policy terms. The policy implications, once clarified, will assist in identifying measures to be taken to keep the equilibrium of deterrence effective.

The states involved share a "strategy"; that is, they both contribute to a common interest in a common strategy, provided through their decision process:

> The term "strategy" is taken here from the theory of games, which distinguishes games of skill, games of chance and games of strategy, the latter being those in which the best course of action for each player depends on what the other players do. The term is intended to focus *on the interdependence of the adversaries' decisions and on their expectations about each other's behavior*. This is not the military usage.[24]

For the purposes of this paper, deterrence can be defined as a strategy shared among states whose common interest, achieved by effective and shared enforcement measures, is to prevent the use of certain weapons, and, in the larger policy sense, to prevent the outbreak of war. Each of these terms requires brief comment.

The strategy as a shared strategy follows the conceptual framework proposed by Professor Schelling. The common interest of rivals who are seeking to make their deterrence effective, mutual and reciprocal, contributes to the peaceful relations or minimum public order shared between them and others. The measures that they have to enforce their shared policy—because strategy, as noted earlier, is a policy-oriented activity—include at this time the weapons at their disposal. But these are measures where the weapons serve a checks and balancing process, offsetting each other through the balancing, and creating deterrence because they offer similar and substantial destruction to both sides.

Though weapons capabilities need not be identical and can be asymmetrical, the perceptions of nations lend themselves toward the greater security afforded through symmetries because there are strong tendencies to favor if not symmetrical weapons capabilities, then reliable processes to make the asymmetries reach symmetrical outcomes. Of course, the results of ineffectively balancing such outcomes are that each side perceives what the other side perceives: the threat, the will, the credibility in carrying out the threat, and the capabilities to inflict catastrophic destruction on the other side and to be subjected to such destruction in turn.

Deterrence is, in summary, established in the following way. Its effectiveness and enforceability are dependent upon the balancing of the major and most destructive nuclear weapons, because all other weapons have a military utility, and could, if used, be targeted discriminately against military objectives, and presumably could meet military needs. Accordingly, the only arms control agreements that are critical in such a process are those relating to the major nuclear weapons.

However, the arms control agreements are treaties. They cover and are reliable solely for the weapons or agents specified. They do not cover other weapons. But they almost always *control* weapons and do not provide for disarmament. Moreover, with regard to nuclear weapons they do not provide for disarmament because this would require measures of inspection, control, and compliance that are beyond what the major rivals find acceptable. The arms control agreements accordingly provide for checks and balancing—the deterrence equilibria—through the weapons themselves, and, as suggested above, the effectiveness is established through a fear of the weapons.

Technological change is a major, and largely uncontrollable, activity among states that leads to processes and products that may have military uses, military support uses, peaceful applications, or combinations of these. The energy unleashed through nuclear power provides a simple example of processes for needed energy, with products that may be used for nuclear explosive devices. The nuclear explosive devices that might be used for surface mining, for canals and so on, also provide the data critical for making nuclear weapons. Technological change provides then an impact— affecting the strategic environment among states in general, but more particularly affecting the processes designed to maintain a deterrence equilibrium.

As the technologies change, and because they cannot be monitored, these changes appear in the "modernization" of weapons and lead to new asymmetries that need balancing, and to the false perception that this constitutes an "arms race," when in fact it constitutes a part of the arms equilibria process or deterrence process. All of the major arms control agreements, unable to provide for the monitoring of research and development, simply make "modernization" one of the permitted activities.

Arms control policy, extending beyond the policy that is associated exclusively with the weapons covered in a given arms control agreement, unquestionably has a wider coverage. But the unresolved issue then remains whether a common interest has been reached in the larger policy, or whether that policy, shared by the United States and the Soviet Union, relates exclusively to the major and most destructive nuclear weapons. Such an issue is not resolved through high expectations, but must be resolved both in the policy and practice of the two states. There is no evidence, at this time, of such resolution, nor of the basis upon which such resolution can depend. In short, there is no global order conception shared by the two rivals leading to and giving some assurance in the future to security that will be based upon such a public order. Both sides, with differing values and value expectations, remain isolated and adversarial—each with its own conception as to what the future global order should be.

Before turning to the operative elements in deterrence and the associated policies, some of the current views on deterrence as strategy should be noted. Bernard Brodie, a leading strategist, declared:

> For one thing, [the new strategy of deterrence] uses a kind of threat which we feel must be absolutely effective, allowing for no breakdowns ever. The sanction is, to say the least, not designed for repeating action. One use of it will be fatally too many. Deterrence now means something as a strategic policy only when we are fairly confident that the retaliatory instrument upon which it relies will not be called upon to function at all.[25]

Brodie, accordingly, takes perspectives that are similar to those of Schelling, and both authors have been relied upon for my discussion above. Brodie indicates that deterrence is the absolute and final policy. There can be no war-fighting policy in the sense that the rivals can ever take the decision to engage in a war with the major nuclear weapons, but the rivals are caught in the paradox that their deterrence is dependent upon each having the reliable "retaliatory instrument." Such an instrument is of course an effective war-fighting instrument.

President Kennedy reflected the same line of argument. In a book review of B. H. Liddell Hart's *Deterrence and Defense,* he said:

> The Soviet acquisition of nuclear weapons and the means for their delivery . . . now makes certain that a nuclear war would be a war of mutual devastation. The notion that the free world can be protected simply by the threat of "massive retaliation" is no longer tenable. . . . [R]esponsible leaders in the West will not and should not deal with limited aggression by unlimited

weapons. . . . [T]he central task of American and Western military policy is to make all forms of Communist aggression irrational and unattractive.[26]

President Kennedy thus raised the broader issue of aggression in his observation. His concern extended beyond that of deterrence itself; it extended to shaping the policy and policy goals of the Soviet Union. He would have attempted this by measures that he does not describe—presumably by instruments of policy other than those employing military measures, though he does not rule out military measures as long as the "unlimited weapons" are never used.

Some complain that we move in this process to "thinking about the unthinkable," and that we incur risks in doing so. In his *The American Way of War*, Russell F. Weigley, speaking of Herman Kahn, one of the principal writers alleged to be such a "thinker about the unthinkable," noted:

> Herman Kahn's *On Thermonuclear War* provoked cries of immorality from those who thought Kahn's coldbloodedness and the "grim jocularity" that attended his dissections of nuclear horror a species of encouragement to itchy nuclear trigger-fingers. The critics of his morality tended to fail to note his repeated insistence that "The greater understanding of nuclear war. . . reduces the danger of accidental war and increases the possibility that any war could be conducted with restraint and terminated relatively soon," and his insistance too that nevertheless the perils were so great we ought to strive to end the arms race through some system of the rule of law.[27]

These citations, though current, go to the formative stage of nuclear strategy, and that strategy, as already noted, is continuing to evolve. But strategy of nuclear weapons lacks the validation of state practice, so speculators, observers, and commentators must attempt to bolster their arguments through reasoning without the benefit of supporting action. The real importance in adopting strategy, both the inclusive strategy of arms control (to the extent it actually exists) and the exclusive strategy of nations opposing each other as rivals, is in its impact on their plans, policies, and programming regarding the weapons and their possible use.

IV.

The relationship of defense and deterrence must be considered—again in terms of their policy orientation—in order to understand the role of nuclear and mass destruction weapons, and the need to maintain the balancing process. The communications between states involved in deterrence include, in addition to diplomatic communications, their procurement policies, their military budgets, the threats and hostile acts (including confrontations) between them, their research and testing capabilities, and the weapons and force capabilities they have, including all of their weapons, conventional and non-conventional alike. These communications differ in form from those associated with diplomacy, or those provided through media or media-oriented instruments. Because such communications are not entirely reliable, the balancing process moves awkwardly, suggesting an arms race. However, in the checks and balancing controls, we perceive only the filling of military capability gaps where weapons imbalances are perceived to exist. Changes in the strategic environment clearly affect these perceptions.

Are the weapons of deterrence needed for defense or war-fighting? In that event, does deterrence offer any control over weapons, or only control in the sense of balancing out capabilities and no more? The answers to these questions depend upon the perceptions regarding the possibility of war, and in the event of war, its conduct, and the processes that might lead to at least some form of reasonable and desirable termination.

First, the distinctions between deterrence and defense should be noted. According to Glenn H. Snyder in his *Deterrence and Defense: Toward A Theory of National Security*:

> The central theoretical problem in the field of national security policy is to clarify and distinguish between the two central concepts of deterrence and defense. Essentially, deterrence means discouraging the enemy from taking military action by posing for him a prospect of cost and risk outweighing his prospective gain. Defense means reducing our own prospective costs and risks in the event that deterrence fails. Deterrence works on the enemy's intentions; the deterrent value of military forces is their effect in reducing the likelihood of enemy military moves. Defense reduces the enemy's capability to damage or deprive us; the defense value of military forces is their effect in mitigating the adverse consequences for us of possible enemy moves, whether such consequences are counted as losses of territory or war damage. The concept of "defense value," therefore, is broader than the mere capacity to hold territory, which might be called "denial capability." Defense value is denial capability plus capacity to alleviate war damage.[28]

Snyder subsequently indicates ways to reallocate the costs and burdens of defense through allies, the balancing of power among allies, and so on. But the fundamental element, regardless of the modalities, is that a clear perception be had of whether the strategy and national power of a nation must be aimed at defense rather than deterrence, and, therefore, whether deterrence without defense meets the requirements of our own policy that arms control be consistent with our national security.

Major states have no choice but to provide for their own defense, and the United States and the Soviet Union, in effect, share a strategy, assimilated as deterrence and arms control policy, in which they are checking their defense, not their deterrence capabilities. As Y. Harkabi in his *Nuclear War And Nuclear Peace* has indicated, they have no choice but to have, each of them, the capabilities to enforce deterrence, so that deterrence becomes enforceable ultimately only through war-fighting capabilities.[29] The reason for this is that while deterrence currently flows from the balancing of the major and most destructive nuclear weapons, the strategy of the two major rivals is that neither can rely on the other for deterrence not breaking down, and because while nuclear weapons might be in balance—and for good reason never invoked—neither side can assume that other military measures will not be invoked, or that these might not lead through escalation to a major war involving the major weapons.

V.

This section will conclude this brief inquiry by examining the legality of nuclear weapons. As already indicated, the deployment and targeting of such weapons is already recognized, and appears in the major arms control agreements between the United States and the Soviet Union such as SALT. For the purposes of those agreements—for arms control policies and for deterrence policies—the two rivals have legitimized their use of nuclear weapons in a posture of continuing threat.

Moreover, it has been suggested that a distinction between deterrence and defense may be inconceivable as a strategy of either side, so that both sides are maintaining the weapons that would ultimately be used for war fighting (regardless, here, of the rationality of such a decision). Furthermore, they have both developed the lesser nuclear weapons, weapons with far less destructive force and with accurate targeting capabilities (avoiding the stigma of indiscriminate weapons), and such weapons clearly would have military utility.

In addition, both sides have maintained an active and vigorous program of research, testing, and development. These are activities that do not lend themselves to compliance procedures and measures, and even direct on-site inspection might prove to be insufficient. The sciences and the rapidly advancing technologies serve such activities and also serve peacetime applications. Distinctions between peacetime outcomes of the sciences and military outcomes cannot readily be made, let alone monitored: lethal chemicals have long been used in industrial processes; nuclear energy spinning off nuclear weapons materials has long been applied for peacetime purposes; and so on.

Nevertheless, limited war between the major rivals offers grave risks. Escalation up the scale toward the major nuclear weapons cannot be controlled, except on paper. The developments since World War II show ever increasing sophistication in the use of private armies, proxies, subversion, and surrogates—particularly by the Soviet Union, but presumably in the future increasingly by the United States as well. Such entities, apart from the undesirable features they offer, also offer the possibility of finding groups that might more congenially merge with the expectations of the peoples with whom they are engaged.

All of these are elements having an impact on deterrence, and compelling us almost by an "iron law" to pursue military activities in the sense of modernization, improved weaponry and delivery systems, research and development of substitutes, and management of weapon substitutes and alternatives. But these are all elements that operate in an environment in which states have traditionally used military measures and they will, in the foreseeable future, continue to resort to military measures as a major instrument of policy. For these reasons the arms control and deterrence equilibria only maintain the checks and balancing equilibria without, in themselves, affecting the relations between the rivals or changing them.

These are the "givens" of current relations, and they set the stage upon which we assess policy, and law, in terms of the expectations of the major participants. While improved communications are crucial to make the process operable, such communications might be diverted toward improving the legal processes.

The legality of nuclear weapons has now been fully established through the treaties and international agreements that cover them for arms control and other purposes. Moreover, their legality is not restricted by treaties relating to the use of such weapons, because such treaties must address the weapons themselves, and none of them do so. It is not enough to find analogies in law, because the practice of states indicates that they do not restrain themselves by analogies, but only by agreements precisely relating to their weapons, or through the application of the law of war. The legality of such weapons (or of mass destruction weapons for that matter) is not affected by resolutions of the U.N. General Assembly because states do not expect that those resolutions have either the authority or controlling effects expected from law: delegations to the General Assembly do not go instructed to reach agreement relating to weapons, but to debate, and maintain positions, or claims, suitable to that forum.

We are compelled to conclude that the control of nuclear weapons is dependent upon the control over the use of force. We are led to this conclusion because only through a more effective control can we be assured of the security needed against the outbreak of nuclear war. The possibilities of escalation of conventional wars between nuclear states are evident, while the inability of states and their military commanders to control the course of warfare, or the weapons used, is clear enough from the practice of belligerent states.

Unquestionably the law of war contains the controls of law, but these controls, except for agreements such as the Hague Regulations, appear largely in the form of general "principles." Among such principles are those of military necessity and of humanity, tending in their operation or application to moderate the destructive impacts of nuclear and mass destruction weapons. However, because these are very general principles, and because their application appears in the reciprocal tolerances of the belligerents during warfare, or, *post hoc*, in the decisions of war crimes tribunals, their application depends upon the perspectives of the belligerents at the time that they are conducting warfare itself. The application of such principles to nuclear and mass destruction weapons in a future war will, accordingly, depend upon such tolerances as the belligerents will reveal during the war. Because nuclear and mass destruction weapons exist, the likelihood that they will be used is very great, and we are thrown back for controls upon what states can achieve through arms control agreements made enforceable and effective during peacetime.

The legal principle of military necessity, in itself a humanitarian principle operating to moderate the destructive force of war and war fighting, is said to have operative force in part because it reflects a "principle of war" identified as the principle of economy of force. Nevertheless, the legal principles operate in a broad and ambiguous way—they do not have the cutting edge that provides any assurance that nuclear weapons or other mass destruction weapons can be identified as indiscriminate under all circumstances, able to operate against target areas so large that they fail the test of relevancy, or can be said to be disproportionate because of their far-reaching destructive capabilities. Such weapons have been assimilated into public opinion and decisions. We can reasonably expect, therefore, that the tolerances regarding their use will be substantial in the event of future war, simply because the expectations of future violence lead to this conclusion.

The U.N. Charter has outlined in prescriptive form the legal order expected of member states and in particular the outlawry of war and acts or threats of aggression. Article 2(4), in which states agree to refrain "from the threat or use of force against the territorial integrity or political independence of any state, or in any other manner inconsistent with the Purposes of the United Nations," establishes the fundamental guidelines.

Professor Myres S. McDougal has concluded that in seeking the security of minimum order these guidelines are in themselves ample, but their weakness lies in the failure to attend to institutional measures to make them effective and hence controlling. As indicated in the following quotation, even the distinction between impermissible and permissible coercion has been achieved:

> In a vast and continuing flow of decision, global constitutive process establishes for any particular territorial community a modest but viable security in relation to all these different features of interaction. . . . The obvious Achilles heel in global public order is in the failure of constitutive process to establish enough effective control over the different nation-states to preclude resort to unauthorized coercion and violence. The number one problem of humankind remains, as we have indicated above, that of security in the sense of establishing a minimum order, in control of unauthorized coercion and violence, which will permit more effective pursuit of an optimum order in maximization of the shaping and sharing of all values. Through articles 2(4) and 51 of the United Nations Charter, and many ancillary prescriptions, the global community has at long last achieved a workable

distinction between impermissible and permissible coercion, admitting of application in particular instances in support of minimum order. It remains, however, for the community to establish an appropriate institutional framework both for disinterested, third-party appraisal of particular instances of alleged impermissible coercion and for the application of appropriate sanctioning measures in preventing and deterring coercion and in restoring and rehabilitating public order. Though contemporary nation-states receive tremendous benefits from constitutive process they have as yet been only imperfectly subjected to its complementary burdens.[30]

We are compelled to conclude that nuclear and mass destruction weapons shape our policy with other states. But we must also conclude that our claims to use those weapons and the policies (and law) relating to those claims are in turn shaped by the existence of the weapons themselves.

The challenge for all states is in establishing and cultivating minimum order. Appropriate institutions must be established among states to address the matters of coercion, and provide, authoritatively, for the distinctions between permissible and impermissible coercion. States that assume all their acts of force are permissible, and that in the last resort they can pass judgment for themselves on the question of permissibility, will continue to do so in the absence of a global structure to prevent these claims.

The policy relationships between law, strategy, deterrence, and defense, and the impacts of these policy-oriented activities of states upon our perceptions of national security have only been briefly sketched in this paper. But it should be borne in mind that had nuclear weapons never been created, the conventional weapons of World War II would have had far more attention—regarding their destructiveness and their targeting capabilities—and would have created a threat far more serious than that of the nuclear weapons. This would have come about from the persisting trends flowing from the vast and tolerated destruction of the Second World War.

Moreover, the risks of major war would also have been greater than exist now in our era of nuclear weapons because of an assumed "familiarity" with conventional weapons. The fear that is still connected with nuclear weapons, and with their untried destructive capabilities, must be nurtured among nations in order to establish their deterrence. The current balance, in short, is consistent with balancing out the products and processes of an advancing technology. Because that technology cannot be effectively monitored and spawns peaceful applications indiscriminately with military applications and weapons, there is little likelihood that security could be based upon monitoring the technologies of rival states, or, even if instituted, that such monitoring processes would be effective. The breakout opportunities in technologies, in the absence of the checks from nuclear weapons already in a balancing process, would rival those with greater and more far-reaching impacts that occurred with the atom bomb of the Second World War.

We cannot rely upon "moral force," because, as Correlli Barnett has declared in his analysis of the decline of British power:

> Moral force, or righteous indignation, was in fact the only means the British left themselves with which to influence the course of world affairs. For their parsonical belief in the powers of moral reprobation was accompanied by an equally parsonical dislike of "immoral" forms of pressure, such as bribery, threats or force. The British ruling class deliberately rejected from their thinking the fundamental operating factor in international relations— power. . . . They had insufficient understanding of the nature of the bargaining process; indeed they eagerly sought to open negotiations when and where their own bargaining position was feeble in the extreme. A negotiation was seen in fact not so much as an arena of pressure and manoeuvre as a meeting of minds in good faith; as an interplay of reasoned persuasion.[31]

According to Barnett, the British were mesmerized by the illusory goals of the League of Nations. They expected the League to be effective even though the global social order upon which it depended had not come into existence:

> It was the ambitious hope and intention of the framers of this document to usher in a new era in the life of mankind. The nobility of their vision is beyond question: a world society regulated by law instead of the power struggle, often violent, that had hitherto shaped the course of history. But its nobility does not redeem its impracticability in the circumstances of the epoch. The new world order rested on nothing more solid than another signed folio of parchment. . . . Naturally enough, in the prevailing atmosphere, much weight was also laid on the moral influence of the League, speaking as the voice of the world's conscience. It appeared therefore that the success of the new system of international law and order depended on there being no lawbreakers. "Covenants without swords are but words," bleakly wrote Thomas Hobbes in the seventeenth century. The League of Nations possessed no sword. How could it? The League, as such, enjoyed no kind of independent existence and authority at all.[32]

In the absence of institutions, states must look to their own capabilities, and, with the time allotted them, seek to shape with those capabilities in existence some form of order and security for that order. Michael Howard noted:

> Perhaps, indeed, it is necessary, in reassessing the place of military force in international affairs, to rid ourselves of the idea that if such force is employed it must necessarily be in a distinct "war," formally declared, ending in a clear decision embodied in a peace treaty, taking place within a precise interval of time during which diplomatic relations between the belligerents are suspended

and military operations proceed according to their own peculiar laws. We reveal the influence of this concept whenever we talk about the "next war" or "if war breaks out" or "the need to deter war." . . . Instead of a formal state of war in which diplomacy was subordinated to the requirements of strategy, [it is more likely] specific military operations might be carried out under the most rigorous political control. It will certainly no longer be enough for the statesman to give general guidance to a military machine which then proceeds according to its own laws. . . . The demands on the military for discipline and self-sacrifice will be great beyond all precedent, and the opportunities for traditional honor and glory negligible.[33]

And Howard concludes, as this paper must conclude:

The power which states exercise in international affairs is compounded of many attributes, economic, diplomatic, cultural and ideological as well as military. But military power, the capacity to use violence for the protection, enforcement or extension of authority, remains an instrument with which no state has yet found it possible completely to dispense. Indeed, it is not easy to see how international relations could be conducted, and international order maintained, if it were totally absent. The capacity of states to defend themselves, and their evident willingness to do so, provides the basic framework within which the business of international negotiations is carried on. That this framework should be as wide and as flexible as possible hardly needs arguing; but if no such limits existed, if it were known that there were no extremes of surrender and humiliation beyond which a state could not be pressed, the maintenance of international order would surely be, not easier, but incalculably more difficult. . . . The ultimate test of national independence remains in the nuclear what it was in the pre-nuclear age: whether people are prepared to risk their lives in order to secure and preserve it.[34]

NOTES

1. *See* Ryiichi Shimoda et al. v. The State (Tokyo, Dec. 1963), *reprinted in* The Law of War vol. II (L. Friedman ed. 1972).

2. *But see* Protocol I Additional to the Geneva Conventions of 12 August 1949, and Relating to the Protection of Victims of International Armed Conflicts, arts. 51 and 57, *opened for signature* Dec. 12, 1977, *reprinted in* 16 Int'l Legal Materials 1391 (1977) (hereinafter Protocol I of 1977), which would moderate attacks whether or not they are denominated "strategic attacks" on cities.

3. According to Department of the Army publication FM 100-1, at 4, "national power" is described, in part, as follows:

National power, the aggregate capacity of a state to achieve its national interests and to influence the behavior of other states, consists of several distinct yet inter-related elements—political, economic, socio-psychological, technical and military. The attainment of national objectives, such as peace among nations on terms not inimical to United States interests, necessarily involves simultaneous employment of these components of national power. Specific goals supporting any national objective are achieved through application of selected combinations of these elements of national power. Military and national goals are therefore inextricably woven together. Application of one or all of the components of national power, including military power, may be required as the nation faces the broad sweep of international relations, ranging from free and harmonious mutual agreements between sovereign nations to unrestrained global military conflict. . . . The United States must prepare itself for the use of military power across the entire spectrum of conflict, from relatively mild policy disagreements, to fairly intense nonwar confrontations of an economic or political nature, to a range of military situations which could conceivably include nuclear war. To achieve maximum effectiveness in support of a coherent national strategy, military power must, however, be applied, in concert with, and in support of, the other relevant elements of national power.

4. C. von Clausewitz, On War (trans. by M. Howard & P. Paret, 1976) (hereinafter Clausewitz).

5. *Id.* at 177 (emphasis added).

6. *Id.* at 90.

7. Sun Tzu, The Art of War 66-71 (1963). Sun Tzu insists that "all warfare is based on deception," *id.* at 66; but he counsels against "protracted war," and, in the offensive strategy, advises against destroying the enemy or his cities unless necessary.

8. *Cf.*, to this end, H. Kissinger, A World Restored (1964).

9. Clausewitz, *supra* note 4, at 605 (emphasis added).

10. *Id.* at 103-04.

11. *Id.* at 119.

12. R. Aron, On War 14 (trans. by T. Kilmartin, 1959).

13. Testimony of James Schlesinger, *quoted in Washington Times,* November 23, 1983, at 5 A.

14. *See generally,* A. de Tocqueville, Democracy in America (1946), particularly Vol. 2, Third Book, Chapters XIII, XXI et seq. On this subject, *see also* the writings of Harold Lasswell, Walter Lippmann, and Gabriel Almond.

15. *See* R. Lebow, Between Peace and War (The Nature of International Crises) (1981) for a view that all wars are deliberate. A short survey on this subject of doctrine is in B. Lambeth, The Elements of Soviet Strategy 7-9 and accompanying notes (1979).

16. *See* Geneva Protocol I of 1977, *supra* note 2, and Protocol II Additional to the Geneva Conventions of 12 August 1949, and Relating to the Protection of Victims of Non-International Armed Conflicts, *opened for signature* Dec. 12, 1977, *reprinted in* 16 Int'l Legal Materials 1442 (1977).

17. A. Mahan, The Influence of Sea Power Upon History 1 (1957). Mahan envisages, in the power process, the competition for power over the seas for the values (resources and control) that the sea affords.

18. S. Gorshkov, The Sea Power of the State, at x (1977). A revolutionizing influence on the development of the armed forces and the art of deploying them has always been exerted by technical discoveries. This expresses the regularity of the impact of the economic development of society and the growth of its productive forces in the military sphere. Lenin wrote: "Military tactics depends on the level of military technology."

Gorshkov gives the larger perspective: For the Soviet Union, the main goal of whose policy is the building of communism and a steady rise in the welfare of its builders, sea power emerges as one of the important factors for strengthening its economy, accelerating scientific and technical development, and consolidating the economic, political, cultural, and scientific links of the Soviet people with the peoples and countries friendly to it. *Id.* at 1.

19. S. Cohen, Geography and Politics in A World Divided 57 (1963).

20. *The Economist* (June 24, 1967), *quoted in* Air Power in the Nuclear Age 172 (M. Armitage & R. Mason eds. 1983).

21. V. Sokolovskiy, Soviet Military Strategy 61-62 (3rd ed. 1975) (emphasis added).

22. Communist ideology and the nature of the Soviet system combine to produce among Soviet decision-makers an extremely pragmatic attitude toward international law. Since international law is very largely a product of the capitalist West, communist doctrine would have justified Soviet decision-makers in totally rejecting it. But in fact they do not openly deny its binding force. They have not even made much overt use of the freedom to accept or reject particular norms and institutions of international law which from time to time the Soviet writers have claimed for them. They frequently use international law as a tool of diplomacy. Soviet textbooks of international law consist in large part of recitals of legal doctrines and practices familiar to Western lawyers. Lissitzyn, Western and Soviet Perspectives, *in* International Law and the Twentieth Century 137 (L. Gross ed. 1969). *See generally id.* at 130 *et seq.*

23. *See* T. Schelling, The Strategy of Conflict (1960).

24. *Id.* at 3 n. 1 (emphasis added).

25. B. Brodie, Strategy in the Missile Age 272-73 (1965).

26. *Quoted in* R. Weigley, The American Way of War 438 (1973).

27. *Id.* at 440.

28. G. Snyder, Deterrence and Defense: Toward a Theory of National Security 3-4 (1961) (emphasis omitted).

29. Y. Harkabi, Nuclear War and Nuclear Peace (1966). Harkabi draws deeply on the views of both Schelling and Snyder. Deterrence in his conception is the active element of policy: its effectiveness depends upon action balancing out changes in circumstances, weapons developments, and the capabilities and actions of the rival that is to be deterred.

30. McDougal, *International Law and the Future,* 50 Miss. L.J. 259, 310 (1980).

31. C. Barnett, The Collapse of British Power 242 (1972).

32. *Id.* at 243.

33. M. Howard, Studies in War and Peace 206-07 (1970).

34. *Id.* at 208-09.

6.
International Law as Law of the Land: Another Constitutional Constraint on Use of Nuclear Weapons*

Martin Feinrider**

Introduction

Concern now focuses on the threat to humankind posed by nuclear weapons to an extent not seen since the days of the Ban-the-Bomb movement of the 1950s.[1] During the past several years, millions of people have taken to the streets in North America and Europe to express this concern.[2] Now, in the United States, physicians, scientists and lawyers are banding together in their own professional organizations to concentrate energies and expertise on this, the greatest problem of our age.[3]

As part of the legal community's effort to address issues presented by nuclear weapons,[4] Professor Arthur S. Miller has written a thought-

---

* Reprinted, with permission, from *Nova Law Journal*, Volume 7, Number 1 (1982).

** Associate Professor of Law, Nova University Center for the Study of Law. The author is a member of the Consultative Council of the Lawyers' Committee on Nuclear Policy. He gratefully acknowledges the assistance provided by Maria Fernandez-Valle, a Goodwin Research Fellow at Nova Law Center, during preparation of this Article for publication.

1. "Concern for the risks of nuclear proliferation (and for the underlying risk of nuclear war) is the beginning of wisdom." Farley, *Nuclear Proliferation,* in SETTING NATIONAL PRIORITIES: THE NEXT TEN YEARS 129, 165 (H. Owen & C. L. Schultze eds. 1976).

During November 1982 elections, Nuclear Freeze proposals were approved in 9 out of 10 state referenda and 27 out of 29 city and county referenda. Union of Concerned Scientists, November 11th Convocation Update, No. 8 (Nov. 5, 1982).

2. *See generally* Butterfield, *Anatomy of the Nuclear Protest,* N.Y. Times, July 11, 1982, § 6 (Magazine), at 14.

3. *E.g.,* Physicians for Social Responsibility, the Union of Concerned Scientists, the Lawyers' Alliance for Nuclear Arms Control, and the New York-based Lawyers' Committee on Nuclear Policy.

4. During the 1982-83 academic year symposia or law review issues dedicated to examination of legal questions raised by nuclear weaponry have been or will be pro-

ful and thought-provoking essay exploring, in a preliminary way, constitutional considerations relevant to American nuclear weapons strategy.[5] In the process of examining implications of the President's Article II responsibilities, Professor Miller asks, "is international law a part of the corpus of laws that the President must faithfully execute?"[6] The answer is, most assuredly, yes.[7]

International law is part of the law of the United States. It binds the United States through its constitutional incorporation into domestic law, and also in its own right, as a self-contained legal system functioning independently of municipal law mechanisms of implementation and enforcement. Substantively, international law binding upon the United States already prohibits the aggressive threat or use of nuclear weapons[8] and by treaty makes illegal a significant number of other uses of nuclear weapons.[9] Additionally there are other evolving international law limitations and prohibitions relevant to nuclear weapons,[10] and, as they crystallize, they will similarly constrain United States nuclear options. International law thus affects the legality of United States nu-

---

duced at Brooklyn Law School, Georgetown University Law School, McGill University Law School, Nova University Law Center, Harvard Law School, and the Association of the Bar of the City of New York. Additionally, at least 37 law schools held events coinciding with November 11, 1982 Veterans' Day anti-nuclear activities cosponsored by the Union of Concerned Scientists, Physicians for Social Responsibility, and the Lawyers' Alliance for Nuclear Arms Control.

5. *See* Miller, *Nuclear Weapons and Constitutional Law*, 7 NOVA L.J. 21 (1982).

6. *Id.* at 33.

7. Paust, *The Seizure and Recovery of the Mayaguez*, 85 YALE L.J. 774, 803 n.131 (1976) ("the President is required to execute treaty and customary obligations faithfully both at home and abroad"). *See* Paust, *Is the President Bound by the Supreme Law of the Land?—Foreign Affairs and National Security Reexamined*, 9 HASTINGS CONST. L.Q. ____ (forthcoming 1982). *Contra*, L. HENKIN, FOREIGN AFFAIRS AND THE CONSTITUTION 221-22 (1972) ("the Constitution does not forbid the President (or the Congress) to violate international law"). For a well-reasoned critique of Henkin's thesis, however, see Paust, 9 HASTINGS CONST. L. Q., *supra*, at ____. For an examination of domestic law implications for the United Kingdom of the international illegality of nuclear weapons see Background Paper, *Nuclear Weapons and the Law*, 5 ST. RESEARCH BULL. (No. 31) 170 (1982).

8. U.N. CHARTER art. 2, para. 4. *See infra* note 55 and accompanying text.

9. *See infra* notes 33-41 and accompanying text.

10. *See infra* notes 43-80 and accompanying text.

clear strategy directly and as another dimension of the constitutional restraints outlined by Professor Miller.

I. International Law as Law of the Land: An Historical Overview

International law was part of eighteenth century English common law received into American law.[11] State courts applied it prior to adoption of the Constitution,[12] and it was thoroughly familiar to partici-

---

11. One finds support for this proposition in the writings of that era's foremost legal scholars, Blackstone and Lord Mansfield among them, "[W]here the individuals of any state violate [the Law of Nations], it is then the interest *as well as the duty* of the government under which they live, to animadvert upon them with a becoming severity, that the peace of the world may be maintained." 4 W. BLACKSTONE, COMMENTARIES 68 (1st ed. 1765-69) (emphasis added). For other examples of Blackstone's writing on this subject, see 1 W. BLACKSTONE, COMMENTARIES 75, 263-64 (1st ed. 1765-69); 3 W. BLACKSTONE, COMMENTARIES 69, 108 (1st ed. 1765-69); 4 W. BLACKSTONE, COMMENTARIES 67-73 (1st ed. 1765-69).

Lord Mansfield wrote extensively and authoritatively on this subject. *See, e.g.,* Luke v. Lyde, 97 Eng. Rep. 614, 617, 2 Burr. 882, 887 (K.B. 1759); Lindo v. Rodney, in LeCaux v. Eden, 99 Eng. Rep. 375, 385, 2 Doug. 594, 613 (1782).

See also the writing of Chief Justice Holt in Mogadara v. Holt, 89 Eng. Rep. 597-98, 1 Show. K.B. 317-19 (K.B. 1691); and the writing of Lord Stowell in The Maria, 165 Eng. Rep. 199, 1 C. Rob 340, 350 (Adm. 1799); and The Recovery, 165 Eng. Rep. 955, 958, 6 C. Rob. 341, 348 (Adm. 1807) ("this is a Court of the Law of Nations, though sitting here under the authority of the King of Great Britain.").

The Act of Anne of 1708 recognized that arrest of an ambassador pursuant to the suit of creditors was "contrary of the Law of Nations" and proceeded to avoid all such suits. Blackstone wrote that the Act was "not to be considered as introductive of any new rule, but merely as declaratory of the old fundamental constitutions of the kingdom; without which it must cease to be a part of the civilized world." 4 W. BLACKSTONE, COMMENTARIES 67 (1st ed. 1765-69). Lord Chancellor Talbot, in Barbuits Case in Chancery, 25 Eng. Rep. 777, 777 (Ch. 1735), wrote that the Act was "only declaratory of the antient universal *jus gentium,*" and Lord Mansfield agreed, observing that the Act of Anne did not vary from international law because "[t]his privilege of foreign ministers . . . depends upon the law of nations," Triquet v. Bath, 97 Eng. Rep. 936, 937, 3 Burr. 1478, 1480 (K.B. 1764).

See generally Dickinson, *The Law of Nations as Part of the National Law of the United States,* 101 U. PA. L. REV. 26, especially at 33 (1952) ("the Law of Nations was part of the law of England").

12. *E.g.,* Respublica v. DeLongschamps, 1 U.S. (1 Dall.) 111 (Pa. Oy. & Term. 1784). "The Law of nations. . ., in its fullest extent, is a part of the law of this state."

pants in the Constitutional Convention.[13] The Framers not only knew common law writings upon the subject, but were also well schooled, as was normal for educated men of their times, in the treatises of such great international law scholars as Grotius, Pufendorf, and Vattel.[14]

What little controversy concerning international law existed during the Constitutional Convention came from the inevitable intertwining of its incorporation with the difficulties of dividing powers between national and state authorities, and between the various branches of the proposed national government.[15] The Constitution finally assigned exclusive responsibility for international relations to the federal government, divided it among the three branches, and specified that, in addition to the Constitution itself and federal statutes, "all Treaties made, or which shall be made, . . . shall be the supreme law of the land."[16]

Id. at 116.

13. *See, e.g.,* THE FEDERALIST No. 3, at 15 (J. Jay) (Bourne ed. 1947). THE FEDERALIST No. 80, at 112, 114 (A. Hamilton) (Bourne ed. 1947); No. 83, at 144 (A. Hamilton) (Bourne ed. 1947); No. 82 (A. Hamilton) (Bourne ed. 1947). *See also* Banco Nacional de Cuba v. Sabbatino, 376 U.S. 398, 451 n.12 (1964) (White, J., dissenting); W. SOLBERG, THE FEDERAL CONVENTION AND THE FORMATION OF THE UNION OF THE AMERICAN STATES (1979). The participants in the Convention

> had a knowledge of contemporary legal thought. . . . It was axiomatic among them that the Law of Nations, applicable to individuals and to states was an integral part of the law which they administered or practiced. . . . Whenever in terms or by implication they spoke or wrote with reference to Law of Nations, they were indulging no mere flight of hopeful rhetoric. . . .

Dickenson, *supra* note 11, at 35-36.

14. Dickenson, *supra* note 11, at 35. *See also* E. DUMBAULD, THOMAS JEFFERSON AND THE LAW 33 (1978); W. SOLBERG, *supra* note 13, at xxx.

15. *See, e.g.,* THE FEDERALIST No. 3, at 15 (J. Jay) (J. Cooke ed. 1977); THE FEDERALIST, No. 80, at 536 (A. Hamilton) (J. Cooke ed. 1977). *See* M. FARRAND, THE FRAMING OF THE CONSTITUTION OF THE UNITED STATES 91-123 (1918). *See also* Dickenson, *supra* note 11, at 26-56.

16. U.S. CONST. art VI., cl. 2. Additionally, the Constitution provides that the President

> shall have the Power, by and with the Advice and Consent of the Senate, to make Treaties, provided two-thirds of the Senators present concur; . . . shall nominate, and by and with the Advise and Consent of the Senate, shall appoint Ambassadors, other public Ministers and Consuls. . . . [art. II, § 2, cl. 2;] shall receive Ambassadors and other public Ministers. . . . [art. II, § 3; and] shall be Commander in Chief of the Army and Navy of

Chief Justice John Marshall little doubted that all international law, no matter what its source, had been incorporated into the law of the United States.[17] American judicial decisions of the last 190 years generally confirm Marshall's understanding of the place of the law of nations in American law.[18] The simplicity and clarity of early court

---

the United States and of the Militia of the Several States. . . . [art. II, § 2, cl. 1].

[Congress has the power to] provide for the common Defense. . . . [art. I, § 8, cl. 1;] regulate Commerce with foreign Nations. . . . [art. I, § 8, cl. 3;] define and punish Piracies and Felonies committed on the high Seas, and Offenses against the Law of Nations. . . . [art. I, § 8, cl. 10;] declare War, grant letters of Marque and Reprisal, and make Rules concerning Captures on Land and Water. . . . [art. I, § 8, cl. 11;] raise and support Armies. . . . [art. I, § 8, cl. 12;] provide and maintain a navy. . . . [art. I, § 8, cl. 13; and] make Rules for the Government and Regulation of the land and naval Forces [art. I, § 8, cl. 14].

The judicial Power shall extend to all Cases, in Law and Equity, arising under this Constitution, the Laws of the United States and Treaties made, or which shall be made, under their Authority;—to all cases affecting Ambassadors, other public Ministers and Consuls;—to all Cases of admiralty and maritime Jurisdiction;—to controversies to which the United States shall be a Party;—. . . to Controversies . . . between a State and the Citizens of another State;—. . . and foreign States, Citizens or Subjects. . . . [art. III, § 2, cl. 1]. In all Cases affecting Ambassadors, other public Ministers and Consuls, and those in which a State shall be a Party, the supreme Court shall have original Jurisdiction. [art. III, § 2, cl. 2].

17. "Marshall accepted the binding force of international law upon courts of the United States with no apparent difficulty. . . ." B. ZIEGLER, THE INTERNATIONAL LAW OF JOHN MARSHALL 5 (1939). See, e.g., the following decisions by Marshall: The Antelope, 23 U.S. (10 Wheat.) 66, 120 (1825) ("[T]he law of nations . . . which has received the assent of all must be the law of all. . . ."); The Nereide, 13 U.S. (9 Cranch) 388, 423 (1815) ("Until such an act be passed, the court is bound by the law of nations, which is a part of the law of the land. . . ."); Rose v. Himely, 8 U.S. (4 Cranch) 241, 277 (1808) ("[T]he law of nations is the law of all tribunals . . . ."); Murray v. The Schooner Charming Betsy, 6 U.S. (2 Cranch) 64, 118 (1804) ("[A]n act of congress ought never to be construed to violate the law of nations, if any other possible construction remains. . . .").

18. See, e.g., Lauritzen v. Larrsen, 345 U.S. 571, 578 (1953); Skiriotes v. Florida, 313 U.S. 69, 72 (1941); Kansas v. Colorado, 206 U.S. 46, 97 (1907); The Paquette Habana, 175 U.S. 677, 700 (1900); Hilton v. Guyot, 159 U.S. 113, 163 (1895); Tag v. Rogers, 267 F.2d 664, 666 (D.C. Cir. 1959); The Lusitania, 251 F. 715, 732 (S.D.N.Y. 1915); The Appam, 234 F. 389, 400 (E.D. Va. 1916); Fernandez v. Wilkinson, 505 F. Supp. 787, 795 (D. Kan. 1980); United States v. Enger, 472 F. Supp. 490,

decisions, however, has been lost as the question of the domestic role of the law of nations became increasingly complicated by other legal issues, including the allocation of competence between national and state governments,[19] the political question doctrine,[20] the self-execution doctrine,[21] and the division of foreign affairs powers among the President and the houses of Congress.[22]

The general principle that international law is part of United States law, however, has survived even the chauvinism of manifest destiny, the banality of American legal positivism, and the arrogance of power that came with American twentieth century global hegemony. Unfortunately, most of the present generation of American lawyers and legal scholars fail to understand the role of international law within

---

504 (D.N.J. 1978); Sociedad Nacional de Marineros de Honduras v. McCulloch, 201 F. Supp. 82, 80 (D.D.C. 1962). *See also* Paust, Litigating Human Rights in U.S. Courts, 4 Hous. J. Int'l L. 137 (1981).

19. *See, e.g.,* Holmes v. Jenninson, 39 U.S. (14 Pet.) 540 (1840) (where despite the absence of an effective federal extradition treaty the governor of Vermont allowed a Canadian resident to be extradited to Canada from Vermont; the Court refused to hear the case because the Justices were equally divided on the meaning of the "Agreement Clause," U.S. Const. art. I, § 10); Missouri v. Holland, 252 U.S. 416 (1920). *See generally,* L. Henkin, *supra* note 7, at 227-49.

20. *See generally,* L. Henkin, *supra* note 7, at 208-16; Gordon, *American Courts, International Law and "Political Questions" Which Touch Foreign Relations,* 14 Int'l L. 297 (1980); Henkin, *Is There a "Political Question" Doctrine?,* 85 Yale L.J. 597 (1976); Wechsler, *Toward Neutral Principles of Constitutional Law,* 73 Harv. L. Rev. 1 (1959). *See, e.g.,* Oetjen v. Central Leather Co., 246 U.S. 297, 302 (1918) ("[C]onduct of the foreign relations of our Government is committed by the Constitution to the Executive and Legislative—'the political'—Departments of the Government, and the propriety of what may be done in the exercise of this political power is not subject to judicial inquiry or decision.").

21. *See, e.g.,* Foster v. Neilson, 27 U.S. (2 Pet.) 253, 314 (1829); Sei Fujii v. State, 38 Cal. 2d 718, 242 P.2d 617 (1952). *See generally* L. Henkin, *supra* note 7, at 156-66. For a discussion of self-execution in the context of human rights treaties, see Feinrider, *Extraterritorial Abductions: A Newly Developing International Standard,* 14 Akron L. Rev. 27, 45 n.121 (1980).

22. "[T]he constitution is especially inarticulate in allocating foreign affairs powers; . . . a particular power can with equal logic and fair constitutional reading be claimed for the president or for Congress. . . ." L. Henkin, *supra* note 7, at 90. *See generally* T. Franck & E. Weisband, Foreign Policy by Congress 135-62 (1979); Feinrider, *America's Oil Pledges to Israel: Illegal But Binding Executive Agreements,* 13 N.Y.U. J. Int'l L. & Pol. 525, 537-49 (1981).

American law; unlike their predecessors and members of the legal profession of other nations, they rarely study it.[23] The significance of international law is lost upon this generation for whom American international political, economic and military power is a ready substitute. Nevertheless, as the world grows smaller and American dominance grows weaker, the relevance of international law may be learned anew.

II. The International Dimension

International law is a law of consent and consensus. The existence of consent given by sovereign nations is demonstrated by treaty, custom and general principle—the primary sources of international law.[24] In the era of the United Nations Charter, when multilateral treaties are common,[25] international debate regular, and global communication rapid, the process of achieving agreement creating international law is

---

23. "[I]t is really only in the past two decades that doubt has been cast on the propriety of judicial invocation of international legal norms." Gordon, *supra* note 20, at 309.

24. The STATUTE OF THE INTERNATIONAL COURT OF JUSTICE, generally recognized as the most authoritative contemporary statement of the sources of international law, directs that the world court shall apply:

a. international conventions, whether general or particular, establishing rules expressly recognized by the contesting states;

b. international custom, as evidence of a general practice accepted as law;

c. the general principles of law recognized by civilized nations;

d. subject to the provisions of Article 59, judicial decisions and the teachings of the most highly qualified publicists of the various nations, as subsidiary means for the determination of rules of law.

THE STATUTE OF THE INTERNATIONAL COURT OF JUSTICE, at art. 38(1). Article 59 of the STATUTE OF THE INTERNATIONAL COURT OF JUSTICE provides that "[t]he decision of the Court has no binding force except between the parties and in respect of that particular case."

A recent International Court of Justice case (Nuclear Tests Case—Australia v. France, 1974) and recent state practice (*see infra* note 41), suggest that even unilateral statements by national representatives may be sources of international obligations.

25. During the first half of the 1960's 6,886 treaties entered into force. P. ROHN, TREATY PROFILES 57 (1976). One hundred forty-eight of them were multilateral. Gamble, *Reservations to Multilateral Treaties: A Macroscopic View of State Practice,* 74 AM. J. INT'L L. 372 (1980).

potentially quicker than in times past.[26] Further, the substance of international law is far greater than in times gone by, reaching nearly all areas of concern to the law.[27] At a time when the globe continues to shrink daily, respect for and adherence to international law is the indisputable prerequisite for international peace and security.

International law is explored and relied upon not only in international tribunals and fora, but also in the courts and legislative chambers of the many nations of the world. This is a function of the fact that at its present state of development international law still, for the most part, relies upon municipal authorities for its enforcement. This, however, does not mean that municipal determinations of the content of international law define international obligations. To the contrary, international law is ultimately determined according to its own sources.[28] If it were otherwise, a law of nations would be an impossibility, drowned in the parochial and often self-serving views of the world's nations.

If a rule of international law exists, it is binding upon the United States. International law, of course, protects against easy imposition of obligations upon a nation without its assent. Once that assent is given, however, or once a peremptory norm is created, binding international obligations exist.[29]

---

26. *See* Cheng, *United Nations Resolutions on Outer Space: "Instant" International Customary Law,* 5 INDIAN J. INT'L L. 23 (1965).

27. International agreements now deal with subjects as diverse as human rights, exploration of the moon, uses of outer space, patents, trade and tariffs, settlement of boundary disputes, arms limitation, protection of non-combatants and civilians during time of international and non-international armed conflict, preservation of the environment, exploration of Antartica, assignment of radio broadcast frequencies, etc.

28. This is not to prejudge whether any particular norm has risen to the level of a rule of international law, nor to minimize the role of the United States as an important actor upon the global scene whose conduct is watched carefully for evidence of relevant state practice by students of international law.

29. Treaties to which the United States is a party, according to the principle *pacta sunt servanda,* are binding. Though subsequent inconsistent United States legislation may negate the incorporation of treaties or customary rules of international law into national law under the last in time doctrine, domestic law may likewise be negated by subsequent inconsistent treaties or customs. RESTATEMENT SECOND OF FOREIGN RELATIONS LAW OF THE UNITED STATES § 135(1) (Tent. Draft No. 1, 1980) (and Reporter's notes 1 & 6); *see* Murphy, *Customary International Law in U.S. Jurisprudence—A Comment on Draft Restatement II,* INT'L PRACTITIONER'S NOTEBOOK (No.

The Judgment at Nuremberg demonstrated the extent to which the international community ascribes individual liability to government officials for breaches of serious international obligations. As a party to the charter which created the Nuremberg Tribunal, the United States commited itself to the international rule of law, a commitment reaffirmed by its ratification of the United Nations charter. Certainly the rule of international law is as binding upon the United States and its government officials as it was binding upon Nazi Germany and the German leaders brought to trial by the Allied Powers.

III. The Limits on and Potential of Law

Before proceeding to an analysis of international legal norms concerning nuclear weaponry, we should first consider of what utility international law can be in the face of nuclear weapons; that is, how might international law affect future use or plans for future use of nuclear weapons? Though demonstration of the illegality of nuclear weapons will not in itself determine the nuclear weapons question or prevent policy planners from detailing conditions of future nuclear weapons use, doctrinal inquiry is far from mere self-delusion.

International law, it is true, has generally not had enforcement mechanisms other than the domestic machinery provided by nation-states, its traditional subjects. Future international criminal law punishment of nuclear weapons users, however, could occur, based on the Nuremberg precedent, but even this would not ensure the efficacy of international legal norms. No law, no matter what its mechanism for enforcement, can prevent illegal behavior other than by threat of negative after-the-fact consequences. The need for *post facto* punishment reflects the inherent inadequacy of all law as an absolute deterrent to proscribed behavior. This would be as true of the international law basis of a Nuremberg-type trial of those responsible for nuclear aggression as it is of the state penal code under which a murderer is brought before some local trial court. Moreover, the nuclear apocalypse, should it ever come to pass, might well preempt forever all possibility of after-

---

20) 17 (Oct. 1982). No matter what the domestic effect of subsequent legislation, however, the international obligations of the United States emanating from treaty or custom remain in force.

the-fact legal consequences, making resort to law futile.

All law, however, receives whatever power it has, not primarily from its threatened enforcement, but from the normative consensus underlying it. In a democracy, according to theory, policy-makers and members of the polity alike share in this consensus;[30] in an authoritarian or totalitarian society the leadership can only retain power by not straying *too far* from the views of those below. Consensus and law, through an interactive process, help create and strengthen each other, thus effectively shaping behavior. Despite the elitist assumptions normally associated with governance and the present nation-state system, consensus and law—even on the international level—can be built from the bottom up. In fact, given the failure of the world's leaders to respond effectively to the challenge of nuclear weapons, we may have no choice but to rely on the efforts and consciousness of the people of the United States, the Soviet Union, and all other nations.[31] International law, and its attempted implementation through domestic legal systems which incorporate it, can effectively assist the popular movement against nuclear weapons.

International law can help limit or even prevent future use of nuclear weapons by defining considerations of policy-makers, swaying public dialogue, providing ammunition for anti-nuclear populist movements, and demonstrating to all willing to listen the complete incompatability of nuclear weaponry with virtually the entire thrust of the post-World War II effort to create structures and norms supportive of international peace and security. Should these ends be accomplished, they could well become means to the creation of law, and no small feat will have been done. Enforcement of international proscriptions of nuclear weaponry may then prove unnecessary in view of a popular anti-nuclear consensus globally reached.

---

30. *See generally* Paust, The Concept of Norm: Toward a Better Understanding of Content, Authority, and Constitutional Choice, 53 TEMPLE L. Q. 226 (1980). For an interesting view of the implications of nuclear weapons for democracy, see Falk, *Nuclear Weapons and the End of Democracy,* 2 PRAXIS INT'L 1 (1982).

31. *But cf.* Hoffman, *International Law and the Control of Force,* in THE RELEVANCE OF INTERNATIONAL LAW: ESSAYS IN HONOR OF LEO GROSS 21 (K. Deutsch & S. Hoffman eds. 1968).

IV. International Law and Nuclear Weapons

Analysis of the international legality of nuclear weapons must take into account the complexities of reality. Nothing in fact or law justifies the *a priori* lumping together, into one neat conceptual category, of all types of nuclear weapons and all their possible uses. Defensive surgical use of a low-yield clean tactical weapon against a clearly military target in an isolated geographical region with low population density, for example, must be viewed, initially at least, as different from strategic first-use of a multi-megaton dirty bomb against a major urban population center.[32] A complex analytic task must be undertaken before we can conclude that all uses and types of nuclear weapons are subject to the same proscriptive norm of international law. Here, the goal is simply to make a small contribution toward accomplishment of that task.

·At present no treaty explicitly prohibits all use of nuclear weapons. It is also probably correct to say that, as yet, no rule of customary international law prohibits all use of nuclear weapons. Nevertheless, a variety of treaties, evidencing global disapprobation, explicitly outlaw or limit a significant number of nuclear weapon uses.[33]

By treaty, international law prohibits nuclear weapons *deployment* or *use* in Antarctica,[34] Latin America,[35] earth orbit, outer space and on

---

32. *See* G. Schwarzenberger, International Law and Order 185-218 (1971). At a recent conference on nuclear weapons held at Brooklyn Law School on September 25, 1982, Professor John Norton Moore, a noted conservative scholar of international law, was forced to admit that the legality of nuclear weapons *per se* remains an open question. Nevertheless, he challenged seriously the analysis of those arguing for illegality by raising hypothetically the odd *de minimus* case. *See* Moore, *Remarks,* 9 Brooklyn J. Int'l L.—(forthcoming 1983). Though his hypothetical did not effectively undermine the basic argument for illegality of strategic use of nuclear weapons, it raised questions concerning less dramatic nuclear uses that must be addressed by any purportedly comprehensive analysis. Intellectual honesty and rigor require no less.

For an early attempt at doctrinal analysis of nuclear legality in light of the variety of nuclear weapons and their possible uses, see G. Schwarzenberger, The Legality of Nuclear Weapons (1958).

33. *See* R. Sivard, World Military and Social Expenditures 13 (1981), *quoted in* Briefing Manual of the Union of Concerned Scientists, Solutions to the Nuclear Arms Race 59-68 (1982).

34. Antarctic Treaty, *signed* Dec. 1, 1959, *entered into force* June 23, 1961, 12 U.S.T. 794, T.I.A.S. No. 4780, 402 U.N.T.S. 71 (ratified, as of Nov. 15, 1982, by 26

celestial bodies,[36] and *deployment* on the seabed beyond the twelve-mile limit of national territorial seas.[37] Further, more than one hundred nations have subjected themselves to a rule of international law prohibiting possessors of nuclear weapons and nuclear weapons technology from *transferring* such weapons or technology to non-nuclear weapons nations.[38] Further yet, states may not even *test* nuclear weapons in outer space, under water or within the earth's atmosphere.[39] In addition, the United States and the Soviet Union have concluded a series of bilateral agreements designed specifically to reduce the risk of accidental or avoidable military use of nuclear weapons during any confrontation between the two superpowers,[40] and also to limit the number of

states).

35.   Treaty of Tlatelolco (Latin American Nuclear Free Zone Treaty), Feb. 14, 1967, 634 U.N.T.S. 281 (ratified, as of Nov. 15, 1982, by 24 states; Argentina and Cuba are the only Latin American states not party to this treaty, and Argentina has signed but not yet ratified it).

36.   Outer Space Treaty, *signed* Jan. 27, 1967, *entered into force* Oct. 10, 1967, 18 U.S.T. 2410, T.I.A.S. No. 6347, 610 U.N.T.S. 205 (ratified, as of Nov. 15, 1982, by 81 states).

37.   Seabed Treaty, *signed* Feb. 11, 1971, *entered into force* June 18, 1972, 23 U.S.T. 701, T.I.A.S. No. 7337 (ratified, as of Nov. 15, 1982, by 70 states).

38.   Non-Proliferation Treaty, *signed* July 1, 1968, *entered into force* March 5, 1970, 21 U.S.T. 483, T.I.A.S. No. 6839, 729 U.N.T.S. 161 (ratified, as of Nov. 15, 1982, by 119 states: bans transfer of nuclear weapons technology to non-nuclear weapons states, and requires controls on "peaceful nuclear facilities" to prevent their being turned to weapons production).

39.   Partial Test Ban Treaty, *signed* Aug. 5, 1963, *entered into force* Oct. 10, 1963, 14 U.S.T. 1313, T.I.A.S. No. 5433 (ratified, as of Nov. 15, 1982, by 110 states).

The United States and the Soviet Union have concluded agreements limiting underground testing of nuclear weapons but have not yet ratified them. *See,* Underground Nuclear Weapon Test Treaty, *signed* July 3, 1974, U.S. Dep't of State, Press Release No. 281 (July 3, 1974), *reprinted in* 13 Int'l Legal Materials 906 (1974), and Peaceful Nuclear Explosions Treaty, *signed* May 28, 1976, U.S. Arms Control & Disarmament Agency, Pub. No. 87 (May 1976), *reprinted in* 15 Int'l Legal Materials 891 (1976). Neither treaty has yet been ratified.

40.   *See* Hot Line Agreement, *signed* and *entered into force* June 20, 1963, 14 U.S.T. 825; T.I.A.S. No. 5362, 472 U.N.T.S. 163; Hot Line Modernization Agreement, *signed* and *entered into force* Sept. 30, 1971, 22 U.S.T. 1598, T.I.A.S. No. 7187, 806 U.N.T.S. 402; Accidents Measures Agreement, *signed* and *entered into force* Sept. 30, 1971, 22 U.S.T. 1590, T.I.A.S. No. 7186, 807 U.N.T.S. 57; Prevention of Nuclear War Agreement, *signed* and *entered into force* June 22, 1973, 24 U.S.T. 1478, T.I.A.S. No. 7654 (agreements between the United States and the Soviet Union).

nuclear weapons allowed to each.[41]

In view of these substantial restrictions on nuclear weaponry explicitly imposed by conventional international law, what remains to be explored are ways in which uses of nuclear weapons still unaddressed by treaty may be subject to implicit legal constraints emanating from the structures and norms of international law generally. In the present context, the result of such examination leads to the conclusion that a rule of customary international law outlawing nuclear weapons *per se* is currently in the process of being created.[42]

A. The Lawyer's Committee Analysis

In the most well-developed analysis currently available,[43] members of the Consultative Council of the Lawyers' Committee on Nuclear Policy rely heavily on the laws of war,[44] Nuremburg principles,[45] Gen-

---

41. Anti-Ballistic Missile Treaty, *signed* May 26, 1972, *entered into force* Oct. 23, 1973, 23 U.S.T. 3435, T.I.A.S. No. 7503, and Protocol of 1974, *signed* July 3, 1974, *entered into force* May 24, 1976, 27 U.S.T. 1645, T.I.A.S. No. 8276; Interim Agreement on Certain Measures with Respect to the Limitation of Strategic Offensive Arms (SALT I), *signed* May 26, 1972, *entered into force* Oct. 3, 1972, 23 U.S.T. 3462, T.I.A.S. No. 7504, *expired* Oct. 2, 1977 (after expiration, the terms of this treaty were continued in force for the United States and the Soviet Union by means of Parallel Unilateral Policy Declarations); SALT II, *signed* June 18, 1979, *not yet ratified*, U.S. DEP'T OF STATE, PUB. 8984, SALT II AGREEMENT, VIENNA (Selected Documents No. 12A, June 18, 1979), *reprinted in* 18 INT'L LEGAL MATERIALS 1138 (1979) (agreements between the United States and the Soviet Union).

42. Law, as Professor Thomas Franck has pointed out, is "congealed politics." T. FRANCK AND M. MUNANSANGO, THE NEW INTERNATIONAL ECONOMIC ORDER: INTERNATIONAL LAW IN THE MAKING? 1 (UNITAR Policy and Efficacy Study No. 6, 1982). Unfortunately, the world social order has only begun the "congealing" necessary to overcome the cultural lag between norm and technology that has thus far retarded development of rules regulating the most awesome of humankind's technological 'achievements.' Examination of politics in the process of congealing, then, becomes incumbent upon those seeking to understand the ways in which international law does and can address the issues raised by nuclear weaponry.

43. *See* R. FALK, L. MEYROWITZ, & J. SANDERSON, NUCLEAR WEAPONS AND INTERNATIONAL LAW (Occasional Paper No. 10, World Order Studies Program, Center of International Studies, Princeton University (1981)). *See also* Meyrowitz, *Nuclear Weapons Policy: The New Tyranny*, 7 NOVA L.J. 93 (1982).

44. *E.g.*, the St. Petersburg Declaration, (1868); the 1889 Hague Declaration Respecting Asphyxiating Gases; the Hague Conventions of 1907, arts. 22, 23(a) and

eral Assembly recommendations (resolutions),[46] and a policy analysis of international law. They convincingly argue international law now limiting war-making by nations equally applies to nuclear war-making, and "any threat or contemplated use of nuclear weapons is contrary to the dictates of international law, and constitutes a crime of state . . . [the continuation of which] should be enjoined by judicial bodies and opposed by citizens and nongovernmental organizations."[47] Elliot L. Meyrowitz, Vice-Chairperson of the Lawyers' Committee sets forth this analysis in greater detail elsewhere in this issue of Nova Law Journal,[48] thus obviating the need for lengthy discussion here.

On the basis of the Lawyers' Committee analysis we can conclude that international law prohibits, at a minimum, those uses and kinds of nuclear weapons violative of the binding principle of proportionality applicable to all warfare and weapons.[49] This general principle of humanitarian law requires that "[b]elligerents shall not inflict harm on their adversaries out of proportion with the object of warfare, which is to destroy or weaken the military strength of the enemy."[50] Proportional-

---

23(e) of the regulations annexed thereto and the famous "de Martens" preambular clause; the Treaty of Versailles (1919), art. 171; the Geneva Gas Protocol of 1925; the four Geneva Conventions of 1949; and, the 1977 Protocol on Humanitarian law Applicable to Armed Conflict, Additional to the Geneva Conventions of 1949. *See* R. FALK, L. MEYROWITZ & J. SANDERSON, *supra* note 43, at 21-33.

45. *See* R. FALK, L. MEYROWITZ & J. SANDERSON, *supra* note 43, at 63-71.

46. G.A. Res. 1380, 14 U.N. GAOR Supp. (No. 16) at 4, U.N. Doc. A/4354 (1959); G.A. Res. 1643, 16 U.N. GAOR Supp. (No. 17) at 34, U.N. Doc. A/5100 (1961); G.A. Res. 2162, 21 U.N. GAOR Supp. (No. 16) at 10, U.N. Doc. A/6316 (1966); G.A. Res. 2936, 27 U.N. GAOR Supp. (No. 30) at 5, U.N. Doc. A/8730 (1972); G.A. Res. 2849, 26 U.N. GAOR Supp. (No. 29) at 70, U.N. Doc. A/8429 (1971); G.A. Res. 3246, 29 U.N. GAOR Supp. (No. 31) at 87, U.N. Doc. A/9631 (1974); G.A. Res. 3154, 28 U.N. GAOR Supp. (No. 30) at 34, U.N. Doc. A/9030 (1973); G.A. Res. 35/152, 35 U.N. GAOR Supp. (No. 48) at 69, U.N. Doc A/3548 (1980). *See* R. FALK, L. MEYROWITZ & J. SANDERSON, *supra* note 43, at 58-62.

47. R. FALK, L. MEYROWITZ & J. SANDERSON, *supra* note 43, at 78.

48. *See* Meyrowitz, *supra* note 43.

49. *See* R. FALK, L. MEYROWITZ & J. SANDERSON, *supra* note 43, at 23-26; Meyrowitz, *supra* note 43, at 93.

50. J. PICTET, THE PRINCIPLES OF INTERNATIONAL HUMANITARIAN LAW 30 (undated; available from the International Committee of the Red Cross). *See* International Committee of the Red Cross, Some International Red Cross Conference Resolutions and ICRC Statements on the Protection of Civilian Population and on Weapons of

ity, and its correlate providing that "[b]elligerents do not have unlimited choice in the means of inflicting damage on the enemy,"[51] have spawned three binding principles of humanitarian law proper to the rules of war:

> [(1)] [b]elligerents will leave non-combatants outside the area of operations and will refrain from attacking them deliberately[;]. . .
> [(2)] [a]ttacks are only legitimate when directed against military objectives, that is to say whose total or partial destruction would constitue a definite military advantage. . .[; and]
> [(3)] [w]eapons and methods of warfare likely to cause excessive suffering are prohibited.[52]

Nuclear weapons, many of which have massive destructive capabilities, long-lasting environmental and genetic effects, and a unique capacity for indiscriminate devastation, are more likely than other weapons to violate proportionality and the three principles derived therefrom. To the extent that certain uses of nuclear weapons would violate these principles, international law, as it exists today, prohibits them.

B.   Charter Restraints on Nuclear Weapons

Article 1 of the Charter of the United Nations, the preeminent international legal document of our time, makes clear that the *raison détre* of the United Nations is, first and foremost, "to maintain international peace and security."[53] The preamble of the Charter reminds us

---

Mass Destruction (August, 1981).

51.   J. PICTET, *supra* note 50, at 32.

52.   *Id.* at 52-55.

53.   U.N. CHARTER art. 1. Article 1, in relevant part, provides;
The Purposes of the United Nations are:
(1) To maintain international peace and security, and to that end: to take effective collective measures for the prevention and removal of threats to the peace, and for the suppression of acts of aggression or other breaches of the peace, and to bring about by peaceful means, and in conformity with the principles of justice and international law, adjustment or settlement of international disputes or situations which might lead to a breach of the peace;
(2) To develop friendly relations among nations based on respect for the principle of equal rights and self-determination of peoples, and to take

that the Organization was brought into being "to save succeeding generations from the scourge of war,"[54] and no scourge could be greater than the one threatened by military use of nuclear weapons.

The article 2(4) prohibition of aggressive war[55] forbids use of nuclear weapons as part of an aggressive war just as it forbids aggressive use of other weapons. Article 51, however, goes further and prohibits even certain defensive uses of nuclear weapons because of their unique capacity for mass destruction. The Charter recognizes the inherent sovereign right of self-defense against armed attack, yet it further provides that the right of self-defense will remain unimpaired by Charter obligations only "until the Security Council has taken measures necessary to maintain international peace and security."[56] Article 51 also requires

---

other appropriate measures to strengthen universal peace . . . .

54.   U.N. CHARTER preamble. The preamble reads as follows:

WE THE PEOPLES OF THE UNITED NATIONS DETERMINED

to save succeeding generations from the scourge of war, which twice in our life-time has brought untold sorrow to mankind, and

to reaffirm faith in fundamental human rights, in the dignity and worth of the human person, in the equal rights of men and women and of nations large and small, and

to establish conditions under which justice and respect for the obligations arising from treaties and other sources of international law can be maintained, and

to promote social progress and better standards of life in larger freedom,

AND FOR THESE ENDS

to practice tolerance and live together in peace with one another as good neighbours, and

to unite our strength to maintain international peace and security, and

to ensure, by the acceptance of principles and the institution of methods, that armed force shall not be used, save in the common interest, and

to employ international machinery for the promotion of the economic and social advancement of all peoples,

HAVE RESOLVED TO COMBINE OUR EFFORTS TO ACCOMPLISH THESE AIMS.

55.   U.N. CHARTER article 2, paragraph 4 reads as follows:

All Members shall refrain in their international relations from the threat or use of force against the territorial integrity or political independence of any state, or in any other manner inconsistent with the Purposes of the United Nations.

56.   U.N. CHARTER art. 51.

that self-defense measures taken before the Security Council becomes seized of a conflict "shall not in any way affect the authority and responsibility of the Security Council . . . to take at any time such action as it deems necessary in order to maintain or restore international peace and security."[57] This apparently further limits the number of situations in which nuclear weapons could lawfully be used. For example, a nuclear attack on New York City resulting in destruction of United Nations headquarters would, to say the least, affect negatively the authority and responsibility of the Security Council in violation of article 51. Similarly, nuclear incineration of Moscow or Washington, D.C., or the capital of any permanent or non-permanent member of the Security Council also would violate the letter and spirit of article 51.[58]

The article 51 limited right to self-defense, and the rest of the United Nations Charter, thus tell us that though the authors of the Charter knew the article 2(4) prohibition of aggressive war would likely be violated, they also envisioned a bottom-line limitation on warmaking in the name of self-defense: the peace-making and peace-restoring machinery of the United Nations must always remain available to serve the needs of humankind. The Charter, in article 2(3), explicitly imposes upon states the duty to respect this bottom line.[59] Any irreparable interference with the functioning or existence of international structures of peace would violate criminally the very object and pur-

---

Article 51, in full, provides that:
  Nothing in the present Charter shall impair the inherent right of individual or collective self-defence if an armed attack occurs against a Member of the United Nations, until the Security Council has taken measures necessary to maintain international peace and security. Measures taken by Members in the exercise of this right of self-defence shall be immediately reported to the Security Council and shall not in any way affect the authority and responsibility of the Security Council under the present Charter to take at any time such action as it deems necessary in order to maintain or restore international peace and security.
See also U.N. CHARTER article 2, paragraph 3 which requires that "all Members shall settle their international disputes by peaceful means in such a manner that international peace and security, and justice, are not endangered."
  57. U.N. CHARTER art. 51.
  58. Is there anyone who would argue, should the analysis presented in the text be correct, that nations "merely" members of the General Assembly would remain legally unprotected against nuclear attack?
  59. *See* U.N. Charter art. 2, para. 3, *supra* note 56.

pose of the United Nations Charter; cynicism concerning the likelihood of effective U.N. action would be no defense. No head of state could violate this international law bottom-line without having need to fear a Nuremberg-type trial.[60] It is inconceivable that the United States Constitution would allow the President to engage in nuclear crimes against the international structures of peace. Consequently, both international and United States domestic law prohibit at least strategic weapons aspects of United States "flexible response" strategy, which provides for escalating first-use of nuclear weapons in the event of Soviet conventional forces attacks in Europe.

C. The Human Rights/Natural Law Right to Survival

War is the ultimate, albeit irrational, act of sovereignty. It is therefore appropriate to look to international law restraints on sovereignty for possible limits on the ultimate act of war—nuclear attack. International human rights law may well serve as a fertile source for such limits on state nuclear war-making powers; human rights law has otherwise been responsible for the most significant limitations upon the sovereignty of states within the world order of the United Nations era.

Since the unanimous adoption by the General Assembly of the Universal Declaration of Human Rights in 1948,[61] numerous treaties of a universal, regional or specialized character have established limitations on the ways in which a national government can (mis)treat its

---

60. Of course, if nuclear war occurs there may well be no survivors to conduct the trial.

61. Universal Declaration of Human Rights, G.A. Res. 271A, U.N. Doc. A/810, at 71 (1948). The Universal Declaration was originally intended as an aspirational statement establishing a "common standard of achievement" for humankind, *id.*; however, many now agree that the terms of the Declaration, or at least some of them have become binding customary international law. *See, e.g.,* R. LILLICH & F. NEWMAN, INTERNATIONAL HUMAN RIGHTS: PROBLEMS OF LAW AND POLICY 7 (1979); Humphrey, *The Universal Declaration of Human Rights: Its History, Impact and Juridical Character,* in HUMAN RIGHTS: THIRTY YEARS AFTER THE UNIVERSAL DECLARATION 22 (B.G. Ramcharan ed. 1979). *See also Montreal Statement of the Assembly for Human Rights* 2 (1968), *reprinted in* 9 J. INT'L COMM. JUR. 94, 95 (1968); Declaration of Teheran, Final Act of the International Conference on Human Rights 3, at 4, para. 2, U.N. Doc. A.Conf. 32/41; G.A. Res. 2442, 23 U.N. GAOR Supp. (No. 18) at 49, U.N. Doc. A/7218 (1968).

own citizenry.[62] Over the last thirty years these treaties have been the subject of more than three hundred fifty separate acts of ratification, changing dramatically the very conceptualization of international law as a law only of nations.[63] Now, individuals too can be subjects of, and direct recipients of rights under international law. Inherent in this development has been recognition that at the heart of all government and law, whether on the international or municipal level, exists a core set of values and rights protecting humankind which emanates from natural law.[64]

The International Covenant on Civil and Political Rights and the International Covenant on Economic, Social and Cultural Rights both speak of the "*inherent* dignity"[65] of the human person and the "*inalienable* rights of all members of the human family."[66] The Preamble to

---

62. *E.g.*, International Covenant on Civil and Political Rights, *adopted* Dec. 19, 1966, *entered into force* March 23, 1976, G.A. Res. 2200, 21 U.N. GAOR Supp. (No. 16) at 52, U.N. Doc. A/6316 (1966) (ratified, as of Nov. 15, 1982, by 72 states); International Covenant on Economic, Social and Cultural Rights, *adopted* Dec. 19, 1966, *entered into force* Mar. 23, 1976, G.A. Res. 2200, 21 U.N. GAOR Supp. (No. 16) at 59, U.N. Doc. A/6316 (1966) (ratified, as of Nov. 15, 1982, by 75 states); [European] Convention for the Protection of Human Rights and Fundamental Freedoms, *signed* Nov. 4, 1950, *entered into force* Sept. 3, 1953, 213 U.N.T.S. 222 (ratified by all 21 members of the Council of Europe); American Convention on Human Rights, *signed* Nov. 22, 1969, *entered into force* July 18, 1978, 36 O.A.S. T.S. No. 1, O.A.S. Off. Rec. OEA/Ser. L/V/II.23 doc. rev. 2 (ratified, as of Nov. 15, 1982, by 17 states); International Convention on the Elimination of All Forms of Racial Discrimination, *opened for signature* Mar. 7, 1966, *entered into force* Jan. 4, 1969, 660 U.N.T.S. 195 (ratified, as of Nov. 15, 1982, by 117 states). For one view of the relationship between human rights and international law, see D'Amato, *The Concept of Human Rights in International Law,* 82 COLUM. L. REV. 1110 (1982).

63. The Vienna Convention on The Law of Treaties recognizes that *some* difference exists between international human rights treaties and other treaties. Vienna Convention on the Law of Treaties, art. 60(5), *opened for signature* May 27, 1969, *entered into force* Jan. 27, 1980, U.N. Conf. on Law of Treaties Off. Rec., 1st & 2d Sess., U.N. Doc. A/Conf./39/27 at 289. *See* Feinrider, *supra* note 21, at 43 n.116. The Vienna Convention has been ratified, as of Nov. 15, 1982, by 43 states; the United States has signed but not yet ratified it.

64. *See infra* notes 65-74 and accompanying text.

65. International Covenant on Civil and Political Rights, *supra* note 62, at preamble (emphasis added); International Covenant on Economic, Social and Cultural Rights, *supra* note 62, at preamble (emphasis added).

66. *See supra* note 65.

the International Convention on the Elimination of All Forms of Racial Discrimination states that the United Nations Charter "is based on the principles of the dignity and equality *inherent* in all human beings,"[67] and, repeating the language of the Universal Declaration, concludes "that all human beings are *born* free and equal in dignity and rights."[68] The American Convention on Human Rights recognizes that "the *essential* rights of man are not derived from one's being the national of a certain state, but are based upon the *attributes of the human personality*."[69] Language such as this indicates comprehension of a natural law basis for human rights,[70] and, when incorporated into treaties, evidences both the state practice and *opinio juris* necessary for creating

---

The common preambular language of the two covenants, in relevant part, reads as follows:

> Considering that, in accordance with the principles proclaimed in the Charter of the United Nations, recognition of the inherent dignity and of the equal and inalienable rights of all members of the human family is the foundation of freedom, justice and peace in the world.
>
> Recognizing that these rights derive from the inherent dignity of the human person,
>
> Recognizing that, in accordance with the Universal Declaration of Human Rights, the ideal of free human beings enjoying civil and political freedom and freedom from fear and want can only be achieved if conditions are created whereby everyone may enjoy his civil and political rights, as well as his economic, social and cultural rights. . . .

67. International Convention on the Elimination of All Forms of Racial Discrimination, *supra* note 62, at preamble (emphasis added).

68. *Id.* (emphasis added).

69. American Convention on Human Rights, *supra* note 62, at preamble (emphasis added).

70. *See* R. FALK, HUMAN RIGHTS AND STATE SOVEREIGNTY 42-45 (1981). *See also* Fernandez v. Wilkinson, 505 F. Supp. 787, 796 (D. Kan. 1980) ("The development of international agreements containing human rights norms which purport to be binding . . . was a significant step in the transformation of natural rights into positive legal rights."), *aff'd on other grounds*, 654 F.2d 1382 (10th Cir. 1981), *discussed in* Note, *Custom and General Principles as Sources of International law in American Courts*, 82 COLUM. L. REV. 751, 773-74 (1982).

The language quoted in the text at notes 65-70 is, admittedly, preambular language. Article 31 of the Vienna Convention on The Law of Treaties, *supra* note 63, however, provides that a preamble is to be considered part of a treaty's text and is among the primary sources for treaty interpretation. *Cf.* Miller, *supra* note 5, at 27-29 (analysis regarding the substantive import of the preamble to the United States Constitution).

customary international law.[71]

Surely, if individuals have inherent and inalienable natural rights superior to the positive international law rights of sovereign states, then so does humankind, if only as holder of the aggregate of rights belonging to its individual members.[72] The superiority of individual and collective natural rights over positive state rights only makes sense if individual and collective survival is assured. Individually and collectively, then, we all have the right not to have our survival threatened by states

---

71. To establish that a norm has become customary international law it is necessary to demonstrate the existence of a substantial number of states acting in conformity with the norm *and* that those states were in conformity because of a belief on their part that their behavior was required by law (*opinio juris*). Here, the norm is one providing that individuals have natural rights limiting the sovereign rights of states. The voluntary subordination of sovereign rights to human rights through the ratification of treaties, (*see supra* note 62) is state practice, and the preambular language of these treaties is clear evidence of *opinio juris,* that is, that the states ratifying them were motivated by the belief they were required to do so by certain preexisting "inherent," "inalienable" "essential" rights, "attributes of the human personality" belonging to beings "born free and equal in dignity and rights." *See supra* notes 65-69 and accompanying text.

The argument for illegality of nuclear weapons presented here should be distinguished from the one Eugene Rostow, Director of the United States Arms Control and Disarmament Agency, was presumably attempting to rebut at the Panel on Strategic Deterrence and Nuclear War of the 1982 Annual Meeting of the American Society of International Law. Rostow, in support of his argument that international law does not prohibit nuclear weapons *per se*, cited The Antelope, 23 U.S. (10 Wheat.) 66 (1825). *See* Panel on Strategic Deterrence and Nuclear War (response of Eugene Rostow to question of Professor Burns Weston) in the Proceedings of the 76th Annual Meeting of the American Society of International Law (Apr. 22, 1982). In *The Antelope,* Chief Justice John Marshall wrote that though slavery was repugnant to natural law, its prohibition *had not yet been incorporated* into international law and therefore was not enforceable in United States courts. Here, the argument is that natural law, by way of custom, *has recently been incorporated* into international law and the natural law right to collective survival is therefore part of United States law. Nothing in *The Antelope* contradicts this assertion.

72. A similar argument to that presented in text, but more palatable to positivists, could be based on the universally recognized "right to life" and the Convention on the Prevention and Punishment of the Crime of Genocide, *opened for signature* Dec. 9, 1948, *entered into force* Jan. 12, 1951, 78 U.N.T.S. 277 (1951) (ratified, as of Nov. 15, 1982, by 84 states). Nuclear holocaust would be seen as murder and genocide multiplied, just as some have suggested that Nuremberg convictions for genocide were not based on ex-post-facto law because murder had long been a crime in all "civilized" nations.

acting out their sovereignty through use of nuclear weapons of mass destruction. Thus, the Universal Declaration of Human Rights provides that "everyone is entitled to a social and international order in which the rights and freedoms set forth in [the] Declaration can be fully realized."[73] Nuclear weapons threaten that order, and even as ardent a positivist as H.L.A. Hart has recognized that at the core of law is the assumption that "the proper end of human activity is survival."[74]

D. The Right to Peace

The "right to peace" is another legal expression of humankind's collective natural right to survive. In 1979, Karel Vasak, the chief legal officer of UNESCO, argued that civil and political rights, and social, economic and cultural rights, are being joined and enhanced by a "third generation of human rights" which includes the "right to peace."[75] Though such "group rights" or "solidarity rights," or "global rights" as Saul Mendlovitz has called them,[76] remain controversial within the international human rights community,[77] they have, in fact,

---

73. Universal Declaration of Human Rights, *supra* note 61, at art. 28.

74. H.L.A. HART, THE CONCEPT OF LAW 187 (1961).

75. *See* Vasak, *Inagural Address: Pour Les Droits de l'Homme de la Troisieme Generation: Les Droits de Solidarité,* in *International Institute of Human Rights, Summary of Lectures—Tenth Study Session* (July 1979).

76. In Mendlovitz' view, the struggle for individual civil and political rights now typical of western liberal (capitalist) democracies marked the 19th century; the struggle for group social and economic rights typical of eastern communist societies marked the 20th century; and the struggle for global, or planetary rights such as those we are now beginning to see develop (e.g., the right to a clean environment and the right to peace) will mark the 21st century. *See* Mendlovitz, *Remarks,* 9 BROOKLYN J. INT'L L. __ (forthcoming 1983).

77. *E.g.,* A. H. Robertson, one-time Acting Secretary General of the International Institute of Human Rights and noted specialist in international human rights law, consistently criticized "third generation rights" during sessions of the Institute's Human Rights Teaching Center because, in his view, they are not susceptible to enforcement by law. Additionally, he wondered against whom such rights might be enforceable.

For a thoughtful critique of the right to peace as a group or solidarity right, see Bilder, *The Right to Peace as a Human Right,* Remarks made at the International Symposium on the Morality and Legality of Nuclear Weapons, in New York City (June 4-5, 1982). (Available in author's file at Nova University Center for the Study of

generated substantial debate and academic inquiry in Europe.[78] Only very recently have they been taken up as the subject of study within the United States.[79] If such rights exist, or are in the process of being created, whether reached inductively as the aggregate of all individual civil, political, social, economic and cultural rights recognized by international law or deductively from the evolving world order of humanity entering the twenty-first century, then the right to peace must be added to the norms limiting nuclear options. Though "peace" may mean more than mere absence of war, it certainly means at least absence of war and assurance of survival. The "right to peace" may thus confirm the integration of H.L.A. Hart's observation regarding the axiomatic relationship of law and survival[80] into the global legal system, meeting effectively, on a conceptual level at least, the threat of planetary eradication by nuclear holocaust.

Conclusion

As has been aptly put by Professor Saul Mendlovitz, "nuclear weapons are disgusting."[81] They are an abomination that must be outlawed by any civilized legal system worthy of the name.

International law already explicitly prohibits many, perhaps most uses of nuclear weapons. The structures and norms of international law and evolving conceptualizations of limits on state sovereignty strongly suggest the illegality of the remaining uses. At the very least these remaining uses should be seen as no more than exceptions which ought not be permitted to devour the emerging proscriptive rule. The international illegality of so many uses of nuclear weapons shifts the burden of persuasion to the proponents of nuclear weaponry. It is they who are on

---

Law).

78. *See, e.g.,* Morehouse, *The Right to Peace or the Right to Live,* 6 HOLDSWORTH L. REV. 120 (1981); and the following articles contained in 1980 BULLETIN OF PEACE PROPOSALS NO. 4, SPECIAL ISSUE: THE RIGHT TO PEACE AND DEVELOPMENT: Alston, *Peace as a Human Right;* Marks, *The Peace—Human Rights—Development Dialectic;* Lopatka, *The Right to Live in Peace as a Human Right.*

79. *See, e.g.,* Bilder, *supra* note 77; Nanda, *Nuclear Weapons and the Right to Peace Under International Law,* 9 BROOKLYN J. INT'L L.—(forthcoming 1983).

80. *See supra* note 73 and accompanying text.

81. Mendlovitz, *supra* note 76.

the defensive now, legally as well as morally, they carry the onus of seeking legal sanction for the remaining nuclear weapons uses.

A comprehensive custom outlawing nuclear weapons *per se* is in the process of being created. It is, hopefully, only a matter of time before municipal as well as international legal systems specifically prohibit all use of nuclear weapons. In the alternative, our present civilization will vaporize in the blinding flash of nuclear explosions forever destroying humankind, its legacy of achievements and its dreams for a future of well-being and peace.

Professor Arthur S. Miller, in his seminal work, has given to American lawyers the hope of promise and the burden of challenge. He calls upon us to help our domestic legal system rise to the task of meeting head-on the nuclear nightmare of our time, a bad dream come true beyond the imagination of even the most pessimistic of eighteenth century apocalypts. By probing our nearly two hundred year old constitution for checks and balances and values that could "secure the Blessings of Liberty to ourselves and our Posterity"[82] he sets a standard of achievement we must all strive to meet.

In response to Professor Miller's challenge, international lawyers must first turn a conservative, slow-moving discipline to face the nuclear challenge just as Miller has so artfully turned the U.S. Constitution. Second, they must help educate American domestic lawyers to the fact that international law is part of the law of the land. Success in the first will make the second all the more important: the United States remains the most powerful nuclear arsenal on earth. Fortunately, law is on the side of those who wish to hold the President to an international rule of law. The Constitution, in this matter, is clear. If, as suggested above, a norm of international law prohibits all, or at least most uses of nuclear weaponry, to answer Professor Miller's question, that norm is "part of the corpus of 'laws' that the President must faithfully execute."[83]

---

82. U.S. Const. preamble.
83. Miller, *supra* note 5 and accompanying text.

7.
Toward a Legal Regime for Nuclear Weapons*

Richard Falk**

I. The Ultimate International Law Challenge

Nuclear weapons have inevitably placed a normative strain on political leaders.[1] This strain was "managed" during the first three decades after 1945 in various ways: by periodic calls for disarmament, by a general Western policy that emphasized defense against aggression and by a diplomacy that from the 1960s onwards sought arms control arrangements to abate the arms race and maintain public confidence in the stability of the overall nuclear situation. More recently, the rising costs and dangers of a quickening arms race have given rise to widespread public anxiety in North America, Western Europe and Japan about the relationship of nuclear weapons to the security of states and to the viability of a global political order constituted principally, but not exclusively, by sovereign states.[2]

---

* Reprinted, with permission, from *McGill Law Journal*, Volume 28, Number 3 (1983).

** Of the Woodrow Wilson School of Public and International Affairs, Princeton University, and co-author, with Robert J. Lifton, of *Indefensible Weapons: The Political and Psychological Case Against Nuclearism* (1982), and a Senior Fellow of the World Policy Institute.

[1] "Normative" is used throughout this article to encompass legal, moral, cultural, and biological standards which help draw boundaries between what is morally permissible and appropriate and what is morally impermissible and inappropriate at different levels of societal organization. The focus of this article is upon the interplay between legal norms and the nation-state, in relation to external uses of military power, and more particularly, to reliance on nuclear weapons. In the context of the law of war, there has always been a strong relationship of coherence among these various sources of normative authority. There has also always been a tension between the power orientation of the modern state and the acceptance of normative guidelines in relation to issues of war and peace. This tension has been made more serious in recent decades as a consequence of the steady application of technological innovation to warfare, in a way that makes adherence to normative guidelines strike political leaders as unrealistic. In a sense, this "unrealistic" demand for a modification of such policy prerogatives lies at the core of the current renewed normative inquiry into the status and role of nuclear weapons.

[2] This anxiety also reflects the erosion of the United Nations' position as a source of normative authority, constituted originally to counterbalance and eventually modify the power-centered, fragmented behavior of independent sovereign states and such alliances of these states which aggregate like-minded and partisan political attitudes. The combined effect of the growing dominance of the state over internal political, economic and cultural spheres of action and belief, and its autonomy (or sovereignty) in relation to supranational frameworks, especially in matters of national security, fosters an impression that such states operate in a normative vacuum, especially the superpowers. For a discussion of these depressing dual aspects of the international situation, see Falk, *Nuclear Weapons and the End of Democracy* (1982) 2 Praxis Int'l 1; and Falk, "The Decline of International Order: Normative Regression and Geopolitical Maelstrom" in *Yearbook of World Affairs 1982* (1982) 10.

This anxiety has taken several forms, but includes important normative dimensions, that is, moral/legal objections to the role currently assigned to nuclear weapons in the strategic thought and actions of the superpowers. Part of this concern has centered on the combined unwillingness and inability of the superpowers to stabilize the arms race in terms of either resource outlays or risks. Another part of this concern has centered on the provocative deployment of specific weapons systems, such as Pershing II and SS-20s in Europe, which appear to invite first strikes or preemptive attacks in periods of acute crisis. This concern has generated as well a wider questioning as to whether any reliance on nuclear weaponry can ever appropriately serve the ends of state power. Implicit in such questioning is a critique of the nuclear encroachment upon the sovereign rights of non-nuclear states and junior alliance partners, whose destinies seem to be entrapped in the dynamics of the rivalry between the United States and the Soviet Union; the old possibility of neutral states opting out of belligerency seems to have become meaningless in a world in which even outer space is understood as a dimension of belligerency, and in which the fallout and the global ecological and economic disruption that would be caused by any major nuclear exchange would certainly ignore national boundaries.

These gathering concerns about the prevailing official thinking on nuclear weapons were most powerfully articulated by Jonathan Schell in his *The Fate of the Earth*.[3] Schell emphasizes the threats to human survival contained in the nuclear standoff, as well as the disproportion between tactics and technology, because nuclear destruction far outweighs the state interests supposedly being served by such weapons. This disproportion has been highlighted during the presidency of Ronald Reagan by loose talk about limited nuclear wars, first-strike weaponry and prevailing or winning in a protracted nuclear war. In fairness to the Reagan Administration, their loose talk, in each instance, builds upon earlier entrenched official thinking and war plans about the role nuclear weapons should play in relation to the foreign policy of the United States. There also exists a growing public realization that the scale and quality of the Soviet missile build-up in the 1970s went well beyond reasonable defensive requirements. This build-up has raised doubts about Soviet motivations, leading analysts to question Moscow's reasons for building and deploying so many missiles, especially in relation to Europe, including the frequent replacement of missile systems. Perhaps in partial explanation of that build-up, it should be noted that, earlier, Soviet strategic inferiority produced a diplomatic humiliation for them at the time of the Cuban Missile Crisis (1962) and this undoubtedly gave rise to an attitude of "never again" in the Kremlin which enabled weapons builders to enlarge their

---

[3] J. Schell, *The Fate of the Earth* (1982).

claims on Soviet resources. Furthermore, the Soviet Union has no "friends", and arguably is surrounded by "enemies", including its East European "satellites" and an antagonistic China with enormous manpower resources and its own growing arsenal of nuclear weapons.[4] Each superpower justifies its own continuous search for more and better weapons by its perception and representation of the other, including profound uncertainties about the other's ultimate and proximate intentions.

In early 1983, normative concerns about nuclear weapons are evident in a variety of forms. There is, first of all, a continuing major Western European grassroots effort to prevent the deployment by NATO of 572 Pershing II and cruise missiles. Additionally, there is Ronald Reagan's somewhat bizarre espousal of an array of twenty-first century advanced defensive weapons, suitably dubbed "Reagan's star wars strategy", which could supposedly provide societies with secure protection against nuclear attack while superseding reliance on deterrence, which is acknowledged for the first time at a leadership level to rest on morally dubious threats to devastate foreign societies.[5] The final adoption of the much discussed Pastoral Letter of the American Catholic bishops, which places the teaching of the Catholic Church on war as applied to nuclear weaponry in direct opposition to many of the principal tenets of prevailing nuclear weapons strategy that have been accepted by NATO and the United States since 1945, also reflects a rising consciousness of these issues.[6]

---

[4] One justification that has been advanced for the Soviet build-up in the European theater is to discourage any Western impulse to intervene in Eastern Europe in the event of future challenges directed at Soviet hegemony.

[5] For the Reagan text, see *President's Speech on Military Spending and a New Defense*, The New York Times (24 March 1983) A 20. The normative aspiration to substitute secure defensive capabilities for current threats to devastate whole societies with weapons of mass destruction is certainly admirable, but there is little reason to suppose that it can ever be made to work with sufficient reliability. Even Reagan talks of this high frontier scenario as a goal for the twenty-first century. We are left with the need for a normative framework that can guide our national security policies at the present time, and lead us toward a safer future. To the extent that high frontier thinking is an alternative to peace and disarmament thinking, it represents one more misguided effort to overcome normative problems by proposing another technological fix. For opposing assessments of the feasibility of such developments, see Teller, *Reagan's Courage*, The New York Times (30 March 1983) A 31; and Garwin, *Reagan's Riskiness*, The New York Times (30 March 1983) A 31.

[6] For a partial text of the Pastoral Letter, *The Challenge of Peace: God's Promise and Our Response*, see The New York Times (5 May 1983) B 16. For earlier assessments from a Catholic perspective, see W. Stein, ed., *Nuclear Weapons and Christian Conscience* (1961). For skeptical assessment, see Voorst, *The Churches and Nuclear Deterrence* (1983) 61 Foreign Affairs 827.

Until this broader political and normative public ferment emerged, international lawyers had been comparatively quiet on these momentous issues. Over the years since 1945 there have been, to be sure, a few scholarly discussions pro and con about the legality of nuclear weaponry, but somehow until the 1980s, the debate never was treated in international law circles as very significant.[7] This neglect has several explanations. The legal issues were clouded from the beginning by the original "popular", and in this sense, legally "non-controversial" use of atomic bombs "to save lives" and bring peace in the closing days of World War II, generally regarded by the victorious powers as a "just" war.[8] It also seemed futile to mount a legal case against weapons so obviously useful and powerful, because of the prevailing realities and track record of geopolitics. Specifically, the inability of the West to develop sufficient non-nuclear means to defend Europe and other vital interests on the Asian mainland, in light of a perceived threat resting upon an overall Soviet superiority in conventional forces, and reinforced by the logistical advantages of Soviet dominance of the Asian land mass, made it seem self-denying for Western powers to question the legal status of nuclear weapons. Furthermore, aside from a brief movement in England a couple of decades ago, there was no political pressure mounted by way of a grassroots normative attack. Defending the legality of nuclear weapons is such a thankless task that it undoubtedly seemed to most international lawyers, who meant to be upholding official policies, to be more desirable to maintain a discreet silence on the subject, as long as this was politically possible. All of these elements contributed to the repression of "the legal question". Nevertheless, it is instructive to realize that legal doubts about the status of nuclear weapons have been objectively "present" ever since the Hiroshima explosion. The importance of posing questions now, in 1983, should not be understood only as a response to a new and more aggravated stage in the nuclear arms race, but also as a belated attempt to consider serious legal issues that, but for the historical circumstances surrounding the original uses, would have been addressed as soon as the first atomic bomb was used as a weapon of war.

If Germany or Japan had developed and used atomic bombs in World War II against the inhabited cities of the victors, the war crimes trials held in Nuremberg or Tokyo would certainly have investigated, and in all probability, condemned, the use of this weapon, and would have punished the

---

[7] Earlier works on the subject include G. Schwarzenberger, *The Legality of Nuclear Weapons* (1958); N. Singh, *Nuclear Weapons and International Law* (1959); and Brownlie, *Some Legal Aspects of the Use of Nuclear Weapons* (1965) 14 Int'l & Comp. L.Q. 437.

[8] A useful depiction of the official thinking surrounding the decision to use the atomic bomb against Japan was made by the influential Secretary of War at the time, Henry L. Stinson. See *The Decision to Use the Atomic Bomb* (1947) 194 Harper's Magazine 97.

officials responsible as war criminals, even had due mitigating account been taken of Allied strategic bombing of Axis cities.[9] The magnitudes of the blasts and the fallout from those original fission bombs would, in my judgment, have led impartial international law experts to regard the atomic attacks on the Japanese cities as having been perpetrated by illegal weapons, or at least as having involved an illegal tactic of war, despite the plausibility of arguments from military necessity and the prior disregard by planners of strategic bombing patterns of the traditional limits of the laws of war. Indeed, the only court that ever investigated the legal arguments surrounding the American attacks on Hiroshima and Nagasaki came clearly and persuasively to the conclusion that they violated international law as it existed in 1945.[10] Nevertheless, despite several relatively obscure legal condemnations over the years, which took place in a variety of international settings, the legal questioning of nuclear weapons has been totally ignored until recently by political leaders and military planners in the nuclear powers, as well as by their publics.

At this time, the international law dimension of the nuclear age is at last becoming prominent, at least in professional and policy-planning circles. A great deal of scholarly work is appearing on all aspects of the topic. International law, as a general rule, is responsive to fluctuations in the political environment, and the last few years have firmly established a climate in which inquiry into the legal status of nuclear weaponry appears "natural", if not unavoidable. The publication of this symposium in the *McGill Law Journal* is one indication of this new prominence.

In fact, some of this legal questioning is coming from strange sources. There exists a hawkish school of nuclear strategists, which has for years wanted to shape nuclear weapons policy around traditional moral/legal notions of "defense" and "military targets", thereby hoping to overcome normative inhibitions against an aggressive foreign policy and also hoping to reconcile normative considerations with a reliance on nuclear weapons. Proponents of this approach emphasize the "immorality" of city-busting

---

[9] Of course, the "criminal" character of the bombing itself was never considered because of "the victors' justice" limitation on the war crimes proceedings; in other words, to have been condemned, the atomic attacks would have had to have been carried out *only* by the losing side. Victor's justice was not extended in an extreme form to punish the losers for war methods *also* used by the victors. For an excellent discussion of the issue, see R. Minear, *Victors' Justice: The Tokyo War Crimes Trial* (1971). For a more sympathetic construction, see T. Taylor, *Nuremberg and Vietnam: An American Tragedy* (1970).

[10] *The Shimoda Case* decided by the District Court of Tokyo on 7 December 1963, reprinted in [1964] Jap. Ann. Int'l L. 212. For comment and interpretation, see Falk, *The Shimoda Case: A Legal Appraisal of the Atomic Attacks Upon Hiroshima and Nagasaki* (1965) 59 Am. J. Int'l L. 759.

weaponry that threatens the indiscriminate devastation of the urban centers of an enemy society, and the "immorality" of apocalyptic thinking that takes no steps to maximize chances of survival should a nuclear war occur. These "normative" critics of mutual terror do not consider abandoning our reliance on nuclear weaponry, but rather argue on behalf of strategic postures which rest upon a provocative mix of civil defense programs (shelters), defensive technologies and accurate weaponry that can concentrate its destructive effect on the enemy's military capabilities, including its command structure.[11] The normative paradox here is evident: this type of reconciliation of nuclear weapons doctrine and weaponry with the core conceptions of the law of war and international morality tends toward a speeding up of the arms race, the design and deployment of first-strike weapons systems, and the adoption of attitudes and doctrines that favor nuclear war-fighting options. In effect, taking international law and morality seriously in *this* manner definitely erodes the crucial firebreak in war-planning that separates conventional and nuclear weaponry, thereby making the outbreak of nuclear war far more likely.

Such a perspective has been recently introduced into international law discourse by a widely noted RAND study.[12] The RAND report has proved irresistible to those international lawyers who are opposed to the legality of nuclear weapons; it seems almost too good to be true. It appears to establish the central point that even a think tank closely aligned with the Pentagon is driven to the conclusion that the principal existing doctrine governing the use of nuclear weapons rests upon a flagrant defiance of international law. In the words of the RAND study, "[d]estruction of societies, destruction as an end in itself, would appear to be directly opposed to the most fundamental principles of international law governing armed conflict".[13] More pointedly: "The concept of Assured Destruction and its derivatives (e.g. economic recovery targeting) appear to be directly opposed to international law and, hence, contrary to both domestic law and DOD directives governing individual actions affecting the acquisition, procurement, and use of weapons."[14] The RAND authors disclose their purpose as being "to help close the chasm that now yawns between international law and U.S. strategic nuclear policies".[15]

---

[11] A clear and influential instance of this perspective is Iklé, *Can Nuclear Deterrence Last Out this Century?* (1973) 51 Foreign Affairs 267. See also C. Gray, *Strategic Studies and Public Policy* [:] *The American Experience* (1982); and K. Payne, *The BMD Debate: Ten Years After* (1980) (a Hudson Institute monograph).

[12] C. Builder & M. Graubard, *The International Law of Armed Conflict: Implications for the Concept of Assured Destruction* (1982) (RAND Publication Series R-2804-FF).

[13] *Ibid.*, vii.

[14] *Ibid.*, ix.

[15] *Ibid.*, xiii.

Indeed, these are extraordinary conclusions, considering their source. In effect, the RAND authors acknowledge an underlying illegality governing United States policy and practice since Hiroshima, a policy and practice characteristic of the United States, of NATO and of Soviet national security.

But it should be noted that this analysis of international law confines itself to a legal condemnation of the doctrine of Mutual Assured Destruction [MAD], and has not been applied to the weapons themselves. The RAND study proposes that "[a]ctual (as opposed to declaratory) U.S. targeting, strike plans, and military forces should be designed only for attacks against military targets and war-supporting activities (i.e. they should be as discriminate as reasonably possible, consistent with their military purposes). What constitutes war-supporting activities is subject to interpretation; but a safe interpretation under the law would not include civilians or civilian industry unless or until they are converted to military activities that could have a direct effect upon the conflict then being waged (i.e. economic recovery targeting would seem a dubious concept under the international law of armed conflict)."[16] The authors spell out the implications for military research and development as leading to an emphasis on "discriminate, militarily effective weapons".[17] The RAND study never genuinely clarifies the extent to which the operational impact of allowing nuclear weapons to be used against military targets is consistent with the fundamental objectives and principles of the law of war. Surely the cumulative effect of nuclear megatonnage and the wide scope of lethal effects creates "problems" for any general validation of nuclear weapons under international law.

The RAND study establishes some important common grounds for inquiry. It affirms the relevance of international law to strategic planning, and it even insists that policymakers and government international lawyers "closely examine" the consistency of "strategic planning concepts. . . with the law of armed conflict".[18] Beyond this, it alerts "defense intellectuals outside the government, in universities and corporations, to appreciate the essentials, if not the details, of the international law as it applies to strategic planning" and urges them to conform their behavior accordingly and on the basis of their opportunity "to be more independent" than those playing official roles. Such a mandate relies expressly on United States Department of Defense official policy, outlined in DOD Instruction 5500.15 which includes the following language: "All action of the Department of Defense with respect to the acquisition and procurement of weapons, and their intended use in armed

---

[16] *Ibid.*, 48.
[17] *Ibid.*, 51. Builder's extremely assertive strategic views confirm this interpretation. See Builder, *Why Not First-Strike Counterforce Capabilities* [1979] Strategic Rev. 35.
[18] Builder & Graubard, *ibid.*, 57.

conflict, shall be consistent with the obligations assumed by the United States Government under all applicable treaties, with customary international law, and, in particular, with the laws of war." [19] In fact, of course, the United States Government position has rested mainly on a facile and unpersuasive application of *Lotus* reasoning, namely, that states are permitted to do anything not expressly prohibited by rules resting on consent, and that in the absence of an express treaty prohibition, joined by the United States, nuclear weapons may be legally employed. [20] It seems ludicrous to extend the reasoning of the *Lotus* case of 1927, developed to assess a very narrow question of jurisprudential competence in a criminal negligence controversy arising out of a collision on the high seas, to the drastically different circumstances surrounding the consideration of the legal status of nuclear weapons. For one thing, on a jurisprudential level, the issue of whether or not a given activity is prohibited by pre-existing rules is partly a matter of how *general* is the level of appraisal chosen. For instance, while nuclear weapons are not the explicit subject of any agreement binding nuclear weapons states, the main instruments of the pre-existing laws of land warfare prohibit *all* methods of warfare having the characteristics associated with contemplated uses of nuclear weapons. The *Lotus* view of the legal status of new weapons and methods of warfare also flies in the face of the "Martens Clause" inserted in the Preamble to *Hague Convention No. IV* of 1907, concerning the Laws and Customs of War on Land, and is itself generally regarded as a binding element of customary international law. The Martens Clause requires governments to assess "cases not covered by the rules adopted by them" by reference to "the general principles of the law of nations, derived from the usages established among civilized peoples, from the laws of humanity, and from the dictates of public conscience". [21] On such a basis, the overwhelming normative consensus now

---

[19] See also United States Dep't of the Air Force, *International Law — The Conduct of Armed Conflict and Air Operations* (1976) 6-11 (AFP. 110-31). The RAND study also relies on the language of art. 36 of 1977 Geneva Protocol I Additional to the 1949 *Geneva Conventions*, which puts parties to the agreement "under an obligation to determine whether" the employment of a new weapon or method of warfare would "in some or all circumstances" violate international law. The study does not note that the United States representative in the treaty negotiations explicitly ruled out the applicability of Protocol I Additional to nuclear weapons. For discussion of the United States Government view on the non-applicability of Protocol I Additional to nuclear weaponry, see Erickson, *Protocol I: A Merging of the Hague and Geneva Law of Armed Conflict* (1979) 19 Va J. Int'l L. 557, 560. For the text of 1977 Geneva Protocol I Additional Relating to the Protection of Victims of International Armed Conflicts, see U.N. Doc. A/32/144, Annex I, reprinted in (1977) 16 I.L.M. 1391.

[20] United States Dep't of the Navy, *U.S. Naval Instructions* (1955), art. 613. See also United States Dep't of the Army, Field Manual 27-10, *The Law of Land Warfare* (1956) 18. For the text of the *Lotus* case, see *The Case of the S.S. "Lotus"* (France v. Turkey) (1927) P.C.I.J., Ser. A., No. 10.

[21] *Hague Convention* [No. IV] *Respecting the Laws and Customs of War on Land*, 18 October 1907, 36 Stat. 2277, T.S. No. 539, 1 Bevans 631, Preamble. For reasoning on the

operative in international society would *legally* condemn all contemplated roles for nuclear weapons, except "possession" as a hedge against nuclear blackmail; not even a retaliatory use of nuclear weapons could be easily reconciled with most interpretations of the laws of war, given the properties of the weaponry and the difficulty of reconciling any actual use with such principles as "necessity", "proportionality", "discrimination", and "humanity".[22]

Official American strategic doctrine and war plans, despite the apparent embrace of Mutual Assured Destruction, has in fact always emphasized military targeting, and hence has been relatively consistent with the position argued in the RAND study. The service manual formulations with regard to legal status validate nuclear weapons only "against enemy combatants and other military objectives". To the extent that existing doctrines and plans rest on a conception of deterrence based on threats to civilian non-combatants and non-military objectives, these would be illegal under even this narrowest definition of the applicability of international law. However, applying such guidelines, the atomic attacks against Hiroshima and Nagasaki should have been clearly repudiated. Furthermore, current counterforce targeting, while it superficially repudiates city-busting options, and therefore is formally consistent with restricting the role of nuclear weapons to military objectives, is in fact deeply misleading in this crucial respect. Because of the magnitude and properties of current nuclear weapons (involving many times the destructiveness of the atomic bombs of World War II), and because of their contemplated use in and around cities (there are, for instance, sixty-two military objectives targeted within the city limits of Moscow!), the cumulative blast and fallout effects from multiple nuclear explosions, the number of targets regarded as "military", and the clustering of military targets near population centers, even an official policy that limits the use of nuclear weapons by reference to the military character of the target is not different in effect from an overtly indiscriminate targeting policy. Furthermore, the World War II experience with the unrestricted bombardment of cities and with unrestricted submarine warfare suggests that a self-limiting framework of policies and tactics confining deliberate destruction to the enemy's military targets gives way in wartime to considerations of battlefield effectiveness, understood to include strikes against cities to weaken the resolve of the enemy society. Either the restriction implicit in counterforce strategy is meaningless, because "military

---

relevance of the Martens Clause to this issue, see Falk, Meyrowitz & Sanderson, *Nuclear Weapons and International Law* (1980) (Occasional Paper No. 10, Princeton World Order Studies Program), reprinted in (1980) 20 Indian J. Int'l L. 541.

[22] For formulations of these principles, see the General Introduction to International Commission to Enquire into Reported Violations of International Law by Israel During its Invasion of the Lebanon, *Israel in Lebanon* (1983) xi.

target" is given such a loose definition that it includes everything pertaining to a war effort, even civilian morale, or the confining effect of a restricted definition is overlooked under pressure, as was the case with the atomic attacks in World War II, whose rationale rested on their overall role in helping to end the war successfully. No serious attempt has ever been made to determine whether the contemplated uses of the atomic bomb might be in violation of the law of war despite the justification provided. Without a more focused inquiry into what is permitted and prohibited by law, the general public conception that *some* uses of nuclear weapons are legal has the primary effect of providing a rationalization or loophole for virtually *any* use of such weapons.

The present affirmation of the applicability and stature of international law is a challenge to prevailing statist attitudes both within and without government.[23] Let the existing situation be clearly stated. The use of atomic bombs against Hiroshima and Nagasaki was never evaluated in relation to this international law framework by planners and leaders, nor has the subsequent diplomacy of the nuclear age, which has included some twenty documented threats to use nuclear weapons, been in any way sensitive to such legal criteria.[24] In the voluminous literature devoted to the Cuban Missile Crisis, only international lawyers have regarded the international law dimension of the crisis as important, except as it was considered in the detailed planning which was associated with the actual carrying out of the strategic decision.[25]

A climate now exists in which to argue the case for the relevance of international law to nuclear issues. This case can be reinforced by action on the part of those who are politically and morally committed to minimizing the role of nuclear weapons. For reasons of state policy, the Soviet Union seems prepared to lend its official support to most efforts to delegitimize nuclear weapons.[26]

---

[23] See sources cited *supra*, note 2; and Falk, *Some Thoughts on the Decline of International Law and Future Prospects* (1981) 9 Hofstra L. Rev. 399.

[24] These uses are documented carefully in an exceptionally important article: Ball, *U.S. Strategic Forces* [:] *How Would They be Used* (1982-83) 7 Int'l Security 31, 41-4 (No. 3).

[25] For a legal maximalist interpretation of the relevance of international law to nuclear weapons that manages to avoid being a legal polemic, see A. Chayes, *The Cuban Missile Crisis* [:] *International Crises and the Role of Law* (1974).

[26] The Soviet position on the nuclear arms race in general has been described well by Soviet dissenters, Roy and Zhores Medvedev, *A Nuclear Samizdat on America's Arms Race*, The Nation [magazine] (16 January 1982) 38. Soviet adoption of an unconditional no-first-use of nuclear weapons pledge is contained in former Communist Party Chairman Brezhnev's "Special Message" of 15 June 1982 to the United Nations General Assembly Second Special Session on Disarmament. The pledge has been reaffirmed by the current Soviet leader, Yuri Andropov.

There remain, however, several serious preliminary difficulties involved in the application of international law to nuclear weapons. First of all, nuclear weaponry is possessed by rival states in a world characterized by acute and pervasive distrust; nuclear disarmament, beyond certain fairly high thresholds, continues to be viewed as unrealistic, because it would create unacceptable political temptations and vulnerabilities. As a consequence of this practical constraint, rival states are likely to retain offsetting nuclear weapons capabilities for the indefinite future, and to insist on at least a posture of minimum deterrence, that is, their possession and a threat, implied at least, to retaliate with nuclear weapons against nuclear attack. Even this form of minimization of the role of nuclear weapons is likely to sustain some type of nuclear arms race, as each side will want to be confident that its nuclear weapons capability and its overall capability for response do not become vulnerable to surprise attack as a result of secret machinations by its rival.[27]

Secondly, as the underlying technology needed to produce nuclear warheads becomes more familiar and refined, the possibility of additional political actors, including dissident armed groups, or even criminal gangs, acquiring nuclear weapons will grow greater. In relation to these prospects of nuclear proliferation, the existing nuclear weapons states are unlikely to give up their hedges against nuclear blackmail by altogether renouncing both nuclear possession and use options. In any event, as long as the technological base persists for producing nuclear weapons, their production and reintroduction into defense arsenals can never be reliably ruled out.

Thirdly, and perhaps most disturbingly, as long as nuclear weapons remain under the control of governments, and as long as armed conflict persists in international relations, there exists a grave danger that any available weapon or tactic, regardless of its normative status, would be introduced into battle, if it were perceived by the leaders involved to be centrally decisive. Throughout the history of modern warfare, going at least as far back as the futile effort to banish the crossbow, weapons that are effective on the battlefield or in relation to defeating an enemy society have been used without consideration of legal (or moral, or cultural) restrictions.[28] Nuclear weapons,

---

[27] The case for nuclear deterrence along present lines is developed ably by Mandlebaum, "International Stability and Nuclear Order: The First Nuclear Regime" in D. Gompert & M. Mandlebaum, *Nuclear Weapons and World Politics* (1977) 13.

[28] Modern war has grown into an unconditional contest of wills, in which every means and tactic of destruction will be used by political leaders with "a clear conscience". The ideological grounding for this secular absolutism is formulated most clearly in the writings of Machiavelli and Clausewitz. For an analysis of this relation, see W. Gallie, *Philosophers of Peace and War* (1978) 37-65; and R. Lifton & R. Falk, *Indefensible Weapons: The Political and Psychological Case Against Nuclearism* (1982) 239-43. Despite the normative doubts now being raised about

whatever else they might be, are regarded as effective, at least in their threat role as guardians of political survival. Indeed, it would be easy to contrive rationalizations that "illegal" *threats* to use nuclear weapons against cities and civilians "save lives", safeguard the prospects of "human survival" and make indispensable peacekeeping contributions by way of the prevention of war. Post-1918 efforts to prohibit the use of poison gas weaponry do not provide much reassurance to the contrary. It is true that the legal prohibition may have operated as a marginal factor in discouraging the use of such weapons and in building moral/legal inhibitions in world leaders against use in wartime. Nevertheless, the evidence suggests overwhelmingly that the non-use of these weapons in major conflicts that have taken place since World War I is related more importantly to doubts about their "effectiveness" under battlefield conditions, and to the existence of alternative methods of carrying out belligerent missions. In essence, the argument I am making rests on the central proposition that because of the way states wage war — the unconditionality of the means they use whenever issues of victory and defeat arise — it is unlikely in the extreme that international law constraints on nuclear weapons by themselves will hold up in times of severe international crisis. Because a large number of these weapons will be retained, under the best of foreseeable circumstances, these weapons will be likely to be used to the extent that it seems to leaders that the outcome of a war is at stake. Countries such as Israel, France and Great Britain presumably possess nuclear weapons as a warning to their enemies not to push them too far, and there is every reason to suppose that rather than accept military defeat, such weapons would be used, regardless of their legal status. To put the matter differently, international law cannot hope to regulate the pursuit of decisive military state interests, and nuclear weapons are manifestly weapons of military decisiveness.

Fourthly, and more obscurely, the indirect reliance on nuclear weaponry to assist in achieving a variety of foreign policy goals is deeply embedded in bureaucratic thinking, at least in the United States and the NATO countries, about upholding "national security" at "acceptable" costs. To relinquish such a reliance will require very determined political leadership in the two superpowers, especially in the West, where first-use nuclear options remain con-

---

nuclear weapons, there has, as yet, been no serious challenge directed at these unrestricted war-making prerogatives of states, and without a "*Magna Carta* for the nuclear age", the legal doubts being currently raised about the status of nuclear weapons, even if they come to be embodied in some authoritative form, will be cast aside in time of emergency. These doubts may, nevertheless, be functional, to the extent that they prompt policies and weapons deployments that operate *as if* these weapons were illegitimate; in effect, the legal challenge may contribute to the replacement of "early use" scenarios, and this by itself would reduce greatly the risks and anxieties associated with the existence of nuclear weapons.

scious premises of existing foreign policy.[29] Nuclear weapons apologists, including those who reaffirm the explicit relevance of international law to such decision making, argue for "defensive" roles for these weapons (against "aggression") and "military" uses (against silos, bases and command centers). These lines of argument are consistent with an *abstract* application of the traditional international law of war to nuclear weapons and tactics in the spirit of the Martens Clause. The strategic implications of such an application are to encourage the development and deployment of neutron bombs, ABM and "high frontier" weaponry, civil defense preparations, increasing the accuracy of weapons, and provocative political plans and strategies. The net effect of such strategies is to overcome inhibitions on the first use of nuclear weapons in a conflict situation, because the inhibitions of terror associated with MAD are weakened.[30] In effect, the nuclear/non-nuclear firebreak is eroded, if not cast aside. The ironic result seems to be that taking international law seriously, given the accompanying implausibility of getting rid of nuclear weapons or of transforming international relations in a more pacific direction, may actually clear the path for nuclear war-fighting doctrines, policies and capabilities.[31] This is the main operative effect of the RAND study, especially

---

[29] For an indication of the extent of reliance on first use options, see Payne, *Deterrence, Arms Control, and U.S. Strategic Doctrine* (1981) 25 Orbis 747. In opposition to such reliance lies the main importance of no-first-use proposals and pledges. A main consequence of renouncing first-use policy options is the refashioning of foreign policy in two directions: reducing the overall nuclear undertaking (that is, precluding any credible defense for certain kinds of attacks on foreign societies) or upholding an earlier commitment by reliance on the sufficiency of non-nuclear military capabilities. To what extent, for instance, are current NATO force requirements for the non-nuclear defense of Western Europe being exaggerated by way of a myth of conventional inferiority? How real, in any event, is the threat of a Soviet armed attack upon Western Europe? Even if denuclearization is the exclusive goal, tactical choices are not self-evident because a process of realignment within NATO could produce the opposite results by restoring first-use options by way of a West German decision to develop its own nuclear strike force. For recent discussion of these issues, see Bundy, Kennan, McNamara & Smith, *Nuclear Weapons and the Atlantic Alliance* (1982) 60 Foreign Affairs 753. For a skeptical response, see Kaiser, Leber, Mertes & Schulze, *Nuclear Weapons and the Preservation of Peace* (1982) 60 Foreign Affairs 1157.

[30] The full implications of the main alternative strategic positions are discussed in Keeny & Panofsky, *MAD Versus NUTS* [:] *Can Doctrine or Weaponry Remedy the Mutual Hostage Relationship of the Superpowers?* (1981) 60 Foreign Affairs 287.

[31] At some level of jurisprudential reflection, this "ironic effect" of international law analysis suggests a defect or bias in the RAND rendering of the law of war *vis-à-vis* nuclear weaponry. See Builder & Graubard, *supra*, note 12. One way out, of course, is to condemn nuclear weaponry as illegal *per se*, because of its attributes, rather than to focus analysis, as had been traditional prior to nuclear weapons, on the probable contexts of their use, that is, on the targets. Another way out would be to formulate a new kind of analysis based upon an interpretation of the hierarchy of objectives pursued by the international law of war in the nuclear age, placing the avoidance of any use of nuclear weapons at the pinnacle of the hierarchy.

in light of the policy directions of those who are presently urging an accelerated arms race and the development and deployment of destabilizing weapons
systems.[32]

The complexity of the fifth obstacle to the application of international
law to these weapons is as follows: some minimalist variant of MAD provides, arguably, the best hope of avoiding any future use of nuclear weapons
and of slowing down the arms race, and yet MAD is presently most flagrantly
in violation of international law, as this law has been generally understood.[33]
Furthermore, MAD does provide potential adversaries with reassurances that
nuclear weapons are being held only against the remote contingency of the
necessity of retaliation against prior nuclear attack. The essence of deterrence
is to make the potential nuclear attacker anticipate with as much certainty as
possible the devastation of his own country. If deterrence is made more
compatible with the RAND reading of international law, then all or some of
the following effects could come about: deterrence would in fact be hypocrit-
ical in its application (that is, because of the nature of the attacking weapons
and of the locations and variety of military targets, counterforce limitations
will not in fact save either cities or the civilian population from nuclear
devastation); MAD would be less effective as a deterrent (that is, the attacker
might regard the prospect of retailiation against those of his military targets
that are separated geographically from places of civilian habitation as an
acceptable and even rational risk to be counted as part of the cost of a nuclear
surprise attack and victory); finally, deterrence would prove less and less
reassuring to a rival in a period of acute crisis (that is, if the other side might
reasonably attack, then pressure to stage a preemptive first strike necessarily
grows).

There may be no fully satisfactory way to circumvent entirely this fifth
obstacle. However, I think there is a line of analysis that more validly uses the
international law heritage to minimize the role of nuclear weapons in diplomacy. The jurisprudential "concession" that will enable this reformulation
is a variant of Catholic "just war" moral reasoning, which allows the choice of
a lesser evil under certain circumstances of belligerency.

---

[32] Indeed, overt doctrine since 1974 has emphasized military targeting, under such rubrics as
"flexible response" and "counterforce". See Leitenberg, *Presidential Directive (P.D.) 59:
United States Nuclear Weapon Targeting Policy* (1981) 18 J. Peace Research 309; Beres,
Tilting Toward Thanatos: America's "Countervailing" Nuclear Strategy (1981) 34 World
Politics 25; and L. Beres, *Mimicking Sisyphus: America's Countervailing Nuclear Strategy*
(1983).

[33] The illegality of nuclear weapons is a firm conclusion of the RAND study. See Builder &
Graubard, *supra*, note 12. This assessment is reinforced by the analysis of the Catholic
Bishops' Pastoral Letter. See *supra*, note 6.

It should be evident by now that serious reflection on the relevance of international law to the status of nuclear weapons will be unavoidably controversial at this stage, and also, that it is, to some extent, both inconclusive and tragic. One is not proceeding on the basis of a clean slate. Thousands of nuclear weapons exist, many thousands more are in the planning and development stages, and it is almost inconceivable that the expenditure of so many billions of dollars and the resulting accumulation of towering structures of bureaucratic influence can be overcome easily. At the same time, the overall normative dimension provides firm grounds upon which to premise a critique of existing nuclear weapons policy and practice. Definite improvements can be made in present policies, and in public expectations governing the use of nuclear weapons without waiting for the darkness of catastrophe or the lightness of utopia to come upon us. Such improvements might increase the prospects for a peaceful transition over time to a denuclearized world.

II.   Toward an International Law Regime for the Nuclear Age

The quest for a legal regime rooted in the dynamics of the state system of world order is adversely conditioned by the continuing predominance of a Machiavellian tradition of political leadership.[34] That is, war as an option of national policy cannot be ruled out by legal fiat, and the legalist efforts of this century to do so, by way of renouncing "aggressive war" options, largely constitute a fraud on the public's consciousness and moral concerns. Because the governments of sovereign states are the highest decision-makers, especially if the political institutions of the United Nations are either inoperative or are discounted as partisan, self-serving interpretations of the legal status of controversial uses of force are made. These circumstances are the rule, not the exception. That is, politically congenial uses of force are routinely characterized as "defensive", whereas politically hostile uses of force are condemned as "aggressive". To some extent, this incoherence flows from polemical uses of the law to serve the interests of state power, but to some extent, it also genuinely reflects a "misperception" that follows from the diversity of perspectives of different states, with different accesses to information, and different ideologies, cultures and worldviews.

This pervasive subjectivity in international politics makes it exceedingly dangerous to tie any restraint on methods of warfare to a characterization of the context of the war as "defensive".[35] The extension of the aggression/

---

[34] See R. Tucker, *Politics as Leadership* (1981) 114-57; and Lifton & Falk, *supra*, note 28, 239-43.

[35] Note that under post-1928 international law, only defensive uses of force in international affairs are "legal". It is also the case that the international law of war is impartial as between the

defense framework to the dimension of nuclear weapons policy is seriously flawed on both conceptual and policy grounds: on conceptual grounds, it regressively merges *jus ad bello* analysis with a determination of relative *jus in bello* rights (that is, it allows the self-styled defending state to use nuclear weapons proportionately and with discrimination);[36] on policy grounds, it weakens the inhibition on the recourse to nuclear weapons, and also dilutes incentives to plan non-nuclear defense strategies.

In articulating the contours of an international law regime responsive to the nuclear age, three goals of policy seem to be paramount: (a) avoiding nuclear war; (b) minimizing crisis instability;[37] and (c) reducing the arms race. These three overriding objectives are phrased so as to take account of the international political setting. Also, they are complementary, but they are not necessarily consistent with one another in all applications. For instance, promoting objective (b) crisis stability, may in certain circumstances require increased defense outlays to maintain an assured invulnerability of retaliatory capabilities to a surprise attack and, hence, represents a setback for objective (c).

Also, each of these objectives requires extensive interpretation to be made operational, and interpretation is necessarily susceptible to a variety of good faith outcomes. One interpreter might argue that the way to avoid nuclear war is to achieve decisive superiority over the other side, because it alone threatens the international *status quo*. Another equally sincere interpreter might contend that only by renouncing all political violence in international affairs is it possible to avoid nuclear war, because participation in any armed conflict contains unacceptable risks of escalation. In effect, this latter position moves in the direction of conceiving the realization of objective (a) as dependent upon the construction of an overall global peace system. Acknowledging these difficulties with the operationalization of these objectives, this framework for a legal regime helps to organize and focus inquiry; it cannot hope to resolve all policy differences, except to the extent that it acts as a value-oriented appeal to a community of scholars and policy-makers to renounce the use of nuclear weapons altogether.

---

permissible tactics relied upon by "aggressor" and "defender". In effect, the law of peace (*jus ad bello*) renounces "aggressive" uses of force, while the law of war (*jus in bello*) accepts a shared framework of restraining rules, principles and agreements.

[36] This is the consequence of Eugene V. Rostow's and John Norton Moore's analyses of these issues. For Rostow's view, see (1982) 76 Proc. Am. Soc. Int'l L. (forthcoming). Moore's views can be found in (1983) 9 Brooklyn J. Int'l L. (forthcoming).

[37] That is, minimizing the temptation in a period of heightened international tensions to have recourse to war or to nuclear weapons, either because it looks as if an advantage could be seized or a dangerous vulnerability neutralized; mutuality as between nuclear rivals is better assurance of stability than military superiority, especially forms of superiority that might be nullified or reduced by a surprise attack.

In order to evolve a useful legal framework for nuclear weaponry, account must also be taken of two features of the international political world: a tendency for states to risk virtually any level of self-destruction in warfare in order to avoid military defeat, and a general willingness by states to use military power to secure positions of privilege, power and wealth in human affairs. There is no way to establish a realistic legal regime that is not sensitive to these geopolitical features of international life, as well as to the three previously delineated specific objectives associated directly with nuclear weapons. That is, given the existence of nuclear weaponry, it is difficult to imagine a major state that possesses such weapons reconciling itself to defeat in a conventional war affecting its perceived core interests. The adoption of nuclear weapons prohibitions, in certain forms, could possibly make the outbreak of major warfare more probable in international life, thereby entailing high human costs, and even quite unintentionally creating an increased net risk that nuclear weapons would in fact come to be used.

Furthermore, in contouring a legal regime for nuclear weapons, the starting point must be the basic principles constituting the customary international laws of war. These principles, emphasizing discriminate and proportionate warfare, seem impossible to reconcile with a nuclear weapons regime that is responsive to our overall guidelines for nuclear weapons. That is, the possession of a small number of invulnerable, inaccurate missiles (second-strike weapons) seems at present the best calculated way to minimize the danger of nuclear war, encourage crisis stability and minimize nuclear arms race incentives. With reasonably credible conventional defensive capabilities, and with the formulation of foreign policy goals in restrained terms, the dangers associated with nuclear weapons would be significantly reduced — but there is a major catch. This type of minimization of initial threat rests on the claim of last resort to engage finally in indiscriminate destruction, at least in a post-attack situation where its execution would be vindictive in the extreme. However, if nuclear weapons are reduced in number, while at the same time they are made accurate enough to strike at military targets, then it is difficult to maintain either crisis or arms race stability, because the nuclear weapons retained by both sides could be used for offensive as well as defensive purposes. If restraining notions were seriously implemented, they might not deter high-risk war and foreign policy initiatives because a probability of military targets being destroyed could still be coupled with a projected favorable outcome of a war. Leaders with intense ambitions or great desperation might conceivably be persuaded to gamble on the unwillingness of an attacked enemy to strike back pointlessly with nuclear weapons, or the attacker might even be prepared to absorb some nuclear retaliation in exchange for a prospect of political victory. Because scenario reasoning (projecting hypothetical future situations) is far-fetched, the uncertainties of political behavior in the nuclear age have been allowed to discourage value-oriented breakthroughs on matters of security.

A legal regime responsive to this background must build upon several interrelated aspects of the existing situation: the possession and retention of some nuclear weapons for use in extreme situations; the mutual distrust of adversary states, and a corresponding lack of sufficient confidence in international institutions that disallows any transfer of control over nuclear weapons beyond the level of the sovereign state; and the authority retained by governments to determine for themselves the occasions warranting recourse to the right of self-defense.

Against this background, a beneficial international law regime for nuclear weapons would have to rest on the following considerations:

(a)   public support for the idea that *any* actual use of nuclear weapons would violate the international law of war and would constitute a crime against humanity;

(b)   public support for the rule that a first use of nuclear weapons, even in a defensive mode in response to or in reasonable anticipation of a prior non-nuclear armed attack, would violate international law and would constitute a crime against humanity;

(c)   it follows from (b) that weapons systems (even at the research and development stage), war plans, strategic doctrines, and diplomatic threats that have first-strike characteristics are *per se* illegal, and that those political leaders, engineers, scientists, and defense workers knowingly associated with such "first-strike" roles are engaged in a continuing criminal enterprise;

(d)   a definite consensus that second or retaliatory uses of nuclear weapons against cities and primarily civilian targets violate international law and constitute a crime against humanity;[38]

(e)   a clear obligation, recognized by all nuclear weapons states and by other states as well, to pursue arms control in the direction of minimizing the role of nuclear weapons in conflict behavior through negotiations in good faith; this obligation is a provision, art. VI, of the

---

[38] There exists a definite normative tension between the legal framework most likely to minimize the risks of the use of nuclear weapons and the legal framework guiding acceptable uses of political violence. The latter framework is most consistent with a *total* prohibition against nuclear weapons, and secondarily, with a prohibition on any use of them directed at non-military targets. The minimizing framework, in contrast, reserves the option for the most legally unacceptable use as the best practical means to avoid any use, and as well, to eliminate arms race pressures and crisis instabilities. This "tension" expresses the impossibility of "living with" nuclear weapons, and highlights the current tragic reality associated with no longer being able to live without them.

widely-ratified *Non-Proliferation Treaty*,[39] and is embodied in general terms as well in the *Charter* of the United Nations and in a variety of formal resolutions adopted over the years by the General Assembly; and

(f)   a definite mandate directed toward citizens to take whatever steps are available to them to achieve a law-oriented foreign policy for their own country, including, as both conscience and good sense dictate, non-violent acts of civil disobedience, and efforts to persuade members of all branches of government to overcome the gap that separates the normative consensus of the public as to the illegality of the use of nuclear weapons from prevailing official policies.

These legal conclusions, taken in conjunction with the background of present political circumstances and the general objectives of a stable world order, underscore the importance of reinforcing the firebreak separating conventional and nuclear weapons. Only by minimizing reliance on nuclear weapons can the destabilizing geopolitical interactions surrounding their possible use be reduced. In this regard, a formal no-first-use pledge, coupled with comprehensive plans for a non-nuclear defense of vital interests, would be the best overall indication that the normative implications of nuclear weaponry are being taken seriously by policy-makers.

The most direct consequence of taking the normative dimension seriously (and law and morality are mutually reinforcing with respect to nuclear weapons), would be to make it "illegal" and "immoral" for a country to seek *any* advantage or positive role for nuclear weapons in relation to national security. From the moral/legal perspective, it is "illegal" to rest national security plans, doctrines or weapons deployments on first-use options or threats, and it is "immoral" for a country to undertake security commitments without developing adequate non-nuclear capabilities. This development of non-nuclear capabilities assumes great importance because no country will accept defeat if that defeat seriously encroaches upon its political independence and territorial integrity. In such a case, it is likely, regardless of the legal status of nuclear weapons, that such weapons would be used, because of overwhelming pressure, if it was thought that their use would alter the outcome of the war, and therefore, rules of prohibition need to be reinforced by making the prohibited activity as unnecessary as possible.

---

[39] *Treaty on the Non-Proliferation of Nuclear Weapons*, 1 July 1968, 21 U.S.T. 483, T.I.A.S. 6839, 729 U.N.T.S. 161.

Furthermore, there already exist "legal" instruments to moderate the arms race and to convey reassurances to other countries that foreign policy and national security planning are based on an unconditional renunciation of nuclear weapons as legitimate instruments of war. Measures of arms control, such as a mutually verifiable freeze, including a comprehensive test ban treaty, seem essential instruments of this approach.

Finally, so long as nuclear weapons are possessed by states, it is important that their possessor act so as not to make these weapons vulnerable to a surprise attack, a theft or a terrorist attack. Making sure that a nuclear retaliatory capability is resonably secure against enemy attack further helps to prevent international situations arising in which the risks of nuclear war are increased.

Within the framework of the present structure of international relations, law and morality cannot do more than to minimize the dangers of nuclear war and the use of nuclear weapons, assuming that strategic conflict is kept within manageable limits. However, if geopolitical rivalry produces a world war, then there is little reason to be hopeful that nuclear weapons will not be introduced into it, either to win an ongoing war more easily or to avoid losing it. In the end, over time, assurances against the "illegal" use of nuclear weapons will depend upon drastic global reform.[40] A legal regime could never purport to supply unconditional protection. It can only help to establish a series of conditions that would make it less likely that international actors will depart from underlying moral and legal guidelines. In this case, the destructive, even ultimate, consequences of a violation make the task of a legal regime for nuclear weapons unique. Its success will depend upon the internalized values, beliefs and interests of political leaders, military bureaucracies and the public. Constructing such a legal regime will depend upon popular pressure, aided by supportive religious groups and changing cultural perspectives. The survival imperatives of our situation suggest the importance of pushing our own leaders, as much as possible, in the direction of adherence to international law guidelines in foreign policy, especially with respect to strategic doctrine and planning. The need for such a framework could perhaps be usefully formulated as a popular demand for a *Magna Carta* for the Nuclear Age. This call is part of a wider conviction on my part that the citizens

---

[40] For some perspectives on this issue, see R. Johansen, *Toward an Alternative Security System* (1983) (Princeton — World Policy Institute Study Paper No. 24); and R. Falk, *A Study of Future Worlds* (1975).

of democratic societies have a selfish interest in assuring that their leaders and institutions adhere to a constraining regime of law, as fully in foreign policy spheres as in domestic domains of public policy.[41] Even such a dramatic resetting of the constitutional order as I have been suggesting here can only hope to achieve, at best, a transitional arrangement, a holding operation. The terrible consequences of the potential use of nuclear weapons place enormous burdens upon our preventive efforts, but even beyond these efforts, building a permanent nuclear peace will depend upon the construction of "a warless world".

Conclusion

A haunting question hovers over the foregoing analysis: Is it possible to reconcile *any* reliance on nuclear weapons simultaneously with minimum security functions and with applicable normative traditions, particularly those contained in the international law of war? The legal regime proposed above confines absolutely the role of nuclear weapons to retaliatory uses and even with respect to such retaliations, offers only a very reluctant, tentative and ambiguous endorsement. The possession of the weapons for purposes of threatening retaliation seems like an unavoidable transitional adjustment, but the normative strain emerges as soon as the character of the threat is specified. If retaliation is restricted in advance to a few *isolated* military targets, then the security function of deterrence is undermined, whereas if it is not so restricted then it seems to be exaggeratedly vindictive and indiscriminate in a manner that is most manifestly at odds with the law of war.

The Catholic Bishops' Pastoral Letter is only "a centimetre of ambiguity" away from an unconditional rejection of nuclear weapons. As the final text emerged, it did leave some political space for a continuing reliance on a much narrowed conception of deterrence, at least for now. In effect, a certain degree of normative incoherence must be accepted in both legal and just war settings, in deference to the realities of our present reliance on nuclear weapons, but with the strong proviso that such deference is a temporary

---

[41] Of course, citizens of non-democratic societies share a similar selfish interest, but realistically, their prior goal, in the nature of a precondition, is to secure for themselves democratic rights. In this regard, the struggle for the democratization of the relations between state and society in the Soviet Union is intimately related to the struggle for the avoidance of nuclear war, yet at the same time, it is partly separable from the preliminary effort needed to construct a legal regime pertaining to nuclear weaponry. This separability arises from the fortunate circumstance that Soviet *state* interests also appear to support minimizing the role of nuclear weapons, and in this critical regard, do not depend upon responsiveness to democratic pressures.

expedient that can be justified even on this qualified basis only if a far stronger effort is made by governments to achieve arms control and nuclear disarmament.[42] If this disarmament effort fails to materialize within this decade, then the burden of persuasion would seem to shift in support of the unconditional prohibition of the threat, use and possession of nuclear weapons, almost regardless of national security claims. The interim position adopted here, in effect, provides governments with a final opportunity to get their normative house in order, by adapting their security policies to an emergent normative consensus that appears to preclude *any* reliance on nuclear weapons.

---

[42] For instance, Bishop Maurice J. Dingman is quoted as saying: "We said this country can keep deterrence only if it works vigorously for arms control. If that isn't achieved, I believe we'll take a far stronger stand." *Is the Pastoral Letter on Nuclear Weapons Only a Beginning?*, The New York Times (8 May 1983) E 5.

8.
Deterrence and International Law*

W. Michael Reisman**

We need to pose three questions concerning nuclear weapons, but they ought to be kept distinct: What is the law in this matter? What should the law be? and, How can we go about changing the law so that it will more nearly approximate our preferences in the future? I suggest that we consider each of these questions separately and be careful not to narcotize ourselves into an imagined bliss by transforming only in our own minds preference into prescription. We no more serve the constituencies to which we are committed in doing that, than we would were we to advise a client whose life or treasure was in jeopardy what the law ought to be rather than what it is.

Observers of international social process should ask themselves whether or not there are expectations of authority and control supporting particular policies and whether those expectations are, in fact, held by politically relevant actors in that setting. If the answer to these questions is in the affirmative, it then becomes useful as scholars, and indispensable as practitioners, to conclude that we are dealing with law, understood not in a documentary but in a socially meaningful sense. An approach based upon such empirically referential tests is particularly necessary in the international system where law does not emerge from predetermined or easily recognizable institutions, and it is not regularly and authoritatively published in collections like the U.S. Code or the Corpus Juris. The observer and practitioner must select what is law from a massive flow of communications, much of it masquerading as law but being no more than just legalistic babble. For the observer looking at a particular process, the test is: Are the communications here sustained by authority and control and have they created coordinate expectations?

---

* This essay is based on remarks delivered at the New York Law School Symposium on Nuclear Arms and World Public Order held October 22, 1982. It is reprinted in edited form with permission from Volume 4, Number 2 of the *New York Law School Journal of International and Comparative Law* (1983).

** Hohfeld Professor of Jurisprudence, Yale Law School.

Many of the international legal scholars who argue for nuclear illegality begin their analysis by selecting a variety of older documents starting with the general principles of the St. Petersburg Declaration and subjecting them to textual analysis. It would be more appropriate to begin by investigating the actual perspectives held by elite members in the United States and the Soviet Union and then attempting to infer certain shared expectations from the fact that these elites are frenetically building, stockpiling, and developing contingency plans for the use of nuclear weapons. If we confirm this behavior and the expectations consistent with it, I think it very perilous to insist that we are not dealing with something that is effectively law.

Let us go a step further and examine a polity in which power is widely shared. If we are to identify the expectations of politically relevant actors in that polity, we must extend our focus of inquiry to include many other community members. I suspect you will discover that in the United States, the vast majority of people who have thought about this problem have routinely assumed that the weapons paid for by their taxes are in fact lawful, and will and should be used under certain circumstances. This does not mean that everyone in that aggregate is ecstatic about the prospect of using them. (I think it unwarranted and unfair to assume that these people are a collection of Dr. Strangeloves.) My impression is that the policy content shared by politically relevant actors in the United States and the Soviet Union is exactly the opposite of what Professor Burns Weston and others associated with the Lawyers' Committee on Nuclear Policy have suggested.[1]

In examining international legal process, we need to consider not only the authority component, but also the communication flow of effective control or control intention. In a decentralized system, without an effective sheriff on whom we can count to secure the implementation of norms, effective control is dispersed among different actors. We determine whether or not there is adequate, effective control to give effect to particular norms by ascertaining whether certain actors have the capacity and will to support those norms through appropriate patterns of reciprocity and retaliation. Retaliation is possible only if you have something akin to what your potential adversary has. Moreover, you must have it when you are suddenly attacked, for nuclear war is a come-as-you-are war. It is ironic and cruel, but there is a Gresham's Law of weapons in international politics: the stability that one seeks in a decentralized system requires the development and maintenance of the very weapons that threaten us and that we would like to eliminate.

Let us now turn to our second question, what should the law be? Our most general preference is for a world public order of human dignity in which there is an abundant production and wide distribution of all the values human beings want; a public order in which those life opportunities, now available to a relatively small stratum of the world's population, are shared much more generously and democratically. Such a public order system requires a low expectation of violence or unauthorized coercion.

Alas, that expectation eludes us. Without a centralized method for securing it, what has been jury-rigged is the so-called system of deterrence. In a system of deterrence, nuclear weapons serve a function unique to a very small category of weapons. The function, as Professor Harry Almond makes clear,[2] is not to be used or, as our German colleagues might put it with enviable precision, to be "not-used." Their function is to deter, to deter comparable use of the same weapon and to deter the initiation of changes in the political balance between parties so substantial that they would force one party to resort to these weapons because it felt its vital interests were being threatened.

This is one hell of a dangerous and anxiety producing way to maintain minimum order! Strategists have yet to come up with something as effective. We lawyers should certainly contribute what we can. The law should seek to banish these weapons. But as Dr. Almond has emphasized, doing this will involve looking not simply at the weapon but at the entire war system of which the weapon is an integral part. Social systems, economic systems, political systems, and personality systems, in addition to the weapon itself, must be changed.[3]

All of us, Americans and Russians alike, wish, in some way compatible with our security, to put this dreadful genie we have released back in the bottle. The third question I am considering here is how can we go about doing it? Legal fiat will not banish the weapons and their supporting systems. One part of the problem, as a number of observers have pointed out, is the deep reciprocal distrust the superpowers have for each other. Even if that distrust is tempered in a period of relative detente, security specialists must continue to be wary. Documents are generally drawn with the expectation that the amicable context prevailing at the time of their conclusion will continue and will sustain the designated behavior in the future. But Professor Myres McDougal has taught us that a critical variable of which to take account in trying to predict future behavior is "crisis," the unanticipated expectation that values critical to an individual or group are at stake in high degree. The intervention of the variable of crisis on agreements means that the terms of agreement presupposing amity are less and less likely to be followed. Hence, even the negotiation and conclusion of documents that limit future arms or that disarm, and even the inception of processes toward that end, must be accompanied by a cogent, effective, and verifiable regime providing the basic deterrence that the current, plainly unsatisfactory system provides. In addition, it must also ward off future crises likely to rend the security system.

Even if there is no norm prohibiting resort to nuclear weapons, international lawyers, by concerted effort, could contribute to fashioning one. Doctrinal writers have long been recognized as a subsidiary source of international law. Before we undertake that responsibility, however, we must ask ourselves first whether the new norm we are proposing is likely to contribute to the realization of the goals of public order in the context I mentioned earlier. Second, will minimum order be enhanced by symmetrical changes urged on both of the major parties? As Professor Francis Boyle has observed,[4] superficially symmetrical relationships may, in terms of the goals sought, be fundamentally asymmetrical. Norms devised to achieve minimum order may have to take that into account.

Many of the basic conceptions on which the norms of the laws of war rest are obsolete. But I do not think they were rendered obsolete in 1945. They began to obsolesce with the French Revolution and the rise of the French Republic. The prototypical modern nation-state is one in which citizen-soldiers are regularly recruited from the entire population and in which the entire nation mobilizes to provide an ongoing flow of people and treasure for the war machine. In that situation the important distinction between combatant and non-combatant begins to blur; the more integrated the people and the war effort become, the harder it is to maintain that distinction. And, of course, the entire doctrine of proportionality, necessity, and capacity to discriminate has, at best, strained application to a deterrence system based on nuclear weapons.

NOTES

1. *See* Weston, Nuclear Weapons and International Law: Prolegomena to General Illegality, 4 N.Y.L.S. J. Int'l & Comp. L. 227 (1983). *See also* Weston, Nuclear Weapons Versus International Law: A Contextual Reassessment, 28 McGill L.J. 542 (1983), *reprinted in* Nuclear Weapons and Law (A. S. Miller & M. Feinrider eds. 1984).

2. *See* Almond, Deterrence Process and Minimum Order, 4 N.Y.L.S. J. Int'l & Comp. L. 283 (1983); *see also* Almond, Deterrence and a Policy-Oriented Perspective on the Legality of Nuclear Weapons *in* Nuclear Weapons and Law (A. S. Miller & M. Feinrider eds. 1984).

3. *See generally* Reisman, Private Armies in a Global War System: Prologue to Decision, 14 Va. J. Int'l L. 1 (1973), *reprinted in* M. McDougal & W. M. Reisman, International Law Essays 142 (1981).

4. *See* Boyle, Nuclear Weapons and International Law: The Arms Control Decision, 4 N.Y.L.S. J. Int'l & Comp. L. 257 (1983).

9.

Nuclear Weapons Versus International Law: A Contextual Reassessment*

Burns H. Weston**

When they shell the telephone building in Madrid it is all right because it is a military objective. When they shell gun positions and observation posts that is war. If the shells fall too long or too short that is war too. But when they shell the city indiscriminately in the middle of the night to try to kill civilians in their beds it is murder.

— Ernest Hemingway [1]

---

* Reprinted, with permission, from *McGill Law Journal*, Volume 28, Number 3 (1983).

** Murray Distinguished Professor of the College of Law, the University of Iowa; Member, Consultative Council, the Lawyers' Committee on Nuclear Policy, and Member of the Lawyers Alliance for Nuclear Arms Control [LANAC]. A.B., 1956, Oberline College; LL.B., 1961, J.S.D., 1970, Yale Law School. I acknowledge with appreciation the gracious help of my former research assistant, Mr. Mark A. Wilson, a recent graduate of The University of Iowa College of Law. I alone, of course, assume full responsibility for what is written.

[1] This quotation is drawn from the typescript of an article entitled *Humanity Will Not Forgive This*, written by Ernest Hemingway for the special 1 August 1938 issue of Pravda on the occasion of the Spanish Civil War. The typescript was discovered recently in the John F. Kennedy Library by Professor of History William B. Watson of the Massachusetts Institute of Technology and first published in English in The Washington Post (28 November 1982) F1. In an accompanying commentary, Professor Watson writes: "The Pravda article that is now being published in English for the first time is exactly as Hemingway wrote it. He wrote it out of anger, and he wrote it for Pravda not only because he was asked to, but because the Russians seemed then the only European power willing to confront Fascism head on." Watson, *Discovering Hemingway's Pravda Article*, The Washington Post (28 November 1982) F1, F13.

Introduction

At the April 1982 Annual Meeting of the American Society of International Law, Eugene V. Rostow, former Director of the United States Arms Control and Disarmament Agency, defended the legality of nuclear weapons against the humanitarian laws of war, in part by invoking an 1825 U.S. Supreme Court decision declaring the then existing African slave trade contrary to the law of nature but permissible under the law of nations. "I rest my case", Rostow said, "on *The Antelope*".[2]

Now surely, in the context of discussing the legalities of truly Plutonic weaponry, one may question the propriety of citing an early nineteenth century decision settling claims for the restitution of some African slaves captured at sea, said to belong to subjects of the kingdoms of Portugal and Spain. No matter how repugnant the African slave trade, hence no matter how analogous to the nuclear arms race it may be, its dehumanizing aspects simply pale in comparison to the treacheries of nuclear war. Still, as we may deduce from the words of Chief Justice Marshall, writing on behalf of *The Antelope* Court, Mr Rostow's point is clear. "However abhorrent this [slave] traffic may be to a mind whose original feelings are not blunted by familiarity with the practice", Marshall wrote,

> it has been sanctioned, in modern times, by the laws of all nations who possess distant colonies, each of whom has engaged in it as a common commercial business, which no other could rightfully interrupt. It has claimed all the sanction which could be derived from long usage and general acquiescence.... Whatever might be the answer of a moralist to this question, a jurist must search for its legal solution, in those principles of action which are sanctioned by the usages, the national acts, and the general assent, of that portion of the world of which he considers himself as a part, and to whose law the appeal is made. If we resort to this standard, as the test of international law, the question...is decided in favor of the legality of the trade.[3]

In short, Rostow's purpose was to observe the classic distinction between the law *lex lata* and the law *de lege ferenda*, to equate the former with "the usages, the national acts, and the general assent of that portion of the world of which he considers himself as a part", and on this basis to decide in favor of the legality of nuclear weapons.

It is, of course, no cause for astonishment that Mr Rostow would favor "the usages, the national acts, and the general assent of that portion of the world of which he considers himself as a part", no more than it is cause for astonishment that Chief Justice Marshall chose to define the uniformities

---

[2] Rostow, remarks, (1982) 76 Proc. Am. Soc. Int'l L. (forthcoming). The case of *The Antelope* may be found in 23 U.S. (10 Wheat.) 66 (1825).

[3] *The Antelope, ibid.*, 115-20.

controlling the slave trade almost exclusively in terms of the elites — the "commercial nations", the "nations who possess distant colonies" — of his time. Jurists, especially jurists with a large stake in the maintenance and expansion of established norms, procedures and institutions, naturally are reluctant to accept significant revaluation or revision of the social order to which they have been accustomed. The legal profession, rather than leading the demand for progressive change, too often opposes it, usually in the name of social stability.

But the point here is not to censure the legal character or profession, as much as this may need doing. The point, rather, is to acknowledge unabashedly the oft-disregarded truth that subjective factors such as position and influence (like culture, class, interest, personality, and past exposure to crisis) commonly condition legal decision, both advertently and inadvertently. They affect not only the substance of our legal judgments; they affect also the evidence we select and the criteria we adopt to reach them — indeed, even our assumptions about the legal system that makes them possible in the first place (the nature of which must be established before we can ascertain the content of the norms that help order our judgments and the system as a whole). Particularly is this so when it comes to assessing the existence or non-existence of a legal rule (for example, a prohibition on a particular use of nuclear weapons) in a juridical system that is predominantly voluntarist in character, hence more or less lacking in putatively impartial command and enforcement structures (for example, the international legal system). In this setting especially, so-called "extra-legal" subjectivities play a critical part.

It is, in any event, from this outlook that the present reassessment is undertaken, proceeding in the belief that, consciously or not, Mr Rostow, like Chief Justice Marshall before him, answered the issue confronting him more according to the dictates of his partisan perspective than to the demands of social reality (although Marshall perhaps may be excused given that the international society of his day consisted entirely of a group of States that shared a common set of interests and normative traditions). By invoking *The Antelope* as he did, Mr Rostow revealed an excessively hegemonic and statist way of thinking about the international legal order and international norm prescription, a way of thinking which, though consistent with his position and influence, is nonetheless unsuited to a world sorely divided by antagonist values and severely threatened by nuclear Armageddon. Thus, he did not close the debate, but invited, instead, a considered — even if here inexhaustive — reply. Concededly, there is a tendency among international lawyers not to take up the debate, due in part to a sense of despondency about the influence of international law upon issues of high policy. But as Ian Brownlie has bravely rejoined, "[a]s a comparative assessment of the role of the law this is incontrovertible and yet it cannot be said to justify the tacit removal of certain subjects from the agenda".[4]

I.   Clarification of the Problem

Let us begin by acknowledging immediately that, despite the aggravated mutilations we call Hiroshima and Nagasaki,[5] which some reputable scholarship says lacked military necessity,[6] the world community has yet to enact an explicit treaty or treaty provision prohibiting generally the development, manufacture, stockpiling, deployment, or actual use of nuclear weapons. This fact is not lost on those who defend the legality of these weapons. Consistent with the traditional State-centric theory of international legal obligation, which requires that prohibitions on international conduct be based on the express or implied consent of States, they rest their claim in substantial part on the proposition drawn from the decision of the Permanent Court of International Justice in *The Case of the S.S. "Lotus"*,[7] *i.e.*, that States are free to do whatever they are not strictly forbidden from doing.[8] Indeed, consistent with Cicero's oft-quoted maxim *inter arma silent leges* (in war the law is silent), some go so far as to contend that nuclear weapons have made the laws of war obsolete.[9]

---

[4] Brownlie, *Some Legal Aspects of the Use of Nuclear Weapons* (1965) 14 Int'l & Comp. L.Q. 437, 437.

[5] For recent important accounts, see The Committee for the Compilation of Materials on Damage Caused by the Atomic Bombs in Hiroshima and Nagasaki, *Hiroshima and Nagasaki: the Physical, Medical and Social Effects of the Atomic Bombings* (E. Ishikawa & D. Swain, trans 1981); Japan Broadcasting Corp., *Unforgettable Fire: Pictures Drawn by Atomic Bomb Survivors* (1981).

[6] See, *e.g.*, United States Strategic Bombing Survey, *Japan's Struggle to End the War* (1946) 13: "Based on a detailed investigation of all the facts and supported by the testimony of the surviving Japanese leaders involved, it is the Survey's opinion that certainly prior to 31 December 1945, and in all probability prior to 1 November 1945, Japan would have surrendered even if the atomic bombs had not been dropped, even if Russia had not entered the war, and even if no invasion had been planned or contemplated." See also G. Alperovitz, *Atomic Diplomacy: Hiroshima and Potsdam* (1965) 236-42; Baldwin, "The Atomic Bomb — The Penalty of Expediency" in E. Fogelman, ed., *Hiroshima: The Decision to Use the A-Bomb* (1964). But see Paust, *The Nuclear Decision in World War II — Truman's Ending and Avoidance of War* (1974) 8 Int'l Law. 160, 179-80.

[7] (1927) P.C.I.J., ser. A., No. 10 (France v.Turkey).

[8] Thus, in this spirit, does United States Army Field Manual No. 27-10 provide: "The use of explosive 'atomic weapons', whether by air, sea, or land forces, cannot *as such* be regarded as violative of international law in the absence of any customary rule of international law or international convention restricting their employment." United States Dep't of the Army, Field Manual 27-10, *The Law of Land Warfare* (1956), para. 35 [emphasis added].

[9] See, *e.g.*, Stowell, *The Laws of War and the Atomic Bomb* (1945) 39 Am. J. Int'l L. 784; Thomas, *Atomic Bombs in International Society* (1945) 39 Am. J. Int'l L. 736; and Thomas, *Atomic Warfare and International Law* (1946) 40 Proc. Am. Soc. Int'l L. 84. *Cf.* Baxter, *The Role of Law in Modern War* (1953) 47 Proc. Am. Soc. Int'l L. 90.

But surely this is not the end of the matter. While the lack of an explicit ban may mean that nuclear weapons are not illegal *per se*,[10] the fact is that restraints on the conduct of war never have been limited to explicit treaty prohibitions alone. As stated by the International Military Tribunal at Nuremberg in September, 1946:

> The law of war is to be found not only in treaties, but in the customs and practices of states which gradually obtained universal recognition, and from the general principles of justice applied by jurists and practiced by military courts.[11]

Indeed, it is precisely the point being made here — that the law of war, like the whole of international law, is composed of more than treaty rules, explicit and otherwise — that prompted Eugene Rostow to certify the pertinence of *The Antelope* to the issue at hand.

It is, at any rate, according to this more true-to-life portrayal of the so-called "sources" or law-creating processes of international law that the argument against the legality of nuclear weapons, qualified or unqualified, is fashioned.[12] While ruing the absence of an explicit treaty or treaty provision that could dispel all doubts, those who deny the legality of nuclear weapons in whole or in part are mindful that historically the law of war has sought to inhibit weapons and tactics that cause aggravated and indiscriminate damage; and accordingly they point to an array of treaty provisions which, they say, implicitly outlaw the use or threat of use of nuclear weapons. Furthermore, they rely upon numerous other "sources" of international authority, such as international custom, general principles, judicial decisions, United Nations declarations and resolutions, and draft rules, to make their case. Some even affirm — correctly, I believe — the appositeness of initiatives by groups having little or no formal status in the international legal order as traditionally conceived.[13]

---

[10] Consider, for example, the emphasis added to the United States Army Field Manual 27-10 quotation, *supra*, note 8.

[11] *Trial of the Major War Criminals Before the International Military Tribunal* (1948), vol. 22, 464 [hereinafter *Trial of the Major War Criminals*].

[12] See, *e.g.*, C. Builder & M. Graubard, *The International Law of Armed Conflict: Implications for the Concept of Assured Destruction* (1982) (RAND Publication Series R-2804-FF); E. Castrén, *The Present Law of War and Neutrality* (1954); G. Draper, *The Red Cross Conventions* (1958) 98-100; M. Greenspan, *The Modern Law of Land Warfare* (1959) 368-77; G. Schwarzenberger, *The Legality of Nuclear Weapons* (1958); N. Singh, *Nuclear Weapons and International Law* (1959); J. Spaight, *The Atomic Problem* (1948); Brownlie, *supra*, note 4; Castrén, *The Illegality of Nuclear Weapons* [1971] U. Tol. L. Rev. 89; Falk, Meyrowitz & Sanderson, *Nuclear Weapons and International Law* (1980) 20 Indian J. Int'l L. 541; Fried, *First Use of Nuclear Weapons* [:] *Existing Prohibitions in International Law* (1981) 12 Bull. Peace Proposals 21; Fujita, *First Use of Nuclear Weapons: Nuclear Strategy vs. International Law* [1982] Kansai U. Rev. L. & Pol. 57 (No. 3); Meyrowitz, *Les juristes devant l'arme nucléaire* (1963) 67 Rev. Gén. Int'l Pub. 820.

[13] See, *e.g.*, Falk, Meyrowitz & Sanderson, *ibid.*, 592-4. See also *infra*, notes 75-9, 105-9 and accompanying text.

Now a distinct advantage of this line of argument — one may even say a virtue — is that it departs from exclusively hegemonic and statist models of international legal process. It therefore helps to discourage the widespread cynicism that international law is or must be only the expression of the will of the strongest. A distinct weakness, however, is its tendency — actually little different from that of its complementary opposite — toward an essentially rule-oriented conception of international law and law-making. Prone to treat international law mainly as a body of rules governing relations between States, rather than as a complex process of authoritative and controlling decision in which rules (and doctrines and principles) are continuously being fashioned and refashioned by a wide variety of global actors to suit the needs of the living and the unborn, this positivist model does not adequately conjoin law and social reality. Hence it makes little or no attempt to ask the question recently and felicitously put by Professor D'Amato: "What 'counts' as law?" [14] Ergo it never really rises to the challenge posed by Mr Rostow, namely, that international custom — by which Rostow meant a general *State* practice accepted as law — simply countermands whatever implicit, even if express, nuclear weapons prohibitions may be said to exist.

It seems evident, then, that the legality or illegality of nuclear weapons is not to be judged simply by the existence or non-existence of an explicit treaty rule or by a mere recitation of other "sources" of world authority, written or unwritten. The issue is not, fundamentally, the explicitness of the rule. Nor is it whether suitable language can be found to support one position or another. The issue is whether any of the authority cited — in this case, the laws of war — is of a sort that "counts as law" insofar as the use and threat of use of nuclear weapons are concerned. The issue is whether any of it, explicit or implicit, comports with what is needed to give it jural quality relative to nuclear weapons, and, if so, how or to what extent it applies.

It is my view (a) that the laws of war indeed do extend to nuclear weapons, and (b) that in fact they severely restrict the use of these weapons in most instances. But of course, merely to assert these propositions is not sufficient; each requires explanation. Before proceeding, however, two preliminary clarifications are in order. Each is necessary to a proper understanding of what follows.

First, we need to be clear about the issue we are *not* addressing, to wit, the lawfulness of using or threatening to use nuclear weapons as part of a campaign or single act of aggression (as that term is defined in the 1974 United Nations General Assembly *Resolution on the Definition of*

---

[14] D'Amato, "What 'Counts' As Law?" in N. Onuf, ed., *Law-making in the Global Community* (1982) 83.

Aggression).[15] Whatever the exact legal status of the Kellogg-Briand Pact [16] and *United Nations Charter* art. 2(4),[17] particularly after the deafening silence that greeted the 1980 Iraqi invasion of Iran, arguably an act of aggression is unlawful irrespective of the kinds of weapons used, nuclear or conventional.[18] Instead, recalling the customary right of individual and collective self-defense (now enshrined in U.N. *Charter* art. 51),[19] and noting that all the nuclear weapon States admit to no other rationale for their arsenals, the question ultimately before us must be whether any *defensive* use or threat of use of nuclear weapons — "first-strike" or "second-strike", "strategic" or "tactical" — may be considered contrary to international law, hence prohibited.[20] Of course, our first duty is, as indicated, to demonstrate that the laws of war, which are the relevant corpus of international law for present purposes, do in fact cover nuclear weapons and warfare, that they are not obsolete in this connection.

Second, we need to be clear about the true nature of nuclear weapons, especially in contrast to so-called conventional weapons. While the horrifying consequences of nuclear warfare are at last beginning to penetrate the popular consciousness, our military leaders and civilian elites seem to think and act as if the nuclear weapon is "just one more weapon", only somewhat more destructive. The fact is, however, that nuclear weapons differ from conventional weapons in at least three very critical respects.[21] First, and most

---

[15] United Nations G.A. Res. 3314, 29 U.N. GAOR, Supp. (No. 31) 142, U.N. Doc. A/9631 (1974).

[16] *General Treaty for Renunciation of War as an Instrument of National Policy*, 27 August 1928, 46 Stat. 2343, T.S. No. 796, 94 L.N.T.S. 57.

[17] *United Nations Charter*, art. 2, para. 4: "All Members shall refrain in their international relations from the threat or use of force against the territorial integrity or political independence of any State, or in any other manner inconsistent with the Purposes of the United Nations."

[18] For pertinent questioning, see Franck, *Who Killed Article 2(4)? or: Changing Norms Governing the Use of Force by States* (1970) 64 Am. J. Int'l L. 809. But see Henkin, *The Reports of the Death of Article 2(4) Are Greatly Exaggerated* (1971) 65 Am. J. Int'l L. 544.

[19] *United Nations Charter*, art. 51: "Nothing in the present Charter shall impair the inherent right of individual or collective self-defence if an armed attack occurs against a Member of the United Nations, until the Security Council has taken measures necessary to maintain international peace and security. Measures taken by Members in the exercise of this right of self-defence shall be immediately reported to the Security Council and shall not in any way affect the authority and responsibility of the Security Council under the present Charter to take at any time such action as it deems necessary in order to maintain or restore international peace and security."

[20] For clarification of these and related terms, as well as substantive discussion on the legal issue posed, see *infra*, text following note 127.

[21] For extensive and detailed information concerning the nature and effects of nuclear weapons, see S. Glasstone & P. Dolan, *The Effects of Nuclear Weapons*, 3d ed. (1977) (prepared and published by the United States Dep't of Defense and the United States Energy Research and Development Administration). See also United Nations, *Comprehensive Study*

obvious, is the fact that most nuclear weapons, certainly all in the "strategic" category,[22] are not just "somewhat more destructive", but many thousands or millions of times more powerful than even the largest conventional high-explosive weapons. One average nuclear weapon by today's standards — a device in the one megaton range — represents about seventy to eighty times the intensity and scale of devastation wrought at Hiroshima and Nagasaki, and it is highly unlikely that any future nuclear exchange would be limited to average size weapons or to one or two "defensive" strikes. Unlike conventional weapons, nuclear weapons risk putting an end to civilization as we know it. Second, the majority of nuclear weapons, "tactical" as well as "strategic",[23] differ from conventional weapons in the variety as well as the intensity and scale of their physical effects. The chief characteristic of conventional weapons is their potential for "blast" or "shock" damage, accompanied by some thermal or heat effects (burns and fires). By contrast, although with variations depending on their yield and place of detonation, nuclear weapons produce "blast" or "shock" damage and, in addition, extended "thermal radiation", "electromagnetic pulse" [EMP] effects, and invisible but highly-penetrating and harmful rays called "initial nuclear radiation", followed by "residual nuclear radiation" in the form of delayed radioactive fallout across potentially great distances and over extended periods of time. The radiation effects, it should be noted, which consist of the transmission of gamma rays, neutrons, beta particles, and some alpha particles, are not unlike — indeed, are very similar to — the effects produced by chemical and biological weapons as opposed to conventional high-explosive weapons.[24] Finally, in still further contrast to conventional weapons, nuclear weapons, even those with fairly low yields, are capable of harming noncombatants (including civilians and neutral parties) virtually inevitably. As George Kennan writes:

> [Conventional] weapons can bring injury to noncombatants by accident or inadvertence or callous indifference; but they don't always have to do it. The nuclear weapon cannot help doing it, and doing it massively, even where the injury is unintended by those who unleash it.[25]

---

on Nuclear Weapons [:] *Report of the Secretary-General*, 35 U.N. GAOR, Annex (Provisional Agenda Item 48(b)) ch. 4, U.N. Doc. A/35/392 (1980), reprinted as United Nations, *Disarmament Study Series No. 1* (1981) ch. 4 [hereinafter *Report of the Secretary-General*; cited to U.N. Doc.].

[22] For clarification of this and related terms, see *infra*, text following note 127.

[23] For clarification of these and related terms, see *infra*, text following note 127.

[24] See, *e.g.*, Lindop & Rotblat, "Consequences of radioactive fallout" in R. Adams & S. Cullen, eds, *The Final Epidemic* [:] *Physicians and Scientists on Nuclear War* (1981) 117. See also Singh, *supra*, note 12, 154-66.

[25] G. Kennan, *The Nuclear Delusion* [:] *Soviet-American Relations in the Atomic Age* (1982) 203.

Mr Kennan might have acknowledged, of course, the possibility of a "surgical strike" with a "clean" low-yield warhead against a purely military target in a region inhabited by few people. But such a scenario would not be common, and thus the third distinction between nuclear and conventional weapons is drawn. Like the first two, it is critical to the legal appraisal that concerns us here.

Now, with these brief clarifications in mind, it is appropriate to turn to the core of our inquiry. We begin, as indicated, with the threshold issue whether the laws of war are obsolete in relation to nuclear weapons and warfare or whether they do in fact apply.

II.   The Matter of Norm Prescription

The traditional approaches to the question whether an international rule of law has in fact been made or does in fact endure, such as the question whether the humanitarian laws of war apply to nuclear weapons and warfare, suffer from not a few disabilities that, at the very least, prompt serious skepticism.[26] The mainsteam *opinio juris* test, for example, which bids inquiry into what States "believe" a rule to be, does not lend itself easily, if at all, to empirical verification. Nor, for that matter, does it rest comfortably in a world increasingly beset by fundamental challenges to the primacy of the nation-state as a global claimant and decision-maker.

Essentially free from such disabilities, however, and therefore worthy of responsible attention, is the "coordinate communication flow" theory of norm prescription espoused by Yale law scholars Myres McDougal and Michael Reisman.[27] Law-making, they write, is "a process of communication which creates, in a target audience, a complex set of expectations comprising three distinctive components: expectations about a policy content; expectations about authority; and expectations about control".[28] And to speak meaningfully of law, they emphasize, "all three components must be copresent".[29] Thus Reisman elaborates:

> [P]rescriptive or law making communications... carry simultaneously three coordinate communication flows in a fashion akin to the coaxial cables of modern telephonic communications. The three flows may be briefly referred to as the policy content, the

---

[26] For insightful criticism, see McDougal & Reisman, *The Prescribing Function in World Constitutive Process: How International Law is Made* (1980) 6 Yale Stud. World Pub. Ord. 249, 256-68.

[27] See *ibid.*, 249-56 and 268-84.

[28] *Ibid.*, 250.

[29] *Ibid.*

authority signal and the control intention. Unless each of these flows is present and effectively mediated to the relevant audience, a prescription does not result.[30]

Equally important, he adds, the three components *"must continue to be communicated* for the prescription, as such, to endure".[31]

In this Part, I attempt to resolve the question whether the laws of war apply to nuclear weapons and warfare according to this tripartite communications model of national and international law-making. I do so, in part, because it does indeed avoid the many pitfalls of the traditional theories. But I do so also, and more importantly, because it demythologizes the business of law-making in favor of a common sense appreciation for the richly textured social and jural environment within which law-making necessarily takes place. So critically significant an issue as the legality of nuclear weapons clearly requires a large dose of jurisprudential realism.

A.   *Policy Content*

As noted earlier, except for a series of treaties prohibiting nuclear weapons in Antarctica, Latin America, outer space, and on the seabed beyond the limit of national territorial seas,[32] plus the *Partial Test Ban Treaty* outlawing the testing of nuclear weapons in outer space, under water, and within the earth's atmosphere,[33] no international covenant forbids expressly the develop-

---

[30] Reisman, *International Lawmaking: A Process of Communication* (1981) 75 Proc. Am. Soc. Int'l L. 101, 108 (The Harold D. Lasswell Memorial Lecture).

[31] *Ibid.*, 108. Reisman explains: "[I]f one or more of the components should cease to be communicated, the prescription undergoes a type of desuetude and is terminated."

[32] See the *Antarctic Treaty*, 12 U.S.T. 794, T.I.A.S. 4780, 402 U.N.T.S. 71, arts I and V (signed 1 December 1959; entered into force 23 June 1961; ratified by 26 states as of 31 December 1982); *Treaty for the Prohibition of Nuclear Weapons in Latin America*, 634 U.N.T.S. 281 (signed 14 February 1967; entered into force for 24 states on 31 December 1982)[hereinafter *Treaty of Tlatelolco*]; *Treaty on Principles Governing the Activities of States in the Exploration and Use of Outer Space, Including the Moon and Other Celestial Bodies*, 18 U.S.T. 2410, T.I.A.S. 6347, 610 U.N.T.S. 205, art. IV (signed 27 January 1967; entered into force 10 October 1967; ratified by 81 states as of 31 December 1982) [hereinafter *Outer Space Treaty*]; *Treaty on the Prohibition of the Emplacement of Nuclear Weapons and Other Weapons of Mass Destruction on the Seabed and the Ocean Floor and in the Subsoil Thereof*, 23 U.S.T. 701, T.I.A.S. 7337, reprinted in (1971) 10 I.L.M. 146 (signed 11 February 1971; entered into force for 70 states on 31 December 1982) [hereinafter *Seabed Arms Control Treaty*].

[33] *Treaty Banning Nuclear Weapon Tests in the Atmosphere, in Outer Space and Under Water*, 14 U.S.T. 1313, T.I.A.S. 5433, 480 U.N.T.S. 43 (signed 5 August 1963; entered into force 10 October 1963; ratified by 110 states as of 31 December 1982)[hereinafter *Partial Test Ban Treaty*].

ment, manufacture, stockpiling, deployment, or use of nuclear weapons *in general*. The United Nations General Assembly has declared the use of nuclear weapons to be "a direct violation of the Charter of the United Nations",[34] "contrary to the rules of international law and to the laws of humanity",[35] "a crime against mankind and civilization",[36] and therefore a matter of "permanent prohibition".[37] In addition, in a much too neglected decision rendered almost twenty years ago, a Japanese tribunal saw fit to condemn as contrary to international law the only instance of actual belligerent use of nuclear weapons to date, the United States bombings of Hiroshima and Nagasaki.[38] But considering that U.N. General Assembly resolutions are presumptively not binding as law and that, ordinarily, a single national tribunal decision cannot alone establish rules of international law, it scarcely can be said that these expressions of legal viewpoint, although certainly evidentiary of customary legal expectation, are by themselves dispositive of the issue at hand. Explicit content does not automatically spell legal prescription, however wise the content communication may be.

Accordingly, if international law has anything useful to say about our topic, as I believe it does, then it will do so implicitly rather than explicitly, through derivations from and analogies to the conventional and customary laws of war, both traditional and modern-day; and highly apropos in this connection are at least six core rules which stand out as *prima facie* relevant [hereinafter usually referred to as "the humanitarian rules of armed conflict"]. Each, to be sure, is susceptible of differing linguistic and contextual interpretation. Also, each involves a balancing of the customary principle of humanity against that of military necessity,[39] which inevitably challenges one's capacity for complete objectivity, be he or she Scholar Laureate or

---

[34] *Declaration on the Prohibition of the Use of Nuclear and Thermo-nuclear Weapons*, United Nations G.A. Res. 1653, 16 U.N. GAOR, Supp. (No. 17) 4, U.N. Doc. A/5100 (1961), para. 1(a).

[35] *Ibid.*, para. 1(b).

[36] *Ibid.*, para. 1(d).

[37] *Declaration on the Non-use of Force in International Relations and Permanent Prohibition of the Use of Nuclear Weapons*, United Nations G.A. Res. 2936, 27 U.N. GAOR, Supp. (No. 30) 5, U.N. Doc. A/8730 (1972), para. 1.

[38] See *The Shimoda Case*, judgment of 7 December 1963, District Court of Tokyo, reprinted in [1964] Jap. Ann. Int'l L. 212 (English translation).

[39] Summarize Adam Roberts and Richard Guelff:

Three general customary principles seek to delineate legal limits on belligerent conduct: the principle of military necessity, the principle of humanity, and what is still called the principle of chivalry. The principle of military necessity provides that, strictly subject to the principles of humanity and chivalry, a belligerent is justified in applying the amount and kind of force necessary to achieve the complete submission of the enemy at the earliest possible moment and with the least expenditure of time, life, and resources. The principle of humanity prohibits the employment of any kind or degree of force not actually necessary for military purposes. The principle of chivalry denounces and forbids

Commander-in-Chief. Nevertheless, I dare to note them here with a brief summary of what I understand to be their contemporary meaning — independent, of course, of the nuclear weapons factor.[40]

Rule 1. It is prohibited to use weapons or tactics that cause unnecessary or aggravated devastation and suffering.[41]

Here the principles of humanity and military necessity meet head-on, highlighting the interest of all States and peoples in simultaneously enhancing

resort to dishonourable means, expedients, or conduct in the course of armed hostility. All three principles are integrally related and require an appropriate balance to be struck. In general, the law which has been codified is the product of such balancing. . . .
A. Roberts & R. Guelff, eds, *Documents on the Laws of War* (1982) 5.

The last of the three principles noted by Roberts and Guelff has tended to lose significance as warfare has become more and more impersonal. McDougal and Feliciano observe:

The principle of chivalry would seem little more than a somewhat romantic inheritance from the Medieval Ages when combat between mailed knights was surrounded by symbolic and ritualistic formalities. In an age increasingly marked by mechanized and automated warfare, the scope of application of chivalry as a principle distinct from humanity may very probably be expected to diminish in corresponding measure.
M. McDougal & F. Feliciano, *Law and Minimum World Public Order* [:] *The Legal Regulation of International Coercion* (1961) 522.

[40] The following summaries, while no substitute for what an appropriately detailed analysis would reveal, are based primarily on the following expertise: S. Bailey, *Prohibitions and Restraints in War* (1972); G. Best, *Humanity in Warfare* [:] *The Modern History of the International Law of Armed Conflicts* (1980); J. Brierly, *The Law of Nations* [:] *An Introduction to the International Law of Peace*, 6th ed. (H. Waldock 1963) ch. 9; A. Cassese, ed., *The New Humanitarian Law of Armed Conflict* (1979); Greenspan, *supra*, note 12; F. Kalshoven, *The Law of Warfare* (1973); McDougal & Feliciano, *ibid.*; L. Oppenheim, *International Law* [:] *A Treatise*, 7th ed. (H. Lauterpacht 1952); J. Pictet, *Humanitarian Law and the Protection of War Victims* (1975); G. Schwarzenberger, *International Law as Applied by International Courts and Tribunals* (1968), vol. 2 — *The Law of Armed Conflict*; J. Stone, *Legal Controls of International Conflict*, 2d ed. (1959).

[41] See, *e.g.*, art. 23 of the 1907 Hague Regulations Respecting the Laws and Customs of War on Land [hereinafter *1907 Hague Regulations*], Annex to the 1907 *Hague Convention* [No. IV] *Respecting the Laws and Customs of War on Land*, 18 October 1907, 36 Stat. 2277, T.S. No. 539, 1 Bevans 631, which provides in part: "In addition to the prohibitions provided by special Conventions, it is especially forbidden. . .(b) To kill or wound treacherously individuals belonging to the hostile nation or army; . . .(e) To employ arms, projectiles, or material calculated to cause unnecessary suffering;. . . [and] (g) To destroy or seize the enemy's property, unless such destruction or seizure be imperatively demanded by the necessities of war". For similar language, see art. 35(2) of Geneva Protocol I Additional Relating to the Protection of Victims of International Armed Conflicts, U.N. Doc. A/32/144, Annex I, reprinted in (1977) 16 I.L.M. 1391 (adopted 12 December 1977; entered into force on 7 December 1978) which prohibits weapons and methods causing "superfluous injury or unnecessary suffering". In addition, see Hague Draft Rules of Aerial Warfare, arts 22-6, reprinted in (1923) 17 Am. J. Int'l L. 245 (Supp.); *Declaration of Brussels*, 27 August 1874, arts 12-3, reprinted in L. Friedman, ed., *The Law of War: A Documentary History* (1972), vol. 2, 194-6; *Declaration on the Prohibition of the Use of Nuclear and Thermo-nuclear Weapons*, *supra*, note 34; *Resolution on Respect for Human Rights in Armed Conflicts*, United Nations G.A.

their security and minimizing the destruction of attendant values. Therefore, it is less the fact of devastation and suffering than the needlessness, the superfluity, the disproportionality of harm relative to military result that is determinative of illegality. This test, of course, is a function of context, and historically, it appears, "the line of compromise has...tended to be located closer to the polar terminus of military necessity than to that of humanity".[42] The relative tolerance heretofore extended to "scorched earth" and "saturation bombing" policies and to incendiary and V-weapons, for example, may well attest to this observation.[43] However, though military necessity may be the leading guide for defining permissible devastation and suffering, its operational scope is not unqualified. Generally speaking, "it...is of the proximate military order of *raison de guerre* rather than of the final political order

---

Res. 2444, 23 U.N. GAOR, Supp. (No. 18) 50, U.N. Doc. A/7218 (1968); *Resolution on Basic Principles for the Protection of Civilian Populations in Armed Conflicts*, United Nations G.A. Res. 2675, 25 U.N. GAOR, Supp. (No. 28) 76, U.N. Doc. A/8028 (1970); International Committee of the Red Cross, *Fundamental Rules of International Humanitarian Law Applicable in Armed Conflicts* (1978) 206 Int'l Rev. Red Cross 248, 249 (Rule 6) [hereinafter *Red Cross Fundamental Rules*].

[42] McDougal & Feliciano, *supra*, note 39, 523. See, *e.g.*, *United States* v. *List*, in *Trials of War Criminals* (1948), vol. 11, 759, 1243-4, and *Law Reports of Trials of War Criminals* (1948), vol. 8, 34, 65-6:

> Military necessity permits a belligerent, subject to the laws of war, to apply any amount and kind of force to compel the complete submission of the enemy with the least possible expenditure of time, life, and money. In general, it sanctions measures by an occupant necessary to protect the safety of his forces and to facilitate the success of his operations. It permits the destruction of life of armed enemies and other persons whose destruction is incidentally unavoidable by the armed conflicts of the war; it allows the capturing of armed enemies and others of peculiar danger, but it does not permit the killing of innocent inhabitants for purposes of revenge or the satisfaction of a lust to kill. The destruction of property to be lawful must be imperatively demanded by the necessities of war. Destruction as an end in itself is a violation of international law. There must be some reasonable connection between the destruction of property and the overcoming of the enemy forces. It is lawful to destroy railways, lines of communication, or any other property that might be utilized by the enemy. Private homes and churches even may be destroyed if necessary for military operations. It does not admit of wanton devastation of a district or the willful infliction of suffering upon its inhabitants for the sake of suffering alone.

[43] Observing that the mass raids on Hamburg and Dresden, with their fire storms, are sometimes said to have been on a scale similar to the devastation at Hiroshima, Brownlie writes: "Of course, it does not follow from this that the mass raids were legal, although this is sometimes the intended inference." *Supra*, note 4, 449, fn. 50. Falk, Meyrowitz & Sanderson elaborate on this theme: "The obvious question is whether the practice of states, victorious in a major war in which accepted rules and standards of war are violated, has the effect of a legislative repeal." *Supra*, note 12, 565.

of *raison d'état*";[44] and in any event, especially when delineation between these two orders proves difficult or impossible, it is shaped by what all agree, after Aristotle, is the proper object of war, namely, the bringing about of those conditions that are needed to establish a just and meaningful and lasting peace.

Rule 2. It is prohibited to use weapons or tactics that cause indiscriminate harm as between combatants and noncombatant military and civilian personnel.[45]

The historic distinction between combatants and noncombatants, military and civilian, once provided what John Bassett Moore called "the vital principle of the modern law of war".[46] Today, however, after four decades of virtually constant conflict in which belligerents everywhere have flaunted the principle in one way or another, its legal status is confused. Although Rome and Paris were declared "open" (*i.e.* undefended) cities during World War II and thereby saved from destruction, ours tends to be an era of "total war" wherein greatly increased civilian participation in "the war effort" and well-known developments in the technical arts of war have rendered application of the principle all but impossible in many instances. At any rate, the more vital the target militarily, the more the law will condone incidental civilian damage; and again, as in the case of *Rule 1*, considerations of military necessity appear to have outweighed considerations of humanity. Nevertheless, demonstrating anew how notions of humanity or proportionality temper claims of military necessity, *Rule 2* appears to pose a genuine legal challenge for at least the following: direct as distinguished from incidental attacks upon civilian populations and upon noncombatant sick and wounded armed forces personnel; raids upon target areas wherein civilian resources and uses of special value, such as cultural, humanitarian and religious institutions, significantly outbalance military and militarily-related resources and uses; assaults upon undefended population centers manifesting little or no effective base of

---

[44] O'Brien, *Legitimate Military Necessity in Nuclear War* (1960) 2 World Polity 35, 51.

[45] See, *e.g.*, 1977 Geneva Protocol I Additional, *supra*, note 41, art. 48 which states: "In order to ensure respect for and protection of the civilian population and civilian objects, the Parties to the conflict shall at all times distinguish between the civilian population and combatants and between civilian objects and military objectives and accordingly shall direct their operations against military objectives." See also *Geneva Convention* [No. IV] *Relative to the Protection of Civilian Persons in Time of War*, 12 August 1949, 6 U.S.T. 3516, T.I.A.S. 3365, 75 U.N.T.S. 287; *1907 Hague Regulations, supra*, note 41, arts 25 and 27; *Resolution on Respect for Human Rights in Armed Conflicts, supra*, note 41; *Resolution on Basic Principles for the Protection of Civilian Populations in Armed Conflicts, supra*, note 41; *Fundamental Rules of International Humanitarian Law Applicable in Armed Conflicts, supra*, note 41, 249.

[46] J.B. Moore, *International Law and Some Current Illusions and Other Essays* (1924) viii.

enemy power; and "terror bombardment" purely or primarily for the purpose of destroying enemy morale.[47] It is, furthermore, appropriate to note art. 6(c) of the *Nuremberg Charter* declaring the extermination of a civilian population, in whole or in part, "a crime against humanity".[48]

Rule 3. It is prohibited to use weapons or tactics that cause widespread, long-term and severe damage to the natural environment. [49]

This prohibitory rule, a new "basic rule" added to the laws of war by 1977 Protocol I Additional to the 1949 *Geneva Conventions*,[50] is emphatically a product of the worldwide environmental reawakening which has taken place since the advent of Sputnik and Rachael Carson's *Silent Spring*. However, with none of the major powers having yet ratified the Protocol and some not even having signed it, its status as general international law is open to some doubt. On the other hand, in view of the sixty-two signatures and twenty-seven ratifications and accessions to date,[51] plus the "common convictions" set forth at the 1972 United Nations Conference on the Human Environment [52] and the mounting efforts since that time to preserve and enhance the human environment for present and future generations, it probably is correct to say that the prohibition is in at least the incipient stage of becoming law, and certainly is a guide to desired conduct.

Rule 4. It is prohibited to effect reprisals that are disproportionate to their antecedent provocation or to legitimate military objectives, or disrespectful of persons, institutions and resources otherwise protected by the laws of war. [53]

---

[47] McDougal & Feliciano, *supra*, note 39, 657 write: "To accept as lawful the deliberate terrorization of the enemy community by the infliction of large-scale destruction comes too close to rendering pointless all legal limitations on the exercise of violence."

[48] *Charter of the International Military Tribunal*, 6 October 1945, 59 Stat. 1555, 1556, E.A.S. No. 472, 13, 14 (1945), art. 6(c).

[49] See 1977 Geneva Protocol I Additional, *supra*, note 41, art. 35(3) which states: "It is prohibited to employ methods or means of warfare which are intended, or may be expected, to cause widespread, long-term and severe damage to the natural environment." See also art. 55(1); and *Stockholm Declaration of the United Nations Conference on the Human Environment*, in *Report of the United Nations Conference on the Human Environment*, U.N. Doc. A/CONF. 48/14, and Corr. 1, reprinted in (1972) 11 I.L.M. 1416, Principles 2 and 26 [hereinafter *Stockholm Declaration*].

[50] *Ibid.*

[51] Information supplied in telephone communications from the Office of the Legal Advisor, United States Dep't of State.

[52] *Supra*, note 49.

[53] See, *e.g.*, 1977 Geneva Protocol I Additional, *supra*, note 41, arts 20, 51, 53 and 55. See also 1954 *Hague Convention for the Protection of Cultural Property in the Event of Armed*

The requirement of proportionality in respect of reprisals [54] is but another manifestation of the interplay of the principles of humanity and military necessity. Accordingly, as in the case of *Rule 1* relative to the limits of permissible destruction in the name of self-defense in general, what constitutes a legitimate reprisal is largely a function of context. Of course, in a legal system dominated by processes of autointerpretation, this fact affords a ready excuse for law evasion by unscrupulous belligerents. Nevertheless, patently disproportionate reprisals, *i.e.* reprisals that are extreme in relation to their provocation or that lack a reasonable connection with the securing of legitimate belligerent objectives, are contrary to *United Nations Charter* art. 51 as well as to international law in general. Moreover, reprisals must be directed at the cobelligerent State, with no adverse impact upon States not party to the conflict;[55] and they may not, besides, be directed against the following persons and objects, among others: wounded and sick persons (military and civilian) who are in need of medical care and who refrain from any act of hostility; the personnel of medical units and establishments, including chaplains; noncombatant civilians and civilian populations; cultural property and places of worship; and works or installations containing dangerous forces such as dams, dykes and nuclear electrical generating stations.[56] Finally, inasmuch as reprisals are extreme measures to be used only as a last resort, every effort must be made, save where military necessity *clearly* compels otherwise, to regulate the conflict by other means.

Rule 5. It is prohibited to use weapons or tactics that violate the neutral jurisdiction of nonparticipating States. [57]

Conflict, 14 May 1954, 249 U.N.T.S. 240, art. 4(4), reprinted in Roberts & Guelff, *supra*, note 39; 1949 *Geneva Convention* [No. IV] *Relative to the Protection of Civilian Persons in Time of War*, *supra*, note 45, art. 33; *Geneva Convention* [No. III] *Relative to the Treatment of Prisoners of War*, 12 August 1949, 6 U.S.T. 3316, T.I.A.S. 3364, 75 U.N.T.S. 135, art. 13; *Geneva Convention* [No. II] *for the Amelioration of the Condition of Wounded, Sick and Shipwrecked Members of the Armed Forces at Sea*, 12 August 1949, 6 U.S.T. 3217, T.I.A.S. 3363, 75 U.N.T.S. 85, art. 47; *Geneva Convention* [No. I] *for the Amelioration of the Condition of the Wounded and Sick in Armed Forces in the Field*, 12 August 1949, 6 U.S.T. 3114, T.I.A.S. 3362, 75 U.N.T.S. 31.

[54] *I.e.* otherwise unlawful acts of retaliation carried out in response to prior illegal acts of warfare and intended to force compliance with the laws of war.

[55] See D. Bowett, *Self-Defence in International Law* (1958) 167-74. See also the discussion of *Rule 5* beginning *infra*, text accompanying note 57.

[56] See 1977 Geneva Protocol I Additional, *supra*, note 41, art. 56.

[57] See *Hague Convention* [No. V] *Respecting the Rights and Duties of Neutrals in War on Land*, 18 October 1907, 36 Stat. 2310, T.S. No. 540, 1 Bevans 654, arts 1, 2, 3, 4 and 10. Article 1 states the basic rule: "The territory of neutral Powers is inviolable." See also *Hague Convention* [No. XIII] *Concerning the Rights and Duties of Neutral Powers in Naval War*, 18 October 1907, 36 Stat. 2415, T.S. No. 545, 1 Bevans 723, arts 1 and 2.

For all the vicissitudes that the law of neutrality has suffered over the years, from the bodyblows of maritime warfare during World War I, to the coming into being of the United Nations collective security system, to the more-or-less routine overflight of planes, rockets and satellites for intelligence retrieval and space exploration purposes, two key claims continue to be honored to substantial degree: the claim that belligerents have no warrant to carry their hostilities into the territory of a nonparticipating State, and the accompanying claim that nonparticipating States have the right to exclude the entry of belligerent forces into their territory. During both World Wars, for example, it was virtually uniform practice for nonparticipants to forbid the entry, deliberate or inadvertent, of belligerent military aircraft into neutral airspace.[58] Of course, as everywhere in the law, different contextual factors make for different applications of the general rule; hence such slippery terms as "absolute neutrality", "nonbelligerence", "qualified neutrality", and the like. On balance, however, the notion that nonparticipants have a legal right to freedom from harm and injury to their territory resulting from interbelligerent activities, and a consequent right to compensation for damages attending violations of that right, appears to have withstood the test of time.

Rule 6.   It is prohibited to use asphyxiating, poisonous or other gases, and all analogous liquids, materials or devices, including bacteriological methods of warfare.[59]

---

[58] See, *e.g.*, G. Hackworth, *Digest of International Law* (1943), vol. 7, 549-57; J. Spaight, *Air Power and War Rights*, 3d ed. (1947) 420-9.

[59] See *Protocol for the Prohibition of the Use in War of Asphyxiating, Poisonous or Other Gases, and of Bacteriological Methods of Warfare*, 17 June 1925, 26 U.S.T. 575, T.I.A.S. 8061, 94 L.N.T.S. 65 [hereinafter *Geneva Gas Protocol*] which states:

Whereas the use in war of asphyxiating, poisonous or other gases, and of all analogous liquids, materials or devices, has been justly condemned by the general opinion of the civilised world; and

Whereas the prohibition of such use has been declared in Treaties to which the majority of Powers of the world are Parties; and

To the end that this prohibition shall be universally accepted as a part of International Law, binding alike the conscience and the practice of nations;

Declare:

That the High Contracting Parties, so far as they are not already Parties to Treaties prohibiting such use, accept this prohibition, agree to extend this prohibition to the use of bacteriological methods of warfare and agree to be bound as between themselves according to the terms of this declaration.

See also *Hague Declaration* [No. IV, 2] *Concerning Asphyxiating Gases*, 29 July 1899, reprinted in Roberts & Guelff, *supra*, note 39, 36; *1907 Hague Regulations*, *supra*, note 41, art. 23(a); *Resolution on the Question of Chemical and Bacteriological (Biological) Weapons*, United Nations G.A. Res. 2603A, 24 U.N. GAOR, Supp. (No. 30) 16, U.N. Doc. A/7630 (1969).

Due partly to fear of retaliation, but also to the opprobrium that surely would attach to the admitted or discovered use of chemical and biological weapons, this prohibition, which is today derived primarily from the *Geneva Gas Protocol* of 1925,[60] has been remarkably well observed since the widespread use of poison gas during World War I. When it has not, as when Italy used poison gas against Ethiopia in 1935-36, or when unobservance is suspected, as presently in the case of the U.S.S.R. in Afghanistan, the aversion and indignation aroused has been substantial. At any rate, given the large number of States that have become party to the 1925 *Protocol* (including the Soviet Union in 1928 and the United States in 1975), the majority view now seems to be that the prohibition should be regarded as part of customary international law, embracing all States whether or not they have formally adhered to the *Protocol* itself. Broad though its prescriptive foundation may be, however, there is some question about the prohibition's substantive scope. For example, some States, including the United States, have taken the position that it does not extend to non-lethal control agents and chemical herbicides.[61] Additionally, because a number of State-parties have attached reservations declaring that the *Protocol* shall be binding upon them only to the extent that it is respected by the other State-parties, some maintain that the prohibition is addressed only to the first use of chemical, biological and equivalent weapons.[62] Probably this is a correct interpretation insofar as these reserving States are concerned, but judging from the all-encompassing tenor of U.N. General Assembly Resolution 2603A which interprets the 1925 *Protocol*, such a construction doubtless should be applied as restrictively as possible.[63]

THUS, despite an obvious erosion over the years of legal inhibitions regarding the conduct as well as the initiation of war, there remains today an inherited commitment to standards of humane conduct within which the reasonable belligerent can operate.[64] Contrary to the repudiated *Kriegsraison*

---

[60] See *ibid*.

[61] See Roberts & Guelff, *supra*, note 39, 138.

[62] *Ibid*.

[63] Resolution 2603A, *supra*, note 59, declares "as contrary to the generally recognized rules of international law", embodied in the 1925 *Geneva Gas Protocol*, the use in international armed conflicts of:

(a) Any chemical agents of warfare — chemical substances, whether gaseous, liquid or solid — which might be employed because of their direct toxic effects on man, animals or plants;

(b) Any biological agents of warfare — living organisms, whatever their nature, or infective material derived from them — which are intended to cause disease or death in man, animals or plants, and which depend for their effects on their ability to multiply in the person, animal or plant attacked.

[64] For a formulation somewhat different, but nonetheless paralleling and complementing the six prohibitory *Rules* summarized above, see *Red Cross Fundamental Rules*, *supra*, note 41.

theory of the German war criminals,[65] there remains the fundamental principle from which all the laws of war derive, including the humanitarian rules of armed conflict noted here, namely, that the right of belligerents to adopt means and methods of warfare is *not* unlimited.[66]

Now when applying this principle in light of the prohibitory rules summarized above, obviously one is not led inevitably to the proposition that nuclear weapons are illegal *per se* — except, I would argue, within the terms of *Rule 6* prohibiting the use of chemical, biological and "analogous" means of warfare. Perhaps not all nuclear weapons which are conceivable, but certainly all nuclear weapons now deployed or planned, including the so-called "neutron bomb" or "enhanced radiation" [ER] weapon, and the "reduced residual-radiation" [RRR] or "minimum residual-radiation" [MRR] weapon, manifest radiation effects that for all intents and purposes are the same as those that result from poison gas and bacteriological means of warfare;[67] and in any event the 1925 *Geneva Gas Protocol* is so comprehensive in its prohibition that it may be said to preclude the use of nuclear weapons altogether.[68] But in the absence of a specific prohibition, one is led, instead, to ask the same basic question that the conscientious belligerent is obliged to ask in any given conflict situation: Is resort to this means or method of warfare proportionate to a legitimate military end?[69] In most if not all nuclear warfare situations, I believe that the answer must be — *no*. It is hard to imagine any nuclear war, except possibly one involving a very restricted use of extremely low-yield battlefield weapons, where this vital link between

---

[65] *I.e.*, the theory that the "necessities of war", or military necessity, override and render inoperative the ordinary laws of war (*Kriegsmanier*).

[66] See, *e.g.*, *1907 Hague Regulations*, *supra*, note 41, art. 22, which provides: "The right of belligerents to adopt means of injuring the enemy is not unlimited." See also 1977 Geneva Protocol I Additional, *supra*, note 41, art. 35(1); *Resolution on Respect for Human Rights in Armed Conflicts*, *supra*, note 41, para. 1(a).

[67] See *supra*, note 24 and accompanying text. For details concerning the so-called "second generation nuclear weapons" mentioned here, including the EMP Bomb [enhanced electromagnetic pulse warhead], see Gsponer, *The Neutron Bomb and the Other New Limited Nuclear War Weapons* (1982) 13 Bull. Peace Proposals 221. The same article describes briefly "third generation direct energy weapons" (laser beam, microwave beam and particle beam weapons) as well.

[68] See Castrén, *The Present Law of War and Neutrality*, *supra*, note 12, 207; Greenspan, *supra*, note 12, 372-3; Schwarzenberger, *supra*, note 12, 37-8; Singh, *supra*, note 12, 162-6; Falk, Meyrowitz & Sanderson, *supra*, note 12, 563; Meyrowitz, *supra*, note 12, 842.

[69] Article 36 of 1977 Geneva Protocol I Additional, *supra*, note 41, extends this inquiry to the longer term, with obvious implications for defense policymakers and operators: "In the study, development, acquisition or adoption of a new weapon, means or method of warfare, a High Contracting Party is under an obligation to determine whether its employment would, in some or all circumstances, be prohibited by this Protocol or by any other rule of international law applicable to the High Contracting Party."

humanity and military necessity — proportionality — would not be breached or threatened in the extreme; and it is especially hard to imagine in the face of the "countervalue" and "counterforce" strategic doctrines that underpin the core of the nuclear deterrence policies of the two superpowers.[70] Given these observations, not to mention the millions of projected deaths and uncontrollable environmental harms that would result from any *probable* use of nuclear weapons, it seems inescapable that nuclear warfare is contrary to the core precepts of international law.

But the point here is not to deal in generalities, as important as the generalities are. Rather, it is to demonstrate, as I believe one can, that the humanitarian rules of armed conflict we have reviewed briefly do in fact apply to nuclear weapons and warfare, and then, to investigate how and to what extent this "policy content" actually operates in concrete contexts. Thus, it is appropriate to turn now to our second "communication flow", the authority signal.

B.   *Authority Signal*

It is one thing to postulate and quite another to establish that the humanitarian rules of armed conflict, both conventional and customary, do extend to or cover nuclear weapons and warfare. A communication of policy content unaccompanied by an authority signal, let alone a communication of control intention, is not law.

But there is, I think, sufficient evidence to confirm that the requisite authority signal is present. The widespread and essentially unqualified adoption of the four 1949 *Geneva Conventions* on the humane conduct of war four years *after* the advent of the nuclear age;[71] U.N. General Assembly Resolution 1653 of 24 November 1961, declaring the use of nuclear weapons to be, *inter alia*, "contrary to the rules of international law and to the laws of humanity";[72] the 1963 *Shimoda Case*, holding that the bombings of Hiroshima and Nagasaki were contrary to international law in general and the laws of war in

---

[70] For a discussion of these doctrines, see *infra*, text accompanying notes 128-32.

[71] See *Geneva Convention* [No. I] *for the Amelioration of the Condition of the Wounded and Sick in the Armed Forces in the Field*, *supra*, note 53; *Geneva Convention* [No. II] *for the Amelioration of the Condition of Wounded, Sick and Shipwrecked Members of the Armed Forces at Sea*, *supra*, note 53; *Geneva Convention* [No. III] *Relative to the Treatment of Prisoners of War*, *supra*, note 53; *Geneva Convention* [No. IV] *Relative to the Protection of Civilian Persons in Time of War*, *supra*, note 45.

[72] *Supra*, note 34 and accompanying text.

particular;[73] resolutions of the International Red Cross;[74] the writings of the vast majority of publicists knowledgeable in the field [75] — these and other communications express a far-flung community consensus that nuclear weapons and warfare do not escape the judgment of the humanitarian rules of armed conflict. True, some will challenge this assertion on the grounds that certain of the communications relied upon are not "true sources" of law, or, in more functional terms, that their communicators do not have the authority to prescribe. But this would be to imply, erroneously I submit, that only State actors have the competence to prescribe internationally respecting issues or values of major and universal significance, a viewpoint that contrasts sharply with the common understanding, certified in the famous Martens Clause of 1907 *Hague Convention No. IV* and reaffirmed in the four 1949 *Geneva Conventions* and the two 1977 Geneva Protocols Additional, that the laws of war are in part a function of "the dictates of the public conscience".[76] Moreover, it is to beg the question of those "sources" that *are* acceptable by statist standards.

In sum, except as noted below, there is little in the authoritative literature to indicate, either explicitly or implicitly, that nuclear weapons and warfare are not or should not be subject to the humanitarian rules of armed conflict; indeed, there is a great deal to indicate that they are and should be. The world community has in no way consented to the abolition of these rules in order to legitimize nuclear war. As Professor Fried has stated emphatically: "It is scurrilous to argue that it is still *forbidden* to kill a *single* innocent enemy civilian with a *bayonet*, or wantonly to destroy a *single* building or enemy territory by *machine-gun* fire — but that it is *legitimate* to kill *millions* of enemy non-combatants and wantonly to destroy entire enemy cities, regions and perhaps countries (including cities, areas or the entire surface of *neutral* States) by *nuclear* weapons." [77]

---

[73] *Supra*, note 38 and accompanying text.

[74] See, *e.g.*, *Resolution XXVIII on the Protection of Civilian Populations Against the Dangers of Indiscriminate Warfare* in *International Conference of the Red Cross, Resolutions* (1965) 22, declaring: "The general principles of the Law of War apply to nuclear and similar weapons".

[75] See, *e.g.*, the many publicists cited *supra*, notes 12 and 40.

[76] The Martens Clause in the Preamble of the 1907 *Hague Convention No. IV*, *supra*, note 41, is quoted in full *infra*, text accompanying note 81. The 1949 versions may be found in *Geneva Convention No. I*, *supra*, note 53, art. 63; *Geneva Convention No. II*, *supra*, note 53, art. 62; *Geneva Convention No. III*, *supra*, note 53, art. 142; *Geneva Convention No. IV*, *supra*, note 45, art. 158. The 1977 versions may be found in 1977 Geneva Protocol I Additional, *supra*, note 41, art. 1; and 1977 Geneva Protocol II Additional Relating to the Protection of Victims of Non-International Armed Conflicts, U.N. Doc. A/32/144, Annex II, art. 1, reprinted in (1977) 16 I.L.M. 1442 (adopted 12 December 1977; entered into force on 7 December 1978).

[77] Fried, *supra*, note 12, 28.

Despite all this evidence, however, at least three negative arguments are heard to deny that the humanitarian rules of armed conflict apply to nuclear weapons and warfare. They merit acknowledgement and rebuttal, if only to demonstrate further the force of what has just been said.

First is the argument that these rules do not apply because, for the most part, they predate the invention of nuclear weapons or otherwise fail to mention them by name. The argument is easily dismissed. As a variant of the spurious thesis that nuclear weapons uses are without legal constraint in the absence of an explicit treaty ban, it fails to heed the multifaceted nature of the international law-creating system, taking a view of legal process that no one would dare accept in the domestic sphere. Moreover, legal rules typically are interpreted to encompass matters not specifically mentioned — often not even contemplated — by their formulators, the Commerce Clause of the *United States Constitution* being a well-known case in point.[78] As stated by the 1945 Nuremberg Tribunal when called to adjudicate complaints about previously undefined "crimes against humanity" and other crimes, "[the law of war] is not static, but by continual adaptation follows the needs of a changing world".[79] Finally, confirming the first point, the well known Martens Clause, partially quoted above,[80] was formulated exactly to cover such lacunae, and accordingly bears quotation in full:

> Until a more complete code of the laws of war has been issued, the High Contracting Parties deem it expedient to declare that, in cases not included in the Regulations adopted by them, the inhabitants and the belligerents remain under the protection and the rule of the principles of the law of nations, as they result from the usages established among civilized peoples, from the laws of humanity, and the dictates of the public conscience.[81]

Weapons and tactics not dealt with specifically in the various texts articulating the laws of war thus remain nonetheless constrained by the principles of international law, including the counterbalancing principles of humanity and military necessity, and — not to be forgotten — "the dictates of the public conscience".

Another negative argument, a variant of the first but not as broadsweeping, is that certain of the humanitarian rules of armed conflict do not apply or are not authoritative simply because they are open to exempting interpretation. For example, notwithstanding that the radiation effects of nuclear

---

[78] Written in the late eighteenth century, before railroads, automobiles and airplanes, the *United States Constitution*, art. I §9, cl. 3, has nonetheless repeatedly been held to regulate virtually every aspect of modern technology operating across federal and state lines.

[79] *Trial of the Major War Criminals*, *supra*, note 11, 464.

[80] See *supra*, text accompanying note 76.

[81] The 1907 *Hague Convention No. IV*, *supra*, note 41, Preamble. For more up-to-date versions, see sources cited, *supra*, note 76.

weapons, initial and residual, produce symptoms and results essentially indistinguishable from the short- and long-term disease and genetic consequences of poison gas and bacteriological weapons,[82] and despite the fact that the omnibus language of the 1925 *Geneva Gas Protocol* ("all analogous liquids, materials or devices") is comprehensive enough to proscribe any weapon whose effects are similar to chemical and biological means of warfare,[83] it still is argued that art. 23(a) of the *1907 Hague Regulations* (forbidding poison or poisoned weapons)[84] and the *Protocol's* omnibus language do not apply to nuclear weapons. It is said that the former reflects an historic revulsion for clandestine instruments of war, which nuclear weapons clearly are not,[85] and that the weapons banned by the latter (presumably the chemical and bacteriological weapons) harbor factual and policy aspects somehow distinguishable from radiological weapons.[86] Similarly, it has been suggested that the radiological consequences of nuclear weapons, far from having any central military importance, are but the "incidental side effects" of nuclear weapons explosions,[87] thus removing nuclear weapons from the reach of such rules as *1907 Hague Regulation* 23(e) forbidding the use of weapons "*calculated* to cause unnecessary suffering".[88] But such interpretive arguments are, I think, self-serving and evasive. As usefully observed by Ian Brownlie, the first argument (relative to chemical and biological weapons) is rather "[like] interpreting older statutes on road traffic in such a way as to confine the word 'vehicle' to the horse and cart";[89] the second argument (relative to the "incidental" versus "calculated" dichotomy) simply ignores that most nuclear weapons, certainly those in the strategic and high-yield tactical classes, are deployed, to quote Brownlie again, "in part with a view to utilizing the destructive effects of radiation and fall-out".[90] On final analysis, these and like arguments tend to beg rather than to justify the conclusions put forward, and are scarcely less preposterous than contending that civil defense arrangements such as air raid shelters make a city defended and thereby beyond the protection of, say, art. 25 of the *1907 Hague Regulations* prohibiting attacks upon "undefended" towns, villages, dwellings, or buildings.[91]

---

[82] See *supra*, note 24 and accompanying text.
[83] See *supra*, note 68 and accompanying text.
[84] See *supra*, note 41.
[85] See McDougal and Feliciano, *supra*, note 39, 662-3.
[86] See *ibid.*, 664-5.
[87] See Phillips, *Air Warfare and Law* (1953) 21 Geo. Wash. L. Rev. 395, 410 and 414.
[88] *Supra*, note 41 [emphasis added].
[89] *Supra*, note 4, 444.
[90] *Ibid.*, 445.
[91] *Supra*, note 41.

Finally, there is the argument that the humanitarian rules of armed conflict do not extend to nuclear weapons and warfare insofar as they are newly expressed in 1977 Protocol I Additional to the four 1949 *Geneva Conventions*. The underlying rationale is twofold: first, that the Protocol has not yet been ratified by the nuclear weapon States, although it has been signed by the majority of them;[92] and second, that at the time of signature, the United Kingdom and the United States stipulated formal "understandings" that the rules established or newly introduced by the Protocol would not regulate or prohibit the use of nuclear weapons, only conventional ones.[93] Now it is true that failure of ratification of a treaty ordinarily prevents its application against a nonratifying State. It also is true that a declaration of understanding, like a reservation, may sometimes effectively qualify a treaty to the degree that it is not incompatible with the treaty's object and purpose. Thus it is arguable that the Protocol's provisions relative to the protection of the natural environment[94] and of civilian populations as a whole,[95] which are among those that supplement and extend the laws of war as previously articulated, may not in fact cover nuclear weapons and warfare at the present time. However, it also is true that a State consenting to a treaty subject to ratification — *e.g.*, the United Kingdom, the United States and the U.S.S.R. in the instant case — is obliged to refrain from acts which would defeat the treaty's object and purpose (at least until such time as it makes clear its intention not to become a party to the treaty)[96] and that a declaration of understanding, in contrast to a reservation, is seen to be essentially a unilateral act and therefore presumptively not binding on parties that fail to object to it.[97] Moreover, in

---

[92] See Roberts & Guelff, *supra*, note 39, 459-60.

[93] Although not yet a signatory of the Protocol, France apparently took the same position during the course of the deliberations over the Protocol. See J. Boyd, ed., *Digest of United States Practice in International Law 1977* (1979) 919. See also M. Bothe, K. Partsch & W. Solf, *New Rules for Victims of Armed Conflicts — Commentary on the Two 1977 Protocols Additional to the Geneva Conventions of 1949* (1982) 189.

[94] See *supra*, note 49 and accompanying text.

[95] See 1977 Geneva Protocol I Additional, *supra*, note 41, pt. IV.

[96] See *Vienna Convention on the Law of Treaties*, U.N. Doc. A/CONF. 39/27, 289 reprinted in (1969) 8 I.L.M. 679 (opened for signature 23 May 1969; entered into force 27 January 1980) [hereinafter *Vienna Convention*]. As of 31 December 1982, the *Vienna Convention* had been ratified by forty-three states. The United States has signed but not yet ratified the *Convention*.

[97] See, *e.g.*, D. O'Connell, *International Law*, 2d ed. (1970), vol. 1, 198-9. The point is important to bear in mind in view of the fact that sixty-two countries besides the United Kingdom and the United States have so far signed the Protocol apparently without formally objecting to the British and American "understandings", but also, it must be noted, without seeking similarly to limit the reach of the Protocol in relation to nuclear weapons. India contradicted the views of the United Kingdom and the United States in a written statement in the final Plenary of the diplomatic conference which negotiated the Protocol. See Bothe, Partsch & Solf, *supra*, note 93, 189-90.

view of such instruments as the 1970 *Stockholm Declaration on the Human Environment* and the 1978 *Red Cross Fundamental Rules*,[98] it is probable that the Protocol's environmental and civilian population protection provisions are declaratory of emerging customary law and are therefore unaffected by the nonratifications and declarations of understanding in question.[99] Finally, because 1977 Geneva Protocol I Additional is directed at the minimization of destruction and suffering in *modern* warfare "without any adverse distinction based on the nature or origin of the armed conflict",[100] and because it regrettably is easy to imagine the use of nuclear weapons in such warfare, it is not unreasonable to conclude that the United Kingdom and the United States declarations vitiate the fundamental objects and purposes of the Protocol and therefore are invalid.[101] At the very least, as remarked by Professor Fujita, "[t]his separation of fields of regulation between conventional warfare and nuclear warfare will produce an odd result not easily imaginable, because conventional weapons and nuclear weapons will be eventually used at the same time and in the same circumstances in a future armed conflict".[102] In sum, the legal effects of nonratifications and declarations of understanding — matters of not a little bewilderment at any time — do not find themselves unequivocally on one side of the present debate. This third argument is highly ambiguous at best, and of course it does not negate any of the prohibitions that predate the Protocol.[103]

On final analysis, then, the humanitarian rules of armed conflict may be said to apply to nuclear weapons and warfare. The counterarguments reviewed represent not a challenge to the essential authoritativeness of this conclusion, but, indeed, an acknowledgment of such authority and a consequent attempt to escape it. Considering the horrifying stakes involved, it seems a misplaced exercise.

---

[98] For the *Stockholm Declaration*, see *supra*, note 49. For the *Red Cross Fundamental Rules*, see *supra*, note 41.

[99] *Cf.* Bothe, Partsch & Solf, *supra*, note 93, 572. It appears, indeed, that the United Kingdom and United States declarations of understanding were perceived as extending only to the Protocol's provisions regarding the use of weapons — *i.e.* paras 35(2) and (3) — and to no others. See Bothe, Partsch & Solf at 190.

[100] *Supra*, note 41, Preamble.

[101] See *Vienna Convention*, *supra*, note 96, art. 19.

[102] Fujita, *supra*, note 12, 77.

[103] *Cf.* Bothe, Partsch & Solf, *supra*, note 93, 190. Mr George H. Aldrich, Chairman of the United States Delegation to the diplomatic conference which drew up and adopted the Protocol, observed at the fourth and final session that the American stand on nuclear weapons applied only to the rules of warfare newly established by the Protocol (in particular, art. 55 on the protection of the natural environment), and not to the already existing customary and conventional laws of war. See Boyd, *supra*, note 93, 919.

C.   *Control Intention*

What we have just observed *vis-à-vis* arguments disputing the applicability to nuclear weapons of the humanitarian rules of armed conflict — namely, that they constitute not a plea of unauthoritativeness but a confession of avoidance — is grist for the proposition that the world community has little or no expectation of allowing the rules of war to regulate the use of nuclear weapons. However solid the authority signal, it would be argued, the intention to make that authority controlling simply does not exist.

This proposition, it must be acknowledged, is no idle one, at least in relation to the nuclear weapon States. Despite abundant rhetoric to the contrary, they appear determined to fight delaying actions against a general legal control of nuclear weapons and warfare. In the name of self-defense and self-preservation, they have built and continue to build enormous nuclear arsenals which presumably they would use if sufficiently provoked. Mutually fearful of evasion, they have shown themselves unable to agree on a comprehensive instrument of prohibition or severe restriction. Except for the Soviet Union, they have declined to renounce the option of first use. And, as noted earlier in connection with 1977 Geneva Protocol I Additional, some of them have sought to exempt nuclear weapons from important provisions of the most recent formal statement on the protection of victims of international conflicts.[104] In other words, on the basis of such facts, there can be genuine doubt about the extent to which the major powers actually have assimilated into their operational codes the authority signal that nuclear weapons and warfare are to be judged according to the humanitarian rules of armed conflict.

This doubt is not the end of the matter, however, although to make the opposite case is not easy, for one must rely for evidence more on acts of omission than of commission. Nevertheless, also germane are three clusters of countervailing factors which, though frequently and perhaps deliberately omitted from the balance of relevant considerations, nonetheless recommend that this third communication flow in law-making relative to nuclear weapons and warfare is not as one sided as at first it may seem. A control intention on the part of the global community as a whole is by no means absent.

In the first place, and perhaps most conspicuous at the present time, there are the initiatives of essentially nonformal members of the international legal community. Emboldened by a variety of inducements, such as the collapse of SALT II, a quantum leap in arms race expenditures, a growing fear of nuclear confrontation in Europe, the Nuremberg precedent, religious teachings, and

---

[104] See *supra*, text following note 91.

secular humanism, increasing numbers of diverse individuals and groups, especially in the West where traditions of petition and redress prevail, have been demanding, if not the complete abolition of nuclear weapons, then the implementation of norms designed to control them. The *Stockholm Declaration* of the U.N. Conference on the Human Environment issued in June 1972 [105] and the *Delhi Declaration* of the International Workshop on Disarmament issued in March 1978 [106] are illustrative. So, too, are the assertions of Vatican II [107] and, more recently, the Pastoral Letter on War, Armaments and Peace of the National Conference of Catholic Bishops of the United States. [108] But perhaps most apposite is the work of the International Committee of the Red Cross [ICRC] which has come to play an important and respected quasi-official role in the implementation as well as the clarification and development of the humanitarian laws of war. [109] Overwhelmingly, the intention is manifest to curtail the growing menace of nuclear militarism and to fashion or reinforce rules of humanitarian conduct in time of war.

Secondly, a control intention is evident in the attitudes and behaviors of the non-nuclear weapon States. Although without the nuclear hardware to prove their restraint unequivocally, still they may be seen to intend the regulation of nuclear weapons and warfare according to the humanitarian rules of armed conflict. For example, under the aegis and with the cooperation of the United Nations, they have on numerous occasions expressed their resolve either to prohibit nuclear weapons *in toto* or to restrict their use severely according to the laws of war. [110] A good illustration, one we already

---

[105] *Supra*, note 49.

[106] For the text, see B. Weston, R. Falk & A. D'Amato, *Basic Documents in International Law and World Order* (1980) 406.

[107] See *Pastoral Constitution on the Church in the Modern World*, ch. 5, reprinted and translated in W. Abbott, ed., *The Documents of Vatican II* (1966).

[108] See National Conference of Catholic Bishops, *The Challenge of Peace: God's Promise and Our Response* (Pastoral Letter on War, Armaments and Peace), 13 Origins — NC Documentary Service No. 1 (19 May 1983).

[109] The ICRC played a major role, as is well known, in the drafting and negotiation of the four 1949 *Geneva Conventions*, *supra*, notes 45 and 53, and the two 1977 Geneva Protocols Additional to the 1949 *Conventions*, *supra*, notes 41 and 76. For further indication of the ICRC's extensive involvement, see Draper, *supra*, note 12; D. Forsythe, *Humanitarian Politics: The International Committee of the Red Cross* (1978); Pictet, *supra*, note 40; and J. Pictet, *The Principles of International Humanitarian Law* (n.d.; available from ICRC). See also ICRC, *Some International Red Cross Conference Resolutions on the Protection of Civilian Populations and on Weapons of Mass Destruction* (1981); and ICRC, *Report on the Work of Experts on Weapons that May Cause Unnecessary Suffering or Have Indiscriminate Effects* (1973).

[110] See, *e.g.*, the 1961 *Declaration on the Prohibition of the Use of Nuclear and Thermonuclear Weapons*, *supra*, note 34, the first time the non-nuclear weapon states expressed their views *via* the United Nations. The recorded vote, analysed in some detail *infra*, note 111, was

have encountered, is found in U.N. General Assembly Resolution 1653 of 24 November 1961, providing, *inter alia*, that the use of nuclear weapons would be "contrary to the rules of international law and to the laws of humanity".[111] Another is found in the history surrounding General Assembly Resolution 2444 of 19 December 1968,[112] involving the deletion, at the request of the Soviet delegation, of a provision "that the general principles of war apply to nuclear and similar weapons". The deletion was allowed, but only over the objections of the United States representative who maintained that the laws and principles of war "apply as well to the use of nuclear and similar weapons", and only on the understanding that the remaining provisions would apply regardless of the nature of the armed conflict "or the kinds of weapons used".[113] But perhaps most telling has been the uniform disinclination of the non-nuclear weapon States to hedge on any of the provisions of 1977 Geneva

---

55 in favor, 20 opposed and 26 abstentions. For General Assembly resolutions on the same themes since 1961, see *Declaration on the Non-use of Force in International Relations and Permanent Prohibition of the Use of Nuclear Weapons, supra*, note 37 (73 in favor; 4 opposed, 46 abstentions); *Resolution on Non-use of Nuclear Weapons and Prevention of Nuclear War*, United Nations G.A. Res. 33/71B, 33 U.N. GAOR, Supp. (No. 45) 48, U.N. Doc. A/33/45 (1978) (103 in favor, 18 opposed, 18 abstentions); *Resolution on the Non-use of Nuclear Weapons and Prevention of Nuclear War*, United Nations G.A. Res. 34/83G, 34 U.N. GAOR, Supp. (No. 46) 56, U.N. Doc. A/34/46 (1979) (112 in favor, 16 opposed, 14 abstentions); *Resolution on Non-use of Nuclear Weapons and Prevention of Nuclear War*, United Nations G.A. Res. 35/152D, 35 U.N. GAOR, Supp. (No. 48) 69, U.N. Doc. A/35/48 (1980) (113 in favor, 19 opposed, 14 abstentions); *Resolution on Non-use of Nuclear Weapons and Prevention of Nuclear War*, United Nations G.A. Res. 36/92I, 36 U.N. GAOR, Supp. (No. 51) 64, U.N. Doc. A/36/51 (1981) (121 in favor, 19 opposed, 6 abstentions). It is significant that the number of states which have voted against the legality of nuclear weapons has increased substantially since 1961.

[111] *Supra*, note 34, para. 1(b). The Resolution was passed by a vote of 55 to 20 with 26 abstentions, which suggests a much smaller consensus than in fact was the case. As Brownlie points out, "[t]he only vote cast against the resolution from Africa and Asia was that of Nationalist China. The Latin-American States largely abstained, as also did the Scandinavian States, Austria, and certain political associates of the West in Asia. What is interesting about the voting pattern is, however, the fact that States representing a variety of political associations are to be found in the majority vote. This was drawn from the 'non-aligned' African and Asian States, some African and Asian States with Western leanings such as Nigeria, Lebanon and Japan, Mexico...and the Communist States. Members of NATO (apart from Denmark and Norway), together with Australia, Ireland, New Zealand, Spain [under Franco], South Africa, three Central American republics and Nationalist China, voted against the resolution." *Supra*, note 4, 438-9. In other words, except for the United States and countries allied with or significantly dependent upon the United States, most of the rest of the world voted *for* the Resolution. Compare the voting patterns in the Resolutions cited *supra*, note 110. Increasingly the non-nuclear weapon states may be seen to oppose the legality of nuclear weapons.

[112] *Resolution on Respect for Human Rights in Armed Conflicts, supra*, note 41.

[113] As recounted in United States Dep't of the Air Force, *International Law — The Conduct of Armed Conflict and Air Operations* (1976) 5-17, fn. 18 (AFP. 110-31).

Protocol I Additional in respect of nuclear weapons as did the United Kingdom and the United States.[114] Not one non-nuclear weapon State has followed suit and none appears inclined to do so. The non-nuclear weapon States, it seems, are variously committed to the wholesale prohibition of nuclear weapons or, in the alternative, to their regulation according to the laws of war as most recently articulated.

Finally, and arguably most importantly, a control intention is evidenced in the words and deeds of the nuclear weapon States themselves. Even while escalating nuclear capabilities and tensions to the point where responsible observers are predicting a nuclear conflagration before the year 2000, the nuclear powers appear to take for granted that nuclear weapons do not escape the scrutiny of the humanitarian rules of armed conflict. For example, a certain responsiveness to these rules, or in any event to the importance of not transgressing them, appears to have been at work, however perversely, in the bombings of Hiroshima and Nagasaki. Each were justified officially on grounds of military necessity.[115] Similarly, the responsiveness seems present, to some extent at least, in the complete non-use of nuclear weapons in Korea, Vietnam, Afghanistan, and the Falkland or Malvinas Islands where, manifestly, superior forces could have been unleashed;[116] and again, to some degree, in the growing interest among American and Soviet strategists in counterforce doctrine and capabilities for damage limitation.[117] But perhaps most unmistakably, the control intention is evident in the military manuals of the major powers, manuals whose purpose it is, *inter alia*, to advise military personnel (particularly those in command positions) on how to comport themselves in time of war. While denying the illegality of nuclear weapons *per se*, the military manuals of the United States and the United Kingdom, for example, consistently instruct that nuclear weapons are to be judged according to the same standards that apply to other weapons in armed conflict.[118]

---

[114] See Cassese, "A Tentative Appraisal of the Old and New Humanitarian Law of Armed Conflict" in Cassese, *supra*, note 40, 461, 475-6. See also *supra*, notes 93, 97 and 99, and accompanying text.

[115] See generally, sources cited *supra*, note 6.

[116] See Meyrowitz, *supra*, note 12, 835.

[117] See, *e.g.*, J. Rose, *The Evolution of U.S. Army Nuclear Doctrine 1945-1980* (1980), including a discussion of Soviet as well as American doctrinal thinking.

[118] See, *e.g.*, United States Dep't of the Air Force, *supra*, note 113, 5-17, fn. 18 and 6-5; United States Dep't of the Army, *International Law* (1962), vol. 2, 42-4 (D.A. PAM 27-161-2) (especially the discussion of the unpublished annotation to United States Dep't of the Army, *supra*, note 8, para. 35); United Kingdom, *Manual of Military Law* (1958), pt. III — *The Laws of War on Land*, para. 113; United States Dep't of the Navy, *Law of Naval Warfare* §613, fn. 1, reprinted in R. Tucker, *The Law of War and Neutrality* (1955). See also Meyrowitz, *supra*, note 12, 836-8.

Thus, there is more to the issue of control intention in the present context than at first meets the eye. The huge emphasis given by the nuclear weapon States to their policies of nuclear deterrence and defense is, of course, theoretically complicating, certainly for anyone who believes law to be no mere body of rules but a complex process of controlling as well as authoritative decision — and the more so when one appreciates how difficult it is for the rest of the world to do much about it. Similarly troublesome, certainly for anyone who accepts the positivist assertion that only States can make, interpret and enforce international law, is any claim of control intention that relies to significant extent upon the words and deeds of actors having uncertain or no formal status in the international system *as traditionally conceived*. But it is crucial to remember that legal norms are prescribed and endure because violators of fundamental community policies do exist; that control intention, as a credible communication, can embrace inducements and pressures not confined to the threat or use of the force we typically associate with power elites; and that, in this burgeoning human rights era especially, when dealing with an issue that involves potentially the fate of human civilization itself, it is not only appropriate but mandated that the legal expectations of all members of human society, official and non-official, be duly taken into account.[119] It is, for example, and by way of analogy, exceedingly difficult to imagine anyone but officials in Pretoria seriously contending that South Africa is not an international outlaw *vis-à-vis* Namibia simply because the World Court's South West Africa decision[120] has not been accompanied by a credible communication that the world community intends to and can make the decision controlling or because the communication which has occurred might be supported by expressions of intent drawn from actors of questionable standing in the international system (*e.g.*, liberation movements). In any event, if recent Western — particularly United States — protests against the Soviet Union in Afghanistan and against Israel in Lebanon for violations of the laws of war are any indication, it is exceedingly difficult to imagine the United States not decrying as a heinous violation of the humanitarian rules of armed conflict an atomic attack by Japan against the United States or Allied territory during World War II, and notwithstanding the "saturation bombings" visited by American air forces at other times during that terrible

---

[119] The point would seem validated by the principle established in the famous Martens Clause that the laws of war are to be determined in part by "the dictates of public conscience". For the Clause in full, see *supra*, text accompanying note 81. And in this spirit, one is tempted to paraphrase American revolutionary patriot Patrick Henry: No incineration without representation!

[120] *Legal Consequences for States of the Continued Presence of South Africa in Namibia (South West Africa) notwithstanding Security Council Resolution 276 (1970), Advisory Opinion* [1971] I.C.J. 16.

conflict. Write Falk, Meyrowitz and Sanderson in a recent essay: "A perspective of role reversal is helpful in orienting our understanding of the present status of nuclear weaponry and strategic doctrine." [121]

Thus, recalling, *inter alia*, the instructions of the military manuals of the major powers and the fact that the incineration of Hiroshima and Nagasaki were rationalized officially on grounds of military necessity, it is not unreasonable to conclude that the large-scale commitment of the nuclear weapon States to their unprecedented destructive arsenals reflects neither a repudiation of the humanitarian laws of armed conflict nor a refusal to make them controlling in respect of nuclear weapons. Rather, it implies an interpretation that nuclear weapons and the laws of war are not necessarily incompatible. The validity of this perception is of course open to debate,[122] but the nuclear weapon, it seems, is nonetheless seen as "just one more weapon", only somewhat more destructive.

* * *

Based on the foregoing "communication flow" analysis, we arrive, at the following three conclusions: first, that the humanitarian rules of armed conflict, though somewhat eroded over the years and obviously susceptible of evasive interpretation, continue as a vital civilizing influence upon the world community's warring propensities; second, that these rules, as contemporaneously understood, are endowed with an authority signal that communicates their applicability to nuclear as well as to conventional weapons and warfare; and third, that there exists on the part of the world community as a whole — evidenced, thankfully, more in words than in deeds — an unmistakable intention to cause the humanitarian rules of armed conflict to govern the use of nuclear weapons should ever that terrible day arrive again. To be sure, there is manifest a certain ambiguity about the extent to which this intention could in fact be fulfilled, and this ambiguity will persist as long as the distribution of the world's effective power remains as oligarchic as it now is. But it would be error to conclude from this ambiguity that there is no prescription or law placing nuclear weapons and warfare under the legal scrutiny of the humanitarian rules of armed conflict.

In the first place, a control *intention* is not synonymous with an unconditional control *capacity*, even though some tangible leverage must be present to make the intention credible. Were it otherwise, many rules we unques-

---

[121] Falk, Meyrowitz & Sanderson, *supra*, note 12, 590.
[122] For pertinent discussion, see *infra*, Part III.

tioningly accept as law would not be law at all. Ours, it should be remembered, is a more-or-less — not an either-or — world.

Secondly, in an essentially voluntarist community such as the world community today, one is well advised to stress the authority element over the control component of prescription, at least in cases where such common inclusive interests as the survival of all or of substantial segments of the community itself are fundamentally threatened, and especially when, in such cases, the community's principal power elites are themselves the cause or source of the threat. Otherwise, assuming the community survives, the danger is very real that the law will become little more than the expression of the will of the strongest. It is true that in minimally integrated communities control may be, as McDougal and Reisman have theorized, "the primary characterizing and sustaining element of prescription" in some — possibly many — instances.[123] But as these scholars also observe, attesting to the more-or-less world in which we live, "[t]he relative importance . . . of the control and authority components [in prescription] may vary with, among other things, the type of prescription being communicated, the level of crisis, and the nature of the community . . . . The interplay between the authority and control elements of prescription is complex and variable."[124]

Finally, in view of the horrifying and potentially irreversible devastation of which nuclear weapons are capable, not to mention the very little time their delivery systems allow for rational thought, it seems only sensible that any doubts about whether they are subject to the humanitarian rules of armed conflict as a matter of law should be answered, as a matter of policy, unequivocally in the affirmative. Such a response seems required, in any event, by a world public order of human dignity in which values are shaped and shared more by persuasion than by coercion. It is in keeping, too, with the major trends of an evolving planetary civilization: for example, the persistent, if uncertain, quest for nuclear arms control and disarmament, and the accelerating struggle for the realization of fundamental human rights, including the emerging right to peace recognized implicitly in art. 28 of the *Universal Declaration of Human Rights*.[125] Also, it is consistent with the spirit, if not always the letter, of the judgment at Nuremberg, the *Genocide Convention*, and, not least, the *United Nations Charter*. The burden of proof, in other words, should be upon those who would contend that the humanitarian norms do not control the use of nuclear weapons.

---

[123] McDougal & Reisman, *supra*, note 26, 251.

[124] *Ibid.*

[125] Article 28 reads: "Everyone is entitled to a social and international order in which the rights and freedoms set forth in this Declaration can be fully realized."

III.   The Matter of Norm Application

We have answered affirmatively the question whether the humanitarian rules of armed conflict apply to nuclear weapons and warfare. It now is appropriate to ask, as posited earlier, whether any *defensive* use or threat of use of nuclear weapons would be in any way contrary to this body of law. The issue subdivides, first, in terms of the actual first- or second-strike defensive use of these weapons for "strategic" or "tactical" purposes;[126] and, second, in terms of the threat of their use by way of research and development, manufacture, stockpiling, or deployment for any defensive use or purpose. The following analytic outline indicates the diversity of considerations involved:

1   *First-strike (initiating/preemptive) defensive uses*
    1.1   *"Strategic" nuclear warfare*
        1.1.1   "Countervalue" (societal) targeting
        1.1.2   "Counterforce" (military) targeting
    1.2   *"Tactical" nuclear warfare*
        1.2.1   "Theater" (intermediate) targeting
        1.2.2   "Battlefield" (limited) targeting

2   *Second-strike (retaliatory) defensive uses*
    2.1   *"Strategic" nuclear warfare*
        2.1.1   "Countervalue" (societal) targeting
        2.1.2   "Counterforce" (military) targeting
    2.2   *"Tactical" nuclear warfare*
        2.2.1   "Theater" (intermediate) targeting
        2.2.2   "Battlefield" (limited) targeting

3   *Threat of first- or second-strike defensive uses*
    3.1   *"Strategic" nuclear warfare*
        3.1.1   Research and development
        3.1.2   Manufacture and stockpiling
        3.1.3   Deployment
    3.2   *"Tactical" nuclear warfare*
        3.2.1   Research and development
        3.2.2   Manufacture and stockpiling
        3.2.3   Deployment

It should be understood, however, that "strategic" objectives and uses have been the centerpiece of United States and Soviet deterrence policies since the late 1940s and early 1950s when the nuclear arms race began. Indeed, despite a growing interest on both sides in counterforce doctrine and capabilities for

---

[126] See *infra*, text following note 127.

damage limitation, the concept of "countervalue" or "assured [societal] destruction" has served at least the United States as the principal rationale for its nuclear arms build-up over the years.[127]

Before proceeding, however, let us be clear about the meaning of the terms "strategic", "tactical", "countervalue", and "counterforce". All figure prominently in any discussion about nuclear weapons and all help to make up the tangled doctrinal web of what popularly is called "nuclear deterrence".[128]

Strategic nuclear weapons are designed to destroy an enemy's entire military, political and economic capacity (or to defend against weapons with such capability) while tactical nuclear weapons are intended for use within more specific and circumscribed objectives. Thus, strategic nuclear weapons and delivery systems include intercontinental ballistic missiles [ICBMs], submarine-launched ballistic missiles [SLBMs] and intercontinental heavy bombers (with and without cruise missiles),[129] whereas tactical nuclear weapons and delivery systems include "theater-level" intermediate-range ballistic missiles, medium-range ballistic missiles and bombers, and strike aircraft,[130] plus weapons planned for use in "battlefield" situations, including short-range ballistic missiles, howitzers, mortars, rockets, and demolition mines.[131] It is important to understand, however, that these distinctions are not altogether unambiguous. For example, while tactical weapons may not possess the range of their strategic counterparts, some of them, as the accompanying notes below reveal, possess yields and side-effects that are nevertheless indistinguishable from strategic weapons. What matters ultimately for

---

[127] See, *e.g.*, Builder & Graubard, *supra*, note 12, 1-3; *Report of the Secretary-General*, *supra*, note 21, 104-13; Beres, *Nuclear Strategy and World Order* (1982) 8 Alternatives — A Journal of World Policy 139.

[128] For definitions of the terms and their relation to specific weapons and weapon systems, see *Report of the Secretary-General*, *ibid.*, chs 2 and 3.

[129] See *Report of the Secretary-General*, *ibid.*, ch. 2, especially Table 1, which shows that strategic weapons generally have strike ranges in excess of 3,000 nautical miles, yields up to twenty megatons, and an accuracy, measured in terms of "circular error probable" [CEP], of 300-2,500 metres. CEP is defined as "the radius of a circle around the target at which a missile is aimed within which the warhead has a .5 probability of falling". United States Arms Control and Disarmament Agency, *SALT Lexicon*, rev'd ed. (1975) 5. In considering CEPs, Krass and Smith write: "[I]t is important to keep in mind, first, that probability does not mean certainty; second, that [it] is also probable that warheads will land further away from the target than the distance of the CEP; and, third, that the accuracy has probably been exaggerated." Krass & Smith, "Nuclear Strategy and Technology" in M. Kaldor & D. Smith, eds, *Disarming Europe* (1982) 19.

[130] Tactical weapons of the "theater" class generally have strike ranges up to 3,000 nautical miles, yields up to one megaton and a CEP accuracy somewhat better than 300 metres. See *Report of the Secretary-General*, *ibid.*, 26-31.

[131] "Battlefield" or limited tactical weapons generally have ranges up to 600 nautical miles, yields up to 100 kilotons and a relatively high accuracy. *Ibid.*

definitional purposes is more the reasons for which these weapons are used than their performance capabilities and characteristics *per se*.

Similar ambiguities attend the distinction between countervalue and counterforce doctrines of nuclear warfare. Generally speaking, countervalue targeting, as embodied in the doctrine of Mutual Assured Destruction [MAD], refers to nuclear attacks upon an adversary's cities and industries, while counterforce targeting refers to attacks upon an enemy's military — usually nuclear — forces. In fact, however, the countervalue doctrines that have informed United States and Soviet nuclear strategy over the years always have included a counterforce component. The central concern, once again, is the ultimate purpose for which the particular weapon is intended. Whereas the essential purpose of counterforce targeting is to threaten military *defeat* (or "denial") as a deterrent to potential aggression or escalation of hostilities, the primary aim of countervalue targeting is to threaten massive *punishment* by way of societal destruction.[132]

Now, with these clarifications in mind, and following loosely the analytic outline set forth above,[133] let us investigate whether, and if so to what extent, the humanitarian laws of war, at least as reflected in the prohibitory rules defined in Part II,[134] may be said to interdict the use of nuclear weapons in specific conflict situations. A proper appreciation of any prescription whether explicitly or implicitly formulated, cannot be had without a conscious understanding of the "real world" contexts within which it has to function.

A.   First Defensive Use of Nuclear Weapons

1.   Strategic Warfare: Countervalue Targeting

As noted above,[135] nuclear weapons designed for countervalue or city-killing purposes tend to be of the strategic class, with known yields of deployed warheads averaging somewhere between two to three times and 1500 times the firepower of the bombs dropped on Hiroshima and Nagasaki. Further, they are "dirty" bombs, capable of producing severe initial nuclear radiation, spatially and temporally dispersed residual radiation (or radioactive fallout), and, in addition, wide-ranging electromagnetic pulse [EMP] effects. Furthermore, their CEP ["circular error probable"] currently averages somewhere between 0.3 to 2.5 kilometers — which is to say that they lack pinpoint

---

[132] *Ibid.*, 100 (discussing the punishment and denial aspects of deterrence).

[133] See *supra*, text following note 126.

[134] See *supra*, Part II(A).

[135] See *supra*, note 129 and accompanying text.

accuracy. Thus, in addition to violating the *Rule 6* prohibition against chemical, biological and "analogous" means of warfare,[136] their capacity for violating all the other prohibitory rules on a truly awesome scale, seems self-evident.[137]

However, when evaluating this defensive option, what really matters, in a certain sense, is less the fact that nuclear weapons would violate one or another of the prohibitory rules mentioned, than the fact that massive nuclear warfare, as a defensive measure, would be unleashed most probably in response to a conventional warfare provocation.[138] By any rational standard, this would constitute a gross violation of the cardinal principle of proportionality. Assuming even the so-called "worst case" scenario — *e.g.*, a Soviet conventional assault against Western Europe or the oilfields of the Middle East — where is the military necessity in incinerating entire urban populations, defiling the territory of neighboring and distant neutral countries, and ravaging the natural environment for generations to come simply for the purpose of containing or repelling a conventional attack? Surely a failure to provide for an adequate conventional defense or to develop alternative energy sources does not excuse these probable results. If so, then we are witness to the demise of Nuremberg, the triumph of *Kriegsraison*, the virtual repudiation of the humanitarian rules of armed conflict in at least large-scale warfare. The very meaning of "proportionality" becomes lost, and we come dangerously close to condoning the crime of genocide, that is, a military campaign directed more towards the extinction of the enemy than towards the winning of a battle or conflict.[139]

---

[136] See *supra*, text following note 59.

[137] For the probable effects, including economic and environmental effects, see *Report of the Secretary-General*, *supra*, note 21, ch. 4; see also Glasstone & Dolan, *supra*, note 21, *passim*; A. Katz, *Life After Nuclear War* [:] *The Economic and Social Impacts of Nuclear Attacks on the United States* (1982), *passim*; J. Schell, *The Fate of the Earth* (1982), ch. 1; S. Zuckerman, *Nuclear Illusion and Reality* (1982), ch. 2.

[138] One assumes, I hope not naively, that a countervalue first strike would not be unleashed for any lesser provocation, for then certainly the principle of proportionality would be violated. For related comment, see *infra*, note 150 and accompanying text.

[139] Genocide, the crime of *deliberately* bringing about the destruction, in whole or in part, of a national, ethnic, racial, or religious group as such, could well be listed among the prohibitory rules considered *supra*, Part II(A). Punished at Nuremberg, it since has become institutionalized in the *Convention on the Prevention and Punishment of the Crime of Genocide*, 78 U.N.T.S. 277 (adopted by the U.N. General Assembly 9 December 1948; entered into force 12 January 1951). China and the United States, as is well known, are alone among the major powers not to have become parties to the *Convention*. But it is accepted generally today that the prohibition has become a matter of customary international law. It does not follow, however, that every large-scale use of the military instrument constitutes genocide. The critical point is the matter of intent.

It is, of course, conceivable that a city-killing first strike might be in response to a perceived but as yet unexecuted threat of nuclear attack — an imminent one, we must assume. Indeed, it is conceivable that the threatened attack would be equivalent in character. Howevermuch the anticipatory or preemptive strike would run afoul of the rules against aggravated and indiscriminate suffering (*Rules 1* and *2* above),[140] it still might be argued to meet the test of proportionality in some rough way. But the argument, I think, would be deceptive. A preemptive strike of the sort contemplated here, particularly if surface bursts are involved, still would inflict large-scale collateral harms beyond the place and moment of immediate conflict.[141] In addition to violating the *Rule 6* ban on chemical, biological and "analogous" weapons,[142] it would likely violate also the minimal safeguards extended to internationally protected persons (*Rules 2* and *4*),[143] nonparticipating neutral States (*Rule 5*),[144] the natural environment (*Rule 3*),[145] and consequently by these excesses would strain severely the principle of proportionality. Moreover, to the extent that U.N. *Charter* art. 51 admonishes recourse to minimally coercive and nonviolent modes of conflict resolution, including resort to the collective conciliation functions of the United Nations,[146] a preemptive strike probably would disproportionately violate *Rules 1* and *2* as well. After all, the threat still would be unexecuted. In any event, the principle of proportionality surely would require that the burden of policy proof be shouldered by those who would unleash the preemptive countervalue strike, and that burden would be a heavy one considering the massive and extended deprivation potentially involved. It is difficult to conceive of any nuclear threat that could not be met by some lesser preemptive mode — except, of course, in the case of foreign policies lacking in creative imagination and insensitive to the magnitude of the human values at stake.

2.   Strategic Warfare: Counterforce Targeting

Involving, as we have seen, the same strategic weapons with the same odious capabilities relied upon for countervalue targeting,[147] a counterforce first strike, like a countervalue first strike, faces the test of proportionality

---

[140] See *supra*, text following notes 41 and 45.

[141] See *Report of the Secretary-General*, *supra*, note 21, ch. 4.

[142] See *supra*, text following note 59.

[143] See *supra*, text following notes 45 and 53.

[144] See *supra*, text following note 57.

[145] See *supra*, text following note 49.

[146] *Cf.*, Feinrider, *International Law as the Law of the Land: Another Constitutional Constraint on Use of Nuclear Weapons* (1982) 7 Nova L.J. 103 (No. 1). For the text of art. 51, see *supra*, note 19.

[147] See *supra*, text following note 128.

with many presumptions against it. Even if intended for essentially military targets alone, it still would have far-reaching EMP and radiation effects that could not be confined to the place and moment of immediate confrontation, thus violating not only the *Rule 6* ban on chemical, biological and "analogous" weapons,[148] but the rights of great numbers of innocent and neutral — including distant — third parties, both living and unborn.[149] And howevermuch actually restricted to essentially military targets, a counterforce first strike still would consist of a massive nuclear retort to what likely would be only a conventional war provocation.[150]

It may be conceded that, because counterforce strategy is a policy of targeting the military, especially nuclear, forces rather than the cities of the other side, there is at least surface plausibility in the argument that a counterforce first strike would not trample unduly upon the *Rule 2* prohibition against indiscriminate injury to noncombatant persons and property.[151] Indeed, a lure of counterforce doctrine is that it makes nuclear weapons more credible as instruments of war in part because, at least theoretically, it is less subject to the legal and moral criticisms that can be levelled against countervalue doctrine. The plausibility of this argument vanishes quickly, however, when it is matched against the available data. An oft-cited Office of Technology Assessment study published in 1979, for example, quotes United States Government studies indicating that between two million and twenty million Americans would be killed within thirty days after a counter-silo attack on United States ICBM sites, due mainly to early radiation fallout from likely surface bursts.[152] The test of proportionality is thus greatly strained once again.

Indeed, when all the dynamics of an actual counterforce first strike are taken into account, the test of proportionality seems to be abrogated completely, particularly when the opposing sides are both nuclear powers, as would likely be the case. In the first place, unless the counterforce attack were an all-out "disarming first strike" aimed at the total incapacitation of the enemy's nuclear forces, which is a highly unlikely achievement, it would virtually guarantee retaliation entailing greater and more widespread devastation and suffering. Second, notwithstanding voguish theories of "intra-war

---

[148] See *supra*, text following note 59.

[149] See *supra*, text following notes 45, 53 and 57.

[150] One assumes, again I hope not naively, that a counterforce first strike would not be the consequence of any lesser provocation, for then without any doubt, the principle of proportionality would be breached. For related comment, see *supra*, note 138 and accompanying text.

[151] For pertinent discussion, see *supra*, text following note 45.

[152] Congress of the United States, Office of Technology Assessment, *The Effects of Nuclear War* (1979) 84.

bargaining", "intra-war deterrence" and "controlled escalation", it is highly improbable that the opposing sides would or could restrict themselves to fighting a "limited" rather than "total" nuclear war, as if somehow governed by the rules of the Marquess of Queensbury.[153] Finally, it seems fairly clear that counterforce targeting, involving missiles that never have been tested over their expected wartime trajectories, is neither as accurate nor as reliable as publicly claimed.[154]

Again, however, it remains to be asked whether different conclusions might not obtain in the case of an anticipatory counterforce first strike as distinguished from an initiating one. Such a strike, designed to preempt, say, an imminent devastation of equivalent or greater dimension, conceivably could meet the test of proportionality precisely because it would be directed, pursuant to counterforce doctrine, against only military targets. Particularly might this be the case where the statistical probability of accurate warhead delivery would be fairly high, that is, where the CEP of the preemptive strike would be fairly low (within 100-200 meters by current standards). This logic, however, is based on a calculation of statistical probability, and probabilities, let us be clear, are not certainties. In addition, it suffers from all the disabilities concerning proportionality that we noted in connection with both the preemptive countervalue strike and the initiating counterforce strike. Again, it is reasonable to conclude that the test of proportionality would not be met or that, at the very least, those who would unleash the preemptive counterforce strike would have the burden of proving otherwise.

3.   Tactical Warfare: Theater/Battlefield Targeting

As noted earlier,[155] there is no clear borderline between so-called "tactical" and so-called "strategic" nuclear weapons, with the yields and consequent effects of the former commonly rising to the level and impact of the latter. The

---

[153] See *Report of the Secretary-General, supra,* note 21, 71-6. Write Krass & Smith, *supra,* note 129, 16:

> [I]t is integral to the idea of limited nuclear warfare, and to the currently fashionable concept of "escalation dominance," that we can mount and dismount the tiger at will. There is a surface plausibility in the idea that since each side will be concerned to limit the damage to itself, both sides will be interested in fighting a limited nuclear war rather than a total war. But this plausibility vanishes once one tries to identify the moment at which one side would decide to leave the other with the final say, the final shot. And if it therefore seems likely that neither side will wish to pull out leaving the other side with the "advantage," then why should either side bother with limited war at all? It is surely more likely that both sides would conclude that, since the most likely outcome is a non-limited war, the best option is to make an all-out strike immediately.

[154] See, *e.g.,* Cockburn & Cockburn, *The Myth of Missile Accuracy,* New York Rev. of Books (20 November 1980) 40.

[155] See *supra,* text following note 128.

public debates and demonstrations in Europe since late 1979, which have related primarily to intermediate-range weapons and weapons systems such as the SS-20 ballistic missile and Backfire bomber on the WTO [Warsaw Pact] side and the planned deployment of Tomahawk ground-launched cruise missiles and Pershing II ballistic missiles on the NATO side, are vivid witness to this fact. Accordingly, it is logical to conclude that the first-strike use of tactical nuclear weapons above, say, the thirteen to twenty-two kiloton range of Hiroshima-Nagasaki, which would include almost sixty *per cent* of the estimated intermediate "theater of war" and more limited "battlefield" nuclear weapons currently deployed by the NATO and WTO countries, should be subject to the same legal judgments that attend the first-strike use of strategic nuclear weapons (both countervalue and counterforce). The first-strike use of such high-yield tactical nuclear weapons, like the first-strike use of their strategic (particularly counterforce) equivalents would appear to violate in the same way and to similar degree, separately and in combination, not only all or most of the humanitarian rules of armed conflict considered in Part II, but also the fundamental principle of proportionality that mediates among them.

But what of tactical nuclear weapons below the thirteen to twenty-two kiloton range of Hiroshima-Nagasaki? Would the first-strike use of such lower yield weapons, particularly those in the one to two kiloton or sub-kiloton range, equally violate the prohibitory rules discussed above? Would such a strike equally violate the principle of proportionality on the grounds that, like its strategic counterparts, it probably would be in response to a conventional warfare provocation — indeed, in likely contrast to its strategic counterparts, probably in response to a conventional warfare provocation by a *non-nuclear* adversary? By common definitional agreement, it will be recalled, the term "tactical nuclear weapons" is intended generally to refer to those weapons systems that are designed or are available for use against essentially military targets in so-called intermediate "theater of war" and more limited "battlefield" situations.[156]

In theory, to be sure, the answers to these questions must depend, *inter alia*, on the characteristics and capabilities of the tactical weapons in question. For example, though the provocation might be a conventional one or, indeed, at the hands of a non-nuclear opponent, it is possible at least to conceive of a low-yield, relatively "clean" and reasonably accurate nuclear weapon or weapon system whose tactical first defensive use actually would save lives and protect property within the meaning of military necessity — that is, without violating the principle of proportionality. This "best case" scenario, however, appears to be a limited one. Judging from the state of the

---

[156] See *supra*, text following note 129.

art as so far publicly revealed, no such option is available among existing intermediate-range theater weapons,[157] although some "progress" in this direction appears to be taking place in connection with limited-range battle-field weapons.[158] The possibility of minimizing destruction and of avoiding indiscriminate harm consonant with *Rules 1* and *2* may be present,[159] but not without substantial and, I submit, disproportionate cost in most circum-stances relative to internationally protected persons (*Rules 2* and *4*),[160] nonparticipating neutral States (*Rule 5*),[161] and the natural environment (*Rule 3*)[162] due to initial and residual radiation. Moreover, except by a process of interpretation that is uninformed by the basic assumptions of a world public order of human dignity, there is no escaping the *Rule 6* prohibition of chemical, biological and "analogous" weapons.[163] By its very nature, a fission weapon must be regarded as "dirty"; and even if a pure fusion weapon with no fission were developed, its explosion in the air and, of course, at ground-level still would result in some radioactive contamination, albeit not as extensive as when nuclear technology was less "tailored" than it is today.

But what truly is damning of the first defensive use of tactical nuclear weapons, whether in theater or battlefield operations, is less the nature of the weapons themselves than the nature of tactical nuclear warfare as a whole. In the first place, as should be apparent to all, if a military campaign defined in part by a first-strike use of nuclear weapons ever were to take place, it surely would not be limited to one or two nuclear strikes, even if only the first user were a nuclear power. Likely as not, as conservatively projected in the 1980 *Report of the Secretary-General* on nuclear weapons,[164] tactical nuclear war-fare, at least at theater level, would result in hundreds and thousands of nuclear explosions and, consequently, untold immediate and long-range, long-term collateral harms. In addition, once unleashed, the probability that tactical nuclear warfare could be kept at theater or battlefield level would be small. A crisis escalating to the first use of even relatively small nuclear

---

[157] This judgment is legitimately inferred not only from descriptions of intermediate-range theater weapons, as in *Report of the Secretary-General, supra*, note 21, 19-22 and ch. 3, but also from recent discussions of new "second generation" and "third generation" nuclear weapons and weapon systems which appear to be designed primarily, if not exclusively, for limited battlefield uses. See Rose, *supra*, note 117; and Gsponer, *supra*, note 67.

[158] See, *e.g.*, Rose, *ibid*. See also W. Van Cleave & S. Cohen, *Tactical Nuclear Weapons* (1978), ch. 4.

[159] See *supra*, text following notes 41 and 45.

[160] See *supra*, text following notes 45 and 53.

[161] See *supra*, text following note 57.

[162] See *supra*, text following note 49.

[163] See *supra*, text following note 59.

[164] See *Report of the Secretary-General, supra*, note 21, 71-6.

weapons would bring us dangerously close to the ultimate stage, a "strategic exchange", particularly if one of the two sides saw itself at a disadvantage in a drawn out "tactical exchange".[165] In sum, once out of the bottle, likely as not even the tactical nuclear genie would quite literally cause "all hell to break loose". This fact, in combination with the observations already made regarding the humanitarian rules of armed conflict, would seem by any rational analysis to run hard up against the principle of proportionality upon which the doctrine of military necessity is premised.

Thus, the first use of nuclear weapons again would appear contrary to the basic laws of war as contemporaneously understood. It need only be added that, for all the reasons noted above, but especially the last two relative to the essential uncontrollability of tactical nuclear warfare in general, this conclusion may be seen to apply to the preemptive first use of tactical nuclear weapons as well as to their initiating first use.

B.   *Second Defensive Use of Nuclear Weapons*

Would a second defensive use of nuclear weapons — one undertaken as a *claimed* "legitimate reprisal" in response to a prior attack unlawfully initiating the use of such weapons — equally or similarly violate the humanitarian rules of armed conflict? In view of the numerous qualifying reservations now attached to the 1925 *Geneva Gas Protocol*, conditioning adherence to it upon reciprocal observance of its terms,[166] it may be that the *Rule 6* ban on chemical, biological and "analogous" means of warfare would not stand in the way. On this point, concededly, there is ambiguity. But what about the *Rule 4* prohibition of reprisals that are disproportionate to legitimate belligerent objectives or that are disrespectful of persons, institutions and resources otherwise protected by the laws of war?[167] Is there ambiguity here as well?

1.   Strategic Warfare: Countervalue Targeting

In the case of a second use of nuclear weapons characterized by countervalue targeting, there is, I submit, no ambiguity. For at least three reasons, such a use may be said to violate the humanitarian rules of armed conflict as contemporaneously understood, especially *Rule 4*.

In the first place, a retaliatory city-killing attack would trample flagrantly upon guarantees extended to civilians and civilian populations, among

---

[165] *Ibid.*, 71.
[166] See *supra*, text accompanying note 62.
[167] See *supra*, text following note 53.

other internationally protected persons, by the most recent formal statements on the laws of war. Article 51(6) of 1977 Protocol I Additional to the 1949 *Geneva Conventions*, for example, is characteristically unequivocal: "Attacks against the civilian population or civilians by way of reprisals are prohibited." [168]

Second, except to destroy enemy morale, which is clearly an impermissible objective under the laws of war,[169] and the more so, one would think, when the result is to terrorize an enemy community through the infliction of literally overwhelming — perhaps irremediable — societal destruction, it is difficult to see how a retaliatory countervalue strike would serve any military necessity whatsoever. To the contrary, even if the antecedent first use were likewise countervalue destructive in character, it would appear to serve mainly the purposes of vengeance rather than the values of proportionate policing (given, at least, the present essentially rural deployment of the world's strategic forces).

Finally, if the history of belligerent reprisals is any indication, there is the near certainty that a retaliatory countervalue strike would lead not to a reduction of hostilities nor to a moderation of tactics, but to an escalatory spiral and spread of countervalue exchanges.[170] At this point, virtually everything for which the principle of proportionality is supposed to stand, including the integrity of the natural environment and the inviolability of neutral state territory,[171] would be threatened; the humanitarian rules of armed conflict would become all but obsolete.

2.   Strategic Warfare: Counterforce Targeting

The case of a second counterforce use of nuclear weapons is not so clear-cut. Because such a response would be directed, pursuant to counterforce doctrine, solely against the military — especially nuclear — forces of the first user, and because the laws of war do not invite national suicide, there is room to contend that such a strike would be compatible with *Rule 4* regarding disproportionate reprisals and the other humanitarian rules of armed conflict, provided that it not be patently excessive relative to the antecedent attack and the goal of law compliance or nonrecurrence. Indeed,

---

[168] 1977 Geneva Protocol I Additional, *supra*, note 41, art. 51(6).

[169] See, *e.g.*, McDougal & Feliciano, *supra*, note 39, 652-9.

[170] See F. Kalshoven, *Belligerent Reprisals* (1971) 375-8; N. Onuf, *Reprisals: Rituals, Rules, Rationales* (1974) 22 (Princeton University Center of International Studies Research Monograph No. 42).

[171] See *supra*, text following notes 49 and 57.

paradoxical though it may seem, it might even be argued that, to ensure a minimum destruction of cherished values (preferably the values of freedom and equality), a nuclear counter-strike of this kind would be required. On the other hand, bearing in mind the characteristics and capabilities of the weapons and weapon systems that constitute today's counterforce arsenals, there remains the problem of reconciling the rights of States not party to the conflict and of persons and property expressly shielded by the law of reprisals and the more general laws of war. "Clean bombs" and "surgical strikes", especially in relation to strategic warfare, exist more in the minds of military planners than they do in reality. Additionally, there is the customary injunction that reprisals be taken only as measures of last resort. In the context of nuclear war, this injunction is all the more imperative.

Thus, the permissibility of a counterforce second strike under the humanitarian rules of armed conflict may be regarded as ambiguous. Of course, because of the essentially uncontrollable dangers involved, one must assume that such a second use, if permissible, would be authorized only in response to an antecedent attack of equivalent or greater proportion, that is, a prior counterforce or countervalue attack. But even then, because of the unrefined nature of the weaponry involved and the likelihood of crisis escalation and spread, the burden of policy proof would again weigh heavily on those who would retaliate in this manner. Let us be candid. As Roger Fisher has written, "honestly, each of us would prefer to have our children in Havana, Belgrade, Beijing, Warsaw, or Leningrad today than in Hiroshima or Nagasaki when the nuclear bombs went off".[172]

3.   Tactical Warfare: Theater/Battlefield Targeting

If there is a case to be made for a use of nuclear weapons that is consistent with the humanitarian rules of warfare, it is here, in respect of the second use of tactical nuclear weapons. Arguably, a second retaliatory use of a low-yield, "clean" and reasonably accurate intermediate- or limited-range nuclear weapon directed only at a military target could be said to meet the requirements of proportionality (or military necessity) that govern the law of reprisals as presently understood. When making the case beyond this highly circumscribed option, however, at least two major complexities arise. First, to the extent that a retaliatory second use would involve theater or battlefield weapons around or above the thirteen to twenty-two kiloton range of Hiroshi-

---

[172] Fisher, "Getting to 'Yes' in the Nuclear Age" in B. Weston, ed., *Toward Nuclear Disarmament and Global Security: A Search for Alternatives* (forthcoming from Westview Press in Autumn 1983).

ma-Nagasaki, there is the problem of having to deal with all the ambiguities and qualifications noted in connection with a second counterforce use of nuclear weapons. And second, regarding all tactical nuclear weapons, including those in the one to two kiloton or sub-kiloton range, there is the problem of establishing upper limits on the number of retaliatory strikes that could be launched at any time without doing violence either to the rights of neutral States (*Rule 5*) [173] and internationally protected persons (*Rules 2* and *4*) [174] or, more generally, to the principle of proportionality. In other words, except in the narrowest of circumstances, the unrefined and unpredictable nature of nuclear weapons and weapon systems continues to call into question the legality of their second use even in tactical warfare. Add to this the extreme dangers that would attend a likely escalatory spiral once the process of reprisal and counter-reprisal were set into motion, and again the burden of proving that this retaliatory approach should be favored over other means of deterring the enemy becomes very heavy.

C.   *Threat of First or Second Defensive Use*

If a given use of nuclear weapons is properly judged to be contrary to the humanitarian rules of armed conflict, then logically any threat of such use — including not only an ostentatious brandishing of arms (such as a menacing "demonstration burst"), but also their research and development, manufacture, stockpiling, and deployment — should be considered contrary to the humanitarian rules of armed conflict as well. In view of our preceding discussion, the threat of a strategic first strike, a tactical first strike, a second countervalue strike, and possibly also a second counterforce strike as well as most tactical second strikes would fit this logic.

A distinct problem with this thesis, however, is that nothing in the traditional rules of warfare prohibits the preparation, in contrast to the actual use of weapons and weapon systems. Also, it flies in the face of the deterrence doctrines which are said to have kept the peace, at least between the superpowers, for the last thirty-odd years — a conflict of major significance because, to be minimally credible, a policy of deterrence requires the research and development, manufacture, stockpiling, and deployment of the weapons upon which it is premised. It is true that the nuclear deterrence policies currently practised between the superpowers especially may be criticized in numerous ways: for involving unacceptably high risks; for building upon an inherently unstable balance; for terrorizing populations and holding them

---

[173] See *supra*, text following note 57.
[174] See *supra*, text following notes 45 and 53.

hostage as a consequence; for detracting from acceptable solutions or alternatives in case of the failure of deterrence; and so forth. But because of the
widespread perception, however much open to debate, that the prevention of
widespread conflict rests on nuclear deterrence and that this system is, in turn,
dependent on credible nuclear threat, it would be difficult to conclude that
measures short of actual use would violate the humanitarian rules of armed
conflict as presently understood. Not even U.N. General Assembly Resolutions 1653 or 2936 which declare, respectively, the use of nuclear weapons "a
crime against mankind and civilization" [175] and a matter of "permanent
prohibition", [176] seek to outlaw measures short of actual use.

Nevertheless, to facilitate a comprehensive outlook, at least three qualifying observations should be borne in mind. First, a number of pathbreaking
treaties do specifically prohibit nuclear weapons preparations short of actual
combat use: the 1959 *Antarctic Treaty*, [177] the 1963 *Partial Test Ban Treaty*, [178]
the 1967 *Treaty of Tlatelolco*, [179] the 1967 *Outer Space Treaty*, [180] the 1971
Seabed Arms Control Treaty, [181] and the 1979 *Draft Moon Treaty*. [182] Second,
where "demonstration bursts" or equivalent menacing tactics are involved,
there is always the possibility of violating the *Rule 6* ban on chemical,
biological and "analogous" weapons [183] and, in addition, of breaching the
other humanitarian rules of armed conflict designed to safeguard internationally protected persons, the natural environment and neutral States. [184]
Finally, because of the high risks and monumental dangers involved, any
nuclear weapons measure short of actual use, but especially those of particularly ostentatious or provocative nature, must be taken with extreme caution.
The history of war is riddled with well-meaning doctrines gone out of control,
and the possibilities of war increase in direct proportion to the effectiveness of
the instruments of war we adopt. It is, no doubt, this viewpoint that lies
behind art. 36 of 1977 Geneva Protocol I Additional to the 1949 *Geneva*

---

[175] *Declaration on the Prohibition of the Use of Nuclear and Thermo-nuclear Weapons*,
supra, note 34, para. 1(d).

[176] *Declaration on the Non-use of Force in International Relations and Permanent Prohibition of the Use of Nuclear Weapons*, *supra*, note 37, para. 1.

[177] *Supra*, note 32.

[178] *Supra*, note 33.

[179] *Supra*, note 32, art. 1.

[180] *Supra*, note 32, art. IV.

[181] *Supra*, note 32, art. I.

[182] *Draft Agreement Governing the Activities of States on the Moon and Other Celestial
Bodies* in *Report of the Committee on the Peaceful Uses of Outer Space*, 34 U.N. GAOR,
Supp. (No. 20) 33, U.N. Doc. A/34/20 Annex II (1979), art. III.

[183] See *supra*, text following note 59.

[184] See *supra*, text following notes 45, 49, 53 and 57.

Conventions: "In the study, development, acquisition or adoption of a new weapon, means or method of warfare, a High Contracting Party is under an obligation to determine whether if employment would, in some or all circumstances, be prohibited by this Protocol or any other rule of international law applicable to the High Contracting Party." [185]

* * *

In summary, while no treaty or treaty provision specifically forbids nuclear warfare *per se*, except in certain essentially isolated whereabouts, almost every use to which nuclear weapons might be put, most notably the standard strategic and theater-level options which dominate United States and Soviet nuclear policy, appear to violate one or more of the laws of war that serve to make up the contemporary humanitarian law of armed conflict, in particular the cardinal principle of proportionality. Whatever legal license is afforded to the development and use of nuclear weapons is restricted to the following:

a)   essentially cautious, long-term preparations for preventing or deterring nuclear war, short of provocative "sabre-rattling" activities;

b)   very limited tactical — mainly battlefield — warfare utilizing low-yield, "clean" and reasonably accurate nuclear weapons for second use, retaliatory purposes only; and

c)   possibly, *but not unambiguously* (until as yet undeveloped technological refinements are achieved), an extremely limited counterforce strike in strategic and theater-level settings for second use retaliatory purposes only.

In short, applying the humanitarian rules of armed conflict to different nuclear weapons options or uses tends to prove rather than disprove the illegality of these weapons generally. And when one adds to this the conclusion at Nuremberg that the extermination of a civilian population in whole or in part is a "crime against humanity",[186] plus the spirit if not also the letter of the 1948 *Convention on the Prevention and Punishment of the Crime of Genocide*,[187] then a presumption of illegality and a commensurate heavy burden of contrary proof relative to the use of nuclear weapons on *any* extended or large-scale basis seems beyond peradventure.

---

[185] 1977 Geneva Protocol I Additional, *supra*, note 41, art. 36.

[186] In the words of the *Charter*, *supra*, note 48.

[187] *Supra*, note 139.

Conclusion

In this essay, two dominant conclusions have been established: first, that the humanitarian rules of armed conflict are not obsolete, that they *do* "count" as law, when it comes to nuclear weapons and warfare; and second, that this body of law restricts severely the use of nuclear weapons and weapon systems in most instances, above all in relation to their first defensive use, and to substantial degree in respect of their second defensive use as well. To be sure, ambiguities exist here and there, especially in the case of limited tactical uses where the venerable test of proportionality must struggle between increasingly "tailored" military technologies and the human propensity for escalatory violence. But, overall, the law opposes resort to these instruments of death, especially in relation to the standard strategic and tactical options which dominate United States and Soviet nuclear policy, and to argue otherwise on the basis of the arguable permissibility of some essentially restricted use is to engage in sheer sophistry. Just as international law came to repeal the African slave trade in the nineteenth century, so now on balance has it come to repeal the legitimacy of nuclear weapons and warfare. Of course, it would be naive to expect that the law alone can make the progressive difference, particularly when, as here, it touches sensitively upon prevailing notions of national security. But more and more the strategic planners among the nuclear weapon States especially — the defense policy-makers, the military operators, the laboratories of military research and development, even the arms controllers — have got to change their modes of thinking. More and more they must come to see the essential incompatibility of nuclear weapons with the core precepts of international law. More and more they must be made to understand that the bell tolls for us all.

10.
International Law, Nuclear Weapons, Arms Control and Disarmament

B.V.A. Röling*

Nuclear weapons have—or rather should have—an impact on almost every field of international relations and international law. Physicists have been aware of this from the very moment it was clear that atomic energy could be used as a weapon. Arthur Holly Compton—to mention one—wrote: "That man shall learn humanity is the condition of survival in the atomic age. He cannot live with the new forces at his disposal without making important adjustments."[1]

In a Memorial Lecture, given at Washington University in honor of Arthur Compton, I tried to spell out some of these necessary adjustments: the limitation of national sovereignty; the ceiling of affluence; a New International Economic Order; the restriction of individual and state liberty in the pursuit of economic prosperity; and, no less important, the limitation of the national freedom of the employment and possession of arms.[2]

The nuclear impact on international law is very broad indeed, too broad to be dealt with in this essay. I will restrict my observations to three fields of international law directly related with nuclear weapons: the *jus ad bellum,* the *jus in bello*, and the international law of arms control and disarmament.

I.

The *jus ad bellum* concerns the right of a state to start war. The right of a sovereign state to use its armed power in promotion or defense of its interests was recognized by positive international law early in this century. Vague notions concerning the doctrine of just war did exist, but it was exclusively the state itself which decided whether it was entitled to go to war.

* Professor Emeritus of International Law and Polemology, University of Groningen; former Netherlands Judge on the International Military Tribunal for the Far East, Tokyo, 1946-48.

The legal position was clearly expressed in article 2 of the 1907 Hague Convention for the Pacific Settlement of International Disputes:

> In case of serious disagreement or dispute, before an appeal to arms, the contracting powers agree to have recourse, as far as circumstances allow, to the good offices or mediation of one or more friendly powers.[3]

War was considered the *ultima ratio*. In a clear case of inferior power the weaker state would give in without fighting, according to the historian Blainey,[4] rather than fight and lose.

National military power formerly was used for acquisitive and for protective purposes, for aggression and for defense. During the first half of our century anti-war sentiments grew. After the First World War the League of Nations declared war to be "a matter of concern" to the whole League. The League's Covenant, however, did not prohibit war. In the Pact of Paris, the Kellogg-Briand Pact of 1928,[5] the parties condemned resort to war and renounced it as an instrument of national policy. The right of self-defense in case of a violation of interests, however, was still recognized and the state itself could determine whether a situation entitled it to go to war in self-defense.

In the U.N. Charter, adopted after the Second World War, article 2(4) totally prohibits the launching of war, while the right to use armed power in self-defense is restricted in article 51 to cases of armed attack "until the Security Council has taken measures necessary to maintain peace and security." A restricted interpretation of the "inherent right" of self-defense was reaffirmed in the Definition of Aggression adopted in 1974, the most important part of which is article 5: "No consideration of whatever nature, whether political, economic, military or otherwise, may serve as a justification of aggression."[6]

This interpretation of the U.N. Charter is not universally accepted. Many scholars maintain that armed defense is permitted as well in cases of threat to, or violation of, vital interests by non-military means. Ideological change may lead to a change of alliances; economic measures or developments in one country may hurt considerable economic interests in other parts of the world. For the industrialized world the existing economic interdependence implies that a considerable part of the needed raw materials must be imported. In short: many scholars and many governments consider not only the provision of "military security," but also of "ideological and economic security," a legitimate function of national armed power.

This is not the place to elaborate on the legal position as formulated by the U.N. Charter. One of the most capable contenders of the above interpretation is Julius Stone.[7] Stone's central theme is that, given the possibility of alternative exegetical approaches to article 2(4) and its related provisions, either approach being defensible on purely textual grounds, we must choose between the possible interpretations in the light of their "consequences" and "their relation to policy and wisdom."

In this regard the "consequences" of nuclear weapons are vital. Considering our political and economic interdependence, every war is more than ever a matter of concern for all mankind. For every war eventually may involve nuclear forces, with the result that a local war could escalate into a world war. This risk is so overwhelming that it adds a new motivation to the existing arguments for strict interpretation of article 2(4) of the U.N. Charter.

Nuclear weapons cannot be used without the unbearable risk of mutual annihilation. Weapons have become unusable between nuclear powers because the use of atomic arms may mean total mutual destruction. One could say: all weapons have become unusable between nuclear powers because every war brings the risk of escalating into nuclear war.

Some pacifists conclude that we must discard these weapons as immoral, inhuman, and too dangerous: "Abolish them altogether, unilaterally, if need be."

However, if one party disarms, the weapons of the opponent become usable once more, for the fear of retaliation no longer exists. The nation-at-arms now has an absolute superiority of force. This is an unacceptable situation. History teaches us that states are inclined to misbehave in proportion to their power, hence the need to possess nuclear arms in order to maintain a power balance and ensure that the opponent's weapons remain unusable.

This is the real weapon dilemma: nuclear arms are unusable, but for the time being indispensable. We know that defense against them is impossible and that their use will lead to mutual total destruction. The only *reasonable* function of armed power in the atomic age clearly is one of deterrence through the prospect of resistance and retaliation in case of attack, to prevent arms being employed, that is, to preserve peace. Such is the status quo, in which there will not be any change until an agreement on mutual arms reduction can be negotiated.

It is also the only *legitimate* function of national arms to provide military security, that is to say, to create a situation in which the state has to fear neither the threat, nor the use of force. When we speak of the function of military power as the guarantee of peace and security, we have in mind the situation in which the state need not fear an attack, nor has to make unreasonable concessions to prevent attack. "Peace and security" means peace and independence.

In short: the nuclear situation of mutual assured destruction (MAD) adds a strong argument in favor of the absolute prohibition of starting war.

That article 2(4) has often been violated is undeniable. In various parts of the world armed force has been used in response to ideological developments unwelcome to one or the other of the "superpowers": Hungary,

Cuba, Guatemala, Czechoslovakia, Vietnam, and Afghanistan are among
the examples. Armed force has been used too in connection with non-
violent infringements on economic interests, as in response to the
nationalization of the Suez Canal Company in 1956. Recently the United
States created the "Rapid Deployment Forces" to be used in various parts
of the world in cases where its economic interests (for example, the
procurement of raw materials) should appear to be threatened.[8]

In the legal field too, national policy has tended to undermine the
authority of the United Nations ground rule. The "Declaration of the States
Parties to the Warsaw Treaty" of May 1980[9] proposed to initiate without
delay businesslike negotiations on the "conclusion of a world treaty on the
non-use of force." The Warsaw Pact Organization proposed on January 5,
1983, to conclude a non-aggression pact between NATO and WPO. One
wonders about the relevance of such treaties, for the parties should
recognize that a treaty on the non-use of force already exists, the most
important and high-ranking treaty of all: the United Nations Charter! And
in this context, what is one to make of the 1973 U.S.-U.S.S.R. Agreement
on the Prevention of Nuclear War,[10] which contains the provision that each
Party will refrain from the threat or use of force against the other Party,
against the Allies of the other Party and against other countries, in
circumstances in which international peace and security may be endangered? As if the threat or use of force were permissible in cases in which
only the national peace and security of the victim was endangered! As if a
general prohibition of force did not already exist in the United Nations
Charter!

The thesis defended in this article maintains that the emergence of nuclear
weapons supports the legal arguments that favor a strengthening of a total
prohibition of war. The emergence of nuclear weapons also promoted the
important General Assembly resolution extending the prohibition of war to
include all nations: the "Declaration on Principles of International Law
Concerning Friendly Relations and Cooperation Among States in Accordance with the Charter of the United Nations."[11] Article 2(6) of the U.N.
Charter formulated a political decision that "[t]he Organization shall
ensure that states which are not Members of the United Nations act in
accordance with [its] principles so far as may be necessary for the maintenance of international peace and security." Non-members now are legally
bound by the existing prohibition of war.

One can even reason that the prohibition of war goes beyond all states
and includes "peoples" as well, even though no official document has
explicitly formulated this point. The license to use force given to those
"peoples" engaged in the struggle for self-determination against colonialism and apartheid, as provided in several General Assembly resolutions,
can only be understood on the assumption that "peoples" in other
situations, such as those of economic exploitation or neo-colonialism, do
not have that right.[12]

II.

A second chapter of international law connected directly to nuclear weapons concerns the law of armed conflict, the *jus in bello* which poses restrictions on the acts of violence justified in case of war. The question is whether international law prohibits, through one of its restrictions, the employment of nuclear arms. Opinions differ on this. According to some jurists their use is already prohibited by international law. Ideas are divided as well, on the question whether such a prohibition is desirable. The answer to that depends on one's conception about the deterrent character of nuclear weapons; that is, whether it is feasible that they might help to ensure peace. Some believe that atomic arms are needed to maintain peace as long as the opponent has superior conventional strength. In NATO this last persuasion finds broad support. Finally there are the jurists who conclude that the use of nuclear arms is not yet prohibited by international law, but that such a prohibition should ardently be sought. This may then imply a general ban that does not preclude a limited employment of nuclear weapons as a "reprisal in kind," or a ban on "first use" which in case of a violation sanctions the unrestricted use of atomic arms in response.

Atomic weapons fall in the category of "dubious weapons,"[13] weapons that clearly are in conflict with the principles accepted in the laws of armed conflict but that are not explicitly prohibited in a general treaty. This dubious character poses the question whether or not these weapons can be considered as already prohibited by the principles of the laws of war, or by resolutions of the General Assembly of the U.N. followed by the practice of some states.

War is an exceptional state of law in which destruction and killing are legally permitted, albeit with restrictions. Hugo Grotius taught that *"in bello omnia licere quae necessaria sunt ad finem belli."*[14] The present *jus in bello* includes the negative aspect of this principle—that is: an act of violence that does not further the aim of war is not permitted. This prohibition of unnecessary suffering is perhaps the only undisputed rule of warfare. The military, too, readily agree to this rule. But opinions differ on which acts are necessary in view of their value for victory or the prevention of defeat. If "coercive warfare" is considered the easiest way to victory—making the war painful beyond endurance to the civilian population in order to compel the government to capitulate—an attack on the civilian population is not viewed as leading to "superfluous suffering." We all know that "coercive warfare" was practiced in World War II, culminating in the atomic bombs dropped on Hiroshima and Nagasaki.[15]

Present international law, however, does accept that everything *ad finem belli* is legal. There are some restrictions. In former times these were based on principles of Christianity, later, on principles of civilization, and at present chiefly on principles of humanity.[16]

The main thrust toward the humanization of warfare was provided by

Henri Dunant. His book *Souvenirs de Solferino* led not only to the establishment of the Red Cross but also to the Conference of Saint Petersburg (1868). It was agreed upon, then, that in principle warfare should be restricted in deference to the laws of civilization and humanity. On that ground some weapons were outlawed and the parties decided to reserve the right, whenever scientific developments were leading toward improvements in armaments "to come to an understanding . . . in order to maintain the principles which they have established, and to conciliate the necessities of war with the laws of humanity." The Geneva Protocol of 1925,[17] concerning the prohibition of the use of biological and chemical weapons, is a clear example of the rejection of weapons that might have great military advantage. These weapons were considered to be so repugnant that the "laws of humanity" prevailed over the "necessities of war."

As the laws of warfare gradually matured from the Hague Conventions of 1899[18] and 1907,[19] to the Red Cross Convention of 1929,[20] Red Cross Conventions of 1949,[21] Protocols Additional I and II of 1977,[22] and the Convention of 1981,[23] the distinction between the civilian population and the military was further elaborated. Respect for the civilian population broadened, and the prohibition on inflicting "unnecessary suffering" expanded to a prohibition on inflicting "disproportionate suffering."

Apart from limitations based on the principles of civilization and humanity, the origin of some limitations of warfare can be traced back to a prohibition of what Kant described as *"sich solcher heimtückischen Mittel zu bedienen, die das Vertrauen, welches zu künftiger Gründung eines dauerhaften Friedens erforderlich ist, vernichten würden."*[24] This principle was adopted in the 1863 Lieber Instructions: Article 16 states that "the military necessity does not include any act of hostility which makes the return to peace unnecessarily difficult."[25]

It is prohibited, then, to perform actions that exclude or obstruct the chances of re-establishment of peaceful relations. While the vagueness of this criterion makes it virtually unfit for direct application, its significance lies in the fact that it has led to the formulation of specific concrete limitations on the use of force. It underlies such limitations as the prohibition "to kill or wound treacherously individuals belonging to the hostile nation or army,"[26] or to misuse the white flag of truce or the uniform of the enemy.[27]

It is, of course, difficult to make a clear distinction between legitimate "ruses of war" and forbidden "acts of treachery." The decisive criterion is given in Protocol I of 1977: acts of perfidy are defined as "[a]cts inviting the confidence of the adversary to lead him to believe that he is entitled to, or is obliged to accord, protection under the rules of international law applicable in armed conflict, with intent to betray that confidence."[28]

This principle of restriction on violence based on the demands of peace has led to the prohibition of certain weapons as some kind of booby trap which would diminish the mutual confidence needed for negotiations.[29]

III.

The relevant principles that might have bearing on the legality of nuclear weapons can be summarized as follows:

1. the prohibition of weapons that cause superfluous injury (unnecessary suffering);

2. the prohibition of weapons that cause disproportionate suffering;

3. the prohibition of weapons of such a repugnant character that the laws of humanity should prevail over the necessities of war;

4. the prohibition of "blind" or indiscriminate weapons;

5. the prohibition of treacherous weapons.

Whether the principles of the prohibition to inflict "disproportionate suffering" or "excessive injury" already have found general recognition is doubtful.[30] They were introduced in the *jus in bello* by Protocol I in 1977,[31] as a supplement to the four Red Cross Conventions concerning the methods of warfare. Nevertheless, in the process of evaluating new weapons this principle of proportionality also should play a role, even as other principles, though not yet adopted into positive international law, need to be taken into consideration. The progressive evolution of international law also has to be manifest in the attitude toward new weapons. The demands of the natural law of the atomic age cannot be ignored!

The modern weapons of mass destruction have introduced a new element in the discussion of the laws of war, namely, that of survival. With the development of weapons of mass destruction—legally recognized as such in the Outer Space Treaty of 1967,[32] the Sea-Bed Treaty of 1971,[33] the Biological Weapons Convention of 1972,[34] as well as the Moon Treaty of 1979[35]—it became necessary to take into account the fact that total war could mean the end of civilization, possibly even of humanity itself.

Some reputable jurists, such as Julius Stone, for example, contend that the principle of self-preservation prevails over all other rules or principles of international law.[36] According to this view, an act of war generally held to be unlawful is no longer so if the existence of the state itself is at stake. This is the extreme example of "military necessity," where the concern is not with winning a battle but with winning the war, that is, with preserving the national existence.

As discussed above, in cases of "military necessity" the conduct of belligerents generally expressed the attitude that *necessitas non habet legem*.[37] Such conduct, however,—so rightly rejected by the courts—merely expressed the principle that for the sake of military purposes, the enemy and the enemy population may be sacrificed.

The question of whether the principle of self-preservation would also justify acts that threaten the very existence of mankind did not arise in

World War II. This is a new issue that arose with the development of biological, nuclear, thermonuclear, and geophysical weapons. Only recently has it become possible to threaten with weapons that if actually used would endanger mankind or a significant portion of it. This concerns not only the fate of the civilian populations in warring nations, but also, because of ensuing radiation or epidemic, the fate of the citizens of neutral countries, perhaps even the fate of future generations.

Related to this issue of survival is the recognition that the *environment* in which man lives deserves the concern of the whole community. The U.N. General Assembly, aware "that the rational management of the environment is of fundamental importance for the future of mankind,"[38] in 1971 affirmed and reaffirmed "the responsibility of the international community to take action to preserve and enhance the environment."[39] Protocol I of 1977 reads: "It is prohibited to employ methods or means of warfare which are intended, or may be expected, to cause widespread, long term and severe damage to the natural environment."[40] It further obliges every party planning the development or adoption of a new weapon "to determine whether its employment would, in some or in all circumstances, be prohibited by this Protocol or by any other rule of international law applicable to the High Contracting Party."[41]

The Convention on the Prohibition of Military or any Other Hostile Use of Environmental Modification Techniques of 1977[42] prohibits the use of weapons "having widespread, long lasting or severe effects."

Responsibility for the environment is recognized in the modern international law of peace. It should be recognized in times of war as well.

Environmental protection should be one of the factors taken into account in the laws of war concerning "dubious weapons." There was little need to do so in former times. But the new weapons that have become available threaten the human environment in its integer biological existence, and technological developments may cause fundamental changes in the earth's ecology. The time is ripe to brand specific acts as international crimes of "ecocide."[43] This new situation requires compliance to the laws of war.

There is a third principle, the principle of the threshold. It is perhaps true that in a number of special cases the use of some specific "dubious" weapon does not violate the existing principles of the laws of war. An example in the case of nuclear weapons might be the use of some type of "mini-nuke" against missiles in outer space. But should the general prohibition of nuclear weapons be rejected because some particular types, in specific circumstances, might be legitimate?

A clear threshold divides conventional from nuclear weapons. If this threshold is crossed, the road is open to the use of all nuclear weapons. In other words, there is a clear danger that any use of a nuclear weapon may lead to an escalation that may end in a total nuclear war.

For the sake of humanity and even for its mere survival, this threshold between conventional and nuclear weapons must be strengthened, even though it may lead to the illegality of all nuclear weapons in all circumstances, including those in which the use in general would not otherwise be illegal.

This principle was applied in the 1925 Geneva Protocol,[44] when chemical weapons were totally banned. This threshold principle, however, never received express recognition. It would have been helpful to have acknowledged this principle: although some specific chemical or nuclear weapons might, in fact, not strictly be contrary to the principles of the law of war, only a total and unconditional prohibition could be effective.

IV.

Here I would like to comment briefly on the "Martens clause" adopted in 1907. The "Martens clause" was inserted in the preamble to the 1907 Hague Convention IV on the laws of warfare, and states that in cases not covered by the Regulations, "the inhabitants and the belligerents remain under the protection and the rule of the principles of the law of nations, as they result from the usages established among civilized peoples, from the laws of humanity, and the dictates of the public conscience."[45] Seemingly, the values generated by the "Martens clause" sources are legally significant each time existing principles of the law of warfare are interpreted or new principles of international law are considered.

It is noteworthy that the "Martens clause" was again explicitly recognized in 1949. Parties to the Geneva Conventions of 1949 were reminded that in case of renunciation of the Conventions, they still remained bound by the rule expressed in the "Martens clause." A similar provision is found in Protocol I of 1977.[46]

It should be noted that Protocol II of 1977,[47] concerning internal wars, contains a formula which, though broader in scope, is similar to the Martens clause. Here is no reference to "principles of the law of nations, as they result from the usages established among civilized peoples, from the laws of humanity, and the dictates of the public conscience"; here, the reference is directly to "the principles of humanity and to the dictates of the public conscience." This is, according to Antonio Cassese, a reference "not to law, but to prejuridical principles, to the sentiments of humanity, to public conscience."[48]

It is clear that the demands of humanity will often conflict with the demands of warfare, with the "necessities of war." Until now, specific prohibitions based on "the laws of humanity and the dictates of the public conscience" have been recognized only when not outweighed by military advantages. Thus chemical and biological weapons are forbidden but no express prohibition exists in respect to nuclear weapons.

Liddell Hart considered it absurd to prohibit chemical weapons "while adopting the use of nuclear weapons—which are weapons of mass-slaughter, and violate the lawful code of warfare on more counts than such a weapon as mustard gas, which is relatively humane."[49] It should be stressed here, however, that the favorable evaluation of chemical weapons by Liddell Hart and others[50] apparently does not take into account the effect of modern nerve gases.

V.

But does all this mean then, that the use of nuclear weapons is already prohibited by international law?

The most important arguments of those who maintain that such a prohibition already is valid are:

1. The weapons under consideration are indiscriminate. They cannot distinguish between civilian and military targets, nor between belligerents and neutrals, nor even between present generations and posterity.

2. Nuclear weapons are odious weapons; they should *a priori* be considered illegal in view of the already valid ban on less repulsive arms such as biological and chemical weapons.

3. The General Assembly of the U.N. has repeatedly, and quite rightly, expressed in resolutions that the use of nuclear arms is illegal, even criminal. The General Assembly of the U.N. declared as early as 1961 that "any State using nuclear and thermonuclear weapons is to be considered as violating the Charter of the United Nations, as acting contrary to the laws of humanity and as committing a crime against mankind and civilization."[51]

In 1966, the General Assembly solemnly declared "the permanent prohibition of the use of nuclear weapons,"[52] and in 1978 again declared any use of nuclear weapons to be a violation of the U.N. Charter and a crime against humanity.[53]

We all know that resolutions of the General Assembly are legally not fully binding, for they are only "recommendations."[54] Nevertheless, even though they may be less than law, they surely mean more than nothing at all. They formulate weak, semi-legal rules, that however only need to be followed by some states or to be recognized in some judicial decisions to become binding law. The recommendations of the League of Nations fared similarly. The tribunals of Nuremberg and Tokyo appealed to the resolutions of the League of Nations to substantiate their decision that the waging of an aggressive war was an international crime. The International Court of Justice has also recognized the law-creating capacity of General Assembly resolutions. It is therefore significant that the General Assembly time and again has declared by large majority votes that the use of nuclear weapons is illegal, even criminal.

4. The dilemmas of survival and protection of the environment confirm the reasonableness, if not the necessity, of a ban on use of nuclear weapons.

VI.

But also those who believe that nuclear arms are not yet prohibited produce strong arguments.

1. In 1868 in St. Petersburg the states recognized that the admissibility of new weapons should be considered in light of the laws of humanity relative to their military importance. The problem was "to conciliate the necessities of war with the laws of humanity." This resulted in later conferences on the ban of the employment of biological and chemical weapons (1925) and of Environmental Modification Treatment (1977). However, a similar conference on nuclear arms has yet to take place.

The International Committee of the Red Cross (ICRC) had already, in 1945, initiated efforts to arrive at such a ban, and a prohibition on the use of nuclear weapons was inserted in its "*Projet de Règles visant à protéger la population civile contre les effets de la guerre indiscriminée.*" But it was exactly this prohibition that squelched the Conference of New Delhi in 1957. Since then, the ICRC has shied away from introducing a regulation for nuclear weapons in its proposals for further humanization of the laws of war. However, the Red Cross Conference of Vienna in 1965 accepted a recommendation to the effect that the general principles of the laws of war would be applicable to nuclear arms. But in its resolution of December 19, 1968,[55] this recommendation was not adopted by the General Assembly of the U.N.[56]

The Red Cross Diplomatic Conferences that resulted in the adoption of Protocols I and II of 1977 asserted from the very start that established regulations had no bearing on nuclear warfare.

If ever a conference on atomic weapons—a conference as envisaged in St. Petersburg—were to take place, it must do more than merely weigh "the necessities of war" versus "the laws of humanity." The effects of nuclear war have gradually become quite clear.[57] Such a war must be avoided. Hence there is emphasis on the deterrent peacekeeping function of atomic weapons: deterrence through the prospect of mutual destruction. The motto of the Strategic Air Command, "Peace is our profession," contains a grain of substance. Though true that the means are repugnant—specifically the threats to annihilate population centers—it is exactly this horror that helps to discourage the waging of war. It is therefore imperative that "the laws of humanity" not only are weighed against "the necessities of war" but also against "the demands of peace."

2. The practice of states is of great importance to international law. The fact is that the nuclear powers and their allies accept the legality of the use, including first-use, of nuclear weapons. China has declared that it will never initiate the use of nuclear arms. The Soviet Union has announced to be ready to negotiate no-first-use agreements. But the nations belonging to NATO have up to now refused even to negotiate such a no-first-use pledge

because they want to retain the freedom to utilize atomic arms against a superior conventional force.

3. Some U.N. resolutions admittedly have declared the use of atomic weapons to be in conflict with international law. On the other hand, however, the General Assembly in 1978, in the first U.N. Special Session devoted to disarmament,[58] apparently assumed that such a prohibition on the use of atomic arms did not exist. In the Final Act, the General Assembly urged the nuclear powers "to pursue efforts to conclude, as appropriate, effective arrangements to assure non-nuclear-weapons States against the use or threat of use of nuclear weapons."[59] In regard to nuclear-weapon-free zones it stated:

> With respect to such zones, the nuclear weapons States are called upon to give undertakings, the modalities of which are to be negotiated with the competent authority of each zone, in particular:
>
> . . .
>
> b. to refrain from the use or threat of use of nuclear weapons against the States of the zone.[60]

What could be the meaning of such special "undertakings," which according to the above statement apparently do not yet exist, if the general obligation to refrain from a first-use of atomic weapons already did exist? The insistence on the adoption of those special obligations denies the existence of the general obligation to refrain from the first-use of atomic weapons.

4. In this connection we must point also to article 3 of Protocol II in the Treaty of Tlatelolco, where the parties agree: "not to use or threaten to use nuclear weapons against the Contracting Parties of the Treaty for the Prohibition of Nuclear Weapons in Latin America."[61] Again, what is the meaning of such a solemn commitment if a general commitment against the use of nuclear arms already has been agreed upon?

5. There are therefore serious arguments in support of the opinion— shared by the present author—that the first-use of nuclear arms is not yet prohibited by international law. However, such use must be banned. In view of the uncertain legal position—for there are arguments on both sides—and in view of the fact that important states do not recognize that such a prohibition already is contained in the existing principles and rules of the *jus in bello*, it is politically advisable to press for a multilateral treaty that entails such a prohibition. To demand such a treaty, while proposing that such a prohibition already is in effect, betrays an uncertainty of one's opinion. Campaigns among the local populations and campaigns in the General Assembly are perhaps more comprehensible and more effective if they point to the need for a prohibition that, unfortunately, up to now is not yet recognized by international law.

VII.

There is yet a third area in which international law has a direct bearing on nuclear weapons: the international law of arms control and disarmament. This concerns the restrictions of freedom of the nation-state to possess national arms forces. Traditional international law deemed this freedom to be unrestricted. If the law of arms control and disarmament becomes a reality, limits will be set to this arms freedom.

The terms arms control and disarmament are used with varying connotations. The U.N. Charter distinguishes in Article 11 between "disarmament" and "the regulation of armaments." Nobel Laureate Alva Myrdal opposes the term arms control and only wants to use the term "disarmament" as an all-embracing concept: "It covers all degrees of reduction of armaments, and it includes the preemption of options for further arms development (non-armament) as well as measures for regulating the production or use of arms quantity or quality."[62]

It seems to me that it is possible to make a reasonable distinction between arms control and disarmament. It is characteristic of the present-day weapon situation that the weapons themselves constitute a danger to peace. Thus an offensive arms build-up produces anxiety in the opponent and contributes to the continuation of the arms race and the resulting overkill. In this context also fits the possession of destabilizing weapon systems, systems which put a premium on haste. The capability to launch a surprise attack can be a temptation to use it, especially when this capability is expected to exist only temporarily. An even greater pressure is generated by a disarming first-strike capability: the capacity to wipe out almost all strategic weapons of the opponent in one strike. It puts an almost irresistible premium on haste. If both parties imagine that they have such a capability, war would be almost inevitable. He who begins wins; fear that the other may begin could lead to direct action.

In short, military power has become a danger in itself because the vulnerability of weapons of mass destruction puts a premium on haste to start the war, or, in the case of an actual war, a premium on escalating the violence.[63] The existing senseless overkill entails another special danger: excessive armed power build-up for deterrence may lead to excessive destruction in case of war.

These features of national armed postures make the weaponry dysfunctional. All arms features that contribute to war and violence should be eliminated by agreements that aim to free military power from the inherent danger that lies in the weapons themselves. Hence it is an error to let negotiations in this area depend on the good political behavior of the opponent. The "linkage" concept must not play a role in the issue of arms control negotiations.

The situation is somewhat different in regard to disarmament, that is a substantial reduction in the general level of armament. U.N. rhetoric expresses hopes for a general and complete disarmament. Linkage can be significant, however, where it concerns disarmament. Radical reduction of armed power is only feasible if both parties can rest assured that neither one is contemplating conquest or planning to use the threat of superior weapons to force other states to make concessions.

In this connection the following question becomes relevant: What function do the states assign to their national arms force?[64] We already concluded, it must be remembered, that the only reasonable and only legitimate function of national arms power is to guarantee "military security," that is, to prevent war and to defuse threats.

A further deliberation is necessary here. "Military security" means in the first place that the nation need not live in terror of the opponent's arms. One might call this "enemy-security." But the arms situation should neither be such that the threat of war is promoted by the weapons. If the military postures themselves do not promote the danger of war or the escalation of the violence, one may then speak of "weapons-security." "Military security" means a combination of "enemy-security" and "weapons-security."

If the states were willing to acknowledge the guarantee of "military security" as the sole national function of their arms power, arms control and disarmament negotiations could most likely be concluded successfully. But thirty-five years of negotiations have shown very meager results. The political will is non-existent. This is especially true where it concerns the superpowers, according to Alva Myrdal. Her book *The Game of Disarmament,* sub-titled *How the United States and Russia Run the Arms Race,*[65] shows that "a major responsibility falls upon the two superpowers, who are so blindly driven by their desire for world hegemony."[66] They act "as if there were between them a conspiracy not to permit a halt, still less a reversal, of the arms race."[67]

But is it possible to clarify this unwillingness to come to an arms control and disarmament agreement? Nations realize that their interests also can be threatened or harmed by non-military events, for example by ideological changes or economic circumstances. The industrialized nations are dependent on raw materials of the Third World countries, a dependence deemed incompatible with "national security." Thus, for the industrialized nations, "national security" embraces not only "military security" (enemy-security and weapons-security), but also "ideological security" and "economic security." This means that the nations who see these securities threatened will be prepared to react with military methods. This requires a military force ready to operate anywhere in the world in order to assure that ideological developments in other countries will be suppressed when they threaten to change existing spheres of influence, and in order to ensure the satisfaction of growing industrial needs for scarce raw materials.

If this extended notion is given to the concept "national security" and consequently a broader function is assigned to the national military force, the reluctance of the great powers becomes more understandable, for the superpowers will strive for an imperial power that can globally be brought into action. They will also continue their pursuit of superiority in relation to each other. Intervention in a country that does not belong to one of the two great alliances creates the danger of involving the other superpower. Thus, the extended function of national military power contributes to the continuation of the mutual arms race.

It is hardly necessary to point out that this extension of the function of national military power is not in accord with the prohibition of war stated in the U.N. Charter and which only permits military reaction in the event of an armed attack. The Charter prohibits therefore the use of violence in cases where interests are threatened by non-military events, such as ideological shifts or economic measures.

VIII.

Traditional international law does not limit the freedom of the sovereign state to possess arms in any way. The Peace Treaty of Utrecht of 1713 adopted as a political maxim a *justum potentiae aequilibrium*: "the peace and tranquility of Christendom may be restored by the just balance of power, which is the best and most solid foundation of mutual friendship and of lasting accord."[68] This maxim, however, did not develop into a legal principle.

A restriction of national arms freedom is found for the first time in peace treaties in which the defeated's freedom to possess arms is curtailed. The Treaty of Versailles[69] denied Germany the right to possess heavy weapons as well as the right to retain any but a very limited armed force.

Disarmament law as the "victor's law" is also to be found in peace treaties concluded after the Second World War with Bulgaria,[70] Finland,[71] Hungary,[72] Italy,[73] and Roumania,[74] and in treaties that admitted the Federal Republic of Germany to NATO[75] and in the Austrian State Treaty.[76] Here we also should point to the constitution of Japan,[77] which was adopted under the influence of the United States and in which Japan yields the right to possess a national armed force.

"Victor's law" in regard to disarmament is inevitably discriminatory. Disarmament law based on mutual agreement most likely is not discriminating, though it may entail accepting unequal positions that are accepted for the sake of maintaining peace. In the era of "peace-loving States"[78] the demands of peace sometimes serve to legitimate unequal legal status. One might think of the Non-Proliferation Treaty, which makes the "nuclear have-nots" legally into "nuclear have-nevers," while the "nuclear weapon states" keep their atomic weapons. Their obligation "to pursue negotiations in good faith on effective measures relating to cessation of the nuclear arms race at an early date and to nuclear disarmament''[79] was not fulfilled.

IX.

The need for agreements on arms control and disarmament was explicitly recognized in the Covenant of the League of Nations. Article 8 stated that "the maintenance of peace requires the reduction of national armaments to the lowest point consistent with national safety." The adoption of the "national safety" standard implied an inadequate willingness to take disarmament seriously: the right of each nation to determine for itself what was needed for its "national security" was affirmed.

The U.N. Charter shows an even lesser interest toward arms control and disarmament. According to Article 11, the General Assembly may discuss "the principles governing disarmament and the regulation of armaments." Article 26 does not give safety, but economic motives for the task of the Security Council to plan "for the establishment of a system for the regulation of armaments," and Article 47 states that the Military Staff Committee shall advise the Security Council concerning "the regulation of armaments, and possible disarmament."

But the U.N. Charter, it must be recalled, dates from the pre-atomic era. The awareness of the existence of atomic weapons has created greater interest in arms control and disarmament. Many negotiations have been entered into, resulting in the signing of a number of treaties.[80] But these did not prevent a constant arms race, which is typified by the fact that in 1982 approximately 700 billion dollars were spent globally on armaments,[81] and an overkill capacity was attained as never before.

Parties to the concluded arms control treaties no longer are entitled to follow their own will in respect to the possession of military power. But not every state is party to these treaties. Moreover, if states want to rearm they can renounce the treaties. Most arms control treaties contain an article with a special version of the *clausula rebus sic stantibus* allowing the states to cancel the treaty if in their opinion "extraordinary events related to the subject matter of the treaty have jeopardized their supreme interests.''[82]

Hence, there is a need for an international law that is generally binding and cannot be cancelled.[83] The gradual development of the international *jus ad bellum* has restricted the right of the State to *use* its armed power. The moment has gradually come to restrict the right of the State to *possess* the means of warfare.

The ground rule of this new chapter of international law should be: "The right of the State to possess armed power is not unlimited." A second rule might be: "The State only has the right to possess such armed power as is needed for the execution of its only legitimate function, that is to provide for military security."

The pertinent restriction will have to be worked out further. It should prohibit the possession of *offensive military weaponry* because that would lead to the continuation of the arms race and hinder the necessary arms control and disarmament. It should prohibit the possession of *destabilizing weapons and weapon systems,* and as such eliminate the danger inherent in the weapons themselves. It should prohibit the possession of *excessive armed power,* weapons that are not needed to fulfill the function of deterrence and defense.

Could such a restriction be workable? Many treaties already make a distinction between offensive and defensive systems; SALT I and SALT II are examples. In SALT II, the United States and the U.S.S.R. agreed that as soon as SALT II was ratified the two powers would start negotiations "to seek measures to strengthen strategic stability by, among other things, limitations on strategic offensive arms most destabilizing to the strategic balance and by measures to reduce and avert the risk of surprise attack." Both powers time and again accuse each other of possessing more arms than needed for defense. The present excessive armed power is, militarily speaking, useless and only dangerous. Deterrence should be reduced to no more than what is indispensable. For a start, strategic weapons could be substantially reduced. In fact, both powers have proposed substantial cuts in strategic missiles.

The new chapter of international law concerning arms control and disarmament should legally restrict the possession of armed power to a level corresponding to the concept of inoffensive or defensive deterrence. The mutual military postures then would be strong in defense and visibly incapable of aggressive conquest. If both parties sincerely agree that the maintenance of peace is their supreme interest they might be willing to enhance their military security in such a way.[84]

Defensive postures have been in bad odor since the experience with the Maginot Line. However, the Maginot Line was a one-sided defensive posture. We are discussing here the effects of mutual or generally accepted defensive postures. The thesis of this paper is that such mutually approved military postures might be the solution to the dilemma of unusable but indispensable nuclear weaponry.

X.

How do we arrive at such a progressive development of international law in the field of arms control and disarmament? The more than thirty-five years of disarmament negotiations have mostly been concerned with topics at the physical peripheries, such as outer space, the antarctic and the seabed, or have aimed at freezing or setting a not yet reached ceiling. The time has come to approach the core of the problem.

Up to now, negotiations have been conducted on the basis of special categories of weapons and armspower. However, technology presents ever more confusing novelties. Bertram directed our attention to "the erosion of the existing weapons categories" which was partly a result of "multi-mission weapons."[85] Hence his plea for "new units of account, missions instead of weapons."[86] The term "mission" is used to describe specific tasks to which military capabilities can be put. Such functions should be the subject of negotiations and agreed-upon prescriptions.

This theory should be applied with the persuasion that the only reasonable and only legitimate national function of armed power is the guarantee of "military security."[87] International law needs to bar any military capability that extends further than necessary for that function.

Another aspect of the negotiations is that they have been dominated by the United States and the U.S.S.R. Are the mightiest the best qualified? Or are they slaves to the instruments of their power? Are perhaps the less powerful more capable of coming to reasonable proposals? In any case, the smaller powers are showing impatience and want to participate. They have expressed their demand "to exercise actively their inalienable right to take part in disarming negotiations."[88]

The U.N. has a task in the progressive development of international law. That task is assigned to the General Assembly.[89] It should execute this responsibility with respect to the law of arms control and disarmament. It is regrettable that the Special Sessions devoted to disarmament did not pay attention to this aspect of the arms problem.

The General Assembly should start by formulating guidelines for disarmament negotiations, linking the legitimate use of national armed power with the legitimate possession of armed power. General principles should be adopted for arms control negotiations concerning the introduction of new offensive, destabilizing, or excessive weapons. These principles should then be applied to existing weapon postures. Gradually these may solidify into rules of binding law concerning national "weapon freedom." In view of the existing inequalities in the world, regional arrangements are needed first of all for the relation between NATO and the Warsaw Pact Organization. These military alliances should be pressed to come to agreements that follow the guiding principles developed by the General Assembly.

The General Assembly should outline, in its resolutions, standards and rules of a new chapter of international law concerning the restriction of weapon freedom. These regulations formulated as resolutions are not yet rules of law, but only recommendations. The General Assembly does not have legislative power; but, by its resolutions it can change the political and juridical climate in the world as it did in respect to colonialization, racial discrimination, and the market-mechanism of the existing international economic order. General Assembly resolutions can bring about this change because they not only influence attitudes of governments directly, but also have direct impact on the people, and through the people they again influence governments. This change in spiritual climate is a pre-condition for the progressive development of international law.

In the field of arms control and disarmament the General Assembly must perform the role of a law-creating agency as it has done in the field of human rights, and as it is in the process of doing in respect to a new international economic order and a new law of the sea.

This law of arms control and disarmament will include nuclear weapons. The contractual accord, which now rests on the terminable Non-Proliferation Treaty, will then have to be founded on interminable international law. The limitation of the right to possess nuclear arms, including limitation of that freedom for the nuclear weapon states, has to be accepted. Nuclear weapons that clearly possess offensive qualities and those that have a destabilizing effect, as well as those that possess an overkill capacity, must be prohibited. The development of an international law that divests these aspects from nuclear armed power needs to be realized.

The question whether all possession of nuclear arms need to be banned can be left out of consideration for now. Succeeding generations will have to decide about that. Such a decision can then be made in view of the existing political climate and the military technology of the time.

NOTES

1. A. H. Compton, Atomic Quest 331 (1956).

2. B.V.A. Röling, The Impact of Nuclear Weapons on International Relations and International Law (Polemological Institute of the University of Groningen, 1982).

3. Hague Convention for the Pacific Settlement of International Disputes, Oct. 18, 1907, 36 Stat. 2199, T.S. No. 536.

4. G. Blainey, The Causes of War 108 (1973).

5. Kellogg-Briand Pact, Aug. 27, 1928, 46 Stat. 2343, T.S. No. 796, 94 L.N.T.S. 57.

6. G.A. Res. 3314, 29 U.N. GAOR Supp. (No. 31) at 142, U.N. Doc. A/9631 (1975), *reprinted in* 13 Int'l Legal Materials 710 (1974).

7. For a survey of Stone's theories and the opposing arguments, *see* Röling, On the Prohibition of the Use of Force *in* Legal Change: Essays in Honour of Julius Stone 274 (A. R. Blackshield ed. 1983). However there is no contention that a case can be made for the diverging interpretations.

8. The thesis that "custom" has changed the legal situation described in the U.N. Charter cannot be maintained. The practice of starting wars cannot be denied. But with respect to these "aggressions" an *opinio juris* does not exist. One of the positive aspects of the "definition of aggression," *supra* note 6, is that it prevents such an opinion.

9. Declaration of the Political Consultative Committee of the State Parties to the Warsaw Treaty (March 15, 1980); *see* U.N. Doc. A/35/558 (1980).

10. Prevention of Nuclear War Agreement, *signed and entered into force* June 22, 1973, U.S.-U.S.S.R., 24 U.S.T. 1478, T.I.A.S. No. 7654.

11. G.A. Res. 2625, 25 U.N. GAOR Supp. (No. 28) at 121, U.N. Doc. A/8028 (1971), *reprinted in* 9 Int'l Legal Materials 1292 (1970).

12. *See* Universal Declaration of the Rights of Peoples/Algiers Declaration (adopted by an international non-governmental conference held in Algiers, July 1-4,

1976), *reprinted in* Basic Documents in International Law and World Order 413 (B. Weston, R. Falk, A. D'Amato eds. 1980). Article 28 of the Declaration recognizes that "[a]ny people whose fundamental rights are seriously disregarded has the right to enforce them . . . even, in the last resort, by the use of force." The text suggests that it is "the people," in auto-interpretation, which decides whether "fundamental rights are seriously disregarded." It seems to me, however, that the right to go to war, denied to "the states," should not be supposed to exist still for "peoples." *See* Röling, *Remarques Critiques sur l'Auto Interprétation du Droit dans la Déclaration d'Alger*, in *Pour un Droit des Peuples* 165 (Cassese & Jouve eds. 1978); *see also* The New Humanitarian Law of Armed Conflict: Proceedings 262 (A. Cassese ed. 1980).

13. B.V.A. Röling & O. Sūkovič, The Law of War and Dubious Weapons (1976).

14. 3 H. Grotius, *De Jure Belli ac Pacis*, ch. 1(2) (1646): "In war, all things are permissible which are necessary to attain the end in view."

15. "These were weapons of terror and shock. . . . The political target of the bomb was not the dead of Hiroshima or the factories they worked in, but the survivors in Tokyo." T. Schelling, Arms and Influence 17 (1976). The bombing of North Vietnam, too, "was the direct exercise of the power to hurt." *Id.* at 171. Schelling concludes, "In the present era non-combatants appear to be not only deliberate targets but primary targets." *Id.* at 27.

16. About the periods of the "Christian Nations" (until the Treaty of Paris, March 30, 1856, 46 B.F.S.P. 8, which admitted Turkey to "the public law and concert of Europe"), the "Civilized Nations" and, since article 4 of the U.N. Charter, the "Peaceloving Nations," *see* B.V.A. Röling, International Law in an Expanded World (1960). One of the functions of the common value (of Christianity, of Civilization, of Peace) is that it provides the motive for the progressive development of international law.

17. Protocol for the Prohibition of the Use of Gas in War or of Asphyxiating, Poisonous or Other Gases, and of Bacteriological Methods of Warfare, June 17, 1925, 26 U.S.T. 571, T.I.A.S. No. 8061, 94 L.N.T.S. 65 (hereinafter Gas Protocol of 1925).

18. Convention for the Pacific Settlement of International Disputes, July 29, 1899, 32 Stat. 1779, T.S. No. 392.

19. Hague Convention (No. IV) Respecting the Laws of War and Customs of War on Land, with Annex of Regulations, Oct. 18, 1907, 36 Stat. 2277, T.S. No. 539, *reprinted in* 1 Bevans 631 (hereinafter Hague Regulations of 1907).

20. Convention for the Amelioration of the Condition of the Wounded and Sick in Armed Forces in the Field, July 27, 1929, 47 Stat. 2074, T.S. No. 847, 118 L.N.T.S. 303; Convention Relative to the Treatment of Prisoners of War, July 27, 1929, 47 Stat. 2021, T.S. No. 846, 118 L.N.T.S. 343.

21. Convention for the Amelioration of the Condition of the Wounded and Sick in Armed Forces in the Field, Aug. 12, 1949, 6 U.S.T. 3114, T.I.A.S. No. 3362, 75 U.N.T.S. 31; Convention for the Amelioration of the Condition of the Wounded, Sick and Shipwrecked Members of Armed Forces at Sea, 6 U.S.T. 3217, T.I.A.S. No. 3363, 75 U.N.T.S. 85; Convention Relative to the Treatment of Prisoners of War, 6 U.S.T. 3316, T.I.A.S. No. 3364, 75 U.N.T.S. 135; Convention Relative to the Protection of Civilian Persons in Time of War, 6 U.S.T. 3516, T.I.A.S. No. 3365, 75 U.N.T.S. 287. These four treaties are known collectively as the Geneva Conventions of 12 August 1949.

22. Protocols Additional to the Geneva Conventions of 12 Aug. 1949, and Relating to the Protection of Victims of International Armed Conflicts (hereinafter Protocol I of 1977), and Relating to the Protection of Victims of Non-International Armed Conflicts (hereinafter Protocol II of 1977), *opened for signature* Dec. 12, 1977, *reprinted in* 16 I.L.M. at 1391 & 1442 (1977).

23. United Nations Convention on Prohibition or Restrictions on the Use of Certain Conventional Weapons Which May Be Deemed To Be Excessively Injurious Or To Have Indiscriminate Effects, *opened for signature* April 10,1981, U.N. Doc. A/Conf. 95/15 (1980) (hereinafter Convention of 1981), *reprinted in* Documents on the Laws of War 467 (R. Adam & R. Guelff eds. 1982).

24. E. Kant, *Die Metaphysik der Sitten* para. 57 (1797): ". . . to manipulate by such treacherous means as would destroy the trust necessary for the establishment of a lasting peace."

25. Lieber, Instructions for the Government of the Armies of the United States in the Field (1863), *reprinted in* Wilson & Tucker, International Law app. 2 (9th ed. 1935).

26. Hague Regulations of 1907, *supra* note 19, art. 23(b).

27. Hague Regulations of 1907, *supra* note 19, art. 23(f).

28. Protocol I of 1977, *supra* note 22, art. 37.

29. *See* Convention of 1981, *supra* note 23.

30. It is questionable whether this principle was ever expressly recognized as a definite rule of international law. Certainly article 26 of the Hague Regulations (1907) required the officer commanding an attacking force to do all in his power to warn the authorities of the impending attack. Article 2 of Hague Convention IX also required definite warning to be given if this were at all possible, but for the rest it permitted "any unavoidable damage." The Hague Rules on Aerial Warfare, formulated in 1923, however, took the principle as a point of departure. Military targets should only be bombed if this could be done "without the indiscriminate bombardment of the civilian population." (Article 24(3)). These rules of air warfare, however, were never confirmed by treaty, and the practice in World War II showed an opposite tendency. Article 35(2) of Protocol I of 1977 states that "It is prohibited to employ weapons . . . of a nature to cause superfluous injury or unnecessary suffering"; it does not mention weapons of a nature to cause disproportionate suffering.

31. Protocol I of 1977, *supra* note 22, art. 51, para. 5(b), art. 57(2) (a) (iii).

32. Outerspace Treaty, *signed* Jan. 27, 1967, *entered into force* Oct. 10, 1967, 18 U.S.T. 2410, T.I.A.S. No. 6347, 610 U.N.T.S. 205.

33. Seabed Treaty, *signed* Feb. 11, 1971, *entered into force* June 18, 1972, 23 U.S.T. 701, T.I.A.S. No. 7337.

34. Biological Weapons Treaty, April 10, 1972, 26 U.S.T. 583, T.I.A.S. No. 8062.

35. Moon Treaty, U.N. Doc. A/34/664, *reprinted in* 18 Int'l Legal Materials 1434 (1979).

36. "Neither practice nor the literature explains satisfactorily how the privilege based on self-preservation in times of peace can be denied to states at war." J. Stone, Legal Control of International Conflict 353 (1959). For a different view of the "right to survival," *see* Feinrider, International Law as Law of the Land: Another Constitutional Constraint on Use of Nuclear Weapons, 7 Nova L.J. 103, 120 (1982), *reprinted in* Nuclear Weapons and Law (A. S. Miller & M. Feinrider eds. 1984).

37. "Necessity has no law."

38. G.A. Res 2849, 26 U.N. GAOR Supp. (No. 29) at 70, U.N. Doc. A/8429 (1972).

39. *Id.*

40. Protocol I of 1977, *supra* note 22, art. 35(3).

41. Protocol I of 1977, *supra* note 22, art. 36.

42. Convention on the Prohibition of Military or Any Other Hostile Use of Environmental Modification Techniques, May 18, 1977, 31 U.S.T. 333, T.I.A.S. No. 9614.

43. *See* R. Falk, This Endangered Planet: Prospects and Proposals for Human Survival 348 (1972).

44. Gas Protocol of 1925, *supra* note 17.

45. Hague Regulations of 1907, *supra* note 19.

46. Protocol I of 1977, *supra* note 22, at art. 1(2).

47. Protocol II of 1977, *supra* note 22.

48. The New Humanitarian Law of Armed Conflict 257 (A. Cassese ed. 1980).

49. B. H. Liddell Hart, Deterrent or Defense: A Fresh Look at the West's Military Position 62 (1960).

50. *See, e.g.*, J. Fuller, The Conduct of War 1789-1961 at 174 (1961).

51. G.A. Res. 1653, 16 U.N. GAOR Supp. (No. 17).

52. G.A. Res. 2936, 27 U.N. GAOR Supp. (No. 30) at 5, U.N. Doc. A/8730 (1966).

53. G.A. Res. 33-71B, 33 U.N. GAOR Supp. (No. 45) at 48, U.N. Doc. A/33/45 (1978).

54. U.N. Charter art. 10.

55. G.A. Res. 2444, 23 U.N. GAOR Supp. (No. 18) at 50, U.N. Doc. A/7218 (1968).

56. *See* Cassese, *supra* note 48, at 63.

57. *See* Office of Technology Assessment, The Effects of Nuclear War (1979).

58. *See* G.A. Res. S-10/2, 10 U.N. GAOR Supp. (No. 4) at 10, U.N. Doc. A/S-10/4 (1978).

59. *Id.* at para. 59.

60. *Id.* at para. 62.

61. Treaty of Tlatelolco, Feb. 14, 1967, 634 U.N.T.S. 281.

62. A. Myrdal, The Game of Disarmament at xvi (1976).

63. This constitutes one of the objections of Europe against the introduction of Euro-strategic weapons. If ever a war were to erupt in Europe—due perhaps to an uncontrollable conflict somewhere else, for example in the Middle East—it would be of the utmost importance to the Soviet Union to destroy these weapons immediately. On the other side the tendency might rise to employ the weapons before they could be destroyed. Both cases involve an escalation of violence that practically excludes the diplomatic negotiations so vitally important to both parties.

64. Here, the international function of the national armed forces to contribute to the realization of "collective security" or "collective diplomacy" is left out of consideration.

65. Myrdal, *supra* note 62.

66. *Id.* at 24.

67. *Id.* at 24; *see id.* at Chapter II, The Superpowers' Game, for examples.

68. This reference is, in fact, to the series of treaties concluded among France, England, Holland, Prussia, Portugal, Savoy, and Spain at the end of the War of the Spanish Succession. Signed, for the most part, between March and August of 1713, they can be found at 27 Parry's T.S. 373-475 and 28 Parry's T.S. 1-359.

69. Treaty of Versailles, June 28, 1919, arts. 159-213, 2 Bevans 43.

70. Treaty of Peace with Bulgaria, Feb. 10, 1947, 61 Stat. 1915, T.I.A.S., No. 1650.

71. Treaty of Peace with Finland, Feb. 10, 1947, 1948 Gr. Brit. T.S. No. 53, 48 U.N.T.S. 203.

72. Treaty of Peace with Hungary, Feb. 10, 1947, 61 Stat. 2065, T.I.A.S. No. 1651.

73. Treaty of Peace with Italy, Feb. 10, 1947, 61 Stat. 1245, T.I.A.S. No. 1648. The stipulation with regard to Italy was cancelled by the Allied Powers in 1951.

74. Treaty of Peace with Roumania, Feb. 10, 1947, 61 Stat. 1757, T.I.A.S. No. 1649.

75. North Atlantic Treaty (Accession of the Federal Republic of Germany), Oct. 23, 1954, 6 U.S.T. 5707, T.I.A.S. No. 3428.

76. Austrian State Treaty, May 15, 1955, 6 U.S.T. 2369, T.I.A.S. No. 3298.

77. *Kenpō* (constitution) art. IX, para. 2 (Japan).

78. U.N. Charter art. 4.

79. Non-Proliferation Treaty, art. VI, *signed* July 1, 1968, *entered into force* March 5, 1970, 21 U.S.T. 483, T.I.A.S. No. 6839, 729 U.N.T.S. 161.

80. *See* J. Goldblat, Agreements for Arms Control (1982).

81. S.I.P.R.I. [1982] Yearbook of Armaments and Disarmaments at xxxvii (1982).

82. *See, e.g.,* Partial Test Ban Treaty, Aug. 5, 1963, art. IV, 14 U.S.T. 1313, T.I.A.S. No. 5433; Treaty of Tlatelolco, *supra* note 61, at art. 30; Non-Proliferation Treaty, *supra* note 79, at art. XIII; Seabed Treaty, *supra* note 33, at art. 8; Biological Weapons Treaty, *supra* note 34, at art. XIII; A.B.M. Treaty, May 26, 1972, art. XV, 23 U.S.T. 3435, T.I.A.S. No. 7503; S.A.L.T. I, May 26, 1972, art. VIII, 23 U.S.T. 3462, T.I.A.S. No. 7504; Threshold Treaty, Jan. 27, 1967, art. XVI, 18 U.S.T. 2410, T.I.A.S. No. 6347, 610 U.N.T.S. 205; Prevention of Incidents on the High Seas, Oct. 20, 1972, art. VIII, 28 U.S.T. 3459, T.I.A.S. No. 8587; Treaty on Underground Tests for Peaceful Purposes, May 28, 1976, art. VIII, *reprinted in* 15 Int'l Legal Materials 891 (1976); Moon Treaty, *supra* note 35, at art. 30.

83. *See* Röling, The International Law of Arms Control and Disarmament *in* Armaments, Arms Control and Disarmament 272 (M. Thee ed. 1981).

84. For further elaboration, *see* Röling, The Feasibility of Inoffensive Deterrence, 9 Bull. Peace Proposals 339 (1978).

85. C. Bertram, Adelphi Paper 5 (The Future of Arms Control and Technological Change No. 146, 1978).

86. *Id.* at 17-31.

87. *See* Röling, The Function of Military Power, *in* Arms Control and Technological Innovation 288 (1977).

88. G.A. Res. 34-88, 34 U.N. GAOR Supp. (No. 46) at 65, U.N. Doc. A/34/46 (1979). *See* Röling, Arms Control, Disarmament and Small Countries, 31 Impact Sci. on Soc'y 97 (1981).

89. U.N. Charter art. 13(1)(a).

11.

"Filling Out" the Right to Peace: A Basic Change in the Nation-State System*

Saul Mendlovitz**

Let me continue some of the questing aspirational emphasis which Ved Nanda has initiated. I shall take his discussion somewhat further afield, but bring it back in a way which I hope will provide an appropriate context for understanding the reality of the right to peace.

I am struck by the fact that when one looks at the question of human rights beginning with what I would call the modern era—and let me fix that at 1648 with the Treaty of Westphalia,[1] so that at least my fellow international law colleagues will have a comfortable, if somewhat cliche, resting place—there are two, perhaps two and one-half, periods in the history of the emergence of human rights. First, and most familiar, are the political and civil rights which arose out of the bourgeois revolutions, the American and the French; one, we should remind ourselves, was a war of "national liberation" of the colonies against a "tyrant" king, the other, a spreading republicanism, or democracy, if you will, against an absolute monarch. For our purposes, the content of these rights, which are associated with western liberal democracies, need not be reviewed. There are, however, three common conditions or attributes in both the United States and French revolutions which are of import in understanding the possibility and content of the right to peace.

First, as already noted, these rights emerged out of violent revolution or armed struggle. Second, in carrying out these struggles, the revolutionaries deemed it of highest importance to issue a statement or declaration—in the one case of Independence,[2] and in the other, the Rights of Man[3]—in which moral

---

* Reprinted, with permission, from the *Brooklyn Journal of International Law,* Volume 9, Number 2 (1983).

** Professor of Law, Rutgers Law School (Newark); Director, World Order Models Project, Institute For World Order. These remarks are the author's restatement and modification of a seminal piece by Stephen P. Marks, *Emerging Human Rights: A New Generation for the 1980's?*, 33 Rutgers L. Rev. 435 (1981) (Symposium Issue on International Conflicts, Law and a Just World Order).

1. Treaty of Westphalia, Oct. 4, 1648, Holy Roman Empire—France, *reprinted in* 1 A. TOYNBEE, MAJOR PEACE TREATIES OF MODERN HISTORY 1648-1967, at 7-49 (F. Israel ed. 1967).

2. The Declaration of Independence (U.S. 1776).

3. Declaration of the Rights of Man and of the Citizen, *reprinted in* A. PEASLEE, CONSTITUTIONS OF NATIONS 20 (2d ed. 1956).

and legal authority were intertwined. And third, these rights were expressed in universal terms, that is, for all human beings.

What is crucial to our understanding of these rights is that they become a part of the nation-state system itself. Thus, they become integrated into the domestic structure of both the United States and France. And, whatever the contradictions and ironies—the imperialism of France, the hegemonic Monroe Doctrine of the United States—this notion of political and civil rights is carried with them to the other parts of the world, and later, as we shall see, comes back to haunt them—in Africa, or in Asia, as witness Vietnam.

Furthermore, from the perspective that is being developed here, it is important to see that these revolutions created an overriding political mythology. And I use the word myth here in its poetic and philosophical sense. That is to say, the kind of image, *Weltanschauung*, or world view that provides the deep meaning to our lives, the meaning we ascribe to our face to face relationships with other human beings, to larger collectivities of humans, to the physical planet, to the meaning of life and death, and to the *mysterium tremendum*. This myth is superstructure of the most significant character, for it provides guidance on how we are willing to deal with our material world. It is the foundation of our political metaphysics—what we consider to be an appropriate political reality—and these two revolutions have had a dramatic, profound psycho-historic penetration on our political being.

We turn now to the second period of rights. They emerge out of the ideological persuasiveness of Marx and Engels of the nineteenth century. They are the rights of economic equality and have become identified with the socialist rights. These rights become politically incarnate through the Soviet revolution in 1917 and the Maoist Chinese revolution some thirty years later. The Soviet Union and China are two major States that play increasingly important roles in the state system. It should be noted once again that these second generation socialist rights emerge out of struggle, are embodied in declarations with moral and legal rationale and bespeak claims on behalf of all of humanity. Similarly, these revolutions have had their profound psycho-historic penetration of humanity intertwined with the first set to make up our political metaphysic.

Two additional points should be noted here. First, both sets of rights have their origin in western society and come as baggage with the domination of western society and civilization throughout the globe. Second, the extent to which the terminology of the French revolution might be said to comprehend these rights is remarkable. The bourgeois rights are to be found in the notion of liberty, and the economic, and perhaps participatory, rights comprehended by the notion of equality.

To complete in only a few sentences what is already a very adumbrated history, I should like to say a few words about the final half of the two and one-half periods. And what I have reference to here is the breakdown of colonialism. Between the end of World War II and the present, the nation-state system has added somewhere between seventy-five and one hundred states under the processes of decolonization and self-determination. It should be noted that this self-determination has an implicit base in both the equality and liberty revolutions of the first two periods, and that this process has created a nation-state system global in scope which has incorporated the ideology of the rights of liberty and equality.

To summarize, then, the rights that we know and cherish emerged in a decentralized international state system dominated by western society. They are, the civil and political rights of the French and American revolutions, and the socialist equality rights of the Soviet Union and the People's Republic of China. Combination of these two major bundles of rights is carried out and forward with the decolonization process, it all being a part and parcel of a global nation-state system.

The argument which I wish to present now stems from the observation that the twentieth century has witnessed the emergence of global or planetary society, and that the next generation of rights will be planetary in scope. Indeed, to carry out the terminological prophecy of the French revolution, we are entering the phase of Solidarity—but this time for the entire human race—and a new bundle of rights are emerging to express the ideology of Solidarity. Let me now attempt to clarify this proposition.

John Dewey, you will recall, stated that "society exists in and through communication," and it is that definition which I believe fixes the twentieth century as the period of history which will be recorded as the epoch in which global or planetary society emerged. And as I have done before in this brief talk, permit me to make a connotative rather than a definitive demonstration of a sweeping proposition.

If you take fifteen hundred as a baseline, there are a half billion people on the face of the earth; perhaps one-tenth of one percent know that the globe is round, and that there are people on the other side. Indeed, there is no way to talk about a common destiny, not even in the ecological sense; "a sparrow may fall" but it has very, very minimal impact even in the organic related sense of Whitehead. It certainly has no impact on your breathing, on your air, your material, let alone common and communal psychological and spiritual being.

Yet less than 500 years have passed—a blip in the history of humanity. Today we are eight times that many people; we are pell-mell rushing toward twelve times, and unless there is a nuclear war or a major catastrophe by the year 2002, there will be 6.5 billion human beings on the face of the earth; indeed, by the year 2022 there will be 7.5 billion. And it will be an extraordinary time. Those 7.5 billion people will be in touch with one another. The fact is that today, the 4.2 billion human beings on the face of the earth already are in touch with one another. Thus, to put the matter simply, granting all the divisiveness, strife, conflict and violence between and amongst nations, races, people, and even sexes, if more than one-tenth of one percent of the human race do not know that the globe is round, that there are people on the other side, and that they share a common destiny, it would be surprising.

It is now becoming increasingly apparent to all of us that somehow we are very interdependent, interpenetrating, and share a common destiny. You cannot go anywhere on the globe, let us say, one hundred miles outside of Lima, Peru, or five hundred miles outside of Delhi, and find the isolated, insular "native." There is no dark Africa for Dr. Livingstone to explore. Instead, there are blue jeans, transistor radios, Scotch whiskey, and everywhere a western-dominated global culture, rightfully bemoaned by many. Yet, I would remind us all that many of our children are yoga-practicing vegetarians, and the fact is that East and West and North and South are coming together. We, the human race, have interpenetrated each other throughout the globe.

We were admonished this morning to talk about reality. Very well. What is the reality of the right to peace? As I have already indicated, my sense of the flow of history leads me to understand the right to peace as an aspect of a new stage or period in the history of rights—both individual and collective—that are going to emerge through the end of this century and the early part of the next. I cannot in this brief comment fill out the full argument here but would like to highlight the main features of this emergence.

First, these are rights which will comprehend and then transcend the present State system. I am very much aware that the State system is at its height, it is at its apotheosis, *but the king, if not dead, is dying.* A decentralized State system, given its structural, material and motivational organization, is no longer capable of dealing with the planetary problems of war, of environment, or what we now call interdependence. To pick up on this latter and most familiar aspect of contemporary global political economy, it is now generally acknowledged that the industrialized world wants the fossil fuels and raw materials possessed by the underindustrialized parts of the globe. The less developed countries, in turn, desire the capital goods necessary to become industrialized. More important, we are all now part of the same global culture. This interpenetration — the fact that we are "into" each other, that we know about each other all over the world, that the normative standards, moral views, and myths that we have of one another are now global and planetary — means that the very kind of conditions under which the first and second generations of rights arose, i.e., revolution and struggle, declarations and statements based on moral and legal ideas, and claims based on universality, are taking place around the face of the world. So when Ved Nanda talks about the aspirational quality and the somewhat "fuzzy" aspect of the right to peace,[4] I believe he is correct. However, we are in a position, on the basis of social trends and developing historical framework, to begin to fill out the content of this right.

Here I wish to make further use of the creative and path-breaking work of Karel Vasak[5] and Steve Marks,[6] who argue that this new "generation of rights" will be based on fraternité or the sense of solidarity—solidarity rights. Again, in synoptic if not too cryptic terms, I believe that Steve Marks is correct when

---

4. Nanda, *Nuclear Weapons and the Right to Peace Under International Law*, 9 BROOKLYN J. INT'L L. 283 (1983).

5. Address given at the Inaugural Lecture to the Tenth Study Session of the International Institute of Human Rights, in Strasbourg, France (July, 1979).

6. Marks, *Emerging Human Rights: A New Generation for the 1980's?*, 33 RUTGERS L. REV. 435, 442-49 (1981) (Symposium Issue on International Conflicts, Law and a Just World Order).

he argues that there are six areas which are likely to become the focus of this new set of rights. They are environment, development, the common heritage, communication, humanitarian assistance, and peace.[7] All of these areas are planetary in scope; and what is likely to emerge over the next twenty-five to fifty years is a new bundle of rights around these substantive areas and with institutional mechanisms to see that they are enforced throughout the world. The developments in these areas will be complementary and mutually supportive, but here I have only the opportunity to discuss the right to peace.

This morning there was a discussion of the criminalization of nuclear weapons which I see as part of a new political mythology that is arising in global society. And with society the questions arise — what kind of governance? what kind of polity? I want to be so bold as to predict — and I am not a world federalist — that my reading of the flow of history, based on the trends we have been discussing, moves us inexorably toward a centralized global system of government by the year 2050. As I have had occasion to argue elsewhere, such centralization may come about in a violent or tyrannical fashion and may be perpetuated in the same manner or, with appropriate human intervention, may be benign and tolerably human-satisfying. International lawyers must find a fitting way to participate in this latter development. Whether you call this *lex ferenda* or not, this is the task that we should have before us, and the right to peace is the cornerstone of that world. Without taking seriously the notion that there will be some way of dismantling the unilateral national security mechanisms of each State of the world, we will not be able to get a centralized system without hegemony or tyranny, but we're going to get there. The only question is, do we have the wit and the wisdom within present polities to dismantle the system of which we are a part?

One cannot help but be very much aware that the escalating arms race is the focus of two major negotiating conferences between the Soviet Union and the United States and that bilateral mutual verifiable freeze has become a cutting edge of the peace movement in western society. I applaud these efforts and expect that the Reagan Administration will make some compromise with the Soviets on intermediate nuclear weapons and perhaps even a small start on START. Yet, my own analysis leads me to

---

7. *Id.*

believe that there is not likely to be a fundamental change without some catastrophe unless some of the actors in the system engage in behavior of bold action. My own feeling is that as an essential matter in filling out the content of the right to peace, American citizens should be demanding of the government national initiatives with regard to a moratorium on nuclear weapons, and even the beginning of the dismantling of some of them.

Now, I understand that there are those who would argue that what we have to worry about is the destabilization, the insecurities, the risks that we would take if we were to initiate dismantling actions in our own society without comparable actions being taken in other nations, whom we frequently call adversaries. I am aware of that. My own response to that is two-fold. To begin with, I have looked at the numbers in the armaments field and perhaps I should present some awkward — for me, at least — credentials. For three years I was on the Social Science Research Advisory Board of the Arms Control and Disarmament Agency under the Nixon Administration. And I have followed, perhaps not as closely as one might, these nuclear and conventional weapons numbers over the intervening years. As a sometime expert, I am absolutely convinced that the dismantling of a strategic weapon by the United States, one a day for the next two years, and announcing that we're doing it, would add more security to the United States than adding a strategic nuclear weapon every day. I am absolutely convinced that we are so swollen, so overly capable of dealing militarily with our "adversary," that at this juncture I conceive it to be an extraordinary blind spot on the part of policy makers throughout the globe, and our own as well, that we fail to see this point. Furthermore, there are good reasons why our "adversary" would like to get out of the arms race.

Perhaps more important, putting this argument aside, I also believe that if you have a cancer in your body, and you're with somebody else who has a cancer, the fact that they are continuing the cancer does not mean that you should continue yours. I believe that at this juncture in history, it is incumbent for someone to step out and to take the lead and to begin now the dismantling. This would be one measure consistent with filling in the content of the right to peace.

In addition, I would have international lawyers relate very closely to the social movement against nuclear weapons and war. Indeed, I believe that the most important thing that has happened in the field of international law with regard to the right to peace is the European peace movement. Ved Nanda alluded to some of the declarations and resolutions that have come from the General Assembly, UNESCO and other governmental and non-governmental fora in connection with the right to peace.[8] These efforts are very important in developing a normative climate and the legal profession should participate fully in them. But this normative climate will become transformed into organization and structure only if the resolutions become intertwined with political demand. In that sense the most significant thing that has happened for the right to peace is that the people of Europe went to the streets in the past two years. In the same spirit, on June 12, 1982 the 750,000 to one million people who went out to the streets of New York added to the possibility of filling out the content of the right to peace. As lawyers, we should be working with these people for the right to peace will emerge from people exercising their demands upon governments throughout the world.

In our own society, I would argue, those of us who are international lawyers should open ourselves to handle the conscientious objecting student; we should open ourselves to handle tax transfer or tax avoidance or tax resistance; we should engage in it ourselves. We should go to Rocky Flats and practice civil disobedience. We should help the people with the King of Prussia case. We should do our own knocking on top of nuclear warheads. We should set up tribunals of the highest moral and legal authority to try the individuals who head our own State, as well as to try the leadership in the Soviet Union, to try any leadership in any society which owns nuclear weapons. We should be as ashamed of being a part of society, of a system that owns nuclear weapons, as we would be if we were part of a system which owned slaves. To own nuclear weapons is more than a violation of international law; it is a shame and embarrassment. It is disgusting, in the same way as it is to own another human being, indeed, to own an army, to be part of a civilized society that wants to do large-scale organized violence upon another unit or polity. Now the content of the right to peace will emerge when enough people internalize this kind of thinking and begin to act on behalf of it.

Finally, we must infuse our efforts with transnational par-

8. Nanda, *supra* note 4, at 289-94.

ticipation. We need to work with like-minded people, professionals, people in the street, with Solidarity, with the dissidents in the Soviet Union, with the Chinese citizens of the People's Republic of China who went to the Peking Wall in 1979 and announced to their leadership "we are citizens of the world." That's what we are. We are citizens of the world, and our first demand is the right to peace.

12.
The Use of Nuclear Weapons Under International Law: An Annotated Bibliography

Carol A. Roehrenbeck*

The dropping of atomic bombs on Hiroshima and Nagasaki raised the curtain on the nuclear age and provided the world with its first view of the effects of nuclear weapons. Despite the horror of that scene the nations of the world continued to develop nuclear arms. In 1952 the United States detonated a fusion device with a yield of about 10 megatons of TNT.[1] In 1961 the Soviet Union exploded a fusion weapon with a yield of about 60 megatons, and by 1981 the world nuclear cache consisted of "a total of between 37,000 and 50,000 warheads with an overall explosive power of 11,000 to 20,000 megatons."[2]

Unfortunately, analysis of the legal issues involved in the use of nuclear weapons did not keep pace with technical developments. In the 1940s authors published almost nothing on the subject. Peace had arrived and society had little interest in the question of the legality of the bomb. In the 1950s some discussion appeared, but it was primarily aimed at furthering nationalistic interests. Authors from countries that lacked nuclear weapons wrote in support of allowing development and use, while authors from countries that had nuclear weapons wanted to limit it.[3] By the 1960s, however, scholars could not ignore the far-reaching problems caused by nuclear weapons buildups, and many looked seriously at the broader related legal issues. Most of the analysis produced during those years focused on the application of the traditional rules of war to the use of nuclear weapons, but, unfortunately, in the 1970s this line of discussion was not followed. Scholars pursued other topics such as the war in Viet Nam, nuclear testing, or the test ban treaties.

---

* Associate Professor of Law, and Law Library Director, Nova University Center for the Study of Law. The author extends her thanks to the library staffs of Columbia, Georgetown, Rutgers, and Nova Law Schools and, in particular, to Pat Harris and Alma Singleton of Nova, for their help in locating and trying to locate materials.

Finally, in the 1980s, they returned to consideration of the legality of nuclear weapons. New draft registration laws, the possibility of nuclear defense of the Persian Gulf, the Reagan administration talk about limited nuclear wars, and the American Catholic Bishops' pastoral letter opposing nuclear weapons all highlighted the need for new approaches. Today scholars are reevaluating the applicability of the old rules of war and also searching for new solutions to the nuclear arms dilemma.[4]

Given the immediacy of this problem it seemed appropriate both to review the earlier writings on this subject and to look at new publications. This bibliography serves as an introductory guide to materials about the subject for researchers.

SCOPE

This bibliography attempts to review thoroughly the materials on international law limiting or prohibiting the use or testing of nuclear weapons. Materials marginally related to the topic, such as those on nuclear energy, nuclear technology, and non-proliferation were omitted. Certain distinctions in the treatment of materials in the main theme are, however, noted below.

Certain areas are treated more extensively than others.[5] For example, the coverage of works applying the conventional rules of war to the use of nuclear weapons is more comprehensive than the coverage of materials dealing with nuclear testing. Testing, at least in the atmosphere, is limited by the Test Ban Treaties,[6] and discussion of the legalities has waned. On the other hand, discussion of the applicability of existing rules of war and the need for new rules is relevant today for several reasons: (1) there is still no general convention that prohibits the use of nuclear weapons;[7] (2) developments in weapons technology have added new dimensions to the question of legality; and (3) there is still wide disagreement on the applicability of these rules to new battlefield tactical weapons although strategic weapons of mass destruction are widely viewed as coming within the purview of customary rules of war.

Treatises, pamphlets, and articles in English and foreign languages are included, but the emphasis is on English language materials which are more readily indexed and available in the United States. Only foreign language materials easily accessible in this country are included.

Some materials could not be discovered through traditional indexes, catalogs, or databases. Entries such as Stein's article on the "Impact of New Weapons Technology" and Rauschning's work, "Nuclear Warfare and Weapons," were discovered by tracing footnotes in indexed articles. Others, such as the Statement of the Lawyers' Committee on Nuclear Policy, were suggested by the authors.[8]

Finally, many of the entries were difficult to obtain. As a result, not every entry was reviewed and annotated. Whenever personal inspection was possible entries were annotated. Those that appear without annotations were included because the authors, or some other authority on the subject, vouched for their relevancy.

CATEGORIES OF PUBLICATIONS

The materials are separated into two categories: those in which the authors discuss the legality of nuclear weapons, and those in which the authors discuss the legality of nuclear testing. Other subdivisions were considered when trying to organize the material for the reader but were rejected because the differences between subdivisions were too inconclusive. For example, one group of authors finds the use of nuclear weapons legal under international law while another group finds their use illegal. Authors such as Bright, Lee, and Stowell fall in the former category, while authors such as Brownlie, Margolis, Smith, Schwarzenberger, and Spaight fall in the latter. Another group of authors, however, including McDougal, Schlei, and O'Brien, supports the use of nuclear weapons only under limited circumstances such as when used for reprisal. Recently, another author, Richard Falk, expressed a fourth viewpoint. In a recent article he intimated that he could condone the use of nuclear weapons in limited situations until international standards of illegality are established. Since these categories are still in flux these distinctions were not used to organize the materials set out below. Nevertheless, they are suggested for the reader's consideration.

NOTES

1. Comprehensive Study on Nuclear Weapons 27 (United Nations, 1981).

2. Rauschning, Nuclear Warfare and Weapons, in 4 Encyclopedia Pub. Int'l L. 45 (1982).

3. *See* Maggs, Soviet Viewpoint on Nuclear Weapons in International Law, 29 L. & Contemp. Probs. 956 (1964).

4. Meyrowitz, The Status of Nuclear Weapons Under International Law, 38 Guild Prac. 67 (1981).

5. The question of the constitutional implication of the use of nuclear weapons appears to be one of first impression. The primary materials on this topic are published in this volume and the *Brooklyn Journal of International Law* and are, therefore, not included here. *See* Miller, Nuclear Weapons and Constitutional Law, *infra,* and Miller, "The Constitutional Challenge of Nuclear Weapons: A Note on the Obligation to Ward Off Extinction," 9 Brooklyn J. Int'l L. 317 (1983).

6. Feinrider, International Law as Law of the Land, 7 Nova L. J. 103, 114 (1982): "States may not even test nuclear weapons in outer space, under water or within the earth's atmosphere."

7. *Id*. at 113.

8. The Statement is available from the Committee.

BIBLIOGRAPHY

I. *BIBIOGRAPHIES*

U.N. Repertory of Disarmament Research, Geneva, UNIDIR, U.N. Directory for
Disarmament, 1982.

This is a good basic reference work containing an extensive collection of
bibliographies, research papers, institutions, and periodicals on the arms race
and disarmament. In Part II there is one section of particular relevance, titled
"Nuclear Disarmament," that includes a list of works on different aspects of
nuclear disarmament and prevention of war. The scope is limited to the
period of the first U.N. Disarmament Decade, 1970-1980. The book is
available in English and French.

Bibliography of International Humanitarian Law Applicable In Armed Conflicts,
Geneva, International Committee of the Red Cross, 1980.

This volume is a comprehensive source for all publications on the law of war.
In Part II, titled "International Armed Conflicts, Methods and Means of
Combat," there is one subsection that deals specifically with nuclear
weapons. Many well known, as well as obscure works, are listed. Entries
include English and foreign language materials.

II. *USE OF NUCLEAR WEAPONS*

A. *TREATISES*

Abranches, Carlos Alberto Dunshee de, *Proscricão Das Armas Nucleares*, Rio
Livraria Freitas Bastos, 1964.

Armaments and Disarmament In the Nuclear Age: A Handbook, Stockholm International Peace Research Institute (SIPRI), Atlantic Highlands, New Jersey,
Humanities Press, 1976 (M. Thee editor).

While the major part of this book deals with the development of nuclear arms
and armaments in general, the editor discusses, in Chapter 8, the need for the
development of new principles in the laws of war in light of the rapid
development of nuclear weapons.

Builder, Carl H., and Graubard, M., *The International Law of Armed Conflict:
Implications for the Concept of Assured Destruction,* Santa Monica,
California, Rand Corp., 1982.

Despite the pro-government alignment of Rand, these authors recognize
illegalities in current U.S. nuclear policy and hope to "help close the chasm
that now yawns between international law and U.S. strategic nuclear
policies." They propose that actual U.S. targeting be designed only for
attacks against strategic military targets and war-supporting activities.

Falk, Richard, *Legal Order In a Violent World,* 374-413, Princeton, Princeton University Press, 1968.

In this treatise the author examines the relevance of international law to the
management of international conflict. In Part III, he focuses on nuclear
weapons and the world order issues they raise. He discusses the *Shimoda* case
(a damages action brought against the Japanese Government for injuries

resulting from the bombing of Hiroshima and Nagasaki), minimizing the use of nuclear weapons, and the first-use doctrine.

Frei, Daniel, *Risks of Unintentional Nuclear War,* Geneva, Institute for Disarmament Research, UNIDIR, U.N., 1982.

This treatise is primarily a policy analysis for general readers. In Chapter Eight, "Existing Agreements to Counter the Risks of Unintentional Nuclear War," however, the author provides a substantial review of agreements that attempt to limit some aspects of nuclear war, and he discusses the impact of each as a deterrent.

Gierycz, D., *Criteria of Prohibition of the Use of Weapons in International Relations,* Studies on International Relations, Warsaw, Polish Institute of International Affairs, 1978.

Glaser, Stefan, *L'arme Nucleaire a la Lumière du Droit International*, Paris, A. Pedone, 1964.

Gotlieb, Allan, *Disarmament and International Law,* Toronto, Canadian Institute of International Affairs, 1965.

The political implications and legal principles of disarmament and arms control are analyzed by the author. He concludes that new rules of law must be drafted that are in the interests of states to uphold and that are consistent with the U.N. Charter.

Hsia, C. L., *War and the Use of Force in International Law,* Great Neck, New York, Harvard Law Books, 1977.

International Association of Democratic Lawyers, *Contributions to the Study of the Problems of Disarmament,* Brussels, I.A.D.L. Publications, 1958.

This collection of essays includes: Bysticky, "The problem of disarmament and international law"; Pokstefl, "The development and present state of negotiations on disarmament"; Standard, "Impact of atomic explosions on international law"; Vitanyi, "Military weapons and targets forbidden by international public law"; Sinha, "Testing of nuclear-fission bombs, is it legal?"; Hirano, "The need for an international agreement on the prohibition of nuclear weapons"; Bramson, "International law and denuclearization."

International Association of Democratic Lawyers, *Legal Problems Arising from the Development and Utilization of Atomic Energy: Proceedings of the Second Commission,* Brussels, I.A.D.L. Publications, 1960.

In this collection of papers the authors explore the international legal aspects of both nuclear energy and nuclear weapons.

International Committee of the Red Cross, *Some International Red Cross Conference Resolutions and I.C.R.C. Statements on the Protection of Civilian Populations and on Weapons of Mass Destruction,* Geneva, Switzerland (undated).

I.C.R.C. has compiled and reprinted the texts of a number of documents relating to limitations on the use of weapons of mass destruction. Of particular interest is the resolution requesting the addition of the atomic bomb to the weapons listed in the Regulations of 1925 on gases and aerial warfare, and the resolution requesting the prohibition of non-directed weapons.

Kapitsa, Mikhail, *What Time Has Shown; Moscow Treaty and New Steps,* Moscow, Novosti Press Agency Publishing House, 1965.

McDougal, Myres, and Feliciano, Florentino, *Law and Minimum World Public Order,* 659-68, New Haven, Connecticut, Yale, 1961.

Despite some reservations the authors express support for the use of nuclear weapons.

Menzel, Eberhard, *Legalität oder Illegalität der Anwendung von Atomwaffen,* Tübingen, J.C.B./Paul Siebeck, 1960.

Nuclear Weapons; Report of the Secretary General of the United Nations, Brookline, Massachusetts, Autumn Press, 1981.

The major portion of the text is devoted to a general discussion of the effects of nuclear weapons and trends in technological development. In Chapter 7, however, the author discusses U.N. resolutions, treaties, and agreements that prohibit or limit nuclear weapons.

Röling, B.V.A., *The Impact of Nuclear Weapons on International Relations and International Law,* Netherlands, Publication of the Polemological Institute of the University of Groningen, 1982.

After demonstrating that the emergence of nuclear weapons has caused fundamental changes in international relations that compel states to live without war, the author turns his attention to the impact of these weapons on international law. He observes that a new chapter is needed, one based on the U.N. Charter and on the groundrule that the right to possess arms is not unlimited.

Röling, B.V.A., and Sūkovič, O., *The Law of War and Dubious Weapons,* Stockholm International Peace Research Institute, Almquist (Stockholm), Humanities Press, 1976.

The authors review the law of war and then look at the legal principles that should be applied to "dubious" weapons such as nuclear, biological, chemical, incendiary, and small-caliber devices. The work is divided into two chapters: a discussion of the principles of the law of war, and an application of those principles to new weapons. The authors conclude that the principles are sound and need only be strengthened.

Schwarzenberger, Georg, *The Legality of Nuclear Weapons,* London, Stevens and Sons, 1958.

In this well-known study on the legal position of a nation using or possessing atomic and hydrogen weapons, the author concludes that scholarly or legal pronouncements will not prevent use and that a world public order that states will obey is needed.

Singh, M. Nagendra, *Nuclear Weapons and International Law,* New York, Praeger, 1959.

The author discusses the origin and development of the laws of war, the effects of nuclear weapons, the application of custom and treaty law to nuclear weapons, and concludes that use of nuclear weapons for reprisal or as a deterrent is illegal.

Spaight, J., *The Atomic Problem*, London, A. Barron, 1948.

This is one of the earliest assessments that the atomic bomb is illegal and that its use is a war crime.

Spetzler, E., *Luftkrieg und Menschlichkeit, Die Völkerrechtliche Stellung der Zivilperson im Luftkrieg,* Göttingen, Musterschmidt Verlag, 1956.

B. *ESSAYS AND JOURNAL ARTICLES*

Almond, Harry, "Deterrence and a Policy-Oriented Perspective on the Legality of Nuclear Weapons,"*supra* at Chapter 5.

In this paper the author analyzes why nuclear weapons are not prohibited under international law and how they affect the choices and policies of states.

Almond, Harry, "Deterrence Process and Minimum Order," 4 *New York Law School Journal of International and Comparative Law* 283 (1984).

Arkadyev, N., "Nuclear Weapons and International Law," *New Times* 9 (Moscow edition, No. 4, 1957).

The author refutes the arguments of apologists for atomic weapons and urges a convention expressly forbidding their use.

Berman, Harold, "Soviet Views on the Legality of Nuclear Weapons," 9 *Brooklyn Journal of International Law* 259 (1983).

The Soviets, according to the author, have always supported a prohibition on the use of nuclear weapons although not necessarily on the threat to use them. He believes that the Soviets depend on an international order and American lawyers should help create, within that order, a structure of peaceful relations between the two countries.

Bilder, Richard, "Distinguishing Human Rights and Humanitarian Law: The Issue of Nuclear Weapons," 31 *American University Law Review* 959 (1982).

The author proposes a treaty outlawing the use of nuclear weapons and massive citizen action to promote such actions.

Bilder, Richard, "Nuclear Weapons and International Law," *supra* at Chapter 1.

International lawyers, whether or not they agree that international law prohibits nuclear weapons, have a special responsibility to help achieve arms control and disarmament, and the author details measures that help accomplish that goal.

Boyle, Francis A., "Nuclear Weapons and International Law: The Arms Control Dimension," 4 *New York Law School Journal of International and Comparative Law* 257 (1984).

Bright, Fred, "Nuclear Weapons as a Lawful Means of Warfare," 30 *Military Law Review* 1 (1965).

This is the traditional government view that the use of nuclear weapons is legal under the existing laws of war. The author concludes that the present state of international law is inadequate to govern either limited or total nuclear war.

Brownlie, Ian, "Some Legal Aspects of the Use of Nuclear Weapons," 14 *International and Comparative Law Quarterly* 437 (1965).

This well-known British author examines the legal aspects of the use of nuclear weapons as instruments of international policy. He reviews the arguments for and against the legality of their use, but he clearly supports those for illegality.

Castren, Erik, "The Illegality of Nuclear Weapons," 1971 *University of Toledo Law Review* 89.

The author discusses: (1) some of the technical problems and devastating effects connected with the use of different types of nuclear weapons; (2) the legality of their use under international law; (3) the harm caused to uninvolved states; and (4) the use of nuclear arms as a means of reprisal.

Charlier, Robert, "La Proscription de l'Arme," 91 *Hague Academy Recueil des Cours* 350 (1957-I).

Courteix, Simone, "La Contrôle de la Prolifération des Armes Nucléaires," 28 *McGill Law Journal* 591 (1983).

Cummings, Edward, "The Role of Humanitarian Law," 9 *Brooklyn Journal of International Law* 269 (1983).

As a representative of the government, the author tries to explain the United States government's position on the relation of international treaties to nuclear weapons. He concludes that, contrary to the position of Elliott Meyrowitz (*see* Meyrowitz, *supra* at Chapter 3), nuclear weapons are not prohibited as a matter of law.

D'Amato, Anthony, "The Purposive Dimension of International Law," 9 *Brooklyn Journal of International Law* 311 (1983).

The author suggests moving away from blanket pronouncements of what the law is and focusing instead on specific international prohibitions in order to develop more useful principles of international law relating to nuclear weapons.

Dobra, Peter, "The Role of Technological Evolution in International Law of Arms Control: Scylla or Charybdis?" 21 *Jurimetrics Journal* 31 (1980).

The author concludes that the introduction of new technology has necessitated new rules of international law and has led to new methods of creating these rules.

Euler, A., "Légalité ou Illégalité des Armes Nucléaires," in *Recueils de la Société Internationale de Droit Pénal Militaire et de Droit de la Guerre,* Vol. II, at 93 (Strasbourg, 1963).

Falk, Richard (with E. Meyrowitz and J. Sanderson), "Nuclear Weapons and International Law," 20 *Indian Journal of International Law* 541 (1980).

In this study the authors consider whether the contemplated uses of nuclear weapons are consistent with international law. After acknowledging an intellectual/moral debt to natural law, they examine various strategic roles contemplated for nuclear weapons and principles of human rights law applicable thereto. They conclude that any use of nuclear weapons violates the principles of international humanitarian law and constitutes a crime of state.

Falk, Richard, "The Shimoda Case: A Legal Appraisal of the Atomic Attacks Upon Hiroshima and Nagasaki," 59 *American Journal of International Law* 759 (1965).

The decision in the *Shimoda* case is analyzed from the standpoint of the continuing relevance of the laws of war to the conduct of nuclear warfare. The author concludes that the court's holding in *Shimoda* supports an unconditional prohibition of the use of nuclear weapons.

Falk, Richard, "Toward a Legal Regime for Nuclear Weapons," *supra* at Chapter 7, and 28 *McGill Law Journal* 519 (1983).

The author proposes a legal regime that confines the role of nuclear weapons to retaliatory uses of non-accurate weapons as an interim measure while governments develop policies that will preclude future reliance on nuclear weapons.

Feinrider, Martin, "International Law as Law of the Land: Another Constitutional Constraint on Use of Nuclear Weapons," *supra* at Chapter 6, and 7 *Nova Law Journal* 103 (1982).

The author traces the history of international law as the law of the land. Next he looks at the law of war, the United Nations Charter, and international human rights law, and he concludes that a customary norm of international law prohibiting nuclear weapons is now crystallizing, thereby limiting lawful nuclear options for the United States.

Fried, John, "First Use of Nuclear Weapons—Existing Prohibitions in International Law," 12 *Bulletin of Peace Proposals* 21 (No. 1, 1981).

The author states that "first-use" and nuclear responses to a non-nuclear attack are prohibited under existing international law.

Fried, John, "International Law Prohibits the First Use of Nuclear Weapons," 1 *Revue Belge de Droit International* 33 (1981-1982).

Fujita, Hisakazu, "First Use of Nuclear Weapons: Nuclear Strategy Versus International Law," 3 *Kansai University Review of Law and Politics* 57 (Osaka, 1982).

After analyzing the nuclear strategy of the United States, its influence on Soviet strategies, and the justifications of first-use put forth by American authorities and legal experts, the author concludes that such justifications are faulty.

Glaser, Stefan, "Arme Atomique et le Problème d'Analogie en Droit International," in *Liber amicorium Prof. Baron Jean van Houtte,* Brussels, Elsevier-Sequoia, 1975.

Goldblat, J., and Lodgaard, S., "Non-use of Nuclear Weapons: Security Assurances for Non-Nuclear Weapons States," 11 *Bulletin of Peace Proposals* 118 (No. 2, 1980).

"ICRC and Nuclear Disarmament," *International Committee of the Red Cross Bulletin* 4 (July 6, 1983 #90).

The I.C.R.C. summarizes its position in favor of complete disarmament and discusses the reasons why it cannot actively participate in disarmament activities.

Kennedy, David, "A Critical Approach to the Nuclear Weapons Problem," 9 *Brooklyn Journal of International Law* 307 (1983).

To date international lawyers have focused on the manipulation of abstractions in the discussion of the use of nuclear weapons under international law, according to the author. It is now time, he concludes, to turn to something more specific such as relentless critique of the strategies of justification presented for the current world order.

Khosla, Dinesh, "Nuclear Weapons, Global Values and International Law," *supra* at Chapter 2.

The author examines international custom and community expectations and raises a number of questions regarding the use of nuclear weapons. He finds the conclusion unavoidable that nuclear weapons are illegal even though specific treaty provisions and case law are lacking.

Lauterpacht, Hersch, "The Problem of the Revision of the Law of War," 29 *British Yearbook of International Law* 360 (1952).

In this paper the author discusses the contributions of the Geneva Conventions of 1949 to the revision of the law of war and reviews the reasons why further codification will be modest. Among these is the fact that in some areas, such as aerial bombardment and atomic warfare, there are no agreed laws to revise.

Lawyers' Committee on Nuclear Policy, "Statement on the Illegality of Nuclear Weapons," (undated).

The committee argues that the use of nuclear weapons is illegal *per se,* and attempts to initiate a dialogue among lawyers on the legitimacy of those weapons under international law.

Lisle, Raymond E., "Nuclear Weapons: A Conservative Approach to Treaty Interpretation," 9 *Brooklyn Journal of International Law* 275 (1983).

The author questions whether our developing rule of law adequately addresses or should address our entitlement to exercise the right of self-defense.

Maggs, Peter, "Soviet Viewpoint on Nuclear Weapons in International Law," 29 *Law and Contemporary Problems* 956 (1964).

This is one of the few English language overviews of the Soviet approach to legal problems connected with the testing, construction, possession, stationing, transit, transfer, and military use of nuclear weapons. The author, after presenting a résumé of the different doctrinal positions of the Soviets, concludes that they use varying legal positions and selected arguments to create a favorable public impression and to support their own power position. Extensive footnoting with many references to Soviet publications is used.

Mallison, W. Thomas, "The Laws of War and Juridical Control of Weapons of Mass Destruction in General and Limited War," 36 *George Washington Law Review* 308 (1968).

The author presents a history of the laws of war and an analysis of the effects of weapons of mass destruction. He supports the continued use of the laws of war to avoid destruction until optimum world order is achieved.

Mendlovitz, Saul, " 'Filling Out' the Right to Peace: A Basic Change in the Nation-State System," *supra* at Chapter 11, and 9 *Brooklyn Journal of International Law* 297 (1983).

After reviewing the history of the development of human rights, the author concludes that a global society is emerging in which ownership of nuclear weapons is not only a violation of human rights but a shame and an embarrassment.

Mendlovitz, Saul, "Nuclear Arms and World Public Order," 4 *New York Law School Journal of International and Comparative Law* 419 (1984).

Menon, P. K., "Legal Limits on the Use of Nuclear Weapons in Armed Conflicts," 18 *Revue de Droit Pénal Militaire et de Droit de la Guerre* 10 (1979).

The author examines the use of nuclear weapons in declared and undeclared wars. He analyzes customary and treaty law, the effects of nuclear weapons, and the actual use of the weapons in an attempt to identify weaknesses in present laws and possibilities for their improvement. There are summaries in French, Dutch, German, Italian, and Spanish, as well as extensive footnotes.

Menzel, Eberhard, "Atomwaffen," 1 *Wörterbuch Des Völkerrechts* (Strupp-Schlochauer) 106.

In this article the author questions whether nations can lawfully resort to nuclear weapons as a means of reprisal.

Meyrowitz, Elliott, "The Laws of War and Nuclear Weapons," *supra* at Chapter 3, and 9 *Brooklyn Journal of International Law* 227 (1983).

Examination of existing international law, the author concludes, supports the belief that all use of nuclear weapons is illegal *per se* and the legal community must play a role in shaping opinion on this issue.

Meyrowitz, Elliott, "Nuclear Weapons Policy: The Ultimate Tyranny," 7 *Nova Law Journal* 93 (1982).

The belief that democratic society is being seriously damaged by nuclear weapons, as stated by Arthur S. Miller, *infra* at Chapter 13, is explored by the author. He concludes that (1) the present nuclear weapons policy is incompatible with a democratic society and threatens its basic structures; and (2) the belief of the public that nuclear weapons are legal under international law is inaccurate.

Meyrowitz, Elliott, "The Status of Nuclear Weapons Under International Law," 38 *National Lawyers Guild Practitioner* 65 (1981).

The author urges the legal community to evaluate the use of nuclear weapons in the light of post-1945 foreign policy developments, and he suggests support for the laws of war and the Nuremberg Principles as constraints on nuclear war-making behavior.

Meyrowitz, Henri, "Les Juristes Devant L'Arme Nucléaire," 67 *Revue General Internationale Public* 820 (1963).

Meyrowitz, Henri, "Problems Juridiques Relatifs à l'Arme a Neutrons," 1981 *Annuaire Français de Droit International* 87.

Moore, John, "Nuclear Weapons and the Law: Enhancing Strategic Stability," *supra* at Chapter 4, and 9 *Brooklyn Journal of International Law* 263 (1983).

In this response to E. Meyrowitz the author supports some uses of nuclear weapons, and he suggests the need to look for proposals that increase strategic stability, rather than pursue those, such as debates on the legality of nuclear weapons, that detract from stability.

Nanda, Ved, "Nuclear Weapons and the Right to Peace Under International Law," 9 *Brooklyn Journal of International Law* 283 (1983).

The author discusses the human right to peace under international law and the implications of the existence of nuclear weapons on the right to peace.

Nincic, D., "Nuclear Weapons and the Charter of the U.N.," 9 *Jugoslovenska Revija za Medunarodno Pravo* 197 (1962).

"Nuclear Weapons and the Law," 5 *State Research Bulletin* 170 (No. 31, 1982).

Any use of nuclear weapons is illegal under international law and could be a basis for criminalizing the manufacture and deployment of such weapons. The authors also discuss the implications of this position within United Kingdom municipal law.

O'Brien, William V., "The Meaning of 'Military Necessity' in Nuclear War," 1 *Yearbook of World Polity* 109 (1957).

O'Brien, William V., "Some Problems of the Law of War in Limited Nuclear War," 14 *Military Law Review* 1 (October 1961).

The author believes that the United States can adapt to the concept of limited nuclear war, but he does not address solutions to the humanitarian problems raised by such a viewpoint.

Paust, Jordan, "Controlling Prohibited Weapons and the Illegal Use of Permitted Weapons," 28 *McGill Law Review* 609 (1983).

Despite numerous direct and indirect international legal prohibitions governing conventional and nuclear weapons, the author concludes that there is an urgent need for additional steps, such as a ban on development, manufacture, sale, and use of nuclear weapons, as well as criminal and civil sanctions.

Paust, Jordan, "The Nuclear Decision in World War II—Truman's Ending and Avoidance of War," 8 *The International Lawyer* 160 (1974).

This article offers a legal and historical analysis of the World War II decision to use the atomic bomb. The author analyzes the *Shimoda* case in terms of legality and military necessity and then looks at the use of the bomb in the context of peace and necessity.

Prusakov, M., "Nuclear-free Zones in Contemporary International Law," 1978 *Soviet Yearbook of International Law* 162.

(In Russian with an English summary.)

Radojkovic, Milos, "Les Armes Nucléaires et le Droit International," *1962 Yearbook of World Affairs* 197 (1962).

Rauschning, Dietrich, "Nuclear Warfare and Weapons," 4 *Encyclopedia of Public International Law* 44 (1982).

The author determines that there is nothing in treaties or general rules of war that expressly prohibits the use of nuclear weapons in war.

Reisman, W. Michael, "Deterrence and International Law," *supra* at Chapter 8.

Using the Yale policy approach to international theory, the author discusses three questions concerning nuclear weapons: what is the law in this matter; what should the law be; and how can the law be changed to approximate our preferences. (This is an edited version of "Nuclear Weapons in International Law," 4 *New York Law School Journal of International and Comparative Law* 339 (1984).)

Röling, B.V.A., "International Law, Nuclear Weapons, Arms Control and Disarmament," *supra* at Chapter 10.

The emergence of nuclear weapons, the author suggests, supports the legal arguments for a total prohibition of war.

Rosas, Allan, "International Law and the Use of Nuclear Weapons," in *Essays in Honour of Erik Castren* 73, Finnish Branch of the International Law Association, Helsinki, Finland (1979).

Sack, Alexander, "ABC—Atomic, Biological, Chemical Warfare in International Law," 10 *Lawyers Guild Review* 161 (1950).

The use of ABC weapons are illegal under principles of international law, and the author concludes that these principles need to be solemnly reaffirmed as binding on all nations.

Sajoo, Amynmohamed, "Human Rights Perspectives on the Arms Race," 28 *McGill Law Review* 628 (1983).

After reviewing the nature of the present arms race and consequent violation of international human rights, the author concludes that only sustained political pressure will force governments to seek alternatives to the present system of international relations.

Setalvad, M. C., "Nuclear Weapons and International Law," 3 *Indian Journal of International Law* 383 (1963).
> This is a survey of the major international law arguments for and against the use of nuclear weapons. Despite the survey format some of the author's views against nuclear weapons come through.

Singh, M. Nagendra, "The Right of Self-Defense in Relation to the Use of Nuclear Weapons," 5 *Indian Yearbook of International Affairs* 3 (1956).
> After analyzing the principles of military survival, self-preservation, and self-defense, the author concludes that the only justifiable use of nuclear weapons is confined to limited exercises of self-defense.

Smith, Gerard C., "Nuclear Arms and Disarmament," 4 *New York Law School Journal of International and Comparative Law* 345 (1984).

Stein, E., "Impact of New Weapons Technology on International Law, Selected Aspects," 133 *Hague Academy Recueil des Cours* 222 (1971-II).
> The major portion of this treatise-length essay is devoted to an analysis of the legal restraints on the arms race imposed by collateral measures. In section II, however, the author looks specifically at international law measures and concludes that the General Assembly resolution prohibiting the use of nuclear weapons represents a consensus that use of nuclear weapons is contrary to international law.

Stowell, Ellery C., "The Laws of War and the Atomic Bomb," 39 *American Journal of International Law* 784 (1945).
> A strong pro-nuclear position is taken by the author who concludes that the most effective means of advancing the cause of civilization is to develop the atomic bomb to prevent aggression, to secure cooperation, and to use as a defense when necessary.

"The United States' Nuclear First-Strike Position: A Legal Appraisal of its Ramifications," 7 *California Western International Law Journal* 508 (1977) (Note by William Lee).
> After a discussion of the use of tactical nuclear weapons in response to a conventional military attack, the author concludes that under certain circumstances such use would be sanctioned by international law.

Vlasic, Iran, "Raison d'État v. Raison de l'Humanité—The United Nations SSOD II and Beyond," 28 *McGill Law Journal* 455 (1983).
> The efforts of the U.N. to prevent arms race escalation, the stalemated U.S.-U.S.S.R. weapons negotiations, and the potential collapse of arms limitations are reviewed by the author. He appeals to jurists to play a more active role in asserting the importance of international law in the maintenance of global peace and security.

Weiss, Peter, "Commentary," 4 *New York Law School Journal of International and Comparative Law* 427 (1984).

Weston, Burns, "Nuclear Weapons Versus International Law: A Contextual Reassessment," *supra* at Chapter 9, and 28 *McGill Law Journal* 542 (1983).
> The humanitarian rules of armed conflict are applied to different offensive nuclear weapons strategies by the author to prove the illegality of nearly all uses of nuclear weapons.

Weston, Burns H., "Nuclear Weapons and International Law: Prolegomenon to General Illegality," 4 *New York Law School Journal of International and Comparative Law* 227 (1984).

III. *TESTING OF NUCLEAR WEAPONS*
A. *TREATISES*

Arx, Herbert, *Atombombenversuche und Völkerrecht,* Basel und Stuttgart: Helbing and Lichtenhahn, 1974.

Asian-African Legal Consultative Committee, *The Legality of Nuclear Tests, Report of the Committee and Background Materials,* New Delhi, Secretariat of the Committee (1966).

> In this report the Committee concludes that nuclear testing in peace time is an abuse of rights. It is contrary to the United Nations Charter, the principles of freedom of the seas, and the Universal Declaration of Human Rights, and should result in liability for damages caused by test explosions.

France, Ministère des Affaires Etrangères, *White Paper on the French Nuclear Tests,* Paris, 1973.

> This is the French government's defense of its nuclear tests. Scientific and technical data and legal issues are reviewed in an effort to prove that the French tests had a sound scientific basis and violated no rule of international law.

Furet, Marie, *Experimentation des Armes Nucléaires et Droit International Public,* Paris, A. Pedone, 1966. (Series: Revue generale de droit international public (Nouvelle ser., no. 9)).

Goldblat, Jozef, *French Nuclear Tests in the Atmosphere: The Question of Legality,* Stockholm, Stockholm International Peace Research Institute (1974) (SIPRI).

> French nuclear tests are evaluated against treaties, peremptory norms, and the International Court of Justice decision. The author explores the legality of French atmospheric testing and atmospheric testing in general.

Sivard, Ruth L., *World Military and Social Expenditures,* Leesburg, Va., World Publications, 1983.

> In this annual the author provides a variety of data on nuclear weapons including statistics on number of missiles held, risks and consequences of explosions, comparisons of nations' expenditures etc., but the chapter of particular relevance is the one on treaties.

B. *ESSAYS AND JOURNAL ARTICLES*

"Explosive Issue in International Law: The French Nuclear Tests," 9 *Melbourne University Law Review* 296 (1973) (note by J. Swan).

> This is an analysis of the international law issues raised by French nuclear tests in the Pacific. The author finds that France invoked state sovereignty in order to avoid relevant international law principles.

Fliess, Peter, "The Legality of Atmospheric Nuclear Tests—Critical View of International Law in the Cold War," 15 *University of Florida Law Review* 21 (1962).

> The author looks at customary and treaty norms to determine whether or not nuclear tests are compatible with international law. Next, he examines state and individual rights affected by atmospheric tests.

Franck, Thomas M., "Word Made Law: The Decision of the I.C.J. in the Nuclear Test Cases," 69 *American Journal of International Law* 612 (1975) (Editorial Comment by Franck).

In the Nuclear Tests Cases the International Court of Justice chose not to confront the issue, but in so doing it made a monumental impact on the international law system. The author concludes that due to the Court's decision states recognize that their public statements become part of the reciprocal expectations that are the basis of the international system.

"International Law—International Court of Justice Has Preliminary Jurisdiction to Indicate Interim Measures of Protection: The Nuclear Tests Cases," 7 *New York University Journal of International Law and Politics* 163 (1974) (Comment by K. Frankel).

The author discusses: (1) the power of the I.C.J. to provide interim protection, (2) the scope of the court's jurisdiction, and (3) the admissibility of these claims under international law.

Khosla, Dinesh, "Nuclear Test Cases: Judicial Valour v. Judicial Discretion," 18 *Indian Journal of International Law* 322 (1978).

The International Court of Justice decision in the Nuclear Tests Cases is analyzed by the author in terms of the value of the unilateral declarations of France. These declarations give rise to expectations which in turn serve as a basis of obligation in international law.

Lee, Luke T., "The Legality of Nuclear Tests and Weapons," 18 *Österreichische Zeitschrift Für Öffentliches Recht* 307 (1968).

Margolis, Emanuel, "The Hydrogen Bomb Experiments and International Law," 64 *Yale Law Journal* 629 (1955).

The author argues in favor of the cessation of further testing or for testing compatible with general tenets of international law.

McDougal, Myres, and Schlei, N., "The Hydrogen Bomb Tests in Perspective: Lawful Measures for Security," 64 *Yale Law Journal* 648 (1955).

After voicing their support for the legality of nuclear testing, the authors conclude that the free world must maintain the capacity to defend institutions until a secure world public order is established.

White, G., "H-Bomb Tests and the International Court," 123 *New Law Journal* 615 (1973).

In this brief article the author discusses the jurisdictional aspects of the World Court proceedings in the French Nuclear Tests Cases.

IV. *OTHER SOURCES OF INFORMATION*

A. *MILITARY MANUALS*

These manuals are a valuable source of information on the official government positions regarding the use of nuclear weapons. They reflect how international law and national law are enforced by each individual country.

A selection of military manuals is included. Many of the entries are taken from the ICRC *Bibliography of International Humanitarian Law*. A complete list of manuals can be found in Chapter 2.7.3. of that work.

FRANCE

Inquiries regarding French publications should be addressed to:

Ministère de la Guerre
14 Rue Saint Dominique
75997 Paris Armées

Ministère de la Marine
2 Rue Royale
75200 Paris Naval

Ministère de la Guerre—*Le droit des gens et les conventions internationales*,
Bulletin Officiel du Ministère de la Guerre, No. 110-0, 1955.
Ministère de la Marine—*Les Instructions navales du 31 decembre 1964 sur l'appli-
cation du droit international en cas de guerre*, No. 2380 E.M.M./2, 1964.
Droit maritime: Instructions sur l'application du droit international en cas de guerre,
Volume No. 102-3, Paris, 1965.
Droit aérien et règlementation aérienne des armées, Volume No. 103, Paris, 1969.

NETHERLANDS

Rules of the law of war, Manual VR 2-1120-11.

UNION OF SOVIET SOCIALIST REPUBLICS

Disciplinary code of the armed forces of the Soviet Union, 1950, in Berman, H. J.,
& Kerner, M., *Documents on Soviet military law and administration, 1955.*

UNITED KINGDOM

Inquiries regarding British military publications should be addressed to:

The Department of Public Information
Ministry of Defense
Main Building
Whitehall, London SW 1

War Office—*The law of war on land, being part III of the manual of military law,*
Code No. 12333, London, Her Majesty's Stationary Office, 1958.
War Office—*Manual of air force law,* vols. I-II, 5th edition, London, 1972.

UNITED STATES

Department of the Army publications may be obtained by writing to the
following address:

Commander U.S. Army
A.G. Publications Center
2800 Eastern Blvd.
Baltimore, MD 21220

Department of the Army—*The U.S. fighting man's code,* Office of Armed Forces,
Washington, D.C., 1955.
Department of the Army—*Field manual: the law of land warfare,* Air Force pamph-
let FM 27-10, Washington. D.C., July 1956.

Department of the Army—*Treaties governing land warfare,* Pamphlet 27-1, Washington, D.C., December 1956.

Department of the Army—*International law, vol. II,* Pamphlet 27-161-2, Washington, D.C., October 1962.

The U.S. Army Combat-Arms Training Board—*Your conduct in combat under the law of war,* Washington, D.C., 1974. (Reprinted as Army Training Circular TC 27-1, 1976).

Department of the Air Force—*International law: The conduct of armed conflict and air operations,* Air Force pamphlet 110-31, Washington, D.C., 1976.

Department of the Army—*Fundamentals of military law,* Washington, D.C., 1976.

Department of the Navy—*Law of armed conflict (law of war): program to insure compliance by the naval establishment,* SECNAVINST 3300 1A, Washington, D.C., May 1980.

Department of the Air Force—*Commander's handbook on the law of armed conflict,* AFP 110-34, Washington, D.C., July 1980.

B. *ORGANIZATIONS*

A list of some organizations that are concerned with the use of nuclear weapons appears below. In addition to playing an active role in the struggle to confront and eliminate these weapons, many of these organizations are a valuable source of information. Addresses are provided and publications are listed when possible.

International Committee of the Red Cross (ICRC/CICR)
   17 Avenue de la Paix
   Geneva, Switzerland

   U.S. Address: 815 Second Avenue
                 Room 510
                 New York, NY 10017
   Publications: *ICRC Bulletin/Annual Report*

International Institute for Strategic Studies (IISS)
   23 Savistock Street
   London WC2E7NG
   England

   The IISS publishes a range of periodicals including *Military Balance, Strategic Survey,* and a series called *Studies in International Security.*

International Peace Research Institute
   Universitetsforlaget
   Box 2959-Toeyen
   Kolstadgt 1
   Oslo, Norway

   U.S. Address: 200 Meachman Ave.
                 Elmont, NY 11003
   Publications: *Bulletin of Peace Proposals, Journal of Peace Research*

Lawyers Alliance for Nuclear Arms Control, Inc. (LANAC)
11 Beacon Street, Suite 719
Boston, MA 02108

The Alliance prepares "white papers" on the history and status of nuclear weapons and arms control. They also publish a quarterly newsletter, bibliographies, and brochures.

Lawyers' Committee on Nuclear Policy (LCNP)
225 Lafayette Street, Suite 207
New York, NY 10012

The organization is composed of lawyers and legal scholars who believe nuclear weapons are prohibited by international law and who dedicate themselves to the prevention of nuclear war and to the abolition of nuclear weapons. They publish a quarterly newsletter, and statements and pamphlets, and often distribute the writings of members of the Committee's Consultative Council.

Physicians for Social Responsibility
639 Massachusetts Avenue
Cambridge, MA 02139

Stockholm International Peace Research Institute (SIPRI)
Sveavagen 166
S-133 46 Stockholm
Sweden

Set up in 1966, SIPRI serves as an independent institute for research into problems of peace and conflict. Research is concentrated on armaments problems, disarmament and arms regulation. The Institute publishes the *Yearbook of Armaments and Disarmaments,* as well as other books and studies.

Union of Concerned Scientists (UCS)
1384 Massachusetts Avenue
Cambridge, MA 02238

United Nations Centre for Disarmament
Palais des Nations
Geneva, Switzerland

The Centre publishes a monthly bibliography of articles on disarmament, peace and security. It also publishes *Disarmament Fact Sheets* in co-operation with the U.N. Department of Public Information.

United Nations Institute for Disarmament Research (UNIDIR)
Palais des Nations
Geneva, Switzerland

(Note: The United Nations publishes a number of items related to this topic. Other publications of note include: *Disarmament* (published quarterly); *Disarmament Yearbook* (published annually since 1976); *Disarmament Studies* (an eight-part set); *Nuclear Weapons,* A/35/392 (a report to the Secretary General on nuclear weapons and policy).)

PART II
Nuclear Weapons and Constitutional Law

13.
Nuclear Weapons and Constitutional Law*

Arthur Selwyn Miller**

Introduction

The time has come for lawyers to confront the question of whether nuclear weapons—their manufacture, deployment, and use—can be justified under either constitutional or international law. Since the explosions of primitive atomic bombs at Hiroshima and Nagasaki in 1945 it has been assumed, without much thought, that there is nothing unlawful about those weapons. This paper is a preliminary statement that suggests the contrary. It is predicated on two observations of Alfred North Whitehead: "The doctrines which best repay critical examinations are those which for the longest period have remained unquestioned;"[1] and "almost all really new ideas have a certain aspect of foolishness when they are first presented."[2] What follows is a brief outline in which I contend that it is not really foolish for law and lawyers to contribute to the growing debate about nuclear war.

People throughout the world live today under the threat of a nuclear arms "race" that is madly out of control. That peril has at long last—almost forty years after the bombs dropped on Hiroshima and Nagasaki—percolated into the thinking of growing numbers of men and women who have swelled into a spontaneous popular movement against the ultimate danger. Their motivations, as perceived by Ambassador George Kennan, include:

---

* Reprinted, with permission, from *Nova Law Journal*, Volume 7, Number 1 (1982).

** 1982-83 Leo Goodwin, Sr., Distinguished Visiting Professor of Law, Center for the Study of Law, Nova University; Professor Emeritus of Law, George Washington University. This essay is based on the author's work in progress, a book tentatively entitled *Getting There From Here: Constitutional Changes for a Sustainable Society.*

1. Whitehead, as *quoted* in Miller, *A Note on the Criticism of Supreme Court Decisions*, 10 J. Pub. L. 139 (1961).

2. Whitehead, as *quoted in* A. Brecht, Political Theory: The Foundations of Twentieth-Century Political Thought 262 (1959) (paperback ed. 1967).

> a growing appreciation by many people of the true horrors of a nuclear war; a determination not to see their children deprived of life, or their civilization destroyed, by a holocaust of this nature; and finally . . ., a very real exasperation with their governments for the rigidity and traditionalism that cause those governments to ignore the fundamental distinction between conventional weapons and weapons of mass destruction and prevents them from finding, or even seriously seeking, ways of escape from the fearful trap into which the cultivation of nuclear weapons is leading us.[3]

Members of the clergy, physicians, scientists, and businessmen have grasped and sought to show to others the meaning of nuclear war.

With rare exceptions, lawyers until very recent times have been mute. They have assumed, if they thought about it, that nuclear weapons are just another means of killing—a bit more powerful but not essentially different from the long bow, the machine gun, the tank, and the airplane. That assumption is simply not accurate.

Some lawyers, mainly those in international law, have begun to challenge the assumption of legality of nuclear weaponry. The Lawyers Committee on Nuclear Policy has recently been formed, with headquarters in New York City. The Committee's position is that nuclear weapons are incompatible "with the core precepts of international law."[4] The Committee believes that "nuclear warfare would lead to results incompatible with fundamental rules of international law, elementary morality, and contrary to any rational conception of national interest and world order. . . . The very nature of nuclear warfare is destructive of all the values which law obligates us to preserve."[5]

---

3. Kennan, *On Nuclear War*, THE N.Y. REVIEW, Jan. 21, 1982, at 8. *See* Molander, *How I Learned to Start Worrying About Nukes*, Manchester Guardian Weekly, April 4, 1982, at 17 (reprint from the Washington Post). For the view of physicians, see Kerzner, *The Last Epidemic*, Miami Herald, March 7, 1982, at E1, col. 1 where it states, "Nuclear war could be the last epidemic our civilization will know. Hundreds of millions of people would be killed or injured, and the economic, ecological and social fabric on which human life depends would be shattered."

4. Weston, *Clergy, Doctors, Business-and now the Lawyers*, Des Moines Register, March 27, 1982, at A9, col. 1. Professor Weston of the University of Iowa quotes Chicago banker Ervin Salk to the effect that the nuclear arms race "is tearing the guts out of our economy just like Vietnam did."

5. LAWYERS COMMITTEE ON NUCLEAR POLICY, STATEMENT ON THE ILLEGALITY OF NUCLEAR WEAPONS 7 (undated). The Committee's purpose is to initiate a dialogue

No one has yet asked the constitutional question: Does the manufacture, deployment, and possible—even probable—use of nuclear weapons contravene the Constitution? This paper is a preliminary inquiry into that question. It is an outline, presenting possible constitutional arguments, rather than a full-dress exposition. In the well-known but little heeded words of Albert Einstein, "the unleashed power of the atom has changed everything save our modes of thinking, and we thus drift toward unparalleled catastrophe."[6] So we do: I contend in this brief paper that the time has come—indeed, it is long past—to change "our modes of thinking" about the constitutionality of nuclear weapons.

My conclusion may be simply stated: An argument based on the goal-seeking nature of constitutionalism, together with at least four other constitutional arguments, invalidate the presumption of constitutionality. These arguments will be discussed in detail later. This is not to say that the Supreme Court would sustain these arguments, were a case to be brought. Rather, it is to say that as a part of the dialogue that is beginning about the legality of nuclear weapons the dimension of constitutional law cannot be ignored—it is not enough to argue that those weapons are incompatible with international law—as surely they are.

At the outset, I readily concede the jurisprudential problem of whether legal norms (rights) can exist absent a means of enforcement. That, however, should not stay the inquiry into the relevance of constitutional prescriptions to the nuclear threat. As long ago as 1803, in the famous case of *Marbury v. Madison*[7] that established the Supreme Court's power of judicial review, Chief Justice John Marshall acknowledged that Mr. Marbury was entitled to his commission as a justice of the peace but went on to assert that there could be no judicial enforcement of that right. Congress, Marshall held, had constitutionally erred in trying to enlarge upon the original jurisdiction of the Supreme Court. Furthermore, until recent decades, a number of now-recognized

---

regarding the legitimacy of nuclear weapons under international law. (The present essay seeks to expand that focus to encompass constitutional law.) The Committee's address is 777 United Nations Plaza (5th Floor), New York, N.Y. 10017. (In the interests of disclosure, I am a member of the Consultative Council of the Committee.)

6. J. SCHELL, THE FATE OF THE EARTH 188 (1982).

7. 5 U.S. (1 Cranch) 137 (1803).

constitutional rights such as the right to privacy, one person/one vote, and racial desegregation were not given judicial cognizance. The history of American constitutional law is one of an expanding number of rights brought into being, in one way or another, by the Supreme Court or other constitutional decisionmakers. In philosophic terms, law—including constitutional law—has always been instrumental. Rather than being a fixed body of pre-existing immutable principles, it is goal-seeking, purposive—a type of human activity that exists for identifiable ends. In addition, constitutional law has been and is relative to circumstances. Necessity is the mother of constitutional law which is constantly in a state of "becoming."[8]

More than 40,000 nuclear weapons now exist, and more are being produced each week. Russia has enough to wipe out every American city of 1500 or more people. The United States has an even larger stockpile. And nuclear capacity is proliferating. France, Great Britain, India, China, for certain, and Israel, South Africa and perhaps Brazil also have significant nuclear weaponry. Enough "overkill" already exists in amounts sufficient to vaporize every living human being on earth today. And yet political officers in the world's capitals continue a mad "race" for supremacy.

This essay is emphatically not a plea for unilateral disarmament. We live in a Hobbesian world, a condition not at all likely to change. The essence of my argument is that those who wield both formal authority and effective control in the American constitutional order have a duty to take action designed to eliminate the nuclear threat throughout the world. The duty, I maintain, is of constitutional dimension. The ultimate goal has been stated recently by Billy Graham as the elimination of *every* weapon of mass destruction in the world.

The Philosophical Basis of Constitutionalism

The text of the ensuing discussion comes from Justice Felix Frankfurter and the French legal philosopher, Leon Duguit. Said Frankfurter in 1949: "It is of the very nature of a free society to advance in its

---

8. For discussion, *see* A. MILLER, DEMOCRATIC DICTATORSHIP: THE EMERGENT CONSTITUTION OF CONTROL (1981); A. MILLER, TOWARD INCREASED JUDICIAL ACTIVISM: THE POLITICAL ROLE OF THE SUPREME COURT (1982).

standards of what is deemed reasonable and right."[9] Said Duguit in 1919: "Any system of public law can be vital only so far as it is based on a given sanction to the following rules: First, the holders of power cannot do certain things; second, there are certain things they must do."[10]

This, then, is an exercise in American constitutionalism. As a concept, constitutionalism has usually had, at least in the United States, a normative connotation, as witness the following definitions. "Constitutionalism," Friedrich Hayek maintains,

> means that all power rests on the understanding that it will be exercised in accordance with commonly accepted principles, that the persons on whom power is conferred are selected because it is thought that they are most likely to do what is right, not in order that whatever they do should be right.[11]

To Daniel Bell it is "the common respect for the framework of law, and acceptance of outcomes under due process."[12] Walter F. Murphy maintains that "[t]he fundamental value that constitutionalism protects is human dignity."[13] And to Charles McIlwain "constitutionalism has one essential quality: it is a legal limitation on government."[14] In sum, constitutionalism in America is more than a process—more than procedure alone—but has a substantive, normative, content looking toward the responsibility, as McIlwain put it, of government to the governed. James Madison said it well in *The Federalist No. 51:* "In framing a government which is to be administered by men over men, the great difficulty lies in this: you must first enable the government to control the governed; and in the next place oblige it to control itself."[15]

As "officers of the courts" lawyers have a quasi-governmental sta-

---

9. Wolf v. Colorado, 338 U.S. 25, 27 (1949).

10. L. DUGUIT, LAW IN THE MODERN STATE 26 (H. Laski trans. 1919).

11. F. HAYEK, THE CONSTITUTION OF LIBERTY 181 (1960).

12. Bell, *The End of American Exceptionalism*, 41 PUB. INTEREST 193 (1975).

13. Murphy, *An Ordering of Constitutional Values*, 53 S. CAL. L. REV. 703, 758 (1980).

14. C. MCILWAIN, CONSTITUTIONALISM: ANCIENT AND MODERN 21 (rev. ed. 1947). McIlwain also said: "All constitutional government is by definition limited government." *Id.*

15. THE FEDERALIST No. 51, at 349 (J. Madison) (J. Cooke ed. 1961).

tus. As such, they should no longer remain on the sidelines, taking no action to seek and, one hopes, to find what Kennan calls "ways of escape."[16] The full force of law, feeble though it may be, should be brought to bear upon the growing peril. Law, to be sure, has shortcomings as a principle of social order. It cannot do everything; there are limits to its effectiveness in changing either the attitudes or behavior of people. But that does not mean that the effort should not be made. Chief Justice Earl Warren once remarked that "law floats in a sea of ethics."[17] So it does: law can be a powerful educational force that will create the climate so necessary to move away from the abyss.

A persuasive case can be made for the proposition that nuclear weapons should be considered to be unlawful under both international law and constitutional law. Since law is instrumental, and a reflection of the circumstances in which it exists, the nuclear peril presents it with a challenge and an opportunity. In the United States, the ultimate purpose of law is human survival under conditions that allow human dignity to be maximized. In familiar legal terms, nuclear weapons are a clear and present danger both to survival and especially to achievement of human dignity. Senator J. W. Fulbright, then chairman of the Senate Foreign Relations Committee, stated the point in 1967 in these well-chosen words: The President, he said,

> by acquiring the authority to commit the country to war, now exercises something approaching absolute power over the life or death of every American—to say nothing of millions of other people all over the world. . . . No human being or group [is] wise and competent enough to be entrusted with such vast power. Plenary powers in the hand of any man or group threatens all other men with tyranny or disaster.[18]

So it does—whether such a power resides in the Kremlin or the White House. The well-known statement of military scientist Karl von Clause-

---

16. *See* Kennan, *supra* note 3, at 8.

17. Address by Earl Warren, Chief Justice of the United States Supreme Court at the Louis Marshall Award Dinner of the Jewish Theological Seminary of America in New York City (Nov. 11, 1962).

18. Fried, *War-Exclusive and War-Inclusive Style in International Conduct,* 11 TEX. INT'L L.J. 1, 26 (1976) (quoting from S. REP. No. 797, 90th Cong., 1st Sess. 1, 26 (1967)).

witz, that "war is diplomacy carried on by other means,"[19] may well have been accurate when made early in the nineteenth century; but it no longer is. Unleashing the atom invalidated it.

Nuclear war cannot by any criterion be "deemed reasonable and right"—to use Justice Frankfurter's words. Not for the United States. Not for the Soviet Union. Nor for any nation. International law merges with constitutional law to proscribe use of such weapons. Once that is seen, *a fortiori* their manufacture and deployment are also outlawed.

Constitutional Challenges to Nuclear Weapons: The Goals of the Preamble

The purposive—goal-seeking—dimension of constitutionalism suggests this argument: the preamble to the Constitution states the ends of government—"to form a more perfect union, establish justice, insure domestic tranquility, provide for the common defense, promote the general welfare, and secure the blessings of liberty to ourselves and our posterity." Nuclear weapons and the delicate balance of terror jeopardize each of those goals; and nuclear war would eradicate them. Surely the framers could not have contemplated such a consequence either for themselves or their posterity.

We are that posterity. The time has come to think seriously about giving substantive content to the preamble. Strictly speaking, to be sure, the preamble is not part of the Constitution. It precedes it. The preamble has never been held to sustain a specific claim of governmental power or of private right. As Justice Joseph Story said in his *Commentaries,* "Its true office is to expound the nature and extent and application of the powers actually conferred by the Constitution, and not substantively to create them."[20] In other words, the preamble sets the tone for the meanings to be given to the specific provisions of the Document of 1787.

Those meanings, first, should be derived from a correct appreciation of present conditions and with the avowed goal of meeting current problems. To quote Chief Justice Marshall's well-known words in *Mc-*

---

19. K. von Clausewitz, On War _ (J. Graham trans., F. Maude ed. 1968).
20. J. Story, Commentaries on the Constitution bk. 3, § 462, at 361 (5th ed. 1981) (1st ed. 1833).

Culloch v. Maryland, "The subject is the execution of those great powers on which the welfare of a nation essentially depends. . . . This provision is made in a constitution intended to endure for ages to come, and, consequently, to be adapted to the various 'crises' of human affairs."[21] The import of that statement, the most important ever uttered on the theory of constitutional interpretation, is clear: The Constitution may validly be considered to be a tacit delegation of power by the framers to enable succeeding generations of Americans to write their own fundamental law—to meet, that is, the exigencies of *their*—not the framers'—times.

The Constitution was drafted for the benefit of "ourselves and our posterity." Since nuclear weapons threaten the goals of the preamble, the meaning is that there will be no posterity left to pick up the pieces after the bombs have exploded. Not only will the constitutional order have vanished, but quite possibly civilization itself. No one can validly argue that threatening the very existence of "posterity" can be constitutional. Posterity has its claims under the Constitution. That is particularly true because the rapid rate of social change, brought about by the scientific-technological revolution, means that most people alive today will be their own posterity. (Those who ask, "what has posterity done for me?", should constantly keep in mind that they are their own posterity.)

I do not suggest, of course, that in and of itself the preamble can be invoked to persuade anyone that nuclear weapons are unconstitutional per se. However, the preamble does provide an initial entry point into a more detailed and more specific analysis. The implication here is that, as William Seward once said, "there is a higher law than the Constitution"; or as Chief Justice Marshall wrote in *Fletcher v. Peck,*[22] Georgia's attempt to revoke a fraudulent land grant disregarded "certain great principles of natural justice."[23] Therefore, Georgia was restrained "either by general principles which are common to our free

---

21. 17 U.S. (4 Wheat.) 216, 421 (1819). *See* E. CORWIN, THE CONSTITUTION AND WHAT IT MEANS TODAY 2 (A. Chase & C. Ducat 13th ed. 1973) where it states, "the Constitution . . . should be interpreted in the light of present conditions and with a view to meeting present problems."

22. 10 U.S. (6 Cranch) 87 (1810).

23. *Id.* at 133.

institutions, or by the particular provisions of the Constitution."[24] Marshall's colleague, Justice William Johnson, went even further, asserting that "a general principle, on the reason and nature of things; a principle which will impose laws even on the deity"[25] invalidated the attempted rescission. In sum, can a principle of natural justice—a concept that has greater currency in Great Britain—be employed to determine the validity of nuclear weapons? The answer can only be "yes." In the language of the famous "Martens Clause" of the fourth Hague Convention of 1907, when no treaty provision specifically forbids a new tactic or weapon, combatants and non-combatants remain nonetheless protected by legal principles derived "from the usages established among civilized peoples, from the laws of humanity, and the dictates of the public conscience."[26]

Without going further into the complex question of natural justice, what particular provisions of the Constitution are conceivably relevant to the nuclear weapons situation? I suggest the following, each of which would require creativity or innovation by a constitutional decision-maker. The points are listed as questions requiring exploration, not as established doctrines. Taken together, however, they point in only one direction: the illegality of nuclear weapons.

The Congressional War Power

First: Can Congress delegate, tacitly or expressly, its war-making power? That there has been a tacit delegation to the President admits of no doubt (as Senator Fulbright said). It is even possible to perceive an express delegation in the War Powers Resolution of 1973, enacted into law over President Richard Nixon's veto, which ironically was intended to place limits over presidential power.[27]

Presidents beginning with George Washington have unilaterally employed violence. All of those instances, however, save perhaps for

---

24. *Id*. at 139.

25. *Id*. at 143 (Johnson, J., concurring).

26. 1 THE LAW OF WAR: A DOCUMENTARY HISTORY 309 (L. Friedman ed. 1972); R. FALK, L. MEYROWITZ, & J. SANDERSON, NUCLEAR WEAPONS AND INTERNATIONAL LAW 15 (Occasional Paper No. 10, World Order Studies Program, Center of International Studies, Princeton University (1981)).

27. *See* Fried, *supra* note 18.

President Abraham Lincoln during the Civil War, were for limited goals. They were taken in accordance with the Principle of the Economy of Means: just enough violence to meet the situation adequately.[28] That Principle is simply not applicable in the age of nuclear warfare. By definition, use of nuclear weapons cannot be limited. Once employed, sooner or later the conflict will escalate into all-out war. The meaning for present purposes is that it is one thing for a President to use limited violence, but that it is quite another thing for the Chief Executive to have absolute power of life and death in the nuclear age. Insofar as there is a constitutional doctrine about delegation of legislative powers, certainly it does not extend to the power to threaten civilization itself.

During the Civil War, the Supreme Court in the *Prize Cases*[29] sustained Lincoln's actions to meet the emergency: "The President was bound to meet it in the shape it presented itself, without waiting for Congress to baptize it with a name, and no name given to it by him or them could change the fact."[30] (What the Court did not say was that Lincoln made absolutely no attempt to call Congress into session to consider a response to Fort Sumter's hostilities; in fact, he waited almost three months—from April until July—before formally telling Congress what was going on.) The most that can be said for the decision in the *Prize Cases* is that the Supreme Court came close to being an arm of the Executive. That decision, furthermore, at best stands for the proposition that a President can *respond* to emergency situations. By no means does it mean that the President can commence a war. First-strike use of nuclear weapons should, as former high officials Robert McNamara, McGeorge Bundy, Gerard Smith and George Kennan recently argued in *Foreign Affairs,* be dropped as a policy option.[31]

The so-called doctrine of anticipatory self-defense, taken pursuant to Article 51 of the United Nations Charter, was cited by American lawyers during the Cuban missile crisis of 1962 (wrongly, in my judgment). That episode is proof positive about the enormity of Congress

---

28. For discussion, *see* A. MILLER, DEMOCRATIC DICTATORSHIP: THE EMERGENT CONSTITUTION OF CONTROL (1981).

29. 67 U.S. (2 Black) 635 (1863).

30. *Id.* at 699.

31. McNamara, Bundy, Smith & Kennan, *Nuclear Weapons and the Atlantic Alliance,* 60 FOREIGN AFF. 753 (Spring 1982).

allowing one man to have the power to eliminate human life. Clearly, the framers did not want the wealth and blood of the nation to be committed by one person (as *The Federalist No. 69* evidences)—even in a day before the invention of such conventional weapons as the machine gun and the tank! During the 1787 Convention, Elbridge Gerry remarked that he "never expected to hear in a republic a motion to empower the President alone to declare war."[32]

We deal, however, with one of the greatest silences of the Constitution; the principle of constitutional reason of State (*raison d'état*), defined as "the doctrine that whatever is required to insure the survival of the State must be done by the individuals responsible for it, no matter how repugnant such an act may be to them in their private capacity as decent and moral men."[33] Political officers of American government have never hesitated to employ that principle—to invoke a constitutional silence—both in external and wholly domestic matter, when they believed that conditions warranted. Franz Neumann put it well:

> No society in recorded history has ever been able to dispense with political power. This is as true of liberalism as of absolutism, as true of laissez faire as of an interventionist state. No greater disservice has been rendered to political science than the statement that the liberal state was a "weak" state. It was precisely as strong as it needed to be in the circumstances. It acquired substantial colonial empires, waged wars, held down internal disorders, and stabilized itself over long periods of time.[34]

Neumann surely was correct on the historical record. Said another way, the Constitution has never been a barrier to what those who wield effective control over governmental actions wanted to do.

Circumstances have changed so radically since 1787, and even since the first primitive atom bombs were exploded in 1945, that old practices and old modes of thinking about constitutional propriety must be re-examined. New doctrine must be discovered: The government

---

32. 2 M. FARRAND: THE RECORDS OF THE FEDERAL CONVENTION OF 1787, at 318 (1911).

33. C. FRIEDRICH, CONSTITUTIONAL REASON OF STATE 4-5 (1957).

34. F. NEUMANN, THE DEMOCRATIC AND THE AUTHORITARIAN STATE 8 (1957). *See* Miller, *Reason of State and the Emergent Constitution of Control,* 64 MINN. L. REV. 585 (1980).

must be obliged, as Madison said, to control itself.[35]

The Bill of Rights was a conscious attempt to resolve the dilemma that *raison d'état* presented to policy-makers. The first ten amendments were inserted for the people's security, to counterbalance extravagant claims of State security. The men who wrote the Bill of Rights were not naive. They knew history and they knew the dark side of man. They opted to make "reasons of freedom and of personal security" explicit, leaving "reason of state" unexpressed. Nuclear warfare means that both personal *and* national security are threatened; neither can long exist while nuclear weapons proliferate. To permit the President alone to have the power to trigger thermonuclear war is contrary both to the letter and the spirit of the Constitution. The failure of Congress to retrieve its war-making authority can no longer be tolerated. In fact, the power to commit the nation to nuclear war is not only presidential; it has actually been delegated to subordinate officers—and on a number of occasions to the vagaries of a computer interpreting radar messages. That is an intolerable situation.

The Congressional Power to Punish Offenses

Second: Can Congress neglect to exercise a delegated power? We have already mentioned the war-making power. Under article I, section 8, clause 10 of the Constitution, Congress has power to punish offenses against "the law of nations." In his famous *Commentaries on American Law,* Chancellor Kent wrote in 1826:

> "When the United States ceased to be a part of the British empire, and assumed the character of an independent nation, they became subject to that system of rules which reason, morality, and custom had established among civilized nations of Europe, as their public law. . . . The faithful observance of this law is essential to national character. . . ."[36]

If, then, it can be shown that international law makes nuclear weaponry illegal, a duty is imposed upon the United States (and other nations) to adhere to that principle.

---

35. THE FEDERALIST No. 51, at 349 (J. Madison) (J. Cooke ed. 1961).
36. J. KENT, COMMENTARIES ON AMERICAN LAW 1 (1826).

The argument would go like this: Congress having been delegated the power to define and punish offenses against international law, has a duty to carry out that power. In *United States v. Arjona,*[37] the Supreme Court said that international law places a duty on every government to prevent a wrong being done within its borders to another nation with which it is at peace, or to the people thereof. That of course is scant legal authority, as lawyers understand authority, to sustain an argument that Congress has a duty to determine the state of international legal norms concerning nuclear warfare and act in pursuance thereof. But the *Arjona* decision does provide a point of entry into a systematic inquiry into the problem. Richard Falk and colleagues have concluded in their monograph *Nuclear Weapons and International Law* that "any threat or contemplated use of nuclear weapons is contrary to the dictates of international law and constitutes a crime of state."[38] If that be so, then the duty that American government has, in all of its branches, becomes clear: to take action to help prevent that "crime of state." As the United Nations has repeatedly said, the threat or use of nuclear weapons is a "crime against mankind and civilization."[39]

The Constitution and International Law

Third: Is international law a part of the corpus of "laws" that the President must faithfully execute (pursuant to Article II of the Constitution)? No one has ever fully explicated the meaning of the word "laws". Usually it is thought of as Congressional statutes. Arguably, however, it has a wider compass. For example, in recent years the Supreme Court has maintained, successfully, that its decisions are the law

---

37. 120 U.S. 479 (1887). The *Arjona* principle was employed by the Supreme Court to hold that Congress may set up a military commission "as it had previously existed in United States Army practice, as an appropriate tribunal for the trial and punishment of offenses against the law of war." In re Yamashita, 327 U.S. 1, 7 (1946); *Ex parte* Quirin, 317 U.S. 1 (1942). *Compare* A. REEL, THE CASE OF GENERAL YAMASHITA (1949) *with* T. TAYLOR, NUREMBERG AND VIETNAM: AN AMERICAN TRAGEDY (1970).

38. *See supra* note 26, at 60.

39. G.A. Res. 1653, 16 U.N. GAOR Supp. (No. 17) at 4, U.N. Doc. A/5100 (1961).

of the land[40]—thus presenting the question of whether the President has a constitutional duty to faithfully execute them. That question is not only unanswered in constitutional theory; it is little discussed in the scholarly literature. If, however, the Supreme Court is correct in its perception of the thrust of its decisions, then the word "laws" must include more than Congressional enactments. If that is so for the Supreme Court, it requires no large mental jump to say the same for norms of "the law of nations."

Imposing duties upon the President is such a new concept that very few judicial decisions are apposite. Since *Mississippi v. Johnson,*[41] it was thought that the writ of courts did not run against the Chief Executive. That, however, changed in 1974 when President Nixon was required to relinquish the infamous White House tapes.[42] Lawsuits against the President have become, if not routine, then certainly not rare.[43] (Even so, litigants tend to hale subordinate executive officers into court, rather than the Chief Executive—as, for example, in the *Iranian Hostage Case.*[44]

A concept of constitutional duty is slowly being developed in American constitutional law. Since *Cooper v. Aaron,*[45] the Justices have maintained that their decisions are "the law of the land." The Justices have more than an umpire's function, as Justice William Brennan noted:

> Under our system, judges are not mere umpires, but, in their own sphere, lawmakers—a coordinate branch of *government*. While individual cases turn upon controversies between parties, or involve particular prosecutions, court rulings impose official and practical

---

40. Cooper v. Aaron, 358 U.S. 1 (1958).

41. 71 U.S. (4 Wall.) 475 (1866).

42. United States v. Nixon, 418 U.S. 683 (1974).

43. *E.g.,* National Treasury Employees Union v. Nixon, 492 F.2d 587 (D.C. Cir. 1974); Goldwater v. Carter, 492 F.2d 587 (D.C. Cir. 1979), *vacated and remanded,* 444 U.S. 996 (1979). *See generally* STAFF OF THE HOUSE COMM. ON THE JUDICIARY, 97th Cong., 1st Sess., REPORT IDENTIFYING COURT PROCEEDINGS AND ACTIONS OF VITAL INTEREST TO THE CONGRESS 11 (Comm. Print 1981).

44. Dames & Moore v. Regan, 453 U.S. 654 (1981) (Regan is the current Secretary of the Treasury). *See* Miller, *Dames & Moore v. Regan: A Political Decision by a Political Court,* 29 U.C.L.A. L. REV. 1104 (1982).

45. 358 U.S. 1 (1958).

consequences upon members of society at large. Moreover, judges bear responsibility for the vitally important task of construing and securing constitutional rights. . . .

The interpretation and application of constitutional and statutory law, while not legislation, is lawmaking, albeit of a kind that is subject to special constraints and informed by unique considerations. Guided and confined by the Constitution and pertinent statutes, judges are obliged to be discerning, to exercise judgment, and to prescribe rules. Indeed, at times judges wield considerable authority to formulate legal policy in designated areas.[46]

My suggestion is that Supreme Court Justices should grasp the nettle and point out to the Executive and the Congress that officials in those branches are charged with a constitutional duty to take action to eliminate threats to the lives, liberties, and properties of the citizenry. Those threats emanate from nuclear weaponry.

The Affirmative Duties of the Federal Government

Fourth: That suggestion of a pervasive governmental duty runs not only to the express provision that the President must faithfully execute the laws but to Congress as well to define and deal with the law of nations and also to the Supreme Court—to make international legal norms judicially cognizable. Of even more importance, a due process question is presented: Does due process of law have a third dimension—in addition to its procedural and substative aspects—that places affirmative duties upon the federal government?

The answer can only be "yes." Some Supreme Court decisions point in that direction. In *West Coast Hotel Co. v. Parrish,*[47] for example, Chief Justice Charles Evans Hughes wrote for the Court that "the liberty safeguarded. . .(by the Constitution) is liberty in a social organization which *requires* the protection of law against the evils which menace the health, safety, morals, and welfare of the people."[48] That statement seems to fit the nuclear weapons situation exactly. And in

---

46. Richmond Newspapers, Inc. v. Virginia, 448 U.S. 555, 595 & n.20 (1980) (Brennan, J., concurring).

47. 300 U.S. 379 (1937).

48. *Id.* at 391 (emphasis added).

Green v. County School Board of Kent,[49] the court held that local school boards were "charged with the affirmative duty"[50] to integrate public schools. Professor Thomas Emerson has argued that the first amendment has an affirmative dimension.[51] The point is that American constitutional law should include not only what governments can and cannot do but also, as Duguit said,[52] what they *must* do if constitutionalism is to survive; and there is precedent for that conclusion.

The argument, in sum, is that the Constitution imposes duties and obligations upon government to control itself—and thus to protect the citizenry. Those obligations run to the American people—the "We, the people . . ." of the preamble. They can be inferred from the Constitution itself, from certain statutes, and from some Supreme Court decisions. The emergent duty that should be recognized is for government officers *not* to take actions that jeopardize the well-being of the populace, or the well-being of "posterity," or indeed, the well-being of peoples of other nations. Nuclear weapons so endanger the lives, liberties, and property of all Americans that they should be considered to be a deprivation contrary to due process.

Conclusion

It would be naive to expect the Supreme Court to intervene in matters such as are discussed above. In general, judges are timorous officers of government. They look upon requests to go beyond the familiar and the expected as "frightful occasions."[53] Judges, however, are not the only guardians of the Constitution. Their reluctance should not foreclose a growing dialogue about the constitutionality of nuclear weapons. Constitutional lawyers and political scientists can no longer remain aloof from the ultimate terror. Political means must be invented by which "the world can peacefully settle the issues that throughout

---

49.   391 U.S. 430 (1968).

50.   *Id.* at 437.

51.   Emerson, *The Affirmative Side of the First Amendment,* 15 GA. L. REV. 795 (1981).

52.   *See supra* note 10.

53.   *See* J. SHKLAR, LEGALISM (1964), particularly at 101-02. *See also* J. STONE, SOCIAL DIMENSIONS OF LAW AND JUSTICE (1966).

history it has settled by war."[54] That is the challenge that nuclear weapons presents to the constitutional lawyer. No more important task exists.

---

54.   J. SCHELL, THE FATE OF THE EARTH 227 (1982).

14.
Commentary on the Constitutional Debate*

Ovid C. Lewis**

Given the complex nature of nuclear weapons strategy for instituting W.W. III,—a subject (survival) for which most of us display intense feelings that tend to cloud our objectivity—I decided to ask my illustrious friend Dr. Jeremiah Pangloss, to write an introductory piece for this symposium. I know no more versatile dilettante. Not weighted down with the myopic effect of very much knowledge, he is able to see the big picture, identifying the worst and the best in any given scenario by employing the simple Procrustean strategy of ignoring the finer points of argumentation. Also, I knew that his distress over the death in 1876 of the last Tasmanian, Lalla Rookh,—an event he perceived as a manifestation of the global movement toward cultural homogeneity and concomitant loss of alternative cultures—made him acutely sensitive to the nuclear threat to our collective existence.[1] Unfortunately, I was unable to convince him to write an introduction but he did read the symposium articles and was willing to permit publication of our subsequent discussion.

OL: Dr. Pangloss, what makes you think that you possess the requisite expertise to evaluate something as technologically complex as nuclear weapons strategy?[2]

JP: Well, first I would point out that my legal education has enhanced

---

* Reprinted, with permission, from *Nova Law Journal*, Volume 7, Number 1 (1982), where it appeared as "An Interview with Jeremiah Pangloss—A Prelude to the Constitutional Debate."

** Dean, Center for the Study of Law, Nova University.

1. *See* Lewis, *Universal Functional Requisites of Society: The Unending Quest,* 3 CASE W. RES. J. INT'L L. 360 (1970).

2. The problem of evaluating the risks in nuclear power generation is equally complex.

> Even if the complex facts [concerning nuclear power] were completely exposed and explained by a neutral group of experts, there is little indication that the public could develop a consensus. For example, little capability exists to weigh the tradeoffs between cheaper electricity produced by nu-

my analytical skills and sense of relevance—especially the capacity to take both sides of any question. And as you know, the legally trained generalist displays the capacity to think of something inextricably connected to something else without thinking about what it is connected to. In this sense, legal analysis is value free.[3] Thus, I can analyze nuclear strategy without thinking about the obscene and grotesque consequences of a nuclear blast for the three hundred million individuals killed or tortured by the blast. The Justices of the Supreme Court have frequently provided evidence of this capacity by employing neutral principles that transcend the immediate result achieved in a particularly hard case.[4]

OL: Are you suggesting that there *are* two sides to the question of survival? I thought that all sane persons agreed that survival is a minimal value without which no other value artifacts can exist! Certified geniuses from Aristotle to H.L.A. Hart have agreed on that!

JP: Well, consider Woody Allen's assessment that mankind is at the crossroads—one road leading to despair and hopelessness, the other to extinction. It's pretty much a Hobson's choice.

OL: But we have made considerable progress since Eve ate from the tree of knowledge, especially if progress is measured by the availability of conceptual schemes for ordering reality. We have solved some of our perennial problems and generally improved our problem-solving capacity. Consider Robert Nozick's assessment:

---

clear power reactors and the small probability of a major catastrophe. Nor does society have the experience to address the delicate question of whether or not any technology that includes a very small attached risk of catastrophe is acceptable. In addition, if all competing values could be completely explicated, no mechanisms are available for resolving strongly held preferences.

PRESIDENT'S COMM'N FOR A NATIONAL AGENDA FOR THE EIGHTIES, PANEL ON SCIENCE AND TECHNOLOGY: PROMISES AND DANGERS IN THE EIGHTIES 58 (1981).

3. *See generally* Miller & Howell, *The Myth of Neutrality in Constitutional Adjudication*, 27 U. CHI. L. REV. 661 (1960).

4. Wechsler, *Toward Neutral Principles of Constitutional Law*, 73 HARV. L. REV. 1, 19 (1959). *See, e.g.*, Hankerson v. North Carolina, 432 U.S. 233, 244 n.8 (1977).

The great reductionist views of Freud and Marx, computer modeling and neurophysiological reduction, behavioral psychology and economic analyses, just join and extend the long list of human accomplishments, striving, and excellence: Shakespeare and Kant and Plato and Goethe and Gandhi and the Baal Shem-Tov and Newton and Picasso and Homer and Rembrandt and Turner and George Eliot and Galileo and Tolstoy and Aurobinde and Weber and Bach and Garrison and the authors of the Hebrew Bible and Sophocles.[5]

The fact is that there "has been striking progress in the control of disease, in the methods of farming, in material productivity, in the reduction of backbreaking labor, in the techniques of rapid mass communication, in the spread of literacy and probably in the reduction in the amount of violence in everyday life."[6]

JP: Actually, there really is no basis for assuming progress. Our exosomatic evolution—autos, telephones, telescopes, computers, etc.—has brought us to what Arthur Miller elsewhere has described as a "climacteric" or convergence of crises. We are drowning in a sea of information. So even with this "progress," or because of it our survival is at best problematical. Probably the most comprehensive statement of the climacteric is provided by Kirkpatrick Sale:

An imperilled ecology, irremediable pollution of atmosphere and ocean, overpopulation, world hunger and starvation, the depletion of resources, environmental diseases, the vanishing wilderness, uncontrolled technologies, chemical toxins in water, air and foods, and endangered species on land and sea.

A deepening suspicion of authority, distrust of established institutions, breakdown of family ties, decline of community, erosion of religious commitment, contempt for law, disregard for tradition, ethical and moral confusion, cultural ignorance, artistic chaos, and aesthetic uncertainty.

Deteriorating cities, megalopolitan sprawls, stifling ghettoes, over-

---

5. R. NOZICK, PHILOSOPHICAL INVESTIGATIONS 644 (1981).

6. Frankel, *The Idea of Progress,* 6 THE ENCYCLOPEDIA OF PHILOSOPHY 483, 486 (1967). The criteria for judging progress are not self-evident. *See* Ginsberg, *Progress in the Modern Era,* 3 DICTIONARY OF THE HISTORY OF IDEAS 633, 649 (1973).

crowding, traffic congestion, untreated wastes, smog and soot, budget insolvency, inadequate schools, mounting illiteracy, declining university standards, dehumanizing welfare systems, police brutality, overcrowded hospitals, clogged court calendars, inhumane prisons, racial injustice, sex discrimination, poverty, crime and vandalism, and fear.

The growth of loneliness, powerlessness, insecurity, anxiety, anomie, boredom, bewilderment, alienation, rudeness, suicide, mental illness, alcoholism, drug usage, divorce, violence, and sexual dysfunction.

Political alienation and discontent, bureaucratic rigidification, administrative inefficiency, legislative ineptitude, judicial inequity, bribery and corruption, inadequate government regulations and enforcement, the use of repressive machinery, abuses of power, ineradicable national debt, collapse of the two-party system, defense overspending, nuclear proliferation, the arms race and arms sales, and the threat of nuclear annihilation.

Economic uncertainty, unemployment, inflation, devaluation and displacement of the dollar, capital shortages, the energy crises, absenteeism, employee sabotage and theft, corporate mismanagement, industrial espionage, business payoffs and bribes, white-collar criminality, shoddy goods, waste and inefficiency, planned obsolescence, fraudulent and incessant advertising, mounting personal debt, and the maldistribution of wealth.

International instability, worldwide inflation, national and civil warfare, arms buildups, nuclear reactors, plutonium stockpiles, disputes over laws of the sea, inadequate international law, the failure of the United Nations, multinational exploitation, Third World poverty and unrepayable debt, and the end of the American imperial arrangement.

Or to put it another way:

Vietnam, Watergate, New York City bankruptcy, gas lines, Mirex, Equity Funding, ITT, riots, Medicaid fraud, redlining, CIA, drugtesting, hostages, price fixing, Vesco, nursing homes, coffee prices, product recalls, assassinations, heroin, the Middle East, Rio Rancho, Kepone, skyjacking, the SLA, Hustler, Spiro Agnew, saccharin, the square tomato, Harlequin books, Los Angeles, OPEC, Wilbur Mills, power failures, My Lai, Charles Manson, PCB, the SST, Andy Warhol, Appalachia, organized crime, Three Mile Island, Valium, the Wilmington 10, REITs, TV violence, strip-mining, FBI break-ins, the Sahel, microwaves, McDonald's, Kent State, Penn Central, Attica, the Torrey Canyon, psychosurgery, mercury, and Chile . . .[7]

OL: But then the dilemma confronting us is of our own making. We have developed a honeycombed store of knowledge, with disciplines segregated to the extent that experts are afflicted with specialized deafness. We question whether it is even possible to see the big picture while applying the knowledge and techniques of the diverse and sophisticated disciplines required to resolve the complex problems of our climacteric era.

Moreover, the classical boundaries of the earth sciences—geology, meteorology, oceanography, and so on—are being eroded and replaced by a planetary multidisciplinary view. For example, portraying and understanding the long-term evolution of climate depends on understanding the movement of crustal plates and the interpretation of deep-sea cores and sediment samples. Understanding and predicting the shorter period changes in climate depends on knowledge of the oceans, their temperature, currents, ability to act as a reservoir, and their role in the global energy cycle.

A central theme is that the new knowledge gained by the vigor of earth sciences and by pertinent technology is now vital to the wise management of our planet. Plate tectonics is essential to the effort to understand and predict earthquakes and to improve reconnaissance for new mineral deposits. Atmospheric chemistry enables us to make a reasoned estimate of the likely future effects of trace amounts of chlorofluoromethanes on trace amounts of ozone in the stratosphere. Basic work in marine biology and ecology is indispensable to structuring effective policies for managing the living resources of the seas. Research on the chemistry of ocean water will enable us to fix more precisely the role of the oceans as a reservoir for CO_2, helping to yield, in time, precise estimates of the climatic effects of CO_2 and a more rational base on which to plan the future

---

7. K. SALE, HUMAN SCALE 21-22 (1980).

use of fossil fuels.

> Our appraisal of recent trends in the earth sciences is dominated by the role of technology and the approach to planetary problems through organized and collaborative efforts of institutions and scientists—big science. There is a current question about big science and its relation to the science of individual investigators. It should be noted that the big science effort described here grew from little science—the ideas of individuals—and provide to individual scientists data that could be obtained in no other way.[8]

JP: The best response to the question you posed concerning my competence in matters as complex as nuclear weapons strategy was supplied by the physicist Erwin Schrodinger: "I can see no escape from this dilemma . . . than that some of us should venture to embark on a synthesis of facts and theories, albeit with second-hand and incomplete knowledge of some of them—and at the risk of making fools of ourselves."[9]

OL: And what then is your assessment of the current state of affairs?

JP: I think the big picture comes into focus by telescoping our finite existence on this globe into a thirty-day span. During the first 29 days, 22-½ hours, mankind was a nomadic predator. Only during the last hour and 25 minutes did he settle into framing and in the last five minutes he finally moved to an urban setting. Within this time frame the Renaissance consumed 4 minutes, the Industrial Revolution 1-½ minutes, and the Electronic Era 10 seconds.[10] The acceleration in rate of change and technological capacity is quite apparent. During the last moments of our 30 days, the ineluctable movement toward annihilation

---

8. SCIENCE AND TECHNOLOGY 50 (National Academy of Sciences 1979). It is suggested that international as well as interdisciplinary collaboration is also necessary for progress. See *id.* at 14-15.

9. E. SCHRODINGER, WHAT IS LIFE? vii (1945).

10. There is considerable disagreement among anthropologists concerning man's first appearance on this planet. "Lucy" appeared 3.5 million years ago, and other hominids over 5 million years ago. See evolutionary chart in D. JOHANSON & M. EDEY, LUCY: THE BEGINNINGS OF HUMANKIND 10-11 (1982). Compare the earlier (and now obviously erroneous) chart in 1 W. DURANT, THE STORY OF CIVILIZATION: OUR ORIENTAL HERITAGE 90 (1954).

of the human species is equally obvious. How clear it now appears, even though each early step was at the time taken, apparently innocuous. Consider the following annihilation schedule:

ANNIHILATION SCHEDULE

	1300:	Cannon
	1440:	Printing Press
	1500:	Rifle
	1776:	Submarine
	1835:	Revolver
	1863:	TNT
	1896:	Radio-Telegraph
	1903:	Airplane
	1905:	Einstein proposes theory for transformation of matter into energy: $E = mc^2$
	1926:	Liquid Fuel Rocket
	1928:	Mechanical Computer
	1933:	Harold Urey isolates heavy hydrogen
	1939:	Fission in uranium discovered
	1942:	First nuclear chain reaction in the Chicago pile
	1945:	First test of A-bomb at Alamorgorda, New Mexico
August 6,	1945:	First obscene use of A-bomb at Hiroshima
	1946:	Electronic numerical integrator and calculator (ENIAC), first all-electronic computer
	1952:	H-bomb tested at Eniwetok
	1954:	H-bomb exploded producing twice anticipated destructive effect. John Foster Dulles propounds strategy of massive retaliation.
October 4,	1957:	Sputnik I

	1960:	Era of nuclear plenty (more than 1000 nuclear weapons available). Atlas Missile has CEP (circular error probable indicating the radius of the circle within which 50% of missiles will land) of several miles.
December,	1960:	SIOP (single integrated operational plan) requires all-cities strategy with estimated death toll of 360-450 million people in communist sphere.
June,	1962:	SIOP II adopts more flexible nuclear strategy of escalation of destruction.
July 8,	1962:	1.4 Megaton H-bomb 248 miles over Johnson Island generates EMP (electromagnetic pulse) of peak 6 megawatts/sq. meter.
October,	1962:	Cuban Missile Crisis
	1969:	NIE (CIA's National Intelligence Estimate of Soviet Nuclear strike capability) assumes parity. Russian SS-9s (armed with 3 warheads each with 7-10 megaton force) are aimed at U.S. LCCs (launch control centers) in the Midwest.
	1970:	U.S. develops MIRVs (multiple independently targetable re-entry vehicles).
	1974:	NSDM 242 (National Security decision memorandum) propounds Schlesinger doctrine of limited nuclear war.
	1975:	NIE assumes nuclear parity not attained by Russians until mid-1980s. U.S. Minuteman III Missile with Mark 12A warhead (350 kiloton force) has CEP of one tenth of a nautical mile.
	1977:	Russia develops MIRVs with low CEP. Window of vulnerability develops.

July,	1980:	PD 59 (presidential directive) sets forth nuclear war strategies.
	1982:	Russian SS-19s acquire new front end with 90% PK (probability of kill) on minuteman missile silos. Opens wider window of vulnerability.
November 22,	1982:	MX dense pack strategy adopted.

The inventiveness of *homo faciens* has produced better and better means of assuring our destruction. But while technological exosomatic evolution has occurred, the human nature of *homo sapiens* has remained unchanged—and in his natural state we know that "the life of man [is] solitary, poore, nasty, brutish, and short."[11] The combination of MIRVs with a low CEP and high PK produced a situation that compelled Carter to issue PD 59, rejecting a MAD strategy in favor of a policy requiring the U.S. military "to be able to undertake precise, limited nuclear strikes against military facilities in the Soviet Union, including missile bases and troop concentration, [and] to develop the capacity to threaten Soviet political leaders in their underground shelters in time of war."[12]

OL: But that sounds as though fighting a nuclear war *is* considered a reasonable option? I would have thought no sane person would even consider that. Do you really believe the leader of a State would initiate a nuclear war and thereby risk destruction of our civilization?

JP: Well, Harry Truman [who authorized Hiroshima's destruction] was sane and he, at the time of the Korean War, contemplated a nuclear attack, although he had removed General MacArthur for urging all-out war. Truman wrote in a January 27, 1952, memorandum:

> It seems to me that the proper approach now would be an ultimatum with a 10-day expiration limit, informing Moscow that we intend to blockade the China coast from the Korean border to Indochina, and that we intend to destroy every military base in

---

11. T. Hobbes, Leviathon or the Matter, Forme & Power of a Commonwealth Ecclesiastical and Civill *62.

12. N.Y. Times, Aug. 6, 1980, at 1, col. 1.

262 Ovid C. Lewis

Manchuria by means now in our control—and if there is further interference we shall eliminate any ports or cities necessary to accomplish our purposes.

This means all-out war. It means that Moscow, St. Petersburg, Mukden, Vladivostok, Peking, Shanghai, Port Arthur, Darien, Odessa, Stalingrad and every manufacturing plant in China and the Soviet Union will be eliminated.[13]

There were, of course, other times when we came close—with Eisenhower in 1953 (Korean War), Kennedy in 1962 (Cuban Missile Crisis), Kissinger in 1973 (Arab-Israeli October War), and Carter in 1979 (Iran Crisis). The fact is that we could end up with a war because of computer error. Tom Wicker recently reported that there were "151 computer false alarms in an 18 month period" and that one false alarm "had American forces on alert for a full six minutes before the error was discovered."[14] Add more powerful missiles and more countries with nuclear weapons and the outcome is bleak at best.[15]

OL: But our civilization would not survive—at least not in any form identifiable by us.

JP: Edward Teller doesn't think a nuclear war would be all that bad. He suggests that we certainly could survive—as long as we acted rationally—including wiping the fallout ash from our skin.[16]

OL: But what about the effects of the EMP?

JP: I suppose all data encoded on microchips would disappear. Given the extent to which our society relies on an information network using microchips, that could be somewhat disastrous.[17] Of course, the mili-

---

13. N.Y. Times, Sunday, Aug. 3, 1980, at 22, col. 1.

14. N.Y. Times, Sunday, Nov. 21, 1982, at EY21, col. 1. Defense experts suggest that the Russian detection systems are even more prone to error. Whew!

15. For an apocalypt's view see H. LINDSEY, THE 1980's: COUNTDOWN TO ARMAGEDDON (1980).

16. "Skin contact with fallout is not necessarily fatal—depending on the intensity of the radiation and the precautions taken. Injuries can be reduced simply by washing off the ash." Teller, *Dangerous Myths About Nuclear Arms*, READERS DIGEST, Nov. 1982, at 139, 141.

17. Daniel Bell reports that by 1980, 51.3 percent of our experienced civilian

tary has taken measures to protect the C^3 of C^3I (command, control, communication, and intelligence) from EMP. I think Thomas Powers' assessment is more accurate than that of Teller:

> Strategic planners hesitate to say what the world would be like after a nuclear war. There are too many variables. But they agree—for planning purposes, at any rate—that both sides would "recover," and that the most probable result of a general nuclear war would be a race to prepare for a second general nuclear war. As a practical matter, then, a general nuclear war would not end the threat of nuclear war. That threat, in fact would be one of the very few things the pre-war and post-war worlds would have in common.[18]

OL: It seems almost inevitable that given our organization for nuclear war, that it will surely occur. There are several haunting stanzas in the Rubaiyat of Omar Khayyam that I can't help but recall:

> We are no other than a moving row
> of magic shadow-shapes that come and go
> Round with the sun-illmin'd lantern held
> In midnight by the master of the show;
>
> But helpless pieces of the game he plays
> Upon this checquer-board of nights and days;
> Hither and thither moves and checks and slays,
> and one by one back in the closet lays.[19]

Do you believe that the probability of nuclear war would be reduced if the Supreme Court persuasively propounded a doctrine that there is a

---

workforce was involved in the information business. Further, that the "axial principles of the post-industrial society, however, is the centrality of theoretical knowledge and its new role, when codified, as the director of social change." Bell, *The Social Framework of the Information Society,* in THE MICROELECTRONICS REVOLUTION 500 (T. Forester ed. 1980).

18. Powers, *Choosing a Strategy for World War III,* 250 THE ATLANTIC, No. 5, Nov. 1982, at 82, 110.

19. THE RUBAIYAT OF OMAR KHAYYAM (E. Fitzgerald trans. 1859).

constitutional duty to avoid a nuclear war?

JP: Well, that question is almost too speculative for me to answer. First, what constitutional provision would impose such a duty? I can agree that a natural law proponent could contend that there is a duty to seek survival. One of the clearest statements appears in the Summa Theologica, where St. Thomas states that "the natural law contains all that makes for the preservation of human life, and all that is opposed to its dissolution."[20] But even for the Thomistic natural law proponent,

---

20. T. AQUINAS, *Summa Theologica,* in AQUINAS: SELECTED POLITICAL WRITINGS 123 (A. D'Entreves ed. 1959). Note: Interestingly, the *Summa Theologica* was incorporated into Catholic doctrine by an encyclical of Pope Leo XIII. *See* C. MORRIS, THE GREAT LEGAL PHILOSOPHERS 57 (1959). Catholics are thus bound, at least in theory, to St. Thomas' call for an active opposition to "dissolution." Catholics do appear to support opposition to nuclear weapons more frequently than Non-Catholics. A recent Gallup Poll indicates the following:

Unilateral Nuclear Freeze

"Do you favor or oppose a freeze on the production of nuclear weapons whether or not the Soviet Union agrees to do the same?"

	Favor	Oppose
National	45	55
Catholics	47	53
Non-Catholics	45	55

Dilateral Nuclear Freeze

"Do you favor or oppose an agreement between the United States and the Soviet Union not to build any more nuclear weapons in the future?"

	Favor	Oppose	No Opinion
National	77	17	6
Catholics	82	13	5
Non-Catholics	76	18	6

Reduce Nuclear Arsenals

"Would you approve or disapprove if President Reagan made a proposal to the Soviet Union that both countries reduce their present stock of nuclear weapons by 50 per cent?"

	Favor	Oppose	No Opinion
National	76	19	5
Catholics	81	16	3
Non-Catholics	73	21	6

there would be many troubling issues before exercising a duty to resist positive law supporting nuclear strike capability.[21] Aquinas' theory of resistance requires only that where positive law is contrary to the common good, it is not to be obeyed *unless* the disobedience is more onerous than the evil occasioned by obedience to an unjust law. Of course, if the Divine law is violated then one must resist—and perhaps survival of God's creation is mandated by the Divine Law requiring man to be "fruitful and multiply."[22] But *which* nuclear weapon strategy will deter a war is a subject of considerable debate. Agreeing to do good and avoid evil is far easier than determining what particular acts will further this primary precept. The same is true for survival.

OL: But what about a constitutional duty? Do you see any realistic argument for establishing such a duty?

JP: There are a number of difficulties. First, what provision in the Constitution is available for serving as a basis for such a duty? Recall that the Court in the *Rodriguez* case stated that only rights explicitly or implicitly guaranteed by the Constitution are to be considered fundamental enough to impose the strict scrutiny standard of review.[23]

OL: If interstate travel, privacy, procreation, voting, and education are fundamental rights implicit in the constitution, then why not a right of

---

Destroy Present Weapons

"Would you favor or oppose an agreement between the U.S. and the Soviet Union to destroy all nuclear weapons that have already been built?"

	Favor	Oppose	No Opinion
National	47	44	9
Catholics	50	42	8
Non-Catholics	46	44	10

Catholics back stand on Missiles, Miami Herald, Sunday, Nov. 21, 1982, at A32, col. 1.

21. Concerning the ambiguities and difficulties inherent in a natural law approach see Kelsen, *Plato and the Natural Law*, 14 VAND. L. REV. 23 (1960); Neilsen, *An Examination of the Thomistic Theory of Natural Moral Law*, 4 NATURAL L.F. 44 (1959). *See infra* note 38.

22. *Genesis* 2:28 (King James).

23. San Antonio School Dist. v. Rodriguez, 411 U.S. 1, 33 (1973).

survival?

JP: You are forgetting that the threat to survival is not a personal right, but one shared by everyone. The Court probably would deny standing to even raise the issue—whether in the context of failure to comply with the "law" on the part of the executive or legislative branch or infringement on the assumed [*arguendo*] right of survival. Recall the recent statement by the Court:

> [The] requirements of standing are not satisfied by "the abstract injury in nonobservance of the Constitution asserted by . . . citizens." *Schlesinger v. Reservists Committee to Stop the War*, 418 U.S. at 223, n. 13, 94 S. Ct., at 2933, n. 13 (1974). This Court repeatedly has rejected claims of standing predicated on " 'the right, possessed by every citizen, to require that the Government be administered according to law. . . .' *Fairchild v. Hughes*, 258 U.S. 126, 129 [42 S. Ct. 274, 275, 66 L. Ed. 499] [1922]." *Baker v. Carr*, 369 U.S. 186, 208, 82 S. Ct. 691, 705 L. Ed. 2d 663 (1962). See *Schlesinger v. Reservists Committee to Stop the War, supra*, 418 U.S. at 216-222, 94 S. Ct. at 2929-2932; *Laird v. Tatum*, 408 U.S. 1, 92 S. Ct. 2318, 33 L. Ed. 2d 154 (1972); *Ex parte Levitt*, 302 U.S. 633, 58 S. Ct. 1, 82 L. Ed. 493 (1937). Such claims amount to little more than attempts "to employ a federal court as a forum in which to air . . . generalized grievances about the conduct of government." *Flast v. Cohen*, 392 U.S., at 106, 88 S. Ct., at 1956.[24]

If standing was found, then the Court still might refuse to reach the merits finding that the issue is a political question because such a case would present either, in the Court's words—

---

24. Valley Forge Christian College v. Americans United for Separation of Church and State, Inc., __ U.S. __, 102 S. Ct. 752, 764 (1982). Another variation on the standing theme relates to the requirement that the judicial resolution of the constitutional issue will produce the relief desired by the plaintiff. *See* Linda R.S. v. Richard D., 410 U.S. 614, 618 (1973). Imposing a duty on *our* government to eliminate the threat of nuclear war would not eliminate the threat from other countries, and indeed, some would contend, would only heighten the likelihood of the apocalypse. One can hear Chairman Andropov paraphrasing President Jackson: "The Court has made its decision. Let it enforce it."

a textually demonstrable constitutional commitment of the issue to a coordinate political department; or a lack of judicially discoverable and manageable standards for resolving it; or the impossibility of deciding without an initial policy determination of a kind clearly for nonjudicial discretion; or the impossibility of a court's undertaking independent resolution without expressing lack of the respect due coordinate branches of government; or an unusual need for questioning adherence to a political decision already made; or the potentiality of embarrassment from multifarious pronouncements by various departments on one question.[25]

Or, given the complexity of the issue and expertise required to appreciate the nuances involved, the Court could invoke some variation of the abstention doctrine. After all, in *Horowitz,* the Court admitted "courts are particularly ill-equipped to evaluate academic performance."[26] *A fortiori*—nuclear weapons strategy! The Court has frequently manifested deference to the Executive Branch in matters of national security.[27]

OL: But assuming, *arguendo,* that the Court would hear the case, why wouldn't the Justices agree that there is a constitutional duty based on the fundamental right of survival.

JP: Frankly, I don't think the predicate exists for establishing such a right. Consider the length of time and number of incremental steps involved in the evolution of constitutional rights of privacy[28] and inter-

---

25.   Baker v. Carr, 369 U.S. 186, 217 (1962). *See also* United States v. Nixon, 418 U.S. 683, 704-05 (1974). The Court would probably apply the same doctrine to arguments of invalid delegation of legislative power to the executive in the area of foreign affairs and national security. Given the temporal proximity to United States v. Curtiss-Wright Export Corp., 299 U.S. 304 (1936) of Panama Refining Co. v. Ryan, 293 U.S. 388 (1935) and Schechter Poultry Corp. v. United States, 295 U.S. 495 (1935), it appears the Court has assumed that even if the delegation doctrine was applicable in other contexts, it would not apply in the area of foreign affairs. Of course, more recently the Court has upheld extremely broad delegations of legislative authority. *See, e.g.,* Lichter v. United States, 334 U.S. 742 (1948).

26.   Board of Curators, Univ. of Mo. v. Horowitz, 435 U.S. 78, 92 (1978).

27.   *See, e.g.,* United States v. Nixon, 418 U.S. 683, 706-07 (1974); United States v. Reynolds, 345 U.S. 1, 11 (1953).

28.   For discussion see Warren & Brandeis, *The Right to Privacy,* 4 HARV.

state travel.[29] And the right of procreation you mentioned is considered as "among the rights of personal privacy protected under the Constitution."[30] By the way, the right to vote in state elections is not a fundamental right. The Court on numerous occasions has indicated that the federal Constitution "does not confer the right of suffrage upon any one."[31] Of course, where the state does grant the right to vote, it must do so on an equal basis.[32] The Court applies a strict scrutiny test in such circumstances because it views the franchise once granted, as "preservative of all [other] rights."[33]

OL: But I recall that the Court actually stated in *Yick Wo* that the political franchise of voting is "a fundamental right because preservative of all rights" and in 1964 in *Reynolds v. Sims,* the Court reaffirmed the same idea, stating:

> Undoubtedly, the right of suffrage is a fundamental matter in a free and democratic society. Especially since the right to exercise

---

L. REV. 193 (1890); Note, *The Right to Privacy Today,* 43 HARV. L. REV. 297 (1929); Bohlen, *Fifty Years of Torts,* 50 HARV. L. REV. 725 (1937); Nizer, *The Right of Privacy—A Half Century's Developments,* 39 MICH. L. REV. 526 (1941); Feinberg, *Recent Development in the Law of Privacy,* 48 COLUM. L. REV. 713 (1948). The Court's discussion of judicial antecedents appears in the various opinions in Griswold v. Connecticut, 381 U.S. 479 (1965). A similar incremental sequence occurred in the development of the fundamental right to marry. *See* Zablocki v. Redhail, 434 U.S. 374, 383-86 (1978). Concerning the development of the fundamental right of personal choice in matters of family life, see Moore v. East Cleveland, 431 U.S. 494, 499 (1977).

29. *See* Crandall v. Nevada, 73 U.S. (6 Wall.) 35 (1868); Edwards v. California, 314 U.S. 160 (1941); Shapiro v. Thompson, 394 U.S. 618 (1969).

30. San Antonio School Dist. v. Rodriguez, 411 U.S. 1, 35 n.76 (1973).

31. Minor v. Happersett, 88 U.S. (21 Wall.) 162, 178 (1875), *quoted with approval in* Rodriguez v. Popular Democratic Party, __ U.S. __, 102 S. Ct. 2194, 2199 (1982). In *Rodriguez,* the Court observed that "the right to vote, *per se,* is not a constitutionally protected right." San Antonio School Dist. v. Rodriguez, 411 U.S. 1, 35 n.78 (1973).

32. Of course the same is true of the right to an appeal. *See* Douglas v. California, 372 U.S. 353 (1963). In situations abridging rights which *where* granted are subject to heightened analysis, the Court often requires that the right be absolutely denied to justify relief. *See* Ross v. Moffitt, 417 U.S. 600 (1974); Plyler v. Doe, __ U.S. __, 102 S. Ct. 2382 (1982).

33. Yick Wo v. Hopkins, 118 U.S. 356, 370 (1886).

the franchise in a free and unimpaired manner is preservative of other basic civil and political rights, any alleged infringement of the right of citizens to vote must be carefully and meticulously scrutinized.[34]

Isn't this true of the right to survive? After all, if we cease to exist, no rights—voting, expression, etc.—are preserved. And given this, why not an implied constitutional duty to eliminate the threat to survival now—since it is absurd to wait until our extinction is certain to occur.[35]

JP: Your analysis might apply in cases where the state grants a right not naturally held by its citizens and where there is a nexus between that right and exercise of other constitutional rights. The Court recently has gone one step further, holding that deprivation of access to a basic education (also not a fundamental right) in certain contexts, is subject to a heightened level of scrutiny.[36] But there, as in the case of voting, a substantive nexus was found between the right granted and other explicit rights in the Constitution—e.g., freedom of expression guaranteed by the First Amendment. There simply is no substantive connection between your proposed right of survival and any existing constitutional rights. Further, your existence is not granted by the State, but is acquired through natural processes beyond the control of the State.[37] Aren't we back to a natural law argument?[38]

---

34. Reynolds v. Sims, 377 U.S. 533, 561-62 (1964). *See also* Harper v. Virginia State Bd. of Elections, 383 U.S. 663, 667 (1966).

35. In another context, less fraught with an imminent threat to national security, the Court adopted the gravity of the evil test, which *mutatis mutandis,* appears applicable here. *See* Dennis v. United States, 341 U.S. 494, 510 (1951). This test was most recently used by Justice Burger in Nebraska Press Assn. v. Stuart, 427 U.S. 539, 562 (1976).

36. Where children of aliens unlawfully present in the United States were absolutely denied access to public education, the Court in Plyler v. Doe, __ U.S. __, 102 S. Ct. 2382 (1982) appears to apply the middle level review utilized in gender discrimination, Craig v. Boren, 429 U.S. 190 (1976); Mississippi Univ. for Women v. Hogan, __ U.S. __, 102 S.Ct. 3331 (1982), and illegitimacy-legitimacy classifications. Mills v. Habluetzel, __ U.S. __, 102 S. Ct. 1549 (1982).

37. *But see* Roe v. Wade, 410 U.S. 113 (1973).

38. Of course, in earlier times incorporation of natural law into our jurisprudence was not unusual. *See generally* Corwin, *The "Higher Law" Back-*

OL: I suggest that there is a clear nexus to the explicit guarantee of a right to life, which cannot be taken without affording due process of law. Further, life cannot be taken in a manner that violates the Eighth Amendment's proscription of cruel and unusual punishments. The Court has held invalid imposition of capital punishment on a robber, even when he is present at a robbery where a murder is committed, since robbery is not a crime "so grievous an affront to humanity that the only response may be the penalty of death."[39] We have not even committed a crime. Where is our due process? Isn't imposition of extinction cruel and unusual? Isn't the psychological torment of a nuclear sword of Damocles itself a cruel and unusual punishment?

JP: The short of it is that the state is not imposing any punishment on anyone. All the provisions you cite were not designed to protect survival of the species. The Court's resolution of the arguments you raise is adumbrated in its opinion in the student paddling (beating) case holding the Eighth Amendment not applicable.

> The prisoner and the school child stand in wholly different circumstances, separated by the harsh facts of criminal conviction and incarceration. The prisoner's conviction entitles the State to classify him as a "criminal," and his incarceration deprives him of the freedom "to be with family and friends and to form the other enduring attachments of normal life." *Morrissey v. Brewer,* 408 U.S. 471 (1972).[40]

I think you can see the difference. It's like the black citizen subjected to the existence of a racially segregated park (unconstitutional),[41] as

---

ground of American Constitutional Law, 42 HARV. L. REV. 149 (1928), 42 HARV. L. REV. 365 (1929). This is no longer fashionable. Today "no one wants to be called a natural lawyer. Natural law insists that what the law is depends in some way on what the law should be. This seems metaphysical or at least vaguely religious. In any case it seems plainly wrong." Dworkin, *"Natural" Law Revisited,* 34 U. FLA. L. REV. 165 (1982).

39. Enmund v. Florida, __ U.S. __, 102 S. Ct. 3368, 3377 (1982) (quoting from Gregg v. Georgia, 428 U.S. 153, 184 (1976)). *See also* Coker v. Georgia, 433 U.S. 584 (1977).

40. Ingraham v. Wright, 430 U.S. 651, 669 (1977).

41. Evans v. Newton, 382 U.S. 296 (1966).

opposed to having no park at all (constitutional).[42] But even if I were to agree that there was a fundamental right somehow involved, and a concomitant duty to eliminate a threat to our individual and collective existence, that would at best only impose a standard of strict scrutiny. This is not an absolute and automatic test invalidating government action or inaction. And in every instance where the state considers its very existence in peril, the Court has found a sufficiently compelling governmental interest to justify subordination of any right proposed—whether under the First Amendment,[43] privacy[44] or even the right not to be subjected to invidious racial classifications subsumed within the due process clause of the Fifth Amendment.[45] As a noted constitutional scholar has concluded: "The Court has never ruled against the state in any matter of consequence."[46]

And so, my friend, our conclusion is that the Court will not involve

---

42.   Evans v. Abney, 396 U.S. 435 (1970).

43.   *See, e.g.,* Barenblatt v. United States, 360 U.S. 109 (1959). A national security interest can justify even a prior restraint. Near v. Minnesota, 283 U.S. 697, 716 (1931). *See also* New York Times Co. v. United States, 403 U.S. 713, 726 (1971) (Brennan, J., concurring).

44.   Roe v. Wade, 410 U.S. 113 (1973). It is interesting that the Court in *Roe* cited favorably *Jacobson* and *Bell:*

[I]t is not clear to us that the claim asserted . . . that one has an unlimited right to do with one's body as one pleases bears a close relationship to the right of privacy previously articulated in the Court's decisions. The Court has refused to recognize an unlimited right of this kind in the past. Jacobson v. Massachusetts, 197 U.S. 11, 49 L. Ed. 643, 255 S. Ct. 358 (1905) (vaccination); Buck v. Bell, 274 U.S. 200, 71 L. Ed. 1000, 47 S. Ct. 584 (1927) (sterilization).

410 U.S. at 154.

45.   The due process clause of the Fifth Amendment prohibits invidious discrimination. Bolling v. Sharpe, 347 U.S. 497, 499 (1954). Accordingly, strict scrutiny is applied where racial classifications are employed—a doctrine that also was developed only incrementally over a considerable period of time. *See* Powell, *Carolene Products Revisited,* 81 COLUM. L. REV. 1087 (1982); Gunther, *Foreword: In Search of Evolving Doctrine on a Changing Court: A Model for a Newer Equal Protection,* 86 HARV. L. REV. 1 (1972). Even so, the Court justified severe restrictions on the rights of citizens of Japanese ancestry during World War II based on "pressing public necessity" and "the military urgency of the situation." Korematsu v. United States, 323 U.S. 214, 216, 223 (1944).

46.   A. MILLER, DEMOCRATIC DICTATORSHIP 194 (1981).

itself in this dispute. This choice is really ours to make. The bottom line is eloquently expressed by Jonathan Schell:

> One day—and it is hard to believe that it will not be soon—we will make our choice. Either we will sink into the final coma and end it all or, as I trust and believe, we will awaken to the truth of our peril, a truth as great as life itself, and, like a person who has swallowed a lethal poison but shakes off his stupor at the last moment and vomits the poison up, we will break through the layers of our denials, put aside our fainthearted excuses, and rise up to cleanse the earth of nuclear weapons.[47]

---

47. J. SCHELL, THE FATE OF THE EARTH 231 (1982).

15.
Protecting Posterity*

Aviam Soifer**

Professor Arthur S. Miller, a master of the genre of creative constitutionalism, contributes an impressive example in his article, *Nuclear Weapons and Constitutional Law*. He advances several provocative arguments for possible constitutional limits on United States participation in the nuclear arms race; these arguments, undoubtedly, will stimulate much thought and development—unless a nuclear catastrophe intervenes.

Miller identifies a particular kind of complacency or cynicism among lawyers that allows many of us to assume that nuclear weapons simply are more powerful ways to kill people. It is surely important to challenge this assumption. On a more basic level, the threat of nuclear disaster invites all citizens—not merely lawyers and judges—to consider and to construe the text and meaning of the United States Constitution.

Law unquestionably serves as a secular religion in our democracy[1] and de Tocqueville's recognition that important political issues tend to

* Reprinted, with permission, from *Nova Law Journal*, Volume 7, Number 1 (1982).

** Professor of Law, Boston University School of Law. This sketch is dedicated to my son Raphael Moshe. In one year he already has given his parents much to consider and to hope for the future. I would also like to express gratitude to the W. K. Kellogg Foundation. A Kellogg National Fellowship allowed me time to read and think about the issues explored below.

1. *See generally* C. MILLER, THE SUPREME COURT AND THE USES OF HISTORY 170-88 (1969); M. LERNER, AMERICA AS A CIVILIZATION 442-43 (1957); Corwin, *The Constitution as Instrument and as Symbol*, 30 AM. POL. SCI. REV. 1071 (1936); T. ARNOLD, THE SYMBOLS OF GOVERNMENT 59-71 (1935) and Llewellyn, *The Constitution as an Institution*, 34 COLUM. L. REV. 1 (1934). Of course, much of Arthur S. Miller's impressive output is also directly on point.

As a young man, Abraham Lincoln urged other young men of Springfield, Illinois to let reverence for law "become the political religion of the nation. . . ." R. HOFSTADTER, THE AMERICAN POLITICAL TRADITION 103 (1948). Alexis de Tocqueville, writing at the same time, but with a bit less reverence, called law in England and America "an occult science." A. TOCQUEVILLE, DEMOCRACY IN AMERICA 287 (P. Bradley ed. 1945).

end up in court is even more accurate today.[2] Our survival and that of our constitutional faith may depend on our willingness to consider the nexus between constitutional values and protecting our posterity.

In the past, slavery, civil rights and, more recently, abortion were the kinds of issues important enough to provoke many people to supplement the views of lawyers with their own constitutional judgments. To the horror of many of those learned in the law, precedential baggage has sometimes been jettisoned in the process. In trying times, judges and their colleagues sometimes behave more like strict constrictionists than strict constructionists.

Realistically, of course, no one today should entertain the notion that a legal challenge to the United States' role in the spread of nuclear weapons is likely to produce an enthusiastic response from the United States Supreme Court. Yet the threat of nuclear conflagration might be just the type of issue to move citizens to seek connections between constitutional language and contemporary values.

Just as it would be a mistake to leave constitutional values entirely to those with legal training, it would also be unwise to ignore the relevance of constitutional language and structure to such a debate. Plainly, as Chief Justice Taney's *Dred Scott* decision tragically demonstrated,[3] there are difficulties and dangers in constitutionalizing debate over public issues. But if the Constitution is relevant to such a debate, attention must be paid.

Miller's article suggests two different kinds of expansive interpretation of constitutional language. The first, more formal type concerns his arguments for the binding nature of international law and for the possible invocation of the non-delegation doctrine, which constitutionally limits the extent to which a branch of government may delegate its powers. Both these lines of analysis involve important legal arguments about the separation of powers in our national government. Miller is a

---

2. A. TOCQUEVILLE, *supra* note 1, at 290. *See also id.* at 102-09. For an introduction to the voluminous recent literature on the litigiousness of Americans, and our propensity to resort to courtroom battles and judicial orders to resolve all manner of disputes, see J. LIBERMAN, THE LITIGIOUS SOCIETY (1981); Manning, *Hyperlexis: Our National Disease,* 71 Nw. U.L. REV. 767 (1977).

3. Dred Scott v. Sandford, 60 U.S. (19 How.) 393 (1857). For a general discussion of this case, its context and its consequences, see D. FEHRENBACHER, THE DRED SCOTT CASE (1978).

leading constitutional law expert on this topic; his thoughts on the subject are surely worthy of consideration. I leave it to others to debate how convincing Miller's specific arguments are.

What interests me more is Miller's second category of argument. Here he suggests that the phrase in the Preamble to the United States Constitution that concerns securing "the Blessing of Liberty to ourselves and our Posterity" may be a meaningful—perhaps even a legally enforceable — concept.

That the Preamble expresses a common theme is underscored when one considers the context in which early state constitutions as well as the federal document were composed and ratified. Those who precipitated a Revolutionary War and established a nation on an innovative constitutional scaffolding intended federal and state governments to provide for and protect not only themselves, but the generations to follow. The influential Virginia Declaration of Rights of 1776, for example, began with the following brave proclamation about equality and the rights of men:

> 1. That all men are by nature equally free and independent and have certain inherent rights, of which, when they enter into a state of society, *they cannot, by any compact, deprive or divest their posterity;* namely, the enjoyment of life and liberty, with the means of acquiring and possessing property, and pursuing *and obtaining happiness and safety.*[4]

A Republican government was formed to secure the happiness and safety of the founders *and of their posterity.* As Thomas Jefferson argued, the living hold the earth in usufruct for future generations.[5] Each

---

4. 10 SOURCES AND DOCUMENTS OF UNITED STATES CONSTITUTIONS 49 (W. Swindler ed. 1979) (emphasis added). Virginia retains this language as Article I of her Bill of Rights.

5. Jefferson's assertion "that the earth belongs in usufruct to the living" appears in his letter to James Madison, written September 6, 1789 but not mailed until January 9, 1790. That letter, and the exchange it provoked between Madison and Jefferson, is discussed in illuminating fashion in A. KOCH, JEFFERSON AND MADISON 62-96 (1950). *See also* D. MALONE, JEFFERSON AND THE RIGHTS OF MAN 179, 291 (1951). Jefferson was sufficiently serious about the obligations of those living to those to follow that he proposed specific legal contraints to guard against waste and other violations of the natural law duty he believed to be owed by the present generation.

generation is morally bound to preserve the inheritance of those to follow. This concept of a responsibility to preserve the earth for the future
was a central tenet in the consciousness and the constitution-making of
the period. It does not take too much stretching across the intervening
two hundred years to see how the early hope and effort of the founders
to preserve and protect their political experiment for posterity is relevant to the threat of nuclear catastrophe today. Provoked in a positive
sense by Miller's analysis, I now turn to an exploration of that idea,
which I will call constitutional protection of posterity. My discussion is
divided into three categories: Preamble, Protection, and Posterity.

Preamble

What legal weight should be accorded the Preamble to the Constitution? This question has seldom been explored in American constitutional law.[6] Like motherhood, the flag, and the Declaration of Independence, the Preamble is honored more by invocation than by observance.
The language of the Preamble is generally relegated to misty patriotic
incantations — appropriate for introductions at political gatherings and
the socialization of immigrants, schoolchildren and the like, but not for
the hardheaded business of those trained in the law. But when debate
about constitutional text becomes particularly heated and spills out into
the streets, as it did in the context of antislavery agitation prior to the
Civil War, for example, citizens-in-the-street often begin to proclaim in
plain language their understanding of the Preamble.[7] Indeed, this tendency helps to explain why the Preamble figures so infrequently in the
constitutional discourse of judges, lawyers and legal scholars. If the
public may parse the Preamble, it begins to appear hopelessly and dangerously open-ended.

The clear possibility of imminent nuclear danger is the appropriate
occasion for reconsideration of what constitutional weight the Preamble
should bear. A full exploration of the issue must await more time and

---

6. A suggestive recent exception appears in Black, *A Round Trip to Eire: Two
Books on the Irish Constitution,* Book Review, 91 YALE L.J. 391 (1981) Black's argument concerning application of the Ninth Amendment clearly relates to, and reinforces, the themes sketched in this essay.

7. *See, e.g.,* W. WIECEK, THE SOURCES OF ANTISLAVERY CONSTITUTIONALISM IN
AMERICA, 1760-1848 (1977) and my review at 56 TEX. L. REV. 1319 (1978).

space; however, Miller makes a significant start. Yet Miller may have dismissed the legal importance of the Preamble a bit too quickly; he also seems not to have weighed adequately the possibility of internally inconsistent commands within the Preamble itself. Miller points to the textual provision about securing the blessings of liberty not merely for ourselves, but also for our posterity. He then quickly moves to a discussion of the concept of natural justice. Thus Miller does not wrestle with other language in the Preamble that commits our government "to provide for the common defence" and to "insure domestic Tranquility." Those who would expand or maintain our nuclear arsenal could certainly argue that the task they have set for themselves is to carry out those directives.

The possibility that both sides might invoke the Preamble in a constitutional argument about nuclear weapons does not make it irrelevant. Internal contradition in the constitutional text is neither as silly nor as strange as it might first appear. Indeed, the phenomenon of conflicting claims, all premised on constitutional language, is a frequent, even prevalent mode of constitutional law argument. The possibility that the Constitution itself contains inconsistent commands and conflicting rights and obligations is an idea not yet adequately explored.[8] A reading of our constitutional history compels recognition of just such problematic interpretations. It also forces those would construe the Constitution's language to consider the structure as well as the words of the document.

In many ways, the Preamble is the obvious place to begin. Its clear indication of transgenerational concern should not be ignored. At a minimum, the Preamble suggests that constitutional meaning should be derived with an eye to the future as well as to the past. Brief consideration of both the specific language and the structure of the Constitution, as they pertain to the obligation of government to protect the populace, illustrates my point that the Preamble suggests the Constitution should be discussed as if posterity were eavesdropping.

---

8.   For useful initial forays, *see generally* Henkin, *Infallibility Under Law: Constitutional Balancing,* 78 COLUM. L. REV. 1022 (1978) and C. MILLER, THE SUPREME COURT AND THE USES OF HISTORY (1969).

Protection

Miller provides a summary of a few recent and controversial decisions by the United States Supreme Court which, taken together, suggest an ill-defined constitutional right to privacy and autonomy. Such a constitutional right, now generally conceded to be a right derived from a revised or revisited idea of substantive due process,[9] could conceivably be extended dramatically to encompass the family of man.

Such a concept of family exceeds the grand old American nuclear family and even the extended family, whose vital role in the American past was essential to the Court's decision in *Moore v. City of East Cleveland*.[10] It is too grandiose a gambit, however, to leap from the Court's groping efforts to define some right to intimate associations[11] to a claim of constitutional contraints that may be invoked to promote group survival.

This jump is troublesome for several reasons. First, most of the Court's recent decisions are premised on a highly individualistic notion of procreative and familial roles. Additionally, the "bad press" that protection of intimate relationships received from the public as well as from constitutional experts soon after its discovery by the Supreme Court makes this particular constitutional claim a somewhat shaky platform upon which to construct an edifice for constitutional protections.

Finally, it is somewhat anomalous to premise an argument advocating constitutional concern for future generations on decisions that are particularly troublesome precisely because, in invalidating state barriers to abortions, the Supreme Court appeared to ignore the future-oriented claim that could be made on behalf of fetuses. This claim implies that the fetus, more than the pregnant woman, is a direct link to future generations; it alleges that the state, as surrogate for and protector of the fetus, best represents posterity.

Needless to say, the nexus between the fetus and the future has

---

9. *See, e.g.,* Moore v. City of East Cleveland, 431 U.S. 494, 502-04 (1977); Ely, *The Wages of Crying Wolf: A Comment on Roe v. Wade,* 82 YALE L.J. 920 (1973).

10. 431 U.S. 494, 503-06 (1977).

11. The most thoughtful effort generally to accept and to develop the implications of the new privacy may be found in Karst, *The Freedom of Intimate Association,* 89 YALE L.J. 624 (1980).

not been a central element of the debate swirling around abortion. But such a connection might be a way to rethink, perhaps even to begin to justify, some of the curious judicial line-drawing in the abortion decisions, even as it suggests new difficulties in *Roe v. Wade*[12] and its misnamed "progeny."

The "privileges or immunities" clause of the Fourteenth Amendment, though not mentioned by Miller, is perhaps more promising, in part, because the meaning of that clause has scarcely ever been explored. The United States Supreme Court vitiated any discernible original intent behind its words in the *Slaughter-House Cases*,[13] which narrowed this protection of the rights of citizens to redundancy and oblivion. But the reasons for disuse of the privileges or immunities clause since that 1873 decision go beyond the burden of distinguishing, overruling or ignoring the Court's dubious initial interpretation. They include the apparent limitation of the phrase to the protection of "citizens" and not — as with other fourteenth amendment protections — protection of all persons. Existing judicial constructions of the seemingly parallel privileges and immunities provision in Article IV of the United States Constitution also complicate new interpretations of the fourteenth amendment language. In recent years, however, a surprising number of constitutional scholars of divergent ideologies have suggested that the hour for privileges or immunities protection has come round at last.[14]

---

12. 410 U.S. 113 (1973).

13. 83 U.S. (16 Wall.) 36 (1873).

14. *See, e.g.,* Kurland, *The Privileges or Immunities Clause: 'Its Hour Come Round at Last,'* 1972 WASH. U.L.Q. 405; J. ELY, DEMOCRACY AND DISTRUST 22-30, 98 (1980). It may be worth noting that Professor Kurland's literary reference is to William Butler Yeats's poem, *The Second Coming,* in which Yeats appears not entirely sanguine about that vision. In fact, the poem may be read as somewhat prophetic on the subject of nuclear annihilation. Perhaps Yeats suggests something emerging from the apocalypse, but he writes of a time when

> Things fall apart; the centre cannot hold;
> Mere anarchy is loosed upon the world,
> The blood-dimmed tide is loosed, and everywhere
> The ceremony of innocence is drowned;
> The best lack all conviction, while the worst
> Are full of passionate intensity.

W.B. YEATS, *The Second Coming,* THE COLLECTED POEMS OF W.B. YEATS 184 (De-

Although the idea that all citizens should share in the constitutional privileges or immunities enjoyed by each citizen is provocative in itself, it is even more so when future citizens are included in the constitutional equation. Yet the Fourteenth Amendment privileges or immunities clause was derived most immediately from the 1866 Civil Rights Act. It is relatively clear that the men of the 39th Congress sought to mandate government protection from grievous harms and to guarantee rights they deemed essential to security.[15] The notion that privileges or immunities has something to do with freedom to choose the means of individual survival, as well as the assurance of minimal personal and group security, merits further attention.

Even more promising, I believe, is the argument that the constitutional text and structure combine to impose a duty on government to guarantee a certain threshold of security to all citizens. This interpretation, while connected to what I suggested about the Preamble, relies primarily upon the package of constitutional amendments ratified in the wake of the Civil War. Elsewhere, I have sought to demonstrate that the framers of the Thirteenth, Fourteenth and Fifteenth Amendments intended to alter existing notions of federalism and to guarantee a range of basic individual rights.[16] They sought to narrow or to eliminate the gap — starkly illustrated for most of them by constitutional protection of slavery — between what they deemed to be natural rights not previously protected, and what the federal Constitution now should and could protect.

Those who wrote, passed, and ratified this second Constitution

---

finitive ed. 1956). A "rough beast," with "gaze blank and pitiless as the sun," now "Slouches toward Bethelehem to be born." After "twenty centuries of stony sleep . . . vexed to nightmare by a rocking cradle," it is this rough beast's hour which is now "come round at last." *Id.*

15. For an elaboration of this theme, and its historical context, see Soifer, *Protecting Civil Rights: A Critique of Raoul Berger's History,* 54 N.Y.U. L. Rev. 651 (1979); *see also* Dimond, *Strict Construction and Judicial Review of Racial Discrimination Under the Equal Protection Clause: Meeting Raoul Berger on Interpretivist Grounds,* 80 Mich. L. Rev. 462 (1982). Raoul Berger's rather vehement response to my article is in, *Soifer to the Rescue of History,* 32 S.C.L. Rev. 427 (1981). For another recent statement of a viewpoint opposed to my own, see *dictum* concerning the negative Constitution in Bowers v. DeVito, 51 U.S.L.W. 2163 (7th Cir. Aug. 20, 1982) (Posner, J.).

16. Soifer, *supra* note 15, at 686-96, 700-06.

hoped that state governments would adequately protect the civil and political rights the federal Constitution now established. By constitutional amendment and by statute, they attempted to assure federal protection in the event that the states failed in their duty to guarantee these newly-recognized rights. To those who sought to constitutionalize the outcome of the Civil War, it was clear that allegiance to government compelled a reciprocal governmental duty to protect basic rights. As they articulated the promise of the second Constitution, they repeatedly included the safety and security of all inhabitants. If the states failed in their obligation to protect those within their borders, it was the federal government's duty to intervene to secure the basic rights of all.

Too frequently, the lawyer's stock-in-trade is a tendency to focus on a single word or phrase to construe a constitutional text. This technique often misses the central message of the constitutional medium. Charles Black made this point convincingly years ago, and it has been developed by several others since.[17] A single example, derived from the Fourteenth Amendment, will illustrate.

In recent years, and for very good reasons, we have devoted primary attention to the "equal" part of "equal protection." Many struggled valiantly, and struggle still, to determine when racial stereotypes and their ilk should be constitutionally forbidden. In this process, the "protection" element of the constitutional text often is ignored. A few scholars have begun to develop the theme of constitutional protection for rights or processes they regard as fundamental, such as the right to political participation and minimal social welfare.[18] Thus far, however, equality remains the dominant motif, and protection is seldom identified as an overarching problem.

I do not mean to suggest that protection is a self-explanatory term, nor that an inquiry about the concept will yield easy answers. Elsewhere I have begun to consider the two-edged nature of arguments about governmental duty to protect. The concept includes both the pos-

---

17. C. BLACK, STRUCTURE AND RELATIONSHIP IN CONSTITUTIONAL LAW (1969); Ely, *supra* note 9, at 73-104; Monaghan, *Of 'Liberty' and 'Property,'* 62 CORNELL L. REV. 405 (1977).

18. *See* Ely, *supra* note 9 (equality in the political process); Michelman, *On Protecting the Poor Through the Fourteenth Amendment,* 83 HARV. L. REV. 7 (1969) (threshold of necessities).

sibility of paternalism, in a pejorative sense, and of parentalism, a more positive counterpart.[19] It can be demonstrated, I believe, that those who wrote and adopted both the initial Constitution and the constitutional innovations after the Civil War operated in contexts that encouraged them to envision something of each kind of protection, without distinguishing clearly between the two.

A right to basic protection can be turned on its head, of course, by those who assert that foreign domination constitutes the vital threat to American security. Even this claim does not easily or convincingly extend to a defense of nuclear weapons proliferation, however. The assertion that in protecting something, we must set in motion the means to destroy it, is familiar enough after Vietnam. By now, such familiarity should breed contempt, not nuclear arms.

My claim is that the threat of nuclear annihilation—like a board bashed across the muzzle of a mule—should be sufficient to get our attention. We may then begin to consider exactly what kinds of obligation to the population we consider essential to the constitutive core of our republican form of government. We will have to confront the vexing issue of how to include posterity in our own generation's calculations.

Posterity

To begin to grapple with the issue of how to deal with our issue, we must wrestle anew with a perplexing philosophic and practical problem, and with a dilemma that deeply concerned eminent American thinkers such as Thomas Jefferson and James Madison. Even to define posterity is a challenge, as Jefferson discovered when he set out to calculate the lifespan of a generation. He tried to use his generational concept to create a legal system to assure that the earth would belong to the living and their posterity, rather than be ruled by the dead hand of the past. Precision about generations was and remains terribly elusive, however. Therefore, Jefferson's more pragmatic friend, James Madison, argued that "the present generation is morally bound to respect the natural rights — the basic needs — of coming generations, however much positive laws in any given society may depart from the

---

19. N.Y. Times, Oct. 19, 1981, at B10, col. 6.

moral ideal."[20]

Concern for future generations was an integral part of constitution-making in the nation's formative years. Koch summarized her discussion of the exchange between Jefferson and Madison as follows: "In general, the fundamental features of the theory that proved acceptable to both Jefferson and Madison were forward-looking and generous in their regard for the liberty and welfare of generations to come in America."[21]

The difficulty of determining exactly what this concern entails remains with us. Neither rights theorists nor utilitarians have met the challenge yet. The nearly total absence of posterity in the calculus done within the school of law and economics is one of the most striking limitations of this new orthodoxy.[22] The challenge of somehow acknowledging and providing for the future is vital, however, and starkly presented through intensified awareness of nuclear terror.

Most judicial analysis employs present presumptions and fact-finding to determine something concrete about the past and to serve a remedial or punitive end. But in constitutional law, the perspective is more often both forward and backward looking. One can lose all sense of balance, of course, in such Janus-like contortions. Yet even self-proclaimed strict constructionists usually acknowledge that the Constitution is a document designed for the future, meant to create a structure for an ongoing Great Experiment. As Chief Justice John Marshall put it, the Constitution was "intended to endure for ages to come."[23]

Failure to heed this future-oriented aspect of American constitutionalism is commonplace. It is particularly glaring, for example, in the

---

20. Koch, *supra* note 5, at 74.

21. *Id.*

22. For philosophic discussions about possible claims upon contemporaries by those to follow, *see, e.g.,* OBLIGATIONS TO FUTURE GENERATIONS (R. Sikora and B. Barry eds. 1978); Kavka, *The Paradox of Future Individuals,* 11 PHIL. & PUB. AFF. 93 (1981) and Parfit, *Future Generations: Future Problems,* 11 PHIL. & PUB. AFF. 113; B. ACKERMAN, SOCIAL JUSTICE IN THE LIBERAL STATE (1980).

The best critical discussion I know about the generational problem in the context of the law and economics debate is found in Heller, *The Importance of Narrative Decision-Making: The Limitations of Legal Economics as a Basis for a Liberal Jurisprudence—As Illustrated by the Regulation of Vacation Home Development,* 1976 WIS. L. REV. 385, 459-68.

23. McCulloch v. Maryland, 17 U.S. (4 Wheat.) 316, 415 (1819).

recent efforts by the Supreme Court to make proof of past discriminatory racial motivation a necessary precondition before courts may recognize violations of rights guaranteed by the Civil War Amendments. This generally serves, as a practical matter, to constitutionalize the *status quo*.[24] It appears to reject the vital combination of symbolic and pragmatic roles the Court often played in the past.

Virtually anything that exists is said to be legitimate under this approach. Existence is viewed as a race of life, which the Court deems to be a fair contest. The nuclear arms race may be perceived in much the same way. Legal protection can be invoked only upon a clear showing of overt, official and effective mistreatment. Victimization alone, even racial victimization, is not sufficient. Exceptions will be made only for those who can actually prove bad motive.

Since the central defense of the expansion of nuclear arms is defense — not only a proper motive, but even an admirable one — an actual constitutional claim that nuclear proliferation endangers rather than enhances the security of ourselves and our posterity appears doomed. If it ever got that far, the current Court would easily dismiss the argument as simply a matter of the claimants' perception of the problem.[25]

Such a response—the idea that any actual harm is simply a matter of one's own subjective perception — is a paraphrase of the way the Court answered the argument in *Plessy v. Ferguson*[26] that to require segregated streetcars was a denial of constitutional rights. Like racial stigma, the danger of nuclear conflagration can be passed over as some-

---

24. For an initial stab at this theme, see Soifer, *Complacency and Constitutional Law,* 42 OHIO ST. L.J. 383 (1981). *See also* Freeman, *Legitimizing Racial Discrimination Through Antidiscrimination Law: A Critical Review of Supreme Court Doctrine,* 62 MINN. L. REV. 1049 (1978).

25. Duke Power Co. v. Carolina Envtl. Study Group, 438 U.S. 59 (1978).

26. 163 U.S. 537 (1896). A disturbing echo of the reasoning in *Plessy* may be found in City of Memphis v. Greene, 451 U.S. 100 (1981), *reh'g denied,* 452 U.S. 955 (1981). Here, too, the United States Supreme Court seemed to believe that any stigma associated with blocking off a street where it traversed a black neighborhood, as it ran from a prosperous white neighborhood to a public park, was to be found only in the perception of the black plaintiffs. After all, Justice Stevens argued, the blacks who complained did not show that blacks ever sought to have streets blocked, only to be refused. Any disparate impact "could not, in any event, be fairly characterized as a badge or incident of slavery." *Id.* at 126.

thing merely in the eyes of the beholder. This is particularly true today, when the Social Darwinian notion of independent individuals freely choosing their own fate again dominates judicial interpretation of constitutional law. Only if we begin to explore and to heed the constitutional directive to protect our posterity, and begin to include future generations in our own constitutional calibrations, can we hope to make certain that the dreaded dead hand of the past does not clasp a future universe full of dead hands.

Exactly where greater recognition of the claims of posterity would lead constitutional law is unclear. It is uncommonly important, though, to consider the organic, direct connection of our founders to subsequent constitutionalists — including ourselves. In turn, we are inevitably the parents and preservers of our posterity. This continuity, and the goal of protecting posterity established in the constitutional framework, suggest that it is neither far-fetched nor unproductive to explore how constitutional values are relevant to the contemporary threat of immediate nuclear annihilation.

Conclusion

The practical visionaries of the past surely could not have anticipated our modern folly. Yet themes of optimistic anticipation and concern for future generations echo through the constitutional scheme they established. The words of 1787 and 1868 provide no crisp, clean answers to any cases and controversies that might be framed to challenge the spread of nuclear weapons. But they do bequeath a still, small call to reason and to hope — for ourselves and for our posterity.

16.
Nuclear War: The End of Law*

Milner S. Ball**

Professor Miller summons us to consider the constitutionality of nuclear weapons. In doing so, he has made an original, provocative contribution to constitutional jurisprudence as well as the humanizing politics of nuclear arms control. He speaks with scholarly responsibility on a subject that has heretofore engendered either silence or nonsense and bombast.

Introduction

By raising the question about the constitutionality of nuclear weapons, Professor Miller augments understanding of constitutional law and how constitutional law is done. Constitutional lawyers take far too crabbed a view of their subject when they merely sift through past court decisions and speculate on how the Supreme Court might decide a case in future. Consideration of the legality of nuclear arms leads Professor Miller to point out that the constitution is not limited to what the Court has said or may say. It includes, he reminds us, the great political realities which are brought partially to textual expression in the preamble and which can be fully satisfied not by judicial opinions but only by the people's decisions and actions and by the operations of all our institutions. To begin with, then, nuclear war violates constitutional law in the Miller dimension, which embraces systemic justice and the fundamental nature of government by the people.[1]

Equally enlarging is Professor Miller's introduction of arguments drawn from specific constitutional provisions. First he exhumes and gives life to the doctrine of delegation, not presently favored in federal

---

* Reprinted, with permission, from *Nova Law Journal*, Volume 7, Number 1 (1982).

** Professor of Law, University of Georgia School of Law.

1. It is to be remembered that Abraham Lincoln characteristically referred to the Declaration of Independence rather than to the Constitution when he addressed the fundamental nature of the American people.

litigation and not before given such expansive, refreshing expression.[2] Article 1, section 8, clause 2 commits to Congress the power to declare war. Presidents, acting without such congressional declarations have, from time to time, authorized responsive, limited military action. Professor Miller proposes that, because limits cannot be maintained once nuclear weapons are employed, Congress may not delegate decisions about their use to the President or to computers and glitsches.[3]

Second, having called attention to the restrictions of delegation, Professor Miller takes note of its responsibilities. Congress may not fail to exercise the powers delegated to it by the constitution. Article I, section 8, clause 10 grants to Congress the power to punish offenses against the law of nations. Accordingly, says Professor Miller, Congress must combat the international crime of threatened or contemplated use of nuclear weapons.[4]

Third, the President has an affirmative constitutional duty similar to that imposed upon Congress. Article II, section 3 directs the chief executive to "take care that the laws be faithfully executed." The word "laws" comprehends international law by implication, analogy or necessity, and so places the President under a duty matching that of Congress. He, too, must act to remove the forbidden threat of nuclear

---

2. Pre-1937 decisions of the Supreme Court occasionally relied upon the doctrine of non-delegation of legislative powers in striking down actions of Congress. *See, e.g.,* A.L.A. Schecter Poultry Corp. v. United States, 295 U.S. 495, 529 (1935). More recently, the Court has avoided invocation of the doctrine by the device of narrow construction of a tested delegation. *See, e.g.,* Federal Energy Admin. v. Algonquin SNG, Inc., 426 U.S. 548 (1976). For a judicial expression of interest in resurrecting the doctrine see Industrial Union v. American Petroleum Inst., 448 U.S. 607 (1980). The doctrine of non-delegation has found a readier audience in state courts where it appears to be alive and well. *See, e.g.,* Howell v. State, 238 Ga. 95, 230 S.E.2d 853 (1976).

3. There is a prior question here about whether Congress itself has the power to declare nuclear war. *See infra* p. 61. If war ever had a human scale, that possibility has grown increasingly remote since the beginning of World War I when technology was let loose relentlessly to grind human life and human flesh.

4. I have reservations about this argument. It may be that legislatures are designed, mercifully, exactly to do nothing. *See, e.g.,* R. NEELY, HOW COURTS GOVERN AMERICA 47-78 (1981). Perhaps the only affirmative duty of Congress that we may safely press is that of the oath of office to support the Constitution (art. VI, § 3). To cite but one example, I think it best that the congressional power to declare war not be viewed as carrying with it an affirmative duty. We want no zealous exercises of that power.

arms.[5]

Last, Professor Miller argues that the due process clause places upon all three branches the requirement actively to prevent nuclear deprivation of life, liberty and property.[6] He then ends as he began: he challenges lawyers to take up the problem of nuclear weapons because it is a matter of law for lawyers, not some distant activity above and beyond the calling of the bar.

The Constitutional Aspects of Nuclear Weapons

If my views diverge from Professor Miller's at certain points, the variance should not be misinterpreted. I wish to pay tribute to him and to do so by heeding his call to speak. How better to express thanks than to do exactly as he urges and take up the debate?

Professor Miller offers his essay as a preliminary exploration of possibilities. My response is in kind. I want to raise some questions about the agenda for discussion of the constitutionality of nuclear weapons.

---

5. This argument has several steps. There must be an affirmative duty; international law must be included in this duty; nuclear weapons must be a violation of international law; the Court must have power to declare the duty. I do not think the argument unworthy of pursuit. But each of its elements will have to be established, and I do not think that an easy task.

6. Such a federal police power might be seen as having two components: an affirmative duty abroad to labor for mutual disarmament and a domestic self-policing duty not to do those things which may trigger nuclear war.

Perhaps the growing interest in an expansion of the public trust doctrine might afford a preferred ground upon which to build the desired affirmative duty.

It is also to be asked if the affirmative duty of government might not include some form of unilateral disarmament. Professor Miller says that his essay is not a plea for selective unilateral disarmament. I would like at least to reserve judgment on the issue of unilateral disarmament. On the one hand, I can imagine a type of selective unilateral disarmament that might be plain, good military policy and actually strengthen our defense posture. On the other hand, as Professor Miller points out, ideas may appear foolish only because they are new and challenge received ways of thinking. Miller, *Nuclear Weapons and Constitutional Law*, 7 NOVA L.J. 21 (1982).

A.   Unconstitutional: Is the Characterization of Nuclear Weapons as Constitutional Adequate?

Fear and befuddlement prevent action. If we are so afraid of the bomb that we suffer ethical paralysis or are so overwhelmed by the claimed complexities of disarmament that we cannot grasp them, then the arms race will run on toward the finish of nuclear apocalypse. Professor Miller cuts the dragon down to size. He gives us hope. He shows us that we can take action, can process the dragon into links of sausage. This is a very lawyerlike approach. It encourages lawyers to understand that nuclear war is something that they can and should prevent. We are enabled to subject the bomb to arguments about constitutional validity the way lawyers reduce any volatile issue to manageable parts bearing blackletter labels.

This is a good and commendable undertaking. Nevertheless there is considerable risk in initiating a dialogue about the legality of nuclear arms. Lawyers suffer a vocational disadvantage in this regard not shared by their colleagues in the medical profession. When a physician describes the effects of a nuclear attack — massive death, mutilated bodies, unbearable suffering, endless contamination — we are horror struck.[7] None but a madman would argue that nuclear war is healthy.

---

7. Physicians are as diverse in their political and social views as any other large group of citizens and rarely speak in unison on matters of public policy. But today they are virtually united in their effort to convey a simple, urgent message about nuclear war to the American public and the Administration. The message is this: Nuclear war—any kind of nuclear war—would cause death and suffering on a scale never seen before in all of history, and modern medicine with all its skills could do little or nothing to help. . . .

Most physicians are convinced that nuclear war is the greatest threat to health and survival that society has ever faced. It would indeed be the 'final epidemic,' for which medicine has no treatment. When there exists no cure for a disease, the only course is to take preventive measures. That is why physicians believe it is their professional responsibility to urge their fellow citizens and their Government to make certain that nuclear weapons are never used. Unlike natural catastrophes, over which man has no control, nuclear war would be a disaster of man's making. It should be preventable.

Realm & Leaf, *Doctors: No Rx's In a War,* N.Y. Times, Aug. 11, 1982, at A23, col. 1.

Not so when our political rather than physical constitution is the subject. No sooner does one lawyer argue that nuclear weapons are not constitutional than another lawyer ventures the counter-argument that they are constitutional.[8] Arguments on both sides of *any* issue are our professional stock-in-trade. To introduce the subject of nuclear weapons into such argumentation is to take the chance that this exercise may, against our deepest wishes, lend nuclear weapons an unwarranted air of legitimacy.[9] Quite apart from any authoritative decision, lawyers' arguments might domesticate the nuclear issue, remove its urgency as well as its terror, and make it, catastrophically, familiar.

Nuclear weapons are monstrous. They may also be illegal. But we dare not lose sight of their unnatural monstrocity. Of course lawyers should address prevention of nuclear war. The assignment is to keep the blasphemy of nuclear war clearly in focus at the same time that we find means for lawyers to reckon with it in lawyerlike ways.

Instead of talking about the unconstitutionality of nuclear weapons, would we not be better advised to describe them as deconstitutionalizing or anti-constitutional?

Professor Miller's own comments — about nuclear war's destruction of underlying values — indicate how we might proceed. Like doctors we would attempt to depict the aftermath of nuclear war. But,

---

8. The arguments in favor of constitutionality are easily imaginable: preambular citation of the need for common defense, Article 1 delegation of the powers to raise and support armies and to provide for the common defense, Article II delegation of certain foreign affairs responsibilities and of command of the armed forces, Articles III limitations of judicial review, etc.

9. Undeniably, nuclear weapons exist. But that certainly does not mean that they are legitimate. Professor Miller refers to an "assumption of constitutionality" of nuclear weapons. Miller, *supra* note 6, at 22. I am not prepared to make or grant that assumption.

Secretary of Energy, James B. Edwards, not only assumes the legitimacy of nuclear weapons but celebrates them. In an unparalleled display of callousness—or was it cynicism?—Secretary Edwards said that he found "exciting" a nuclear bomb exploded on the eve of the anniversary of the bombing of Hiroshima. *"Cabinet Officer says U.S. will continue Atom Arms Testing,"* N.Y. Times, Aug. 6, 1982, at 1, col. 1. Secretary Edwards seems to regard nuclear arms as an adjunct of the first amendment: the nuclear bomb "is the weapon that can preserve their ability for free political discussion." *Id.* at B4, col. 6. It is an alarming point of view and helps to indicate why I wish to overthrow the ideological statement that we live in a Hobbesian world. *See infra* note 10.

instead of taking up the medical consequences, we would address the legal consequences.

For example: What would become of western legal order? Would there be a legal system? How would it function? Would there be government? Would there be courts? What of police? What would happen to the practice of law? Would there be law schools left? What would legal education become when all the major law schools in major urban target areas had been destroyed? And what of democratic government? Is it not likely that any surviving remnant would find abhorrent and reject our way of life and Constitution that had permitted this thing to happen?[10]

These are the kinds of questions that might be taken up and debated if we realized that nuclear weapons are de-constitutionalizing. We would be asked to portray those things known to us as lawyers that would be lost. Lawyerly argument would then be stripped of its potential to legitimate nuclear weapons for the arguments would proceed from the premise of destruction. The subject for debate would be not whether nuclear weapons are legal, but rather, the extent to which they destroy law and lawyers.

---

10.   Professor Miller says that we live in a Hobbesian world. Miller, *supra* note 6, at 24. I disagree for two reasons. First, a Hobbesian world is what we would have *after* nuclear war. Hobbes' account is sobering:

> In such condition, there is no place for industry; because the fruit thereof is uncertain: and consequently no culture of the earth; no navigation, nor use of the commodities that may be imported by sea; no commodius building; no instruments of moving, and removing, such things as require much force; no knowledge of the face of the earth; no account of time; no arts; no letters; no society; and which is worst of all, continual fear, and danger of violent death; and the life of man, solitary, poor, nasty, brutish and short.

T. HOBBES, LEVIATHAN 100 (M. Oakeshott ed. 1962). That is a pretty fair description of a post-nuclear war world, not the one we have now, and it serves to help us understand what we would lose.

The second reason for disagreeing with the statement that we live in a Hobbesian world is this: We are made to believe that we live in a Hobbesian world through propaganda and ideology, and it is a kind of self-fulfilling prophecy. We need desperately to find a more satisfactory description for reality, one that would not lead us to accept as rational the self-contradictory statement that we must have nuclear arms if we are to survive.

B. Decision-Makers: The Nuclear Problem as an Opportunity for Popular Revolution.

Professor Miller, with his strategy of hope, points out that nuclear weapons present us with an opportunity. He makes of them an opportunity for broadening and deepening our conception of constitutional jurisprudence and for heightening our sense of legal ethics. May there not be another opportunity in the making, opportunity for a kind of positive democratic revolution?

Thomas Jefferson had thought that liberty in America might be enriched by a revolution every generation. Nuclear arms may provide occasion for this generation's revolution if the growing disarmament movement among the people continues.[11]

Professor Miller makes reference to those who have authority and control in the government and their duty to take action. And he says that lawyers are no longer on the sidelines because they have quasi-governmental status and a share in the action. This is to accept the fact of government by an elite and to say that lawyers have some attachment to that elite.

The problem of truly popular government is one that we have not solved. We have done a more or less satisfactory job of providing government of and for the people. We do not provide government by the people. Periodic elections, polls and interest groups are means of bringing influence to bear upon government. They are not a participation in government. The nearest thing the people have to a place within government is the street — marches and rallies before the United Nations, below the Washington monument, etc. The street is not a satisfactory forum for the formation and expression of opinion.

It is in this sense that nuclear weapons and the people's movement to control them offers a governmental opportunity, the opportunity to think about and explore government by the people.

President Eisenhower pointed to the gap between what the government is planning and doing and what the people are dreaming and hoping. He said that the people want peace so much that one day govern-

---

11. Letter from Thomas Jefferson to W. S. Smith (Nov. 13, 1787) in THE PAPERS OF THOMAS JEFFERSON 356-57 (J. Boyd ed. 1955). *See also* THE LIFE AND SELECTED WRITINGS OF THOMAS JEFFERSON 488, 492, 674-75, 714 (A. Koch & W. Peden eds. 1944).

ments "had better get out of their way and let them have it."[12] We keep reciting the refrain that in this government the people are sovereign. If the people are indeed the governors as well as the governed, then they and not an elite should be the decision-makers with the duty to act. Perhaps the issue of nuclear arms control will bring the day for piercing the veil of rhetoric and reaching the reality of popular government. At least we are given the opportunity to consider it.

Lawyers have a critical role to play in the democratic governing of affairs, especially nuclear affairs.[13] They have this role not because of ties to a governing elite but because of their original ties to the people. If we have governmental status with responsibility to act, then this is so because as officers of the court we have a singular duty in generally-shared citizenship.

With respect to the nuclear disarmament opportunity, lawyers might wish to reflect upon and develop juridical means for giving expression to what the people are dreaming and hoping. We might also wish to consider whether conceptions of how to train lawyers in the skills of representation have been too narrowly confined. Legal representation of the people may entail something altogether different from (and in addition to) courtroom advocacy, negotiation, drafting, etc. Would this be subject matter for a professional skills course? Constitutional law? Some other? As a minimum, lawyers ought to be asked to devise, for a matter as urgent and immediate as nuclear war, a more efficacious mode of participation than polls, litigation, demonstrations, or a letter to one's congressman. (The force of such a letter is fully spent in triggering a machine-extruded standard-form response bearing a machine-impressed signature.)

C.   Process: Are the Procedures Leading Up To and Resulting From Nuclear War Constitutional?

Professor Miller observes that constitutionalism in the United

---

12.   D. EISENHOWER, THE QUOTABLE DWIGHT D. EISENHOWER 55 (1967); B. COOK, THE DECLASSIFIED EISENHOWER 149 (1981) (quoting a statement of Eisenhower to Harold Macmillan in a televised talk, London (Sept. 6, 1959)).

13.   I am a member of the Lawyer's Alliance for Nuclear Arms Control. I do not represent or speak for this organization. My opinions led me to join this group; my membership did not lead me to hold these opinions.

States is more than process, i.e. law has normative content. This may well be true. But are there not procedural issues yet to be fully exploited?

(1) If we project the aftermath of a hypothetical nuclear war (assuming there would be an aftermath), the barren legal landscape exhibits several procedural features. One of these is the absence of appeal or recourse.

In *Nixon v. Fitzgerald*,[14] the Supreme Court held that the President is absolutely immune from damage suits for actions taken in connection with official duty. Writing for the Court, Justice Powell averred that the Court had not placed the President above the law.[15] He said that the possibility that the President was above the law was a chilling but unjustified contention.[16] He said that it was unjustified because there remains the remedy of impeachment.[17] Regardless of what one thinks about *Nixon v. Fitzgerald,* it does help us to see the chilling fact that nuclear war would put the President above the law, and above politics for that matter. There would be no legal or political redress. Impeachment would have no materiality or relevance. Elections, if they were ever held again, would not recall the devastation.

We can see that Congress cannot delegate to the President such an unlimited power. But then we can also see that Congress cannot exercise this power either. In fact, the real reason that Congress cannot delegate this power is that it does not have such a power. The essence of constitutionalism, says Professor Miller is limited government. Article I of the Constitution does not contain the grant of unlimited power. When we committed to Congress the power to declare war, we did not grant the power to declare Armageddon. There would be no appeal from such a declaration. We have given neither the President nor the Congress the right to use unbounded violence or violence without legal and political control. Self-destruction, if it is a right, is one retained by the people.

(2) If we start with nuclear war and think back rather than beyond, we find other procedural issues. For example, what is the process

---

14.   50 U.S.L.W. 4797 (U.S. June 24, 1982).

15.   *Id.* at 4804 & n.41.

16.   *Id.* at 4804 n.41.

17.   *Id.* at 4804.

by which nuclear war comes about? Research on this subject by constitutional scholars could be divided into two phases: one from the present back to the origin of the nuclear possibility; the other forward to a projected hypothetical nuclear war.

With respect to phase one: How has today's situation come to be? Through what processes was our policy or lack of policy given shape? What defaults in constitutional process does this history expose? With respect to phase two: What exactly are the procedures by which nuclear war happens? Do these procedures entail nuclear war, or do faulty procedures allow nuclear strikes to take place in constitutionally suspect ways? (I hazard the guess that secrecy in these areas — such as chains of command — has far less legitimate scope than we are led to suppose.)

(3) If there are procedural arguments and procedural research remaining to be pursued, are there not also procedural actions to be considered? In addition to debating the subject, what ought lawyers do? What judicial, political or other steps should we take? For a start, would it not be lawyerlike to press for the procedural device of requiring impact statements detailing the effects of nuclear war and the arms race upon the environment?

Conclusion

Professor Miller's essay precipitates a final, unresolved thought: What if nuclear weapons are constitutional and nuclear war is legal? What might that reveal to us about our constitution? About our legal-political system? About ourselves? All the answers within range of my powers of vision appear utterly joyless. Ultimate honesty compels us to face those answers howsoever bitterly we may rue their content.[18]

---

18. Such honesty would be the contemporary form of repentance. As such, it would not be easily accomplished. One of the difficulties is the way in which people use God. As George Kennan has noted, during this century's world wars, both sides appealed to God for support of their military efforts. Kennan, *A Christian View of the Arms Race*, THEOLOGY TODAY 162, 170 (July, 1982). Howsoever questionable "this combination of religious faith and secular chauvinism . . . in those past instances" and howsoever it may appear that "modern military technology has now created conditions which allow only one (godly) answer to the possibility of a Soviet-American war," *Id.* I believe that history offers every reason to suppose that some people will nevertheless

appeal to God in support of even nuclear arms. There has long been an intimate involvement of religion in both American constitutionalism and warfare. This is neither the place nor the forum for trying to confront that controversial, complicated involvement. However, these matters are an issue in the question of the constitutionality of nuclear weapons. Suffice it to say here that the honesty necessary to face the answers to the questions posed in the text seems to me available only in the context of the biblical faith. But I also believe that the biblical tradition is to be understood by us in nonreligious terms. As Dietrich Bonhoeffer proposed: "Man's religiosity makes him look in his distress to the power of God in the world: God is *deus ex machina*. The bible directs man to God's powerlessness and suffering; only the suffering God can help." D. BONHOEFFER, LETTERS AND PAPERS FROM PRISON 197 (E. Bethge ed. 1967). A *deus ex machina* is the ally of nuclear weaponry; the suffering God is the ally of its victims. (My own attempts at a theological understanding of law, first addressed in M. BALL, THE PROMISE OF AMERICAN LAW (1981), are the subject for continued exploration in another book now in progress.)

17.
The Frail Constitution of Good Intentions*

Stanley C. Brubaker**

If I understand the architecture of Professor Miller's argument correctly, his lofty conclusion rests on two pillars, either of which he regards as adequate to support it; these pillars in turn arise from a single foundational premise. The conclusion, of course, is that the manufacture, deployment, or use of nuclear weapons is unconstitutional. The premise is that nuclear war is "[b]y definition" unlimited.[1] The first pillar is constructed from clauses of the Constitution reinforced with good intentions. The second is of similar construction, but is also girded by a novel interpretation of international law.

His essay is admittedly only a "preliminary inquiry"[2] into the constitutionality of nuclear weapons, but the architectural design must be examined to see if it affords any reasonable hope of supporting his conclusion.

Pillar I: The Well Intended Constitution

It is the leitmotif of Professor Miller's argument that the Constitution is not to be interpreted simply according to the terms of its text, but informed by the Constitution's intentions.[3] These intentions, we learn, are not simply those of the people who wrote the text, but also, and primarily, those present and future generations who live under its authority.[4] The ultimate end—stated vaguely enough to spark little opposition—emerges as "human survival under conditions that allow human dignity to be maximized."[5] But the proper and good intention

---

* Reprinted, with permission, from *Nova Law Journal*, Volume 7, Number 1 (1982).

** Assistant Professor of Political Science, Colgate University.

1. Miller, *Nuclear Weapons and Constitutional Law,* 7 NOVA L.J. 21, 30 (1982).

2. *Id.* at 23.

3. *Id.* at 27.

4. *Id.*

5. *Id.* at 26.

accompanying this end is to be found among the "clergy, physicians, scientists, and businessmen [who] have grasped and [seek] to show others the meaning of nuclear war."[6] Lawyers are thus invited to share their intentions and, so inspired, to read the text of the Constitution.

Three aspects of the Constitution contribute to the first pillar of support—the Preamble, the nondelegation doctrine, and the Due Process clause. Apparently Professor Miller believes each is independently capable of supporting his conclusion, for he does not indicate how they fit together except that they are each to be read with the Constitution's "intention" in mind.

The most curious of these is the nondelegation doctrine. Professor Miller suggests that it is unconstitutional for Congress "tacitly or expressly"[7] to delegate the authority to the President to declare nuclear war. One must wonder from what use of the nondelegation doctrine Professor Miller expects to draw support. The oldest and most straightforward use of the nondelegation doctrine is, as the term implies, to require that certain decisions can be made by Congress alone, that it cannot delegate these to any other body.[8] But this argument can provide no support for Professor Miller's conclusion that nuclear weapons are unconstitutional because it implies that Congress does have the constitutional authority to manufacture, deploy, and use nuclear weapons.

Perhaps Professor Miller has in mind a more recent use of the nondelegation doctrine, one which hinges on individual rights rather than congressional duty.[9] It implies that an individual has a right to the careful reflection of Congress before his or her liberty is abridged. Conceivably that liberty could be expanded to the liberty to be free from nuclear threat. This use of the nondelegation doctrine could, like the first use, imply that Congress does have the authority to wage nuclear war. But the doctrine so used, unlike the first use, usually harbors a serious reservation about the power that Congress has exercised. While

---

6. *Id.* at 22.

7. *Id.* at 29.

8. *See, e.g.,* Field v. Clark, 143 U.S. 649 (1892) and The Brig Aurora v. United States, 11 U.S. (7 Cranch) 383 (1813). On the nondelegation doctrine generally, see S. BARBER, THE CONSTITUTION AND THE DELEGATION OF CONGRESSIONAL POWER (1975).

9. *See, e.g.,* Kent v. Dulles, 357 U.S. 116 (1958).

an actual constitutional limit to that power must be established independently of the nondelegation doctrine, the nondelegation doctrine is at least supposed to elevate the sensitivity, or "raise the consciousness," of Congress to constitutional limitations.[10] Again, however, the nondelegation doctrine offers no support, in itself, for Professor Miller's conclusion.

And one must further wonder how this use of the nondelegation doctrine could function towards "consciousness raising." Following a nuclear exchange should the Supreme Court declare the war to have been unconstitutional? If Professor Miller is serious about his fundamental premise that nuclear war is by definition unlimited, then there would be no Congress left to have its consciousness raised. But perhaps the remedy lies in equity rather than in law. Should an injunction be issued to halt the President from contemplating a nuclear exchange until Congress explicitly assumes its constitutional obligation to set forth the conditions, if any, in which it thinks nuclear war proper? Until Congress makes up its mind, nuclear war would be limited, assuming improbably that the President heeds the injunction, but hardly in a way that Professor Miller or most any United States citizen can think desirable.[11]

There is a third use of the nondelegation doctrine that might be thought to question the constitutionality of nuclear weapons, which would run as follows: only the President can act quickly enough to use nuclear weapons; only Congress can decide in each instance whether that use is justified. Aside from its wholly disingenuous use of the nondelegation doctrine, this argument requires propositions of fact and value that Professor Miller does not even assert, much less establish. Thus, under any of the three possible uses of the nondelegation doctrine, it lends no support to his conclusion and must be regarded as mere facade.

Infused with good intentions, the Preamble and the Due Process clause are also pressed into impossible duties. "Nuclear weapons and the delicate balance of terror jeopardize,"[12] he tells us, each of the

---

10. It is used, as Professor Alexander Bickel has noted, "in the candid service of avoiding a serious constitutional doubt." A. BICKEL, THE LEAST DANGEROUS BRANCH 165 (1962) (quoting United States v. Rumely, 345 U.S. 41, 47 (1953)).

11. Miller, *supra* note 1.

12. *Id.* at 27.

goals of the Preamble, especially in the sense that there might be no "posterity" remaining to enjoy them. Similarly, "[n]uclear weapons so endanger the lives, liberties, and properties of all Americans that they should be considered to be a deprivation contrary to Due Process."[13] No doubt nuclear weapons do in some way jeopardize our goals and do endanger our lives, liberties, and properties. But we have to ask, compared to what?

Compared to a world in which there are only conventional weapons? Clearly this is what Professor Miller hopes for, but our posterity and our lives, liberties, and properties would not necessarily be rendered more secure. One must discount the gravity of nuclear war by its improbability,[14] and one must remember that it was with conventional weapons that Rome lowered Carthage to dust.

But let's grant the preferability of a world without nuclear weapons. Can one discover a course of constitutionally mandated action? Professor Miller declares that guiding the course is a "duty to take action designed to eliminate the nuclear threat throughout the world."[15] One might wonder how Professor Miller can leap from the Constitution's rights and goals to world duties, but if the United States had sovereignty commensurate with that duty throughout the world, the duty would not be difficult to follow. The problem, of course, is that such authority is lacking. What then can the United States do? We can unilaterally disarm and achieve peace through submission. But Professor Miller implicitly agrees that while this might eliminate the nuclear threat, it would sacrifice the nation's goals. We could take the initiative in reducing our forces, but there is no guarantee that the Soviet Union would follow suit and thus the delicate balance of terror could be rendered an indelicate imbalance. We could negotiate in good faith, but again there is no guarantee that the Soviet Union would do likewise. Finally the United States could attempt to achieve nuclear superiority and either negotiate from strength or, with a clear superiority, force the Soviet Union into submission. Professor Miller might wish the courts to appoint a special master to oversee the SALT negotiations, but what

---

13. *Id.* at 36.

14. Apologies to then Chief Judge Learned Hand, United States v. Dennis, 183 F.2d 201, 212 (2d Cir. 1950).

15. Miller, *supra* note 1, at 24.

course of action that court appointee would mandate is far from clear.

In short, all that this pillar can support is a requirement to make a good faith effort to reduce the risk of nuclear war while not jeopardizing the nation's way of life. By no means is this a trivial obligation. But first, it does not differ in kind from the sort of duty we have assumed the Constitution to place on our public officials concerning conventional weapons, and second, the duty, involving in its essence questions of prudence and discretion, is wholly improper for judicial enforcement.

Pillar II: The Constitution Girded with International Law

Perhaps the most creative aspect of Professor Miller's argument is found in the construction of this second pillar where he attempts to argue that the Constitution imports a duty, to be judicially enforced, to obey international law, which he asserts is "surely"[16] incompatible with nuclear weapons. The argument begins with the proposition that "Congress having been delegated the power to define and punish offenses against international law, has a duty to carry out that power."[17] The thought continues that the President also might as well be assigned a duty "faithfully to execute" international law.[18] And then why not have the Supreme Court "grasp the nettle and point out to the Executive and the Congress that officials in those branches are charged with [this] constitutional duty"?[19]

Putting aside the question of whether what is called international law, lacking both an authoritative interpreter and a means of enforcement, can be considered law—putting aside the fact that it is only in the recent writings of a few academic commentators that nuclear weapons are regarded as contrary to international law[20]—putting aside all of

---

16. *Id.*at 23.

17. *Id.* at 33.

18. *Id.*

19. *Id.* at 35.

20. Professor Miller is apparently depending on the work of R. FALK, L. MEYROWITZ, & J. SANDERSON, NUCLEAR WEAPONS AND INTERNATIONAL LAW (Occasional Paper No. 10, World Order Studies Program, Center of International Studies, Princeton University (1981)). Other than this work, it is hard to discover much that can be used to support Professor Miller's claim that nuclear weapons are unconstitutional. There is the 1961 United Nations General Assembly Resolution 1653, 16 U.N. GAOR Supp. (No. 17) at 4, U.N. Doc. A/5100 (1961) asserting the use of nuclear

this—the argument that international law has a place in the Constitution superior to ordinary legislation and presidential action is wholly without foundation in the text of the Constitution, precedent, or the Framers' intent. The text of the Constitution does grant Congress the *authority* "to define and punish Piracies and Offenses against the Law of Nations;"[21] but this authority implies a *duty* to enforce international law about as much as the authority of Congress to borrow money[22] mandates a duty of deficit spending.

Recognizing the discretionary authority of Congress to define and punish offenses against the law of nations and recognizing that this requires the principle *leges posteriores priores contraries abrogant* (later laws abrogate prior laws that are contrary to them), the Court has consistently held that Congress has the authority, to which courts will give effect, to violate international law—even treaties—the most fundamental datum of international law. What international law provides, wrote Chief Justice John Marshall, "is a guide the sovereign follows or abandons at his will. The rule is addressed to the judgment of the sovereign: and although it cannot be disregarded by him without obloquy, yet it may be disregarded."[23] The fact that Congress violates international law is, as Professor Louis Henkin has succinctly made the point, "constitutionally irrelevant."[24]

Nor has Professor Miller produced one shred of evidence that the Framers wished to subordinate national sovereignty to the dictates of international law. The wisdom of the contrary position—that occasionally it is necessary to subordinate international law to national sovereignty—is reinforced when we see that some, such as Professor Miller, are willing to see as a dictate of international law the freshest idealisms

---

weapons to be illegal (55 states voting in favor of the resolution, 20 states against, and 26 states abstaining). But as Professor Michael Akehurst points out in A MODERN INTRODUCTION TO INTERNATIONAL LAW 252 (1978 3d ed), "A General Assembly resolution of this type is, at most, merely evidence of customary law; but the voting figures for this resolution show the absence of a generally accepted custom." The United States voted *no* while the U.S.S.R. voted *yes,* possibly because of the latter's nuclear inferiority at the time. *Id.*

21.   U.S. CONST. art. I, § 8.
22.   *Id.*
23.   Brown v. United States, 12 U.S. (8 Cranch) 110, 128 (1814).
24.   L. HENKIN, FOREIGN AFFAIRS AND THE CONSTITUTION 410 n.11 (1972).

of a few academic commentators regardless of the consequences for national security.

To say that his interpretation is without foundation in conventional construction of the Constitution may leave Professor Miller undaunted, for again he understands the Constitution in terms of its "intentions" and he understands these intentions to be those of the well intended "clergy, physicians, scientists, and businessmen"[25] rather than the more modest ones of the Framers. If this beneficent sentiment proved insufficient to bestir the Due Process clause and the Preamble to join the march against the bomb, perhaps it is sufficiently engaging to disarm the world through international law. But again, even if we grant momentarily that Congressional authority to define and punish offenses against the law of nations could be puffed into a duty, which the courts could enforce, we confront the problems of limited power. Court injunctions could only extend to the United States government, and thus we would simply have to return to the prudential alternatives discussed above, running from submission to dominance.

Pursuing Professor Miller's apparent assumption that good intentions make up for what, under conventional interpretations of the Constitution, would be usurpation of authority, there may be, however, a way in which the Supreme Court could grasp the nettle and eliminate threats to the lives, liberties, and properties of the citizenry. It could make itself the authoritative interpreter of international law. It could secretly authorize a Super Manhattan project which would culminate in the construction of a nuclear weapon awesome and accurate enough to cow into submission all nuclear powers. Then the Court would be able to give clout to the special masters it appoints to strategic negotiations and to back the injunctions it would issue around the world in the name of enforcing international law.

Other than with this reinforcement, I can see no way that the superstructure of Miller's argument can withstand even minimal scrutiny.

The Foundation

My inquiry thus far has focused on the superstructure of Professor Miller's argument, though I have indirectly touched on the adequacy of

---

25. Miller, *supra* note 1, at 22.

its foundation. It is time to examine more closely his contention that nuclear war is "by definition" "unlimited."[26] If we fully grant this premise then the superstructure becomes ironically superfluous. For if nuclear war is "definitionally" unlimitable, it must be obviously unlimitable. If it is obviously unlimitable, no one with a modicum of intelligence and concern for self-interest would consider risking it, for one's missiles would in effect be directed towards oneself and all that one wishes to preserve. If such a person would not even contemplate the use of nuclear weapons, we are rendered about as secure against nuclear weapons as we could ever expect to be through any judicially enforced pronouncements.

But only as an exercise in abstract logic should we grant Professor Miller his premise. As a military analyst has recently argued, it is utterly ridiculous to believe that generals and politicians "would become so absorbed in the conflict-as-a-game that they would reply tit for tat, move by move, instead of stopping the war as soon as it had become nuclear, before it could destroy their own cities and their own families."[27] One would have to believe that mankind both in the battlefield and in civilian authority had become robots. And if we thus reasonably deny Professor Miller his premise, the structure of the argument collapses.

This is not to say that in several respects, I do not share Professor Miller's wistful yearning for a world free of nuclear weapons. There was at least dignity in the defense of Carthage in a way there can never be in a defense against nuclear destruction. But to allow this yearning for dignity to inform one's interpretation of the Constitution and judicial power, is to lay bare the frailty of good intentions.

Can Lawyers Contribute to the Debate?

Although Professor Miller urges the Supreme Court to "grasp the nettle"[28] on the question of the constitutionality of nuclear weapons, he realizes that it is "naive"[29] to expect the Justices presently to do so. His

---

26. *Id.* at 30.
27. Luttwak, *How to Think About Nuclear War,* 74 COMMENTARY 21, 26 (Aug. 1982).
28. Miller, *supra* note 1, at 35.
29. *Id.* at 36.

apparent hope is to foster a "dialogue about the constitutionality of nuclear weapons,"[30] which in a fashion akin to the reapportionment cases will move the Court closer to his wished for declaration. He asks then rhetorically: "Is it really foolish to contend that law and lawyers have something useful to contribute to the growing debate about nuclear war?"[31]

Lawyers should be able to contribute to this debate. They should be able to remind us of the relevance of constitutional principles to changing circumstances. But to do so in the case of nuclear strategy, they must not only be aware of constitutional principles and of the relevance of those principles to the larger ends and limits of law and politics; they must also be knowledgeable as to the nature of those changing circumstances, which in this case means knowledge of diplomacy and strategy in the nuclear age. These are demanding criteria, but occasionally lawyers do meet them and make valuable contributions.[32]

On that concluding point I find myself in partial accord with Professor Miller. It is not entirely foolish to contend that lawyers have something useful to contribute to the growing debate about nuclear war. But it is foolish to believe that many who meet the above criteria will agree with Professor Miller.

---

30. *Id.* at 36.
31. *Id.* at 21.
32. *Cf.* S. TALBOTT, ENDGAME 20-21 (1979).

18.
Wisdom, Constitutionality, and Nuclear Weapons Policy*

Dean Alfange, Jr.**

In a well-known passage in his famous dissent in the flag-salute case of 1943, Justice Felix Frankfurter wrote:

> Our constant preoccupation with the constitutionality of legislation rather than with its wisdom tends to preoccupation of the American mind with a false value. The tendency of focussing attention on constitutionality is to make constitutionality synonymous with wisdom, to regard a law as all right if it is constitutional. Such an attitude is a great enemy of liberalism. . . . Reliance for the most precious interests of civilization, therefore, must be found outside of their vindication in courts of law.[1]

Arthur Miller does not subscribe to any such notion. For him, the principal function of courts of law is precisely to vindicate the most precious interests of civilization. In his view, the Constitution is not a finite set of narrow commands that establish a framework within which policy is to be determined. Rather, it is an expansive body of rules which, at any given time, require the adoption of the specific policy choices that would then best serve to achieve "the avowed goal of meeting current problems."[2] What wisdom dictates to be the most desirable way of attaining important social goals is what the Constitution demands. When applied to the issue of nuclear weapons, that approach yields the conclusion that since "the ultimate purpose of law [including constitutional law] is human survival under conditions that allow human dignity to be maximized"[3] and since wisdom (indeed, common sense) tells

---

* Reprinted, with permission, from *Nova Law Journal*, Volume 7, Number 1 (1982).

** Professor of Political Science, University of Massachusetts.

1. **West Virginia State Bd. of Educ. v. Barnette, 319 U.S. 624, 670-71 (1943)** (Frankfurter, J., dissenting).

2. Miller, *Nuclear Weapons and Constitutional Law,* 7 Nova L.J. 21, 27 (1982).

3. *Id.* at 26.

us that the continued manufacture and deployment of nuclear weapons involves the increasing risk that eventually, by design or error, they will be employed and that their use would threaten the complete destruction of human civilization, the Constitution must forbid the government of the United States from following a policy that perpetuates the possibility of such a catastrophe. In addition, the Constitution must impose a "duty [upon the government] to take action designed to eliminate the nuclear threat throughout the world."[4]

Professor Miller is, of course, well aware that, despite its substantial appeal (particularly to those like me who agree as to the danger posed by the continued existence of nuclear weapons and the urgent need to eliminate the threat), such a conclusion is at odds with traditional approaches to constitutional interpretation. He recognizes that adoption of any of his points "would require creativity or innovation by a constitutional decision-maker,"[5] and concedes it is unreasonable to expect that they would be accepted by the Supreme Court.[6] Indeed, the novelty of his arguments is obvious. To Congress is delegated the power to declare war, to raise and support armies, and to provide and maintain a navy. No language in the Constitution nor any judicial decision known to me suggests that those powers do not carry with them the power to select the weapons with which the armies and the navy are to be equipped. And, however much we may pray that no President would ever again make the choice to employ atomic or nuclear weapons in war, surely, according to the accepted understanding of the Constitution, the authority of the Commander-in-Chief includes the power to decide which of the weapons provided by Congress are to be employed once hostilities have commenced.[7] Moreover, much more precedent can be marshalled against, rather than for, the proposition that the Constitution obligates the three branches of the national government to ob-

---

4. *Id.* at 24.

5. *Id.* at 29.

6. *Id.* at 23.

7. The power delegated to Congress to declare war obviously limits the authority of the President to employ weapons *before* hostilities have commenced. *See* L. HENKIN, FOREIGN AFFAIRS AND THE CONSTITUTION 80-81 (1972). But that limitation goes to the use of *any* weapons; it has no special significance with respect to nuclear weapons, even though it may apply with greater moral force where nuclear weapons are concerned.

serve and enforce norms of international law even where these are contrary to national law or national policy.[8]

The fact that a constitutional lawyer would be strongly tempted to employ constitutional argument to shape public policy on so vital an issue is certainly understandable.[9] But Professor Miller faces a serious dilemma in that his argument is likely to be persuasive only to those who already agree with his policy position. Those who hold opposing views on the policy question are many and influential. They sincerely believe, however misguidedly, that the maintenance of a nuclear arsenal and the willingness to employ it where necessary are absolutely essential to the cause of peace and the security of our nation and its allies, and can readily dismiss Miller's argument with the accurate observation that settled constitutional law is to the contrary. Even those whose minds are not yet made up are unlikely to be won over by a constitutional contention that can be rebutted so effectively by arguments with impeccable traditional credentials.

If Professor Miller's purpose is simply to reinforce the resolve and commitment of those who already agree with him on the policy question by telling them that their views are not only supported by good sense, ultimate morality, and perhaps the norms of international law, but also reflect authentic constitutional commands, he may well be successful. But if his purpose is to change public opinion through constitutional argument, he must be able to convince his audience of the authoritativeness of that argument, and the authoritativeness of a legal argument can be demonstrated in only two ways: consensual agreement

---

8. *See id.* at 460-61 n.61. Professor Henkin flatly states that "the Constitution does not forbid the President (or the Congress) to violate international law and the courts will give effect to acts within the constitutional powers of the political branches without regard to international law." *Id.* at 221-22. *See* Feinrider, *International Law as the Law of the Land,* 7 NOVA L. J. 103 (1982) for opposing view.

9. The insightful observation of Felix Cohen seems squarely on point here:
   Clearly, for the sanitary engineer, the existence of untreated swamps is the cause of malaria. For the king's attendant with the palm-leaf fans, the bite of the mosquito is the only relevant cause. For the pathologist, the effect of the malaria virus upon red blood corpuscles is the cause. In each case the cause is the point at which effort can be usefully applied.

Cohen, *Field Theory and Judicial Logic,* 59 YALE L.J. 238, 255 (1950). For Professor Miller, as constitutional lawyer, the relevant cause of the nuclear weapons crisis must be the failure to recognize and apply proper principles of constitutional law.

among a substantial majority of those generally recognized as know-ledgeable in the field or acceptance by a court—preferably an appellate court and most preferably the Supreme Court. Quite plainly, Professor Miller is in a position to make neither demonstration. Novel constitu-tional arguments designed to win the day for the adherents of one side of a controversial policy issue will, by their nature, be unable to com-mand broad acceptance, and, as noted, Professor Miller concedes that his argument will be unlikely to find judicial favor. Even a favorable judicial ruling may, of course, be insufficient to resolve a disputed con-stitutional issue, as long ago demonstrated by the categorical rejection by the North of the Dred Scott decision of 1857,[10] and as may clearly be seen today in the ongoing debates over such questions as abortion policy,[11] the exclusionary rule,[12] and school bussing for the achievement of racial desegregation.[13] But the instances in which public opinion and public policy have been changed by constitutional reasoning[14] have nec-essarily involved judicial pronouncements which have given moral force to debatable constitutional arguments by converting them into rules of law. Without such legitimation,[15] mere argument, no matter how co-gent and thoughtful, lacks the authority necessary to lead persons of differing views to abandon their prior positions on policy questions.

Professor Miller is surely right in his observation that "[i]t would be naive to expect the Supreme Court to intervene"[16] on the issue of nuclear weapons policy. But is this merely because, as he suggests, "judges are timorous officers of government . . . [who] look upon re-quests to go beyond the familiar and the expected as frightful occa-

---

10.   Dred Scott v. Sandford, 60 U.S. (19 How.) 393 (1857). For a description and discussion of the political reaction engendered by this decision, see D. FEHRENBACHER, THE DRED SCOTT CASE 417-567 (1978).

11.   See, e.g., F. JAFFE, B. LINDHEIM & P. LEE, ABORTION POLITICS (1981); E. RUBIN, ABORTION, POLITICS, AND THE COURTS 87-161 (1982).

12.   See, e.g., S. SCHLESINGER, EXCLUSIONARY INJUSTICE (1977).

13.   See, e.g., the antijudicial diatribe of L. GRAGLIA, DISASTER BY DECREE (1976).

14.   The paradigm case is, of course, the effect of Brown v. Bd. of Educ., 347 U.S. 483 (1954) in ending de jure racial segregation.

15.   The classic discussion of the legitimating function of the Supreme Court is in C. BLACK, THE PEOPLE AND THE COURT 56-86 (1960).

16.   Miller, supra note 2, at 36.

sions"?[17] Is the problem really only one of judicial timidity? It does seem severe to label as timorous a federal judiciary which has, in recent years, recognized abortion as a constitutional right,[18] ordered the President of the United States to relinquish evidence that would incriminate him with regard to the commission of impeachable offenses,[19] drastically curtailed the imposition of the death penalty,[20] required unwilling school boards to implement sweeping remedial plans for bringing about the desegregation of public schools,[21] and taken over the administration of particular prisons or of entire prison systems in some 24 states.[22] It is thus a good deal less likely that the anticipated judicial reluctance to intervene in nuclear weapons policy is to be attributed to the inherent timorousness of judges than to their probable views on the proper role of courts in the governmental process and on the relationship between the wisdom of a policy and its constitutionality.

This leads to the inevitable question: what *is* the proper relationship between the wisdom of a policy and its constitutionality? Or, to put the same question somewhat more directly, when should judges insist, as a matter of constitutional law, upon the adoption of a policy they deem wise or the rejection of a policy they deem unwise? When should they be prepared to remove a policy issue from the political forum, where numbers count, in order to decide it in the judicial forum, where numbers can be ignored? These issues have been exercising constitutional scholars a great deal in recent years, yielding a wide variety of answers across a spectrum that finds Arthur Miller perhaps closest to one end[23] and Raoul Berger closest to the other.[24] The answers at

---

17.   *Id.*

18.   Roe v. Wade, 410 U.S. 113 (1973); Doe v. Bolton, 410 U.S. 179 (1973).

19.   United States v. Nixon, 418 U.S. 683 (1974).

20.   *See, e.g.,* Woodson v. North Carolina, 428 U.S. 280 (1976). A listing of cases in which the Supreme Court invalidated the imposition of death sentences between 1976 and May, 1980, may be found in the concurring opinion of Justice Marshall in Godfrey v. Georgia, 446 U.S. 420, 438 n.5 (1980).

21.   See the discussion in Columbus Bd. of Educ. v. Penick, 443 U.S. 449, 458-61 (1979).

22.   For a comprehensive list of states in which courts had taken over the administration of prisons as of 1981 and of the decisions which brought these results about, see the concurring opinion of Justice Brennan in Rhodes v. Chapman, 452 U.S. 337, 353-54 n.1 (1981).

23.   *See* A. MILLER, TOWARD INCREASED JUDICIAL ACTIVISM (1982); Miller,

the very extremes of the spectrum are "never" and "whenever they want," but both of these are unacceptable. To answer "never" is to oblige the judiciary to treat as constitutional such policies and practices as "separate but equal" racial segregation, gross legislative malapportionment, and the maintenance of prison systems in which inmates are confined in conditions of ghastly and barbaric inhumanity.[25] To cite the wise counsel of Justice Harlan Fiske Stone, refraining in all cases "from passing upon the legislative judgment 'as long as the remedial channels of the democratic process remain open and unobstructed' . . . seems . . . no less than the surrender of the constitutional protection of the liberty of small minorities to the popular will."[26]

On the other hand, to answer "whenever they want" is to maintain that judges, rather than the branches of government responsive to the electorate, should have the ultimate authority to decide the content of government policy — an authority which they would exercise by invoking the Constitution whenever they disagreed with the manner in which Congress or the President proposed to deal with a national problem. It is clear that Professor Miller does not find that answer unattractive, nor its consequences undesirable.[27] Unlike Learned Hand, he would have no misgivings about being "ruled by a bevy of Platonic Guardians,"[28] for he would have no doubt that Platonic Guardians could be counted on to do better in insuring "human survival under conditions

---

The Case for Judicial Activism, in SUPREME COURT ACTIVISM AND RESTRAINT 167 (S. Halpern & C. Lamb eds. 1982).

24. R. BERGER, GOVERNMENT BY JUDICIARY (1977). Berger's view is that judicial policymaking is never legitimate, and that the only proper function of courts in constitutional adjudication is to ascertain and faithfully (slavishly) to apply the original intention of those who framed and ratified the constitutional provision at issue. I have elsewhere criticized Berger's position at some length. *See* Alfange, *Another Look at the "Original Intent" Theory of Constitutional,* 5 HASTINGS CONST. L.Q. 603 (1978).

25. For a lengthy and disturbing, but not exhaustive, list of the policies and practices that would have to be constitutionally tolerated if the answer to this question were "never," see Grey, *Do We Have An Unwritten Constitution?,* 27 STAN. L. REV. 703, 710-14 (1975).

26. Minersville School Dist. v. Gobitis, 310 U.S. 586, 605-06 (1940) (Stone, J., dissenting).

27. *See* the works cited *supra* note 23.

28. L. HAND, THE BILL OF RIGHTS 73 (1958).

that allow human dignity to be maximized"[29] than would individuals whose continuation in office depends on their attentiveness to the pressures of interest-group politics. Perhaps he is right. Nevertheless, that answer has implications that are profoundly troubling.

It is likely that Platonic Guardians would be fallible; it is certain that judges are.[30] There is no abstract reason for believing that the policies judges might choose, after considering the arguments of lawyers on behalf of their clients, will in fact be wiser than the policies enacted into law by Congress after considering the representations of interest-group spokesmen on behalf of their constituents, or than the policies adopted by the President after considering the counsel of his advisers. But the argument that judges should assume authority to invalidate laws or policies they deem unwise is rarely, if ever, based on abstract considerations. There is no mystery as to who may be expected to advocate or oppose that argument. Those who suspect that the democratic political process will yield policies with which they disagree, and that, if courts were allowed to decide, more favorable policies would be adopted, will argue for the equation of wisdom and constitutionality and for judges to protect us all from the folly of majoritarianism. Those who believe that the policies the political branches are likely to adopt will be reasonably sound, and that judicial involvement will probably result in actions that are retrogressive and unenlightened, will argue for the strict separation of wisdom and constitutionality and for judges to refrain from deciding constitutional questions on the basis of their own views of wise public policy. It is thus no coincidence that in the period from the 1880s to the New Deal, when judicial review was perceived as a major obstacle to the cause of social and economic reform, liberal opinion was united in its criticism of the courts for their failure to respect the distinction between wisdom and constitutionality.[31] Similarly, the enthusiasm of liberals for judicial intervention in

---

29. *See supra* note 3 and accompanying text.

30. The classic statement of this proposition is that of Justice Jackson: "We [the Supreme Court] are not final because we are infallible, but we are infallible only because we are final." Brown v. Allen, 344 U.S. 443, 540 (1953) (Jackson, J., concurring).

31. As Robert Jackson noted shortly after the end of this period, the "long-smouldering intellectual revolt against the philosophy of many of the Supreme Court's decisions [equating wisdom and constitutionality] . . . was led by outspoken and

policy matters that blossomed during the era of the Warren Court can hardly be unrelated to their preference for the policies that present-day judges can sometimes be persuaded to adopt.[32] Conversely, conservatives, who once looked upon courts as a bastion for the protection of property rights against legislative policies they abhorred,[33] have come to see the virtue of distinguishing wisdom from constitutionality now that they perceive that policies favored by the courts may be less to their liking than those of the legislature.[34] Over the years, the argument that courts should ignore the distinction between wisdom and constitutionality by substituting their own policy choices for those of the political branches has been made and opposed on behalf of causes both noble and not so noble.

The belief that judges can reliably be counted on to share one's own conception of wise public policy may be both rational and accurate with regard to specific issues at specific times. It is a more dubious basis, however, for a defense of judicial policymaking on all public questions in all periods. Given the fact that there is no *a priori* reason to assume that the policy choices of courts will be objectively better than those of the legislature, or that judges, who vary widely in philosophy and perspective, will consistently share one's values on public mat-

---

respected members of the Court itself . . . [and was joined by] those in our universities distinguished for disinterested legal scholarship . . . many thoughtful conservatives and practically all liberals and labor leadership." R. JACKSON, THE STRUGGLE FOR JUDICIAL SUPREMACY v (1941).

32. *See, e.g.,* L. TRIBE, AMERICAN CONSTITUTIONAL LAW iv-v (1978).

33. The clearest statement of this view was perhaps that of Justice Brewer:
I am firmly persuaded that the salvation of the nation, the permanence of government of and by the people, rests upon the independence and vigor of the judiciary. To stay the waves of popular feeling, to restrain the greedy hand of the many from filching from the few that which they have honestly acquired, and to protect in every man's possession and enjoyment, be he rich or poor, that which he hath, demands a tribunal as strong as is consistent with the freedom of human action and as free from all influences and suggestions other than is compassed in the thought of justice, as can be created out of the infirmities of human nature. To that end courts exist . . . .

Brewer, *The Nation's Safeguard,* PROCEEDINGS OF THE NEW YORK STATE BAR ASSOCIATION 37, 47 (1893).

34. *See, e.g.,* Graglia, *In Defense of Judicial Restraint,* in SUPREME COURT ACTIVISM AND RESTRAINT, *supra* note 23, at 135-37.

ters, it would seem difficult to argue for a broad judicial policymaking role in all areas. Certainly even the most optimistic judicial activist today can feel no assurance that courts, given freedom to make their own policy choices "whenever they want," will no longer use that power to block legislative efforts at social, political, or economic reform.[35] To invite judges to equate their own notions of wise policy with the requirements of the Constitution, and to do so on their own terms, is to run the risk of opening a Pandora's Box of unforeseeable content.

If an understandable basis for advocating judicial activism in all areas of policy is difficult to perceive, it is easy to see a principled justification for an across-the-board opposition to judicial policymaking—it seems squarely inconsistent with democratic theory. As Terrance Sandalow has written: "Reducing the influence of politics upon governmental policy is, in short, a means of reducing the influence on policy of those whose lives are affected by it."[36] The observation that judicial policymaking is antidemocratic is, of course, not new,[37] nor has it gone unchallenged.[38] The basis of the challenge, as it is most commonly made, is that democracy, at least in its pure form, was not the form of government chosen by the framers of the Constitution, who, through such means as the electoral college, the imposition of constitutional re-

---

35. For recent examples of transparent exercises of judicial policymaking in which legislative efforts at social, economic, or political reform were thwarted, *see, e.g., Buckley v. Valeo,* 424 U.S. 1 (1976) (declaring invalid, on first amendment grounds, the critical expenditure-limitation provisions of the Federal Election Campaign Act Amendments of 1974 through which the Congress had sought to protect the integrity of the federal election process against the kinds of abuses that came to light as a result of the Watergate scandals); *National League of Cities v. Usery,* 426 U.S. 833 (1976) (striking down, apparently on tenth amendment grounds, the extension by Congress of the coverage of the Fair Labor Standards Act of 1938, as amended, to the employees of state and local governments); *First Nat'l Bank of Boston v. Bellotti,* 435 U.S. 765 (1978) (striking down, on first amendment grounds, a Massachusetts law intended to control the impact of corporate spending on referendum elections); *Allied Structural Steel Co. v. Spannaus,* 438 U.S. 234 (1978) (striking down, on contract clause grounds, a Minnesota law intended to protect the pension benefits of employees against the risk of plant shutdowns prior to the establishment of their pension eligibility).

36. Sandalow, *The Distrust of Politics,* 56 N.Y.U. L. Rev. 446, 459 (1981).

37. *See, e.g.,* the discussion in A. Bickel, The Least Dangerous Branch 16-23 (1962).

38. *See, e.g.,* C. Black, *supra* note 15, at 179-81; Bishin, *Judicial Review in Democratic Theory,* 50 S. Cal. L. Rev. 1099 (1977).

straints on certain types of majority action, and the creation of an appointed and life-tenured judiciary, sought to guarantee that the will of the people would be held within tolerable bounds.[39] Judicial review, the argument goes, although not specifically mentioned in the Constitution, is simply another of the checks in the constitutional framework. Moreover, since its exercise has been warmly accepted by the people, it must be seen as having been approved by democratic choice, and thus cannot be said to be undemocratic.[40] In addition, it is claimed that the whole argument that courts should defer to the policy judgments of the political branches in order to respect the will of the majority is misconceived because, even if it could be assumed that there is such a thing as the majority will and that it is possible to ascertain in practice what that will actually is, the political branches (particularly Congress) are selected and organized in such a way as to insure its frustration, not its effectuation.[41]

These challenges to the claim that judicial policymaking is antidemocratic have been answered meticulously and effectively by Jesse Choper,[42] whose argument cannot even be summarized here. Suffice it to say that, while one must concede the existence of myriad ways in which the political branches can function undemocratically and escape public accountability, Congress and the President remain vastly more responsive to public opinion than the federal courts. And, while the American people clearly favor judicial review and expect the courts to hold the other branches of government within constitutional limits, it requires an enormous jump to conclude from that observation that the public would approve the courts' use of that power to invalidate presidential or congressional action in any case in which the judges deemed the policy underlying that action to be mistaken.[43] While the framers

---

39. *See id.* at 1104-08.

40. C. BLACK, *supra* note 15, at 178-79, 210-12.

41. The best, and perhaps now the classic, statement of this argument is in M. SHAPIRO, FREEDOM OF SPEECH 17-25 (1966).

42. J. CHOPER, JUDICIAL REVIEW AND THE NATIONAL POLITICAL PROCESS 29-59 (1980).

43. There is more than a little merit in the observation of Robert Bork:

The Supreme Court regularly insists that its results, and most particularly its controversial results, do not spring from the mere will of the Justices in the majority but are supported, indeed compelled, by a proper understand-

undoubtedly were uneasy about some of the possible ramifications of majority rule and sought to guard against its potential excesses, they did so, as Gordon Wood describes it, "without repudiating the republicanism and the popular basis of government that nearly all devoutly believed in."[44] That the action of the people's representatives may need to be checked from time to time and in particular ways does not render unlimited judicial policymaking legitimate. If judges may freely substitute their own policy preferences for those of the legislature, we should no longer claim to be a democracy, and should seek to find a new name and a new theory for the governmental system which has evolved.

If judicial policymaking—the equation of wisdom with constitutionality—is sometimes imperative but not always permissible, just when is it proper and defensible? My own choice for the proper starting place in the search for the answer is Justice Stone's justly celebrated Carolene Products footnote of 1938.[45] There Stone suggested that the political process was the proper area for the resolution of policy questions[46] except where effective access to it is wholly or partially closed off to the persons affected by the policy at issue or where "prejudice against discrete and insular minorities"[47] seems likely to have been the motivation for its adoption or enforcement. In those cases, courts may legitimately view with skepticism the results arrived at through the political process and undertake to assess for themselves

---

ing of the Constitution of the United States. Value choices are attributed to the Founding Fathers, not to the Court. The way an institution advertises tells you what it thinks its customers demand.

Bork, *Neutral Principles and Some First Amendment Problems*, 47 IND. L.J. 1, 3-4 (1971).

44.   Wood, *Democracy and the Constitution*, in HOW DEMOCRATIC IS THE CONSTITUTION? 1, 16 (R. Goldwin & W. Schambra eds. 1980).

45.   United States v. Carolene Products Co., 304 U.S. 144, 152-53 n.4 (1938). It is precisely because it uses the *Carolene Products* footnote as the starting place in the search for the answer that I find J. ELY, DEMOCRACY AND DISTRUST (1980) to be the most pregnant and insightful of the recent writings on the legitimate role of judicial review in a democratic society. Professor Miller is, of course, not of the same opinion. *See* Miller, Book Review, 32 U. FLA. L. REV. 369 (1980).

46.   Stone's view of the proper locus of policymaking authority in the ordinary case was forcefully expressed in his dissenting opinion in United States v. Butler, 297 U.S. 1, 78-88 (1936).

47.   The term comes from the third paragraph of the *Carolene Products* footnote, 304 U.S. at 153 n.4.

the desirability of the policy outcome.[48] The thrust of Stone's Carolene Products approach (at least the approach described in the second and third paragraphs of the footnote)[49] may be characterized as resting upon a "legislative failure" theory[50]—that is, the theory that judicial resolution of the policy questions inherent in constitutional adjudication becomes permissible when the political process (most commonly the legislative process) fails adequately to perform its function of attaining a just and fair compromise among competing interests because of imperfect access or prejudice.

It may be that a legislative failure theory alone is insufficient to cover all of the circumstances in which the policy judgments of the legislature may be judicially disregarded. Institutional considerations may undoubtedly justify a greater role for courts in the evaluation of procedural, as opposed to substantive, rules,[51] and there should be some

---

48. As Stone was to write two years after *Carolene Products:*
   History teaches us that there have been but few infringements of personal liberty by the state which have not been justified . . . in the name of righteousness and the public good, and few which have not been directed . . . at politically helpless minorities.
Minersville School Dist. v. Gobitis, 310 U.S. 586, 604 (1940) (Stone, J., dissenting).

49. There is another paragraph — the first — which suggests that courts might be justified in not accepting the policy judgments of the political branches where the action being challenged appears to violate one of the specific prohibitions of the Constitution. This paragraph was not in Justice Stone's original version of the footnote but was added later at the urging of Chief Justice Hughes. *See* L. LUSKY, BY WHAT RIGHT? 108-11 (1975). It is somewhat at odds with the portion of the footnote that Stone had conceived because it seeks to justify judicial rejection of legislative policy judgments, not on the basis of any reason to believe that the legislative process may not have functioned fairly, but solely on the text of the Constitution. *See id.* at 111-12. Since the text is usually not self-defining, ascribing meaning to its provisions is an act of policymaking. If, as Stone believed, courts should defer to the policy judgments of the political branches in the ordinary case, why not in these cases as well? That is, as long as there is no ground for suspicion that the political branches may be unjustly disfavoring those without an effective voice in the political process or those toward whom majoritarian prejudice may be directed.

50. It has, in fact, been so characterized by Owen Fiss. *See* Fiss, *Foreword: The Forms of Justice,* 93 HARV. L. REV. 1, 6-11 (1979). Professor Fiss is extremely critical of the *Carolene Products* approach because he rejects its "general presumption in favor of majoritarianism." *Id.* at 6.

51. Even Justice Frankfurter, who saw no room for judicial reexamination of the substantive policy choices of the legislature as long as these choices could be said to be

room for judicial invalidation of statutes touching on individual rights where these cannot be said to serve any legitimate public purpose[52] or where, in the classic formulation of Justice Oliver Wendell Holmes, "a rational and fair man necessarily would admit that the statute proposed would infringe fundamental principles as they have been understood by the traditions of our people and our law."[53] But surely the protection of the powerless and the unrepresented from a hostile or unsympathetic majority is manifestly the great and vital function of judicial review. It is the fulfillment of that function that amply justifies judicial policymaking in certain situations: defending the right to hold and to express beliefs that the majority may regard as abhorrent;[54] eliminating gross legislative malapportionment[55] or discriminatory gerrymandering;[56] abolishing all vestiges of racial discrimination that stigmatizes its victims;[57] taking whatever affirmative action may be required to insure

---

rationally related to the achievement of a proper public purpose, *see, e.g.,* West Virginia State Bd. of Educ. v. Barnette, 319 U.S. 624, 647 (1943) (Frankfurter, J., dissenting), conceded the propriety of "the exercise of judgment" by courts in the evaluation of procedures employed in criminal trials "to ascertain whether they offend those canons of decency and fairness which express the notions of justice of English-speaking peoples." Adamson v. California, 332 U.S. 46, 67 (1947) (Frankfurter, J., concurring).

52. *E.g.,* Griswold v. Connecticut, 381 U.S. 479 (1965), invalidating Connecticut's anti-contraception law. *Cf.* Justice Harlan's statement in Poe v. Ullman, 367 U.S. 497, 543 (1961) (dissenting opinion), that due process forbids "all substantial arbitrary impositions and purposeless restraints." The abortion cases, Roe v. Wade, 410 U.S. 113 (1973) and Doe v. Bolton, 410 U.S. 197 (1973), cannot be said to involve purposeless restraints and thus present a far more difficult issue than *Griswold. See, e.g.,* Epstein, *Substantive Due Process By Any Other Name: The Abortion Cases,* 1973 SUPREME COURT REVIEW 157.

53. Lochner v. New York, 198 U.S. 45, 76 (1905) (Holmes, J., dissenting).

54. That is, the kind of protection that the Supreme Court, to its discredit, did not provide in the years following both World Wars. *See, e.g.,* Schenck v. United States, 249 U.S. 47 (1919); Dennis v. United States, 341 U.S. 494 (1951). *Cf.* Collin v. Smith, 578 F.2d 1197 (7th Cir. 1978), *cert. denied,* 439 U.S. 916 (1978).

55. *See* Reynolds v. Sims, 377 U.S. 533 (1964).

56. *See* Gomillion v. Lightfoot, 364 U.S. 339 (1960).

57. *See* Brown v. Bd. of Educ., 347 U.S. 483 (1954). Race-conscious legislation that does not stigmatize those who may be adversely affected is another matter. *See* Regents of the University of California v. Bakke, 438 U.S. 265, 373-76 (1978) (opinion of Brennan, White, Marshall, and Blackmun, JJ.). As Laurence Tribe has noted: "When the group in control of the political process adopts classifications which protect or benefit a minority and burden itself, the reasons are absent for regarding the govern-

that public school authorities meet their constitutional responsibility to establish and maintain school systems "in which racial discrimination would be eliminated root and branch;"[58] and guaranteeing that conditions of confinement in state prisons are not so inhumane and barbaric as to constitute cruel and unusual punishment.[59] At the same time, recognition that legislative failure to protect the rights of those who have suffered from prejudice or inadequate representation provides the fundamental justification for judicial policymaking would spare us judicial interference with the policy decisions of the political branches in cases where those who seek judicial protection from the effects of those policies are themselves in command of substantial political resources and cannot reasonably be looked upon as the targets of irrational majority hostility.[60]

But under almost any theory that recognizes some limitations on judicial discretion, it is difficult to understand how the issue of nuclear weapons policy could be said to fall within the range of questions that may be deemed appropriate for judicial, as opposed to political, resolution. I am not disposed to deny that the issue is one on which human survival may ultimately depend, or that the policy of increasing our stockpiles of missiles and warheads (while seeking to negotiate for their overall limitation) and of maintaining a first-strike capability is one that carries with it the terrible risk of the eradication of civilization.

---

mental choice with suspicion, and therefore for strictly scrutinizing the results." L. TRIBE, *supra* note 32, at 1044.

58.   Green v. County School Bd., 391 U.S. 430, 438 (1968).

59.   Prisoners clearly fall within the scope of both the second and third paragraphs of Justice Stone's *Carolene Products* footnote (*see supra* text accompanying note 47). They have no access to the political process and they are a "discrete and insular" minority. They are "voteless, politically unpopular, and socially threatening." Rhodes v. Chapman, 452 U.S. 337, 358 (1981) (Brennan, J., concurring).

60.   Among the recent judicial excrescences that might have been avoided under a legislative failure theory are Buckley v. Valeo, 424 U.S. 1 (1976) (declaring invalid the expenditure limitations in the Federal Election Campaign Act Amendments of 1974, even as applied to the campaigns of the Republican and Democratic candidates for federal office — individuals who, as a group, are probably the least lacking in political efficacy of anyone in the country); National League of Cities v. Usery, 426 U.S. 833 (1976) (declaring invalid the application of the Fair Labor Standards Act of 1938 to employees of state and local governments, in disregard of what Justice Brennan, in dissent, described as "the enormous impact of the States' political power" when exercised in the federal political process. *Id.* at 878 (Brennan, J., dissenting)).

But the urgency of the issue and the potentially frightful consequences of miscalculation are not what should determine whether the matter is one for the political or the judicial process. In fact, recalling the observation of Terrance Sandalow, one might reasonably conclude that the more urgent the issue, the more vital it is to avoid "reducing the influence on policy of those whose lives are affected by it."[61] Shifting the question to the judicial forum converts it into a dispute to which most of us become bystanders; leaving it in the political process can nurture a sense of public responsibility—such as is currently being manifested in the rapid growth of the grass-roots movement for a nuclear freeze. Moreover, raising the issue in the courts carries its own risks, which ought not to be minimized. As Charles Black has shown, judicial action can do much to legitimize governmental policy.[62] A ruling by the Supreme Court that the maintenance of a nuclear weapons arsenal is constitutional (which is the only ruling realistically to be expected should the question actually reach the Court and be decided on the merits) could, in light of the public tendency noted by Justice Frankfurter "to regard a law as all right if it is constitutional,"[63] seriously undermine the cause of opposition to nuclear weapons[64] by raising doubts in the minds of many persons about the point of continuing to object to a policy whose validity has been judicially affirmed.

Obviously, the issue of nuclear weapons policy is not one where access to the political process is in some way closed off to those whose interests are affected.[65] Nor is it one where the government's policy is

---

61. *See supra* note 36 and accompanying text.

62. *See supra* note 15.

63. *See supra* note 1 and accompanying text.

64. The legitimating function of the Supreme Court has already dealt a blow to the opponents of nuclear power plants. Ignoring serious questions of standing in order to reach the merits of a suit brought by groups seeking to block plant construction, the Court gave advance validation to the Price-Anderson Act of 1957, which limits the total amount of a company's liability in the event of a nuclear accident. As long as the validity of the act was an open question, companies had a strong motivation for caution in entering the nuclear power industry. The legitimation of the act took away that need for caution and gave the companies concerned a significant stimulus to proceed. *See* Duke Power Co. v. Carolina Envtl. Study Group, 438 U.S. 59 (1978).

65. Of course, human survival is not a question about which only citizens of the United States have an interest. Every person in the world may well have a life-or-death interest in what the policy of the United States is with regard to nuclear weapons, but

aimed at, or may be expected to have its harshest effects upon, a disadvantaged minority. If nuclear war should come, the costs will be shared evenly by all, including the officials responsible for developing and supporting the policy that may have led to it. Judicial intervention thus cannot be justified on the basis of a theory of legislative failure. Indeed, the issue is not, in the traditional sense, one of individual liberties at all. For, despite the potential costs to us all, the government is not seeking to deprive anyone of life, liberty, or property; it is seeking—beyond a doubt, sincerely—to protect the nation, its people, and its allies from a possible external threat, and, presumably, to advance the cause of world peace through nuclear deterrence. In that regard, it cannot be said that the government's policy is unrelated to the attainment of a legitimate public purpose or that it is rationally insupportable. As strongly as I believe that a policy which accepts the risk of nuclear war is intolerable, and as easily as I may talk in private about "nuclear madness," I would find it impossible to assert that no rational and fair man could subscribe to the government's policy or could conscientiously accept its assumption that the surest way of avoiding nuclear war—a goal, I trust, that everyone shares—is to maintain a nuclear force of sufficient strength to deter the use of such weapons by anyone else.

What is more, it is not clear what courts could do even if they undertook to call into question the validity of the government's policy. They could presumably hold that it is unconstitutional for the United States to maintain nuclear weapons, but what then? Professor Miller emphatically states that he is not advocating unilateral disarmament, but merely urging a recognition of the government's constitutional duty "to take action designed to eliminate the nuclear threat throughout the world"[66] —which means, I presume, a duty to negotiate with other nations to effect the abolition of nuclear weapons. Similarly, no court could be expected to order unilateral disarmament; the most it could do would be to order the government to enter into disarmament negotiations. But I fail to see how such an order would markedly alter the

---

only United States citizens have direct access to the American political process. However, since the interest of all persons in survival is identical, the claims of nonresidents of the United States may be fully represented by their counterparts among United States citizens. This is a genuine class-action matter regardless of whether it is heard in the political process or the judicial process.

66.   Miller, *supra* note 2, at 24.

existing situation. Nuclear weapons would continue to exist (and presumably, to be manufactured and deployed) during the course of whatever negotiations would be held. The negotiations themselves would be carried out by the President (for I doubt that even Professor Miller is yet prepared to urge that federal courts oust the President from the process and commence their own negotiations with foreign governments), and would in all likelihood go on pretty much as at present. Because any judicial declaration of the unconstitutionality of nuclear weapons would have no effect until the completion of successful negotiations, it could not be expected either to cause the government to negotiate differently than it otherwise would or to cause the public to put greater pressure on it to conclude an agreement. The President would be no more willing to sign a treaty except on terms that he would consider to be fully consistent with the security interests of the United States and the public would be no more prepared to insist that the government accept less than the most favorable possible agreement. Nuclear weapons are already generally perceived as abominable; yet, as long as they are possessed by other nations, considerations of national security make the abominable seem tolerable. It is extremely doubtful that a judicial declaration of unconstitutionality would do more to cancel out these national security concerns than abhorrence already does.

In sum, regardless of the magnitude of the stakes, what our nuclear weapons policy should be seems clearly to be a question of wisdom, not of constitutionality. The policy area is one where responsibility for decision making is squarely and unequivocally delegated to the political branches by the Constitution. The soundness of the policy raises questions about which reasonable men may differ. The hazards that the policy generates must be faced as fully by the policymakers themselves as by any inadequately represented or disadvantaged minority group. All of these factors point to the appropriateness of a political resolution, as courts undoubtedly would recognize should the issue somehow be brought before them.

It seems likely that the ultimate purpose of Professor Miller's breathtaking exercise in constitutional reasoning is not the futile and misdirected effort to involve the courts in the resolution of this question,[67] but the generation of additional political pressure for a reversal of current governmental policy. If that is his purpose, I wish him well. But it is essential to remember that the horse must be kept in front of the cart. It may well be that in some saner future, if humanity does eventually manage to overcome the threat of nuclear devastation, it will be the common understanding that nuclear weapons are wholly unacceptable in a civilized world. That understanding may then come to be recognized as an integral part of our constitutional law. When that time is reached, Professor Miller's article may well be looked back upon as the first groundbreaking step leading us to the path of higher constitutional wisdom. But that higher constitutional wisdom will not be achieved unless we first become convinced of the absolute necessity of abolishing nuclear weapons as a matter of policy. Until the day has been won on the policy question, the argument for the unconstitutionality of nuclear weapons will remain a curiosity except to those who already share its underlying policy premises. It is indispensable, therefore, that current efforts to change national policy be directed at persuading those who do not yet agree that continued reliance on nuclear weapons is unwise rather than unconstitutional.

---

67. It might be argued, with some merit, that the opponents of current nuclear weapons policy have little to lose by trying to raise the issue of the constitutional merits of that policy in the courts as well as in the political process. If they lose in the political process, they just might win in court; on the other hand, if they win in the political process, there is no danger that the courts would overturn that victory. It is certainly true that courts would not overturn such a political victory as long as the traditional limitations on judicial authority are respected. But, while fanciful, it is possible to imagine judges appointed by Ronald Reagan and holding the views on the scope of judicial power and the concept of affirmative constitutional duty espoused by Arthur Miller (see Miller, *Toward a Concept of Constitutional Duty,* 1968 SUPREME COURT REVIEW 199) who might assert that since the Constitution imposes upon the federal government the affirmative constitutional duty to protect human dignity, and since human dignity is only possible in a non-Communist society, the Constitution requires the United States to maintain and deploy an arsenal of nuclear weapons sufficient to guard against the possibility of successful Communist aggression. Why is it necessary to assume that the policy decisions of judges will be ones that we would embrace? That was certainly not the case prior to 1937. It is not always the case today. It need not be the case in the future.

19.
Admirable Ends—Questionable Means*

Iredell Jenkins**

I agree, of course, with the thrust of Professor Miller's paper and with the conclusion at which he arrives. There can be no question that nuclear weapons pose a threat not only to civilization and to all human beings, but even to the life process itself. It follows, then, that the proliferation of such weapons contravenes the fundamental principles of morality, the accepted rules of international law, and any sane idea of national interest and policy. Furthermore, I think that Professor Miller's five arguments make out a cogent case for his conclusion that "the manufacture, deployment, and possible — even probable — use of nuclear weapons contravene the Constitution".[1] Each of these arguments is closely reasoned and well supported; together they present a persuasive defense of his claim, which might on its face appear unreasonable to the point of absurdity.

One may be tempted to object that the time-honored doctrine of *raison d'etat* makes these arguments and this conclusion meaningless: for this doctrine holds that any state is justified in taking—and is certainly going to take—whatever steps it deems necessary for its own protection. However, this argument fails for the simple reason that when several states possess significant numbers of nuclear weapons, then their use by any one state would quite surely lead to retaliation and hence to its own destruction. And this goes directly against the purpose of *raison d'etat,* which is to guarantee the existence of the society of which the state is the agent.

Consequently, and as a point of departure for this response, I am prepared to stipulate Professor Miller's conclusion that "those who wield both formal authority and effective control in the American constitutional order have a duty to take action designed to eliminate the nuclear threat throughout the world" and that "the duty . . . is of con-

---

* Reprinted, with permission, from *Nova Law Journal*, Volume 7, Number 1 (1982), where it appeared as "Admirable Ends—Ineffective Means."
** Professor Emeritus of Philosophy, University of Alabama.
1. Miller, *Nuclear Weapons and the Constitution,* 7 Nova L.J. 21, 23 (1982).

stitutional dimension."[2] However, despite all of this, I fear that the conclusion itself will be inconsequential because it has no precise and positive content. Stated more explicitly, the nature of this "constitutional duty" is both unspecified and devoid of sanctions; it does not impose any clearly defined obligations, either positive or negative, upon those to whom it is addressed; and it does not suggest any ways in which these "obligations" could be enforced and derelictions therefrom punished. This judgment must be qualified by pointing out, as Professor Miller stresses, that this essay is a "preliminary inquiry," not a "full-dress exposition."[3] Its purpose is to raise an issue rather than settle it, and so to initiate a cooperative discussion of legal (constitutional) procedures as a possible means to control the deployment and use of nuclear weapons. A final judgment, therefore, must be held in abeyance; but as the case now stands, I fear that however admirable the end sought, the means proposed will prove ineffective.

The argument that supports this judgment stands on three legs. Each of these is itself based upon a contention or concession that is central to Professor Miller's case and essential to its understanding and evaluation. My purpose in developing this argument is to indicate the difficulties I perceive in his position and thus to contribute as best I can to the discussion he seeks. He has made an admirably provocative start, and the undertaking is eminently worthwhile.

I take my first step with Professor Miller's statement that his paper "is emphatically not a plea for unilateral disarmament. We live in a Hobbesian world, a condition that is not at all likely to change."[4] Since the nations of the world have rejected the irenic precept of live and let live, adopting instead a policy of dog eat dog, the international climate is poisoned by mistrust and fear. Given this atmosphere, any suggestion of unilateral disarmament would be tantamount to putting one's self at the mercy of one's enemies. If nuclear disarmament is to be safe and acceptable, it must be mutual, with every nation disposing of its entire arsenal: "every weapon of mass destruction in the world"[5] must be eliminated. This is the outcome that the Constitution is held to

---

2. *Id.* at 24.
3. *Id.* at 23.
4. *Id.* at 24.
5. *Id.*

require. This is made quite explicit in the passage quoted earlier, where it is stated that the "constitutional duty" imposed on the government is "to take action designed to eliminate the nuclear threat *throughout the world*"[6] (Emphasis added). Since nuclear weapons anywhere clearly pose a threat to our lives, liberties, and properties, we, as American citizens, have a right to be free of them, and the government has the duty to see that we are.

Standing by itself, this contention appears self-evident. If the government owes us protection against arbitrary search and seizure, double jeopardy, self-incrimination, and cruel and unusual punishment — not to mention such benefits as clean air, pure water, adequate diet, and proper health care — then it would certainly seem to owe us protection against instant immolation. Therefore one is inclined to take this first step without hesitation.

This brings me to my second step. Here I take as my text Professor Miller's statement on page 23: "At the outset, I readily concede the jurisprudential problem of whether legal norms (rights) can exist absent a means of enforcement". It is, or course, traditional doctrine that a right accorded to some is barren without a corresponding duty imposed on others. It is further recognized that both the right and the duty are bootless unless there are sanctions to enforce the latter and make good the former. It is difficult to see just what legal (constitutional) means are available to secure to the people this right to the worldwide elimination of nuclear weapons. If the Supreme Court were to issue orders to this effect, how is it to enforce them against this government, let alone the governments of other sovereign states?

To this objection, Professor Miller offers two rebuttals, both sound in principle. He first points out that there are both constitutional and legislative duties that cannot be judicially enforced or for the neglect of which no penalty is even provided.[7] Secondly, he reminds us that the law is instrumental and living, and that the courts are continually recognizing new rights and creating new duties as the occasion seems (to them) to require. These points are well taken, but I do not think they are applicable in the present context. When the courts accord rights to privacy, abortion, racial integration, and so forth, they impose duties

---

6. *Id.* at 24 (emphasis added).
7. *Id.* at 23.

that are at least within the claimed and granted (albeit reluctantly) jurisdiction of the federal government, and to enforce these rights they can create sanctions, however ineffective and difficult to enforce they may be. But when the courts recognize the right of American citizens to the elimination of *all* nuclear weapons *everywhere,* they impose duties that are altogether beyond both the legal jurisdiction and the practical reach of the federal government. For the courts now tell the government of this country to achieve certain outcomes in other countries whose governments recognize no authority superior to themselves and which command power commensurate with that of this country. Without a common sovereign which holds both ultimate authority and a monopoly of power, rights and duties become mere words. The gist of the matter is this: the writ of the federal courts simply does not run in other sovereign states.

I now take my third step, which raises the most concrete and practical issues. This is again based on the passage previously cited from page 23 and also on another passage of similar import with which professor Miller summarizes his argument. The latter runs as follows:

> "My suggestion is that Supreme Court Justices should grasp the nettle and point out to the Executive and the Congress that officials in those branches are charged with a constitutional duty to take action to eliminate threats to the lives, liberties, and properties of the citizenry. Those threats emanate from nuclear weaponry."[8]

In both of these passages, it is the phrase "take action" that I want to emphasize: the government is to be told that it has a "constitutional duty" to "take action" to "eliminate the nuclear threat throughout the world." Even if we grant that the Supreme Court should in principle and does in fact issue orders to this effect, the critical question remains: *What action?*

Precisely what actions are the Executive and the Congress to be ordered to take? A duty which is hopelessly vague or with which compliance is impossible to determine is as empty as one that is unenforceable. And simply to order "action" would be the epitome of vagueness: the government could claim compliance on the basis of virtually any effort whatever; or it could refuse to disclose the "actions" it had taken,

---

8. *Id.* at 35.

justifying its refusal by invoking the sacred cow of the "national security". One could answer this objection by arguing that the Supreme Court decision mandating this new duty would be similar to that in the 1954 school desegregation opinion: the Court would simply order the President and the Congress to take steps to effect universal nuclear disarmament "with all deliberate speed".[9] The specifics of this mandate would then be left to be worked out in a series of suits and rulings.

But I do not believe that this argument would stand up. Mutual nuclear disarmament by numerous sovereign states is obviously a matter of foreign policy; and the conduct of foreign policy is, by the Constitution itself, conferred on the President with the advice and consent of the Senate. What actions this country could and should take in this area are matters of high policy, involving diplomatic, political, military, and economic dimensions: intelligent decisions require wide experience, vast amounts of detailed information, and the cooperation of experts from numerous esoteric fields. It seems doubtful if even those omniscient legal deities, the Justices of the United States Supreme Court, could muster the data and acquire the familarity that would be needed to issue reasonable and effective orders regarding nuclear disarmament. The Court could, of course, solicit *amicus* briefs from innumerable experts; and they could subpoena witnesses and documents from the several executive departments. But much of this information is strictly classified, hardly suitable to be aired in legal briefs, open hearings, and the Supreme Court reports; and the advice that the Justices would receive would certainly be so diverse and contradictory that they would, in the last analysis, have to rely upon their own judgment, untrained as that is in this field. Even if all of these hurdles could be surmounted, it is difficult to see what "action" the Court could order. In negotiating the reduction of nuclear weapons with other sovereign states, there are only two procedures this government can employ: it can threaten and it can deal. And that is precisely what every President for at least the past thirty years has been doing.

There are two further issues that should be considered briefly. The first concerns Professor Miller's alternative proposal that the "first-strike use of nuclear weapons should . . . be dropped as a policy op-

---

9.   Brown v. Bd. of Educ., 347 U.S. 483 (1954).

tion."[10] This is a more moderate suggestion. And it is an "action" that the Supreme Court could easily order, since it is simple and specific—enforcing the order, however, would be another matter. But quite apart from the wisdom and practicality of such a step, I fear that it would prove ineffective as an instrument of peace and ineffective as an inducement to other states to take similar action, for the government that adopted such a policy of renunciation could not bind future goverments. The state is an enduring entity; but circumstances change, and so do governments and their perceptions of these circumstances. Consequently, the announcement of such a policy would have little meaning or impact. It would offer no lasting guarantee to the society that adopted it and even less to other states and their governments.

The second of these issues concerns the idea—suggested but not developed in Professor Miller's paper—that a Supreme Court decision condemning nuclear weapons on constitutional grounds and mandating action to effect their worldwide elimination would have great moral force and persuasive power. Even if the Court could not enforce such an order or specify its meaning, its mere announcement might serve to make the public more conscious of the terrible dangers and the ultimate evils inherent in the proliferation of nuclear arms. This is a possibility that should not be dismissed lightly. There is not the slightest doubt that past Supreme Court decisions have had just such an impact on this society, and even on the international order: one thinks particularly of decisions on racial integration, the equality of women, access to the political process, and human rights in general.

However, I do have serious doubts, based on two grounds, whether a Supreme Court ruling on nuclear weapons would have a similar impact. One of these grounds concerns the context of such a ruling. Intense suspicion of Russian policy and intentions, and hence an obsessive fear of Russia gaining nuclear superiority, are endemic in this country. Given this atmosphere, any such Court ruling would almost certainly be interpreted as mandating unilateral disarmament; so it would be greeted with outrage and dismissed with contempt.

The other ground of my doubts concerns the present public standing of the Supreme Court, for I do not think that the Court now enjoys anything like the respect and moral authority that it once did. The

---

10. Miller, *supra* note 1, at 30.

mystique of the Court—the sense that it was somehow above the political process, untainted by ordinary human passions, and immune to outside pressures—has been largely stripped from it. Once the Supreme Court was thought to be concerned only with the Eternal Law writ large in the Constitution, and the Justices were seen as moved only by constitutional considerations. But now we are only too aware that the Court is concerned with the same social issues that occupy us; and we have learned that the justices are as much influenced by their biases and personal backgrounds as the rest of us.

This shift in view is due partly to the greatly enhanced publicity accorded the Court, and to an increasing public cynicism regarding all institutions. It is also due very largely to the extreme activism of the Supreme Court in recent decades. The Court has intervened in so many moral and social questions that touch people deeply, and it has issued decisions that have aroused such resentment, that it is now widely regarded not as a pure servant of the law, but rather as the tool of special interests, especially those of an ultra-"liberal" persuasion. The Supreme Court and the federal judiciary have been extremely courageous in intervening to correct social ills that had been neglected and ignored by all of the governmental authorities that bore responsibility for them. But this fact does not lessen the resentment and mistrust that have been directed against the Supreme Court.

Be all this as it may, I doubt if a Supreme Court ruling on nuclear disarmament would have any significant moral force or persuasive power. When survival is thought to be in question, even the strongest moral voice falls on deaf ears, and even the most perfect argument fails to assuage fear.

Professor Miller made it very clear that he wanted his respondents to offer criticisms and suggestions that could fuel a further dialogue. I have certainly offered criticisms, though suggestions, alas, have been sadly lacking. But I would not wish to close on this negative note, for I think Professor Miller's proposal could be extremely important: whether it will be, only the ensuing dialogue can tell.

If we are to consider Professor Miller's paper at all sanely and sympathetically, we must take seriously the quotations from A. N. Whitehead with which he introduces his proposal; these set the necessary tone for his suggestion. It is precisely our fundamental and unquestioned assumptions that most need to be brought into the open and re-examined. And when some hardy soul does this, and proposes fresh ideas, these are apt to appear patently absurd. And so it is with this idea that nuclear weapons pose a constitutional issue to which lawyers and the courts should address themselves. It has long been assumed that the conduct of foreign policy and the care and nurture of the national security were to be left to the President and his military and diplomatic advisors. The Congress was held to have very little business meddling in these matters, and the federal courts to have none at all: these latter need only recognize that treaties duly ratified were part of the law of the land.

That is no longer a safe assumption. Professor Miller's view that judges are "timorous creatures" who "look upon requests to go beyond the familiar and the expected as frightful occasions"[11] may be sound as a general proposition. But it seems clearly not applicable to the federal judiciary as a whole, nor especially to the justices of the Supreme Court. During the past thirty years or so, these men have not hesitated to assert that they have the highest wisdom and hold the ultimate authority in such matters as school integration, racial balance, abortion, the prevention and punishment of capital crimes, reapportionment, and the treatment of the mentally ill and prison inmates.[12] All of these issues were regarded as altogether beyond either the jurisdiction or the competence of judges and courts: they were the proper and ordained domains of other experts and authorities. But in all of these contexts, the federal courts have intervened—"meddled"—to correct persistent and intolerable ills. I hold no strong brief for federal judges as arbiters of moral, social, economic, and other such problems: their reach often exceeds their grasp, and their discretion fails to match their valor. But these judges have, time after time, acted to repair gross injustices and initiate significant reforms.

So despite the reservations voiced above, I am sympathetic to Professor Miller's proposal and I am prepared to be optimistic that it might bear fine fruit. I would anticipate two great obstacles to this happy outcome. First, I do not see what measures—what "action"—the

---

11. *Id.* at 36.

12. Brown v. Bd. of Educ., 347 U.S. 483 (1954); Columbus Bd. of Educ. v. Penick, 443 U.S. 449 (1979); Roe v. Wade, 410 U.S. 113 (1973); Woodson v. North Carolina, 428 U.S. 280 (1960); Reynolds v. Sims, 377 U.S. 533 (1964); Wyatt v. Stickney, 344 F. Supp. 373 (1972), *aff'd in part sub nom.* Wyatt v. Aderholt, 503 F.2d 1305 (1974); Rhodes v. Chapman, 452 U.S. 337 (1981).

Supreme Court could mandate, aside from those that every administration has employed: to deal and to threaten. (Though I certainly acknowledge that several of these administrations, and especially the present one, could be a great deal more restrained, constructive, and cooperative in their dealings with the Soviets instead of treating them as avowed enemies.) Second, and more serious, is the fact that some of the parties—sovereign states—whose agreement is essential to nuclear disarmament, are altogether beyond not only the grasp, but even the reach, of the Supreme Court. Judges have encountered more than enough recalcitrance and open defiance from state legislatures and governors. It would be interesting to be hidden behind an arras, like some hero of a gothic romance, when some diplomat hands a Supreme Court writ to Yuri Andropov (Brezhnev's successor), Indira Ghandi, or Menachem Begin.

But any such event as this lies in a distant time and a different clime. And if it ever occurs, the writ will come from a court serving as the agent of a single world sovereign. For the foreseeable future, the Supreme Court will have to contend itself with enhancing public consciousness of the enormity of the threat and with putting incessant pressure on the other branches of government. On first acquaintance, Professor Miller's proposal does such violence to our political and legal presuppositions that it has the aura of the judicial equivalent of science fiction. But we all know how often the science fiction of one year is the technological fact of the next. And when I recall the changes that the federal courts have wrought in recent decades, I think that this may well be an idea whose time has come.

20.
Letter from the Government*

William H. Taft, IV**

July 15, 1982

Articles Editor
Nova Law Review
3100 S.W. 9th Avenue
Fort Lauderdale, Florida 33315

You have written to both Secretary Weinberger and me inviting us to comment in your law review on the issues raised in Professor Arthur Miller's article "Nuclear Weapons and Constitutional Law." This letter is in response to both invitations. We appreciate very much the opportunity thus provided.

Professor Miller's article suggests that officers of the federal government are under a constitutional duty to take action to eliminate the threat to American lives, liberty, and property posed by nuclear weapons. It is not necessary to agree with Professor Miller's constitutional analysis, much of which he himself characterizes as tentative and even far-fetched, to recognize the responsibility of government officials in this regard. Quite apart from the implicit powers and duties derived from the doctrine of *raison d'état*, which Professor Miller evidently views with some ambivalence,***

---

* Reprinted, with permission, from *Nova Law Journal*, Volume 7, Number 1 (1982).

** General Counsel of the Department of Defense.

*** Professor Miller's ambivalence arises, I believe, from a misunderstanding of the relationship between national security in the context of international affairs and personal security. Professor Miller perceives a tension between the interests of the state in maintaining its authority and individual rights. While this tension undoubtedly exists in a domestic context, with regard to threats to individual rights by foreign countries, national security and personal security are interdependent: the survival of the state is what in this context preserves the individual rights secured by the Constitution. Threats from nuclear weapons arise, needless to say, only in an international context.

there is an explicit provision in the Constitution that bears on this matter. Section 4 of Article IV provides that

> "The United States shall guarantee to every State in this Union a Republican Form of Government, and shall protect each of them against Invasion. . . ."

2

In addition, the Constitution requires both the President and Members of Congress to swear that they will support the Constitution.

These provisions together sufficiently establish the existence of the constitutional duty to reduce and, if possible, eliminate the threat that nuclear weapons pose to the individual freedom and rights of Americans set out in the Constitution. The Reagan Administration has, of course, recognized its responsibilities in this regard. Its policy has been and continues to be to deter the use of nuclear weapons first by assuring that any adversary knows that we have sufficient strength to inflict unacceptable damage in retaliation against any attack that may be made on us and, secondly, by entering into negotiations with the Soviet Union to reduce substantially the arsenals of nuclear weapons held by both that country and the United States.

Sincerely,

William H. Taft, IV

21.
Presidential Power and Nuclear Defense*

Arval A. Morris**

It is becoming common knowledge[1] that the combined nuclear arsenals of the United States and the Soviet Union contain more than 50,000 warheads, having a destructive power more than one million times greater than the atomic bomb that destroyed Hiroshima. In terms of blast equivalences, these weapons represent four tons of TNT for every living person on earth. One United States Polaris submarine can destroy 128 Soviet sites, and carries more firepower than all the weapons used in World War II. The new Trident submarines are still more powerful. These new weapon systems and the underlying strategic planning leave old notions of deterrence behind. These weapons are building toward a capacity to fight as well as to deter nuclear war, and some civilian and military analysts are even asserting that a nuclear war can be fought and "won". The United States and NATO have long expressed their policy to use nuclear weapons first — especially "tactical" nuclear weapons — if necessary, to stop a Soviet invasion of Europe.[2]

The United States is improving and developing more and more precise missiles and anti-submarine systems, thereby affording the

---

* Reprinted, with permission, from *Nova Law Journal*, Volume 7, Number 1 (1982), where it appeared as "The Constitution and Nuclear Defense."
** Professor of Law, University of Washington.

1. The next several pages draw heavily on the literature of the Lawyers Alliance for Nuclear Arms Control, Inc., 11 Beacon Street, Suite 719, Boston, Mass., 02108, but any one of dozens of contemporary sources would have done as well. This group seeks to end lawyer apathy in the area. This is especially critical since lawyers learn and practice the skills of conflict resolution which are the very skills that must be applied to the nuclear arms race if we are to avoid nuclear war. Lawyers separate fact from fancy, distinguish the relevant from the irrelevant, and negotiate lasting agreements building upon common or compatible interests in efforts to obtain peaceful solutions to problems of conflict. Nowhere are these skills more in need today than in nuclear arms limitation, reduction and elimination.

2. *See* Mossberg, Wall St. J., Oct. 15, 1982, at 4, col. 1, Haig and Weinberger here confirmed this policy under the heading *Nato Chief Warns of New Soviet Strategy to Deny the West the Use of Its Nuclear Punch.*

United States a theoretical first-strike attack capability. It will be a "counterforce" capability having the power to destroy all or most of the Soviet Union's nuclear arsenal. This "counterforce" capability is claimed to be defensive only, but since the weapons can deliver a first-strike, it can be seen as offensive as well. Military analysts expect the Soviet Union to have this same first-strike capability sometime before the end of this decade.[3]

The possibility of intentional full-scale nuclear war hangs by a hair trigger. Such a war would last only a matter of hours. If launched from the Atlantic Ocean, missiles from the new Trident submarine could hit Moscow in just ten minutes. Morever, Pershing II missiles are currently scheduled for deployment in West Germany. They could hit targets in the Soviet Union in a mere four minutes. The Soviets have similar capabilities. Thus, it is obvious that the White House or the Kremlin will have only a few minutes in which to evaluate a report of an incoming missile attack and decide whether to launch a nuclear strike in response. It is quite possible that technological advances will force this decision to be delegated to computers and their "specialists". Indeed, if a non-first-strike nuclear power is confronted by another nuclear power possessing a first-strike counterforce capability, it can be considered "rational for the non-first strike power to adopt a "launch on attack" or "launch on report" policy. It is widely feared the Soviets may adopt such a policy if the United States maintains its present philosophy. The destiny of mankind would then have been turned over to machines.

The probability of accidental nuclear war is genuine and increasing. The warning system of the United States Air Command has reported hundreds of false alarms about incoming missiles, and has otherwise malfunctioned. No American actually knows the reliability of the Soviet Union's command and control systems. Yet, ironically, for all the billions they have spent on defense, the American people must rely every day on the Soviet systems to prevent our destruction. So far, the Soviet systems have been sufficiently reliable to protect Americans from a wave of nuclear weapons launched because of an accident or malfunction. But how long will security last? Currently, six countries

---

3. *See supra* note 1.

admit they have atomic arms.[4] By the end of this century, an additional two dozen countries are expected to have nuclear weapons, thereby increasing dramatically the probability of accidental, or intentional, nuclear war.

Indeed, the existence of a "counterforce" first-strike nuclear capability that could destroy most of an opponent's nuclear weapons while they remain on the ground, makes nuclear war appear "rational" under certain circumstances. Suppose for example that Iran, with Soviet backing, masses its military forces to invade Saudi Arabia and the Arab Emerites, thereby eliminating most of Europe's and Japan's oil supply, as well as much of our own. Irreparably crippled, the United States, invoking the Carter Doctrine,[5] declares its vital security interest threatened and prepares to intervene. It can do so effectively only by using American troops. The Soviet Union threatens the United States, saying it will not tolerate U.S. troops fighting in Iran or Saudi Arabia, which are just below its southern border. It then masses its troops on the Iranian border. Perceiving this development as further threatening its vital interests, the United States responds by placing its nuclear forces on a "red" ready alert. The Soviet Union responds by placing its nuclear forces on ready alert. Negotiations between the Soviet Union and the United States deteriorate and finally break down. Iran's troops begin to cross the border and invade Saudi Arabia.

IF either the United States or the Soviet Union concludes that: (1) negotiations have irretrievably broken down and are of no further avail and (2) war is surely coming, then, under these circumstances, voices on both sides will be raised declaring that a nuclear first-strike is fully "rational". It is better, it will be argued, for us to attack first and destroy as many Soviet missiles as possible, thereby suffering only 25 to 30 million dead Americans from a crippled Soviet nuclear response, than to lose fifty to eighty million or more Americans and most of our nuclear weapons, by waiting and absorbing a full power Soviet nuclear

---

4. United States, Soviet Union, United Kingdom, France, China, India and although she does not admit it, most people believe Israel has them as well.

5. The Carter Doctrine, 16 WEEKLY COMP. PRES. DOC. 197 (Jan. 23, 1980) which states: "Let our position be absolutely clear: An attempt by any outside force to gain control of the Persian Gulf region will be regarded as an assault on the vital interests of the United States of America, and such assault will be repelled by any means necessary, including military force."

first-strike attack.

Once war is perceived as inevitable in a world where the United States and the Soviet Union each possesses a first-strike capability, it will be declared "rational" to initiate nuclear war in a deteriorating crisis situation in order to destroy the other side's missiles and limit casualties. If one accepts this analysis, is there any American who knows the Soviet mind well enough to predict the exact point at which, in a deteriorating crisis situation, the Soviets will perceive war as inevitable, or vice-versa? Assuming one side or the other perceives war as inevitable, on which side does prudence lie? Shall millions of preventable deaths be risked by not striking first, or shall it be a race between Americans and Soviets to press the button first? A bilateral first-strike situation is inherently unstable, especially during a deteriorating crisis. How should a democracy like the United States respond?

In foreign and military affairs, the general will of the population of a democracy is what the leaders determine it to be, and particularly for nuclear war prospects, what the President determines it to be. In a free society, no president normally would reach any momentous decision without consultation, without considering the widest scope of available opinions, without the best information he can obtain, and without patient and deep reflection on where the common interests of the people lie. But all of this takes time, much time, and time is precisely what is not available in the nuclear timetable. Neither the Congress, the people, nor any other authority, can make the decision for the President. The decision is essentially individual, and therefore autocratic. In the logic of nuclear war, the President, by circumstances of mutual, first-strike capability, is condemned to be a dictator. That is contrary to our democratic order, and a question arises, therefore, as to whether the Constitution applies to this situation.

The War Power

The Constitutional Convention was convened on May 25, 1787, and was concluded on September 17, less than four months later.[6]

---

6. 2 RECORDS OF THE FEDERAL CONVENTION OF 1787, at 649 (M. Farrand ed. 1911) [hereinafter cited as 2 RECORDS]. There is no complete or entirely reliable record of the Convention's deliberations. The Convention's delegates met in secret and resolved to communicate nothing to non-delegates. 1 RECORDS OF THE FEDERAL CON-

Fifty-five men attended in all, but the significant work was done by far fewer. For the first two months, the Convention devoted itself mainly to discussions, developing and perfecting resolutions. In late July, those resolutions on which agreement had been reached were turned over to the Committee on Detail, and on July 26, the Convention adjourned for ten days, until August 6, to permit that Committee of five to create a draft of the Constitution.[7]

The Committee's draft constitution assigned Congress the power "to make war."[8] Later on August 17, Charles Pinkney opposed vesting the power to make war in Congress, saying "its proceedings were too slow."[9] He argued that the "Senate would be the best depository, being more acquainted with foreign affairs and most capable of proper resolution."[10] Pierce Butler countered, saying that if informed judgment and efficiency were the standards to be applied, then the Senate suffered the same disabilities as Congress; consequently, he was "for vesting the power in the President. . . ."[11] Thereafter, James Madison and Elbridge Gerry "moved to insert 'declare', striking out 'make' war; leaving to the Executive the power to repel sudden attacks."[12] Roger Sherman thought it stood very well. "The Executive [should] be able to repel and not commence war."[13] Elbridge Gerry said that he "never expected to hear in a republic a motion to empower th Executive alone to declare war."[14] Oliver Ellsworth observed that "there is a material

---

VENTION OF 1787, at 10 n.4, xi (M. Farrand ed. 1911) [hereinafter cited as 1 RECORDS]. The Journal of the Convention recorded only the formal motions and the votes thereon. Extensive, but incomplete notes were taken by several delegates — Rufus King, James McHenry, William Pierce, William Paterson, Alexander Hamilton, and George Mason. *Id.* at xvi-xxiv. The most important record, James Madison's notes, was revised thirty years after the convention. *Id.* at vii.

7. 1 RECORDS, *supra* note 6, at xxii. John Rutledge of South Carolina was Chairman, and James Wilson of Pennsylvania an important member.

8. 2 RECORDS, *supra* note 6, at 318: "Mr. Pinkney opposed vesting this power in the legislature. . . ."

9. *Id.*

10. *Id.*

11. *Id.*

12. *Id.*

13. *Id. See also* Bas v. Tingy, 4 U.S. (4 Dall.) 37, 40-43 (1800) where Justice Samuel Chase wrote: "Congress is empowered to declare a general war or Congress may wage a limited war. . . ."

14. 2 RECORDS, *supra* note 6, at 318.

difference between the cases of making *war* and making *peace,*"[15] and that "it should be more easy to get out of a war, than into it."[16] George Mason "was against giving the power of war to the Executive, because not [safely] to be trusted with it . . . he was for clogging rather than facilitating war; but for facilitating peace;"[17] thus, "he preferred '*declare*' to '*make*.' "[18] Thereafter, the vote was called and "the motion to insert '*declare*' in place of '*make*' passed."[19]

This result is not surprising because the authors of our Constitution had all been reared with the axiom, endlessly repeated before and after the American Revolution, that standing armies and their commanders are always a menace to the liberties of a free people. The dangers posed by a standing army were repeatedly dealt with during the ratification debates, and it accounted for significant opposition to the proposed constitution.

There is no ambiguity or uncertainty about the general intent of the framers of the Constitution with respect to the war power.

> [It] was understood by the framers — and subsequent usage confirmed their understanding — that the President in his capacity as commander in chief of the armed forces would have the right, indeed the duty, to use the armed forces to repel sudden attacks on the United States, even in advance of Congressional authorization to do so . . . [and] . . . that he would direct and lead the armed forces and put them to any use specified by Congress but that this did not extend to the initiation of hostilities. . . .[20]

---

15. *Id.* at 319 (emphasis original).

16. *Id.*

17. *Id.*

18. *Id.* (emphasis original).

19. *Id.* (emphasis original). By defining the issue in terms of the power to "declare" war, the framers may have confused later generations. The real issue was congressional authorization of hostilities, full or partial, against a foreign sovereign state. The framers meant to vest that power as well as the power ultimately to control general or limited war in the hands of Congress. The President was to be the commander-in-chief, subject to Congress' ultimate control.

20. National Commitments, S. REP. No. 797, 90th Cong., 1st Sess. (1957), *quoted in* G. GUNTHER, CASES AND MATERIALS ON CONSTITUTIONAL LAW 417 (10th ed. 1980). In 1801, Chief Justice Marshall, writing for the Court, ruled that the "whole powers of war being, by the Constitution of the United States, vested in Congress . . . the Congress may authorize general hostilities . . . or partial hostili-

In a letter to Madison in 1789, Thomas Jefferson wrote: "We have already given in example one effectual check to the Dog of War by transferring the power of letting him loose from the Executive to the Legislative body. . . ."[21]

One conclusion is clear: the so-called doctrine of a President attacking first and making war as anticipatory self- defense, allegedly justified by Article 51 of the United Nations' Charter, has no historical standing in American Constitutional law.

The United States had a puny, regular military force of less than 840 men when George Washington assumed the Presidency under the new constitution,[22] nevertheless, the framers sorely worried about war and the dangers posed by the military. They denied the President the power to initiate hostilities and embroil the nation in war. Presidents in the 19th Century interpreted their commander-in-chief powers differently, but on the whole, the basic constitutional framework was generally observed. Presidents did not initiate war. Summarizing the war power in the 19th Century, Robert William Russell wrote:

> It is not a simple matter to arrive at conclusions concerning this period in which the constitutional interpretation was far from consistent, where Grant's extreme view is sandwiched between the conservative views of Buchanan and Cleveland. But there was one opinion that enjoyed wide acceptance: the President could constitutionally employ American military force outside the nation as long as he did not use it to commit "acts of war." While the term was never precisely defined, an "act of war" in this context usually meant the use of military force against a sovereign nation without that nation's consent and without that nation's having declared war upon or used force against The United States. To perform acts of war, the President needed the authorization of Congress . . . .
>
> This dividing line between the proper spheres of legislative and executive authority was sufficiently flexible to permit the President to use military force in unimportant cases, while preserving the role of Congress in important decisions. The acts of war doctrine was probably a step beyond what the framers intended when they changed the Congressional power from "make" war to "declare"

---

ties. . . ." Talbot v. Seaman, 5 U.S. (1 Cranch.) 1, 28 (1801).

21. *See* G. GUNTHER, *supra* note 20, at 418.

22. A. SOIFER, FOREIGN AFFAIRS AND CONSTITUTIONAL POWER 116 (1976).

war, and was certainly a move in the direction of Presidential power compared to the cautious stance of Washington, Adams, Jefferson, and Madison. The central objective which the Constitution sought — Congressional authority to approve the initiation of major conflicts — was undamaged, but certain fraying of the edges had occurred. This slight deterioration was greatly accelerated during the following 50 years.[23]

The 19th Century presidents used the military forces in "hot pursuit" of bands of pirates or bandits or to protect American lives and property under treaties conferring rights and obligations on the United States. But early 20th Century presidents — Theodore Roosevelt, Taft, and Wilson — expanded the scope of presidential power by using military force against small sovereign states, and Congress did not resist.[24] Later, in 1941, "President Roosevelt, on his own authority, committed American forces to the defense of Greenland and Iceland and authorized American naval vessels to escort convoys to Iceland";[25] thus, "by the time Germany and Italy declared war on the United States, in the wake of the Japanese attack on Pearl Harbor, the United States had already been committed by its president, acting on his own authority, to an undeclared naval war in the Atlantic."[26]

The trend begun by Theodore Roosevelt, Taft, and Wilson, and accelerated by Franklin Roosevelt, increasingly continued under Presidents Truman, Eisenhower, Kennedy, Johnson, and Nixon, "bringing the country to the point at which the real power to commit the country to war is now in the hands of the president."[27] thus, the power to conduct foreign affiars,[28] the campaign for government secrecy, and the

---

23. R. Russell, The United States Congress and the Power to Use Military Force Abroad (Ph.D. thesis, Fletcher School of Law and Diplomacy, 1967) *reported in* NATIONAL SENATE COMM. ON FOREIGN COMMITMENTS, S. REP. NO. 797, 90th Cong., 1st Sess. (1967); *quoted in* G. GUNTHER, CONSTITUTIONAL LAW 416, 418 (10th ed. 1980).

24. G. GUNTHER, *supra* note 23, at 419.

25. *Id.*

26. *Id.*

27. *Id. See also* United States v. Curtis-Wright Corp., 299 U.S. 304 (1936) where the Court seemingly affirmed an inherent superior presidential power over foreign affairs, not derived from constitutional or statutory sources. *Compare* Bestor, *infra* note 28.

28. For an enlightening analysis of this power, and the meaning of the King's

commander-in-chief powers were combined and used in ways that eventually produced the current "Imperial Presidency":[29]

> The imperial presidency was essentially the creation of foreign policy. A combination of doctrines and emotions — belief in permanent and universal crisis, fear of communism, faith in the duty and the right of the United States to intervene swiftly in every part of the world — had brought about the unprecedented centralization of decisions over war and peace in the presidency. With this there came an unprecedented exclusion of the rest of the executive branch, of Congress, of the press and of public opinion in general from these decisions. Prolonged war in Vietnam strengthened the tendencies toward both centralization and exlusion. So the imperial presidency grew at the expense of the constitutional order. Like the cowbird, it hatched its own eggs and pushed the others out of the nest. And, as it overwhelmed the traditional separation of powers in foreign affairs, it began to aspire toward an equivalent centralization of power in the domestic polity.[30]

However, the war powers as spelled out in the Constitution and its balances between Congress and the President are not obsolete. All that is required is for Congress actively and continually to reassert its constitutional authority over the use of American military force. Ultimately, congressional action will be founded upon enlightened, press influenced public opinion. This opinion obviously will affect the presidency since that office is also highly susceptible to public influence.

A first step was taken by Congress when it passed the War Powers Resolution in 1973, stating its purpose was

> to fulfill the intent of the framers of the Constitution of the United States and insure that the collective judgment of both the Congress and the President will apply to the introduction of United States Armed Forces into hostilities, or into situations where imminent involvement in hostilities is clearly indicated by the circumstances, and to the continued use of such forces in hostilities or in such

---

power of "advice and consent," see Bestor, *Separation of Powers in the Domain of Foreign Affairs*, 5 SETON HALL L. REV. 527 (1974).

29.   For discussion, *see* A. SCHLESINGER JR., THE IMPERIAL PRESIDENCY (1973).

30.   *Id.* at 207.

situations.[31]

This legislation, however, does not fully restore the intent of the framers. The framers did not rely on the *collective* judgment of Congress and President to initiate hostilities, but solely on Congressional declaration to introduce military forces into hostilities, except in limited cases of presidential repulsion of a sudden attack on the United States. Nevertheless, the statute is useful, so long as it is seen as a first step to be followed by others. It confirms the constitutional position that the doctrine of presidentially created war as anticipatory self-defense has no constitutional standing, and it helps to restore part of the constitutional balance. The rest of the balance can be restored if the American people have the will and have the vision to do so. Alexander Hamilton was prophetic in seeing the consequences of a people living in a garrison state. He implied the need for continuous vigilance by the people. In a striking passage, Hamilton observed "safety from external danger is the most powerful director of national conduct, . . . [and] . . . [e]ven the ardent love of liberty will, after a time, give way to its dictates."[32] Hamilton prophetically concluded that the "violent destruction of life and property incident to war—the continual effort and alarm attendant on a state of continual danger, will compel nations the most attached to liberty, to resort for repose and security, to institutions, which have a tendency to destroy their civil and political rights."[33]

---

31. The constitutional powers of the President as Commander-in-Chief to introduce United States Armed Forces into hostilities, or into situations where imminent involvement in hostilities is clearly indicated by the circumstances are exercised only pursuant to (1) a declaration of war, (2) specific statutory authorization, or (3) a national emergency created by attack upon the United States, its territories or possessions, or its armed forces.

Pub. L. No. 93-148, § 2, 87 Stat. 555, 93d Cong., 1st Sess., 1488 (H.R.J. Res. 542, 93d Cong., 1st Sess. adopted over Presidential veto on Nov. 7, 1973). (This statute is an unusual, quasi-constitutional variety of congressional action, not setting forth substantive policy but processes and relationships. Query: is it clear, is it not, that Congress did not go far enough and failed to restore the original intent?)

32. THE FEDERALIST No. 8, at 45 (A. Hamilton) (J. Cooke ed. 1961).

33. *Id.*

Presidential Power and Nuclear War

It seems relatively straightforward to conclude that the President has no constitutional power to initiate a nuclear war by authorizing a preemptive nuclear first-strike. That clearly would be a functional "declaration" of war in its most emphatic and destructive form, and only Congress has that power under our Constitution. Moreover, as the United Nations repeatedly has declared, the threat or use of nuclear weapons is a "crime against mankind and civilization."[34]

But does the President, after receiving a radar or other report of an incoming wave of nuclear missiles, have constitutional power to authorize a responsive nuclear missile strike? The War Powers Resolution of 1973 permits the President "to introduce United States Armed Forces into hostilities"[35] in the event of "a national emergency created by attack upon the United States . . . or its armed forces."[36] this provision clearly contemplates the use of military manpower and it may be so limited, but arguably it may also include hardware, such as nuclear missiles. Thus, the statutory situation is somewhat murky. Yet clearly, a nuclear attack on the Soviet Union based on radar alone, or some other report, does not come within the statute because the reports may, like others in the past, be in error. At that moment only a report exists and neither the United States nor its armed forces have actually been "attacked". The doctrine of anticipatory self-defense by a President is ruled out. Likewise, the situation would not fall within the provision of the President's Constitutional power to repel sudden attacks because the "attack" had not yet occurred. On the other hand, if the reports were true and if the President waited until after the "attack" on the United States actually occurred, he may be left with very few, if any, missiles with which to respond. Of course, in such a situation, a question exists concerning the good to be achieved by authorizing a responding nuclear attack with the remaining missiles, which would only produce another nuclear attack on the United States with the Soviet Union's remaining missiles.

---

34. G.A. Res. 1653, 16 U.N. GAOR Supp. (No. 17) at 4, U.N. Doc A/5100 (1961). This resolution was adopted Nov. 24, 1961, by a vote of 55-20, with 26 abstentions. The United States voted "No". The U.S.S.R. voted "yes".

35. *See supra,* note 31.

36. *Id.*

It may be true that neither the Constitution nor the War Powers Resolution was designed to apply to the conditions of nuclear war. Nuclear war is fundamentally different from warfare by tank, machine gun, and airplane. It is a crime against humanity. But, under the Constitution as it currently exists, it appears reasonably correct to conclude (1) that the President has no constitutional power to order a pre-emptive, nuclear first-strike and thereby initiate nuclear war; (2) that the President has no constitutional power to order a nuclear attack solely in response to reports of an incoming wave of missiles, and (3) that the President has no emergency power to "repel" a nuclear attack already fully completed. If the President has any power, it would only be to repel a nuclear attack on the United States that is in process by authorizing a responding nuclear attack after the United States actually has been attacked. Of course, by then, there may be very little left with which to respond or little reason to do so. It is difficult to see how an American nuclear attack on the Soviet Union authorized during or following a nuclear attack on the United States by the Soviet Union can be characterized as "repelling" the initial attack. Nothing is "repelled", and the concept loses its meaning in a nuclear context. Moreover, the whole concept of presidential power "to repel a sudden attack" on the United States presupposes (1) that the purpose of such presidential power is to gain time sufficient for Congress to convene and act, and (2) that things called "Congress", "the United States", and "the American people" will continue to exist after the President exercises his power to repel sudden attack. If neither of these two presuppositions exist, as neither would if we absorbed a full, nuclear strike from the Soviet Union, then the whole rationale for the concept of presidential power "to repel sudden attack" disappears. Rather clearly, it seems, the existence of a first-strike posture in the possible use of nuclear weapons is unconstitutional and should be dropped as a policy option.[37]

A president may act contrary to the constitutional requirements in each of the above three situations, arguing emergency presidential prerogative,[38] a doctrine dangerous to a free society. The founding fathers

---

37. For a recent discussion of this point solely as a matter of policy, see Bundy, *Nuclear Weapons and the Atlantic Alliance,* 60 FOREIGN AFFAIRS 753 (Spring 1982).

38. Machiavelli argued that all republics in times of crisis need a dictatorship

did not completely deny power to use military force to the President. They permitted him to repel a sudden attack, and this recognizes, in part, an emergency power in the President, but the prerogative is not unqualified. Nevertheless, some presidents have gone well beyond their carefully circumscribed power. It appears that Lincoln acted on a theory of wide presidential prerogative during the Civil War,[39] as did Roosevelt during World War II,[40] and Kennedy during the Cuban Missile Crisis.

So long as presidents believe they will be successful in their actions, they will continue to claim emergency prerogative. But, what would count as "success" in any of the above three situations involving nuclear war? Our safety may turn on the quirks of mind of a particular president and on how he judges "success" and how he sees himself in the annals of history. The pathway to real "success" is set forth in Professor Arthur Miller's article.

Professor Miller's stimulating and welcome analysis, seeking to change our modes of thinking about nuclear war, goes well beyond my argument set forth above. He holds that the manufacture, deployment, and use of nuclear weapons are unconstitutional. By focusing solely on

---

and that it was better to provide for one by law than to have power usurped. "[R]epublics which, when in imminent danger," Machiavelli said, "have recourse neither to a dictatorship, nor to some form of authority analagous to it, will be ruined when grave misfortune befalls them." 1 N. MACHIAVELLI, THE DISCOURSE ch. 34, 291 (Routledge ed. 1950). Two and a half centuries later, Rousseau argued that the "ability to foresee that some things cannot be foreseen is a very necessary quality;" that the "sacrosanct nature of the laws never should be interfered with save when the safety of the state is in question," and at that point "the People's first concern must be to see that the State shall not perish." 4 J. ROUSSEAU, SOCIAL CONTRACT ch. 6, 415-16 (Oxford ed. 1947). Even John Stuart Mill stated he was "far from condemning, in cases of extreme exigency, the assumption of absolute power in the form of a temporary dictatorship." J. MILL, *Considerations on Representative Government*, THE PHILOSOPHY OF JOHN STUART MILL 408 (M. Cohen ed. 1961).

39. *See Emancipation Proclamation, Jan. 1, 1863*, VIII A. LINCOLN, COMPLETE WORKS OF ABRAHAM LINCOLN 161 (Nicolay & Hay eds. 1894), and letter from Abraham Lincoln to Secretary Chase (Sept. 2, 1863) (which appears in IX A. LINCOLN, COMPLETE WORKS OF ABRAHAM LINCOLN 108 (Nicolay & Hay eds. 1894)); E. CORWIN, THE PRESIDENT: OFFICE AND POWERS 382 (1940).

40. *See* Murphy, Request of the Senate for an Opinion as to the Powers of the President In Emergency or State of War, 39 Op. Att'y Gen. 343-48 (1939); 10 F. ROOSEVELT, PUBLIC PAPERS AND ADDRESSES 1941, at 195 (1950).

the limited presidential power to repel attack, my argument is narrower but parallels his, seeking to demonstrate only that the presidential core of our nuclear first-strike capability strategy is unconstitutional. Professor Miller broadly attacks the nuclear establishment as a whole, arguing boldly that constitutional law is instrumental and that it places a duty on government officers NOT to take any action that, on balance, unreasonably jeopardizes the well-being of the populace or "posterity." He argues that constitutional law imposes a duty of negative content. Although this part of the argument is neither set forth comprehensively nor definitively, I find Professor Miller's preliminary statement persuasive.

Two additional arguments and a general conclusion present some surmountable difficulties. First, Professor Miller argues that international law partially defines the duties the Constitution places on governmental officers because it is incorporated into our constitutional law.[41] Second, he argues that international law, as stated by Richard Falk and his colleagues, declares that any threat or contemplated use of nuclear weapons constitutes a crime of state.[42] The duty of government officials, he argues, then becomes clear: "to take action to help prevent that 'crime of state.' "[43] Accepting the validity of the above two arguments for discussion purposes, the requirement that government officials "take action" does not follow from the prior general duty of negative content that officials take no action that unreasonably jeopardizes the well-being of the American people. Another step is needed, a constitutional judgment from the Supreme Court that the current manufacture, deployment, and contemplated use of nuclear weapons unreasonably jeopardizes American well-being. Once that reasonable judgment is made, then Professor Miller's arguments take hold and Congress comes under a duty to act to undo the jeopardy to the American people. In doing so, it prevents a "crime of state". Such judgment from the Supreme Court of the United States is, however, most unlikely. That prospect, though, should not deter vigorous discussion of this vital subject.

Should international law be part of constitutional law? Professor

---

41. Miller, *Nuclear Weapons and the Constitution,* 7 Nova L.J. 21 (1982).
42. *Id.* at 33.
43. *Id.*

Miller argues it should. Surely, the part of international law that conflicts with the Constitution cannot be. My argument above indicates, however, that part of international law outlawing a nuclear first-strike position does not conflict with American constitutional law. Thus, that portion of international law could be incorporated into American constitutional law. Professor Miller's preliminary, creative, result-oriented affirmative argument is intriguing indeed. Anyone who takes law and humankind seriously must agree with his goal to eliminate nuclear weapons. Yet, I suspect American officials will not accept Professor Miller's argument without also knowing it has been agreed to by the Soviets. Nevertheless, by opening debate, Professor Miller puts us in his debt.

Professor Miller is quite right when he states that we must invent the legal means, whether his or others, by which the world can peacefully settle the issues that previously have been settled by war. Until the necessary legal means are created and institutionalized, any reduction in the steadily increasing probability of nuclear catastrophe is unlikely in the absence of effective negotiations on the control, reduction and elimination of arms. The limited progress that has been made to control nuclear arms has come as a result of direct negotiations between the nuclear powers, and, in this country, has been accompanied by enlightened citizen demands. In the United States, citizen enlightenment in the area of arms control is crucial, but, happily, as John Jay saw long ago, citizen interest in this area endures. "Among the many objects to which a wise and free people find it necessary to direct their attention," Jay declared, "that of providing for their *safety* seems to be first"; and that means their "security for the preservation of peace and tranquility, as well as against dangers from *foreign arms and influence,* as from dangers of the *like kind* arising from domestic causes."[44] Thus, the legal profession becomes deeply implicated because it consists of professionals whose skills are necessary to save mankind from nuclear war. Lawyers have skills to separate fact from fancy; they can understand nuclear strategies, and they can explain to the public the dangers and constitutional status of our current nuclear posture. Lawyers also are negotiators and indispensible advisors to policy makers. They nego-

---

44. THE FEDERALIST No. 3, at 14 (J. Jay) (J. Cooke ed. 1961) (emphasis original).

tiate lasting agreements founded on the existence of common or compatible interests, including common and compatible interests of the Soviet Union and the United States. It is these lawyerly skills, employed in the service of Professor Miller's vision, that are sorely needed today by the American people for their posterity. May they be forthcoming.

22.
The Power to Use Nuclear Weapons: A Response to Professor Miller*

Jack M. Goldklang**

I have given some thought previously to the legal issues involved in fighting World War III. My specialties include emergency powers, war powers, constitutional law, and international law. It strikes me as fascinating therefore that we are here confronting a question—the constitutionality of nuclear weapons—that has never been considered a difficult one.

The fact that this question does not come up often is not really surprising. It probably was never asked in real life by Harry Truman of the Attorney General in 1945 when atomic warfare began. That is because, judged by the same standards by which we judge other constitutional issues, there is no realistic case that can be made that nuclear weapons are unconstitutional *per se.*[1]

Before I go too far, I want to make clear that I am not discussing the *policy* that the President and the Congress or the rest of the world ought to adopt concerning the construction and use of nuclear weapons. My own position is not an issue here. I am not an expert on nuclear weapons and I do not attempt to follow the details of the many debates on weapons systems.

However one may feel about nuclear weapons, the conclusion is unavoidable: A wish that nuclear weapons would go away cannot be translated into the conclusion that they are unconstitutional. The thesis that has been presented by Professor Miller[2] does not demonstrate that any single section of the Constitution *provides* or has been interpreted in a way which would even lead one to believe that nuclear weapons are

---

* This essay is based on remarks delivered at the Conference on Nuclear Weapons and Law held at Nova University Center for the Study of Law on February 5, 1983.

** Attorney-Advisor, Office of Legal Counsel of the United States Department of Justice. The views expressed here are those of the author in his personal capacity and are not necessarily those of the U.S. Department of Justice.

unconstitutional. If one starts with the assumption that nuclear weapons must be unconstitutional, then it is, of course, possible to embroider almost *any* part of the Constitution with a similar message, not just the ones that Professor Miller has mentioned.

One thing that strikes me about Professor Miller's paper is that it discusses the issues surrounding nuclear weapons as if they were executive decisions alone. The President, of course, has substantial powers as commander-in-chief and as chief executive. But the decision to develop, build, and deploy nuclear weapons has involved congressional involvement at every step.

It would be useful, therefore, to review some basic constitutional doctrine. Perhaps the most widely used analysis concerning the war powers comes from a concurring opinion by Justice Jackson in the 1952 *Steel Seizure Case*.[3] Although his opinion was not the opinion of the Court, it has, because Jackson wrote so well, become much better known than the majority opinion. It is frequently used as a point of departure by students of the Constitution and by the Supreme Court itself.[4] President Truman, you may recall, was told by the Supreme Court that he could not seize the Youngstown Sheet & Tube Company even though, in his judgment, it was necessary to fight the Korean War. Congress had declined to give him express statutory power to do this even though it had given the President a variety of emergency economic powers when the war first broke out.

Justice Jackson mentioned that the constitutional assumptions one made depended on the interaction between Congress and the Executive:

1. When the President acts pursuant to an express or implied authorization of Congress, his authority is at its maximum, for it includes all that he possesses in his own right plus all that Congress can delegate. In these circumstances, and in these only, may he be said (for what it may be worth) to personify the federal sovereignty. If his act is held unconstitutional under these circumstances, it usually means that the Federal government as an undivided whole lacks power.
2. When the President acts in the absence of either a congressional grant or denial of authority, he can only rely upon his own independent powers, but there is a zone of twilight in which he and Congress may have concurrent authority, or in which its distribution is uncertain.
3. When the President takes measures *incompatible* with the express or implied will of Congress, his power is at its lowest ebb, for then he can rely only upon his own constitutional powers minus any constitutional powers of Congress over the matter. Courts can sustain exclusive presidential control in such a case only by disabling the Congress from acting upon the subject.[5]

In the *Steel Seizure Case* Justice Jackson concluded that President Truman's action belonged in category three. The President's actions were inconsistent with legislation on the subject and the seizure was not upheld.

The present case is, of course, totally different. Congress did not know just what it was funding at the Manhattan Project during World War II although individual members were briefed.[6] It certainly knew, however, that the United States dropped two atomic bombs in 1945, and it has continued to authorize and appropriate funds for nuclear research, development, and deployment ever since. We can turn to the records of virtually each and every Congress and find hearings and debates supporting authorizations and appropriations for missiles, submarines, and various other nuclear defense systems.[7]

We therefore have, in Justice Jackson's terms, a case one situation. We have the power of the President as commander-in-chief and chief executive combined with legislation passed by Congress pursuant to its constitutional authority to raise and support armies, to provide and maintain a navy, to provide for the common defense, to make rules for the government and regulation of the land and naval forces, and to make all laws "which shall be necessary and proper" for carrying out all of the other powers just mentioned.

Thus, "the sovereignty of the United States," to use Jackson's term, lies behind the decision to construct and deploy nuclear weapons systems.

Our legal system also deals with the decision to take this country to war. The classic model is the declaration of war. But there never was, in fact, a classic period, no matter what people would like to believe today, when American troops fought only under declarations of war. The possibility of undeclared war was foreseen by the Framers at the Convention of 1787 when the Federal Convention discussed language that would have empowered Congress "to make war."[8] The Convention, of course, ultimately decided to give Congress the power to "declare" war in Article I, section 8 of the Constitution.

The records we have show that this difference was crucial. James Madison and Elbridge Gerry jointly moved to substitute the word "declare" for the word "make," thus "leaving the Executive," in their words, "the power to repel sudden attacks."[9] This shows the foresight of the Framers who realized that they were writing a document that might have to last for a long time. In 1787, very little could happen that was truly "sudden"; getting from one place to another took a long time then. Today "sudden" can *really* mean "sudden."

The theory behind the decision made by the Framers is not just something to be discussed by students reading Madison's Notes on the Federal Convention. When Congress passed the War Powers Resolution less than ten years ago, it explicitly recognized that the President had the constitutional power to introduce forces into hostilities if there were an emergency "created by an attack upon the United States."[10]

Thus, here again we see that the President possesses constitutional powers, reinforced by the Congress of the United States, to make the judgments (1) that the United States deploy nuclear weapons and (2) that the President may respond to attacks upon the United States with nuclear weapons. In terms of constitutional analysis, we have a case one situation—the total power of the United States supporting these decisions.

Several other constitutional issues have been raised by Professor Miller that deserve comment. One is the relevance of Article I, section 8, clause 10 of the Constitution—the power of Congress to "define and punish . . . Offenses against the Law of Nations." It has been used to outlaw assault against ambassadors, counterfeiting of foreign currency, and piracies. One can find all of these offenses in the criminal code because of this constitutional provision. Congress has passed the necessary statutes to create these offenses.[11] But Congress has never enacted a statute to punish the use of nuclear weapons by the armed forces of the United States. Perhaps this is what Professor Miller really wants. Under this theory, we would have a very interesting case three situation (the power of the President minus the power of the Congress).

Professor Miller seeks to bypass the lack of legislation on this subject by asking "Can Congress neglect to exercise a delegated power?"[12] The short and unequivocal answer is yes, and Professor Miller should understand that. Congress has no obligation to pass every law it might conceivably pass under all clauses of the Constitution. No case under any clause of the Constitution suggests that a law is as good as passed merely because Congress might have passed it, or ought to have passed it. In fact, the closest authority that I can find for that proposition appears in Gilbert and Sullivan's operetta, *The Mikado*. The Mikado, the Emperor of Japan, had ordered that an execution take place in the town of Titipu or else the city would be reduced in rank to a mere village. The villagers therefore reported that an execution had taken place. When it turned out that there had been none and that something of a fraud had been committed, Ko-Ko, speaking to the Mikado explained it all thusly:

> When your Majesty says, "Let a thing be done," it's as good as done—practically it *is* done—because your Majesty's will is law. Your Majesty says, "Kill a gentleman," and a gentleman is told off to be killed. Consequently, that gentleman is as good as dead—practically he *is* dead—and if he is dead, why not say so?[13]

Professor Miller cannot argue that simply because he proclaims that Congress has power to ban nuclear weapons that therefore it is as if Congress had *in fact* banned them; unless, of course, he believes himself, or perhaps the Supreme Court, endowed with the imperial powers of the Mikado.

In real life one must instead look to what Congress has actually done. Congress *has* passed legislation, but that legislation is designed to make sure that the Executive does *not*, by itself, give up the nuclear arsenal that Congress has created. Thus, in the Arms Control and Disarmament Act, Congress has *expressly* provided that:

no action shall be taken under this or any other law that will obligate the United States to disarm or to reduce or to limit the Armed Forces or armaments of the United States, except pursuant to the treaty-making power of the President under the Constitution or unless authorized by further affirmative legislation by the Congress of the United States."[14]

Congress made sure that it would not wake up one morning and be surprised by the headline: "NO NUKES."

Professor Miller also raises the issue as to whether international law is part of the laws of the land that the President must, under Article II, faithfully execute.[15] He states that no one has explicated the meaning of the word "laws" and that it requires no large mental jump to include international law *norms* under Article II. Being an international lawyer I know that new norms can sometimes arrive as quickly as a mushroom cloud can form over the beach, but even if a new norm banning nuclear weapons should be developed, the courts have made clear when and how such a norm would become part of our domestic legal system. This issue is not, as the paper suggests, a matter of first impression.

As long ago as 1814, in *Armitz Brown v. United States,*[16] Chief Justice Marshall had occasion to discuss the relationship between international custom and the war powers. He pointed out that the usage of the law of nations is a guide which the sovereign follows or abandons *at his will.* It, "like other precepts of morality, of humanity, and even of wisdom, is addressed to the judgment of the sovereign; and although it cannot be disregarded by him, without obloquy, yet," he said, "it may be disregarded."[17]

Subsequently, the Supreme Court, in *The Paquete Habana,*[18] a prize case from the Spanish-American War, handed down a decision widely recognized as the leading statement on when international law applies domestically. During the war President McKinley had proclaimed a blockade of Cuba. In the proclamation he said that the blockade should be carried out "in pursuance of the laws of the United States *and the law of nations applicable to such cases.*"[19] Prize cases, such as this one, review the legality of a capture made during wartime; the capture in this case was of a small Cuban fishing boat.

The text of the proclamation, mandating obedience to the law of nations, gave the Supreme Court an opening to review in great detail all of the precedents, starting in 1403, about whether small fishing boats like the *Habana* could be captured in wartime. It concluded that honest fishermen peacefully bringing in fresh fish were exempt from capture.

The Court said, in language that is often quoted, that "international law is part of our law," but it also said that courts would apply it only where there was "no controlling *executive* or *legislative* act or judicial decision."[20] As the Court noted, it could rely on international law "in the absence of any treaty or *other public act*"[21] of the government in relation to the matter. In its decision the court thus made clear that if the President had, as an act of military necessity, "expressly authorized"[22] the seizure of similar fishing boats, this would have been a *controlling executive act,* taking precedence over international norms to the contrary, which would have *bound the court.* (Similarly, had the President *banned* the seizure of fishing boats that would have been the law of the case and would have concluded the matter as far as the court was concerned.) Had Congress legislated on the subject or had there been a treaty, that also would have taken precedence over customary international law under our constitutional system.

Thus, even assuming, for the sake of argument, that there is an international law "norm" against the use of nuclear weapons, it cannot, under our law as set down by our highest court, displace the acts taken by Congress and the President under their constitutional powers.[23]

What Professor Miller seems to want is *not* a continuation of legal tradition within any of the rules previously recognized, but a decision to disarm without regard to the Constitution or laws of the United States.

NOTES

1. This paper does not explore the side issues, addressed by others, of whether a court would hear or decide such cases. All three branches of government take the same oath to uphold the Constitution. Thus, if the Executive were persuaded that use of nuclear weapons was unconstitutional, it should abandon their use, whether or not the question could be litigated.

2. *See* Miller, Nuclear Weapons and Constitutional Law, 7 Nova L.J. 21 (1982), *reprinted in* Nuclear Weapons and Law (A.S. Miller & M. Feinrider eds. 1984).

3. Youngstown Sheet & Tube Co. v. Sawyer, 343 U.S. 579, 634 (1952).

4. The Supreme Court followed the Jackson opinion closely in upholding the hostage agreement with Iran, noting that both parties agreed that it "brings together as much combination of analysis and common sense as there is in this area." Dames & Moore v. Regan, 453 U.S. 654 (1981).

5. 343 U.S. at 635-38 (emphasis added).

6. In fact the information had been kept from Truman when he was a Senator. L. Giovannitti & F. Freed, The Decision to Drop the Bomb 27-28 (1965). The funds for the venture were disguised in the federal budget. G. Thomas & M. Witts, Enola Gay at x (1978).

7. Despite this frequent participation, some have questioned, as a policy matter, the quality of congressional review. *See, e.g.,* H. Kissinger, Nuclear Weapons and Foreign Policy 412-16 (1957).

8. 2 M. Farrand, The Records of the Federal Convention of 1787 at 318 (1974).

9. *Id.*

10. 50 U.S.C. § 1541(c), 87 Stat. 555.

11. *See* 18 U.S.C. §§ 1116, 478-83, 1651.

12. Miller, *supra* note 2, at 32.

13. W. S. Gilbert & A. Sullivan, The Mikado, Act II, *in* The Complete Plays of Gilbert & Sullivan (The Modern Library, Random House, undated) at 399 (emphasis in original).

14. 11 U.S.C. § 2573. There are some historical examples of arms limitation agreements by Executive action alone based on the power of the President as chief executive and commander-in-chief. *See* W. McClure, International Executive Agreements 122-23 (1941); Bunn, Missile Limitation: By Treaty or Otherwise?, 70 Colum. L. Rev. 1, 27-30 (1970); Levitan, Executive Agreements: A Study of the Executive in the Control of the Foreign Relations of the United States, 25 Nw. U. L. Rev. 364, 376 (1940). The Executive has not, however, challenged this provision as a restriction on its powers since its enactment in 1961. Congress was concerned that its own constitutional powers to raise and maintain armed forces, Art. I, § 8, might be compromised by a President acting on his own. 107 Cong. Rec. 20293, 20308 (1961). These powers oᶠ Congress were inserted in the Constitution as a reaction to the English experience ᴡhere the King alone could raise and maintain armies and navies. Constitution of the United States of America: Analysis and Interpretation, S. Doc. No. 82, 92d Cong., 2d Sess. 329 (1972). The Framers did not, of course, fear that the President might disperse forces that Congress had raised. Thus, the present situation is quite different from that which motivated the original constitutional provision. The placement of the ultimate power of decision in Congress seems clear, however. *Cf.* Ex parte Milligan, 71 U.S. 2, 139 (1866).

15. *See* Miller, *supra* note 2, at 33; *see also* Feinrider, International Law as Law of the Land: Another Constitutional Constraint on Use of Nuclear Weapons, 7 Nova L.J. 103 (1982), *reprinted in* Nuclear Weapons and Law (A. S. Miller & M. Feinrider eds. 1984).

16. 12 U.S. (8 Cranch) 110 (1814).

17. *Id.* at 128.

18. 175 U.S. 677 (1900).

19. *Id.* at 712 (emphasis added).

20. *Id.* at 700 (emphasis added).

21. *Id.* at 708 (emphasis added).

22. *Id.* at 711.

23. This discussion only addresses the issue raised by Professor Miller as to whether international norms are law that must be "faithfully executed" under Article II, § 3 of the Constitution. It does not deal with possible violations of international law.

The Restatement of Foreign Relations Law of the United States, Revised Tent. Draft No. 1 (1980). Section 135, Reporters' Note 5, recognizes that the President has the power to disregard rules of international law when acting within his constitutional power and says that the courts will not compel him to observe customary law although the draft *Restatement* also maintains that customary norms are laws in the Article II sense. This seems to be a contradiction in terms. *See* Tag v. Rogers, 267 F.2d 664, 666 (D.C. Cir. 1959), *cert. denied,* 362 U.S. 904 (1960) ("it has long been settled in the United States that the federal courts are bound to recognize any one of the three sources of law [treaty, statute, or constitutional provision] as superior to the canons of international law.")

23.
The President, the Constitution and Nuclear Weapons*

Thomas M. Franck**

We need to analyze the possibility of constitutional constraints on the President's ability to resort to use of nuclear weapons in terms of three issues:

1. whether the Constitution has anything to say about the right of a President to use nuclear weapons;
2. whether the Constitution has anything to say about presidential war-making; and,
3. whether the Constitution has anything to say about the power of Congress, if it so chose, to restrict the power of the President to make war and/or the power to employ nuclear weapons.

Professor Miller strives mightily, in his stimulating paper,[1] to find an affirmative answer to the first of these questions: does the Constitution have anything to say about the President's *choice of weapons* in a situation of legitimate hostilities. Let me emphasize that this question, both literally and in historical practice, is treated differently in constitutional theory from the second question: does the Constitution limit the President's power to initiate hostilities, whatever his choice of weapons.

I must confess that I do not find myself convinced by the "right to life" argument adduced by Professor Miller from the spirit and penumbra of that long-suffering document, the Constitution. *If*, and that's a big "if," the United States is lawfully engaged in hostilities, it is within the power of the President to determine the strategic military means by which the war is to be prosecuted.

That proposition has the support of the black-letter law of the Constitution's "Commander-in-Chief" clause, which was written precisely to mend

---

* This essay is based on remarks delivered at the Conference on Nuclear Weapons and Law held at Nova University Center for the Study of Law on February 5, 1983.

** Professor of Law and Director, Center for International Studies, New York University School of Law.

the perceived deficiencies of war-making by the Continental Congress. It is clarified by the founders' debate on the clause, which involved an informed and deliberate choice between giving the Congress the power to "make," that is, to manage, or merely to "declare" war.

It also has the support of an unbroken line of historical acquiescence by Congress. In 1867, Congress tried and failed to remove certain powers from the first President Johnson and to vest them in General Grant—a failed attempt rarely repeated and only to the same non-effect. Even in peacetime these efforts have not been successful, even when they were only ranged against the more ephemeral presidential power to conduct foreign affairs. Nothing happened when President Roosevelt stationed U.S. troops in Greenland and Iceland in violation of the Selective Service Act after the fall of Denmark in 1940. Note that these conflicts pit the President's plenary powers against not just the Constitution but the Constitution underscored with specific congressional legislation.

Above all, it has the support of common sense. For the United States to tell the Russians that the Constitution forbids our Head of State recourse to nuclear weapons if we are legitimately at war is tantamount to unilateral disarmament. How tantamount depends upon the speaker. If the speaker is the Supreme Court, I believe it *would be wholly* tantamount to a policy of saying to the Kremlin: "come and get it." If the speaker is one, or a group, of distinguished unofficial legal authorities, the effect is less tantamount because the Russians may discount their views as, presumably, would the President. But it sends a confusing signal, at best, to the other side. Whether such a signal advances or hurts the chances of avoiding a war depends on whether you think we or they are more likely to start one.

If some Russians, or whomever, were to take seriously (or *mistake* seriously) the argument that the Constitution totally bars the President from using nuclear weapons, they might feel less inhibited about pursuing their aims with force—with or without use of nuclear weapons. Then what if they found out, as they probably would, that the prognosis was wrong? But I am not here going to explore the relationship between deterrence theory and law, except to say that the worst of all possible strategic balances is one in which you signal the other side that you won't react to a particular initiative and then you do—as when Dean Acheson, in a public speech, drew a defensive perimeter in the Asian Pacific that did not include South Korea just before the North Koreans struck, or as when the British in 1982 withdrew their only naval vessel from duty in the Falklands.

I believe that any signal suggesting a constitutional restriction on the power of the Commander-in-Chief to use nuclear, or any other, weapons in an otherwise lawful war, is dangerous precisely because it is an incorrect prediction not only of the law but also of the potential consequences of aggression against us or our allies in Western Europe and Japan.

That brings us to the next issue: does the Constitution circumscribe the power of the President to *initiate* hostilities? The answer is that the

Constitution prohibits the initiation of hostilities by a President acting without Congress in certain circumstances. These circumstances do not—with one important exception to be discussed later—include the President's choice of weapons. I do believe that there is such a thing as an unconstitutional war, at least in legal theory. The *Holtzman* case[2] suggests that courts can understand this, although they may not know exactly what to do about it.

But I find nothing to support the theory that a President's use of force which is not otherwise unconstitutional can become unconstitutional because of the weapons he chooses to employ. Again, I think there is one caveat to that statement which I will discuss later.

Let me emphasize that asking whether presidential war-making may be unconstitutional is not the same as asking whether the Constitution protects or prohibits his nuclear first-strike option. I agree with the senatorial draft version of the War Powers Act, that the President may use force—any kind of force—when Congress has declared war, when the United States or its citizens have been attacked, or when war has otherwise been made upon us, or is about to be, by a foreign power. In other circumstances, presidential war-making is unconstitutional. The historic record to support this senatorial enumeration is well developed by Professor Louis Henkin[3] and Judge Abraham Sofaer,[4] as well as by the staff of the Senate Foreign Relations Committee.

But, as always, there is a grey area: that blessed hunting preserve of the legal scholar. That brings me back to the confusing difference between a nuclear first-strike option, and the initiation of hostilities with nuclear weapons. A first-strike option merely implies first use of nuclear weapons, which could either initiate hostilities or else be an escalation of already on-going hostilities. The initiation of hostilities with nuclear weapons is a narrower concept which implies not only first-use, but the offensive or initiatory first-use in a situation where armed hostilities did not already pre-exist.

As you will by now have surmised, I believe that nothing in the Constitution, the practice (at the time of Hiroshima and Nagasaki or thereafter), or the War Powers Act supports a distinction between the powers of the President to use either nuclear or non-nuclear weapons as an exercise of his power to *make*, i.e., conduct war as the Commander-in-Chief. But the Constitution, the practice, and the War Powers Act do at least suggest that he may not, except in very limited circumstances, alone *initiate* hostilities: whether by use of conventional or nuclear forces. But note that I am speaking of aggressive war-making, the initiation of hostilities by a President, and not of first-use of nuclear weapons in circumstances where hostilities have been initiated by someone else.

The grey area is created by two factors: the recent history of presidential war-making and by the vagueness of the word "initiate."

In the twentieth century, presidents have used force to initiate hostilities in circumstances where they were not merely responding to an act of armed hostility against us. Korea is the salient case and, if the Pentagon Papers really did show that the Tonkin Gulf incident was provoked by us, then so also was the Vietnam War. The latter also shows up the fragile fabric of facts on which turns the constitutionally crucial difference between presidential "initiating" and "responding to" hostilities.

These instances do not prove, as Nicholas Katzenbach once insisted, that congressional action has become irrelevant to constitutional use of force by the President. Congress did act to endorse both uses of force.

There is another sense in which the word "initiate" creates problems of line-drawing. Suppose the President is certain that we are about to be attacked and decides to use force pre-emptively. Is he acting unconstitutionally by failing to get congressional authority, or is he acting in "anticipatory self-defense"? Is he "initiating" or "responding"?

The issue is comparable to another: whether he would be acting within or outside the spirit of article 51 of the U.N. Charter which prohibits the use of self-defense except against an actual armed attack.

Can any light be shed on this grey area? I think so.

To begin with, it should be noted that the Constitution is not a blank page on this question. Article I, section 10, says that states of the union may not engage in war "unless actually invaded, or in such imminent Danger as will not admit of delay." It is inconceivable that the authors of the Constitution meant, as an unenunciated by-product of the congressional war power, to deny the President the very power to initiate that they had given the Governors of the States. Rather, Article I, section 10, seems to me a pretty good effort to define what was then, and remains today, the popular understanding of the right of nations to self-defense as permitted by international usage. It answers the question: When is an anticipatory initiation really a constructive response, in which case the President's unfettered commander's power comes into its own?

Well, not quite. International law, as pointed out in Professor Feinrider's excellent work,[5] also has a voice. It enunciates the concept of proportionality. Paraphrased, this says "don't swat a fly with a mallet."

My problem is that the Constitution seems to leave this choice to the President, whenever we are lawfully engaged in hostilities. While international law may help fill the Constitution's interstices, it cannot repeal its intent by deleting or altering the President's power to "make," i.e., conduct war.

But perhaps proportionality can be introduced more narrowly, not to limit the Commander-in-Chief's constitutionally unfettered choice of weapons, but to help define the circumstances in which the President, without congressional declaration of war, may strike first. It can be used to flush out the bare-boned limitation on plenary war-making power. It is surely limited to situations when we are "in such imminent Danger as will not admit of delay."

International law informs the Constitution that, today, this means that nuclear weapons may not be used to preempt anything except an imminent attack by nuclear force, so long as the threat, in other words, can be dealt with in other ways. The Presidential use of nuclear weapons to neutralize Cuba during the missile crisis would have been unconstitutional and grounds for impeachment because there was no evidence that the Soviet missiles were ready to be used against us.

This brings me to my final point: does the Constitution permit Congress an anticipatory legislative role in determining whether, when, and how nuclear weapons may in future contingencies be used by the President? Put another way, may Congress write a guide to the grey area? My answer to that question is evident from what I have already said. Despite the precedent of Franklin Roosevelt's dispatch of troops in 1940 to places prohibited by Congress, I believe Congress shares with the President the power to set policy governing the initiative (as opposed to reactive) use of the armed forces; forces which Congress "raises" and the deployment of weapons systems for which Congress votes appropriations. I believe this power over deployment, when we have not been attacked, is clearly in the grey area of concurrent powers and that it would be perfectly constitutional to enact a congressional rider stating, for example, that nuclear weapons may not be used by the President except in the event of a congressional declaration of war or an attack, or apprehended attack, made against either the United States or on a country for the defense of which the United States had assumed legal responsibility by a ratified treaty or congressionally authorized executive agreement.

A comparable limitation on weapon and troop deployment was contained in numerous authorizations and appropriations which, toward the end of the Vietnam War, forbade the use of U.S. forces "in, over or off" Indochina and in laws, still in effect, forbidding clandestine military activities in Angola and Nicaragua. These laws were signed by the President. Alas, the record of obedience to the laws is mixed—they were willfully disobeyed in the *Mayaguez* rescue and are probably being bent even now in Nicaragua. But a good case can be made for their constitutionality. And we would not be sending misleading signals to Moscow if Congress were to prohibit the President from doing what only a madman would contemplate: using nuclear weapons to initiate aggressive, unprovoked hostilities. Deterrence does not require the Presidium or the President to be in doubt about that.

The utility, the efficacy of such legislation is rooted in the doctrine enunciated by Mr. Justice Jackson in the *Steel Seizure Case*:[6] that, in the grey area, presidential discretionary power is at its greatest when backed by a congressional delegation, at its middling in the event of congressional silence, and at its nadir in the face of a congressional enactment which precludes the exercise of presidential discretion. Let us opt for the attainable nadir.

Which leads me to a further point. Whether or not a use of nuclear weapons is unconstitutional in the sense of not proportional or not prescient, depends ultimately on strategic and political circumstances. If the other side has deployed overwhelming conventional force against the United States, it may leave the Commander-in-Chief with only two options—both of which, I believe, would then be fully within his constitutional authority: to await attack and then surrender or to initiate a preemptive nuclear first-strike.

Which he does would depend on the politics of those making or shaping the decision.

But the real effort should not go into trying to preshape the outcome of this improbable doomsday scenario now: certainly not by inventing an answer and planting it between the lines of the Constitution.

The real effort should be directed toward making the choice to respond with nuclear weapons not merely improbable but unnecessary and thus clearly not prescient. This can only be done by strengthening our conventional capability so that it, rather than the nuclear stockpile, becomes the effective deterrent.

McGeorge Bundy and George Kennan, et al., are fervently cited for their proposal in *Foreign Affairs* that we take the "no first use pledge."[7] But those who cheer this proposal usually fall silent when Bundy and Kennan expound its inevitable concomitant: the need for a more convincing conventional deterrent.

Why is this passed over in silence? Is it because the movement for renunciation of nuclear weaponry consists of a loose coalition of four factions? First, there are those who, like Bundy, think there is a danger from the Soviets but that it can be met by more reliance, although not exclusive reliance, on conventional force deterrence. Second, some don't think that there is a problem: that we are not in any danger from the Soviets, who are seen either as benevolent or as mired in their own failures. And, third, there are some who concede that the Russians might take advantage of a decisive military (nuclear and conventional) advantage but believe that it is better to be red than dead, even if the mere embracing of this pose helps to force that choice upon us. Finally, fourth, we have those who think that we would just be better off under a different system.

In the days of the anti-Vietnam War movement, it did not seem to matter much why a person was against the war. We could all roughly agree that the conflict was bad for America. But the nuclear ban movement is different. Whether the President is some day faced with nothing but a last clear chance to defeat a foreign aggressor by recourse to a nuclear preemptive strike will depend on whether he was denied or given a credible non-nuclear alternative to defeat. That means a conventional weapons system which, in the words of the Constitution, does "admit of delay" in escalation.

Congress and the mainstream of the nuclear ban movement, even at the risk of losing the fringe, have an obligation to ensure that such an alternative is timely and credibily made manifest. The demand of good lawyering is to seek to ensure that the questions Professor Miller raises need never be resolved in an actual instance.

NOTES

1. *See* Miller, Nuclear Weapons and Constitutional Law, 7 Nova L.J. 21 (1982), *reprinted in* Nuclear Weapons and Law (A. S. Miller & M. Feinrider eds. 1984).

2. *See* Holtzman v. Richardson, 361 F. Supp. 544 (E.D. N.Y. 1973), *supplemented by* Holtzman v. Schlesinger, 361 F. Supp. 553 (E.D. N.Y. 1973) (granting summary judgment, holding U.S. military forces to be enjoined from engaging in combat operations in Cambodia, but postponing issuance of an injunction to allow defendant to apply for stay); *rev'd* 484 F.2d 1307 (2d Cir. 1973); *application to vacate stay,* 414 U.S. 1304 (1973); *reapplication to vacate stay,* 414 U.S. 1306 (1973); *application for stay,* 414 U.S. 1321 (1973); *cert. denied,* 416 U.S. 936 (1974).

3. *See, e.g.,* L. Henkin, Foreign Affairs and the Constitution (1972).

4. *See, e.g.,* A. Sofaer, War, Foreign Affairs and Constitutional Power: The Origins (1976); Sofaer, The Presidency, War and Foreign Affairs: Practice Under the Framers, L. & Contemp. Soc. Probs., Sp. 1976, at 12.

5. *See* Feinrider, International Law as Law of the Land: Another Constitutional Constraint on Use of Nuclear Weapons, 7 Nova L.J. 103 (1982), *reprinted in* Nuclear Weapons and Law (A. S. Miller & M. Feinrider eds. 1984).

6. *See* Youngstown Sheet & Tube Co. v. Sawyer, 343 U.S. 579 (1952) (Jackson, J., concurring).

7. *See* Bundy, Kennan, McNamara & Smith, Nuclear Weapons and the Atlantic Alliance, 60 Foreign Aff. 753 (1982).

24.

A Commentary on *Nuclear Weapons and Constitutional Law*[*]

Fletcher N. Baldwin, Jr.[**]

The issue before us is the relationship of the Constitution of the United States to the manufacture and use of nuclear weapons. Perhaps we can find that relationship by examining specific provisions in the Constitution, though some would argue that such an examination is precluded by the war-making powers found in Article I, Section 8, clauses 11 through 16.

I'm not so sure we are talking here about the war-making powers. General Eisenhower planning and carrying out the invasion of France would be construed a culmination of the war-making power. I think we are talking about annihilation that isn't covered in Article I or Article II. Annihilation is somewhat different from carrying on a war; when we engage in war we expect to win. Therefore, it would seem that it's more a task of ours to try to identify some of the areas where we the people might have some input and further to examine various ways in which a platform might be constitutionally constructed so that we might be able to call for a halt to the madness of the nuclear arms race.

Though there are many lobbying groups in Washington, we as lawyers tend to be more comfortable in the courtroom. Yet, except for the various civil rights movements, or labor movements, we've never really had a very effective platform in the courtroom open to the people to articulate their real hopes and fears. So what I'd like to do is first of all identify some of the problems I see and then briefly respond to Professor Miller's thesis.[1]

In point of fact, I think that our courts, especially the Supreme Court of the United States, when utilizing what is available generally under the Constitution, and what is available specifically to them under Article III, as a guide, can't even solve the problems that they are paid to solve. They can't even solve domestic problems, much less the nuclear proliferation issue.

---

[*] This essay is based on remarks delivered at the Conference on Nuclear Weapons and Law held at Nova University Center for the Study of Law on February 5, 1983.

[**] Professor of Law, University of Florida, Spessard L. Holland Law Center.

The tasks well-suited for the court, one would think, deal with equal protection, with the rights of poor people, with due process and the exclusionary rule, yet the courts are very ill-equipped to solve, much less identify, even those basic problems. So when you talk about the court and constitutionalizing the nuclear weapons issue, please keep in mind what court you're talking about. Perhaps what the subject matter here should be is not so much the Constitution and nuclear proliferation, but the Court and how we go about selecting our Justices and creating an intellectual hierarchy available to the appointments process.

The Supreme Court is now, as I think it has almost always been, with some brief detours, a very defensive Court; defensive in its posture and defensive about its power. Our Court throws words around such as comity and federalism in order to avoid taking jurisdiction over cases. Thus, they leave matters of grave national concern to state courts, courts that are equally ill-equipped to deal with most of the constitutional issues that people in good faith bring to them. The United States Supreme Court won't give standing in many areas; most recently, for example, the Court decided to narrow standing so that we can no longer go into court when we are challenging the giveaway of government property to church groups to train ministers of the Bible. The Court, indeed, has tried, with some success, to eliminate parts of our Constitution. The thinking of a majority appears to be that sections of that compact deserve very little respect. Once when I was in the Supreme Court the Chief Justice looked at me, and said "Why are you wasting this Court's time with a technicality?" The technicality he was referring to was the double jeopardy provision of the Fifth Amendment. He should have said "technicalities" because I would like to have talked about the fourth amendment exclusionary rule as well if he'd given me the time. But the concept of technicalities as articulated by the Chief Justice, incredibly, is shared by a slim majority of his colleagues. It does not seem to matter that it is the Bill of Rights we are talking about.

I have little hope that the present Supreme Court, and I'm afraid to say it will be with us until the turn of the century, is going to hear cases like those suggested by Professor Miller. The Court is ill-equipped intellectually, procedurally, and emotionally, to hear this type of case which would require creative thinking to an extreme degree. I would suggest, in fact, that the Justices, instead of wanting to deal with the real issues plaguing our society, seem to have a death wish with respect to certain provisions of the Constitution.

Nevertheless, it has always amazed me how in times of extreme crisis in this country, people, non-lawyers mainly, continue to have faith in the Court and continue to press the Court. Indeed, as you well know, when President Roosevelt tried to "pack" the Supreme Court, it was the people who in effect prevented him from doing it. The faith that people have in the Court, I believe, was reflected in the civil rights movement. People who simply continue to have faith in the judicial structure are telling us that they want, no, they demand an arena. They want a safety valve, if nothing else. They want to air their political or social views, and they can't afford high-priced lobbying groups. But they do need a platform and, indeed, in some arenas they are given one. Some lower court judges, for example, are quite receptive to original concepts; lower court platforms are often rendered moot on appeal, however. But at least the people do not want to feel politically powerless about nuclear weapons; an issue of enormous magnitude, and to argue what has gone before us, to say what the Constitution tells us now, I think is terribly irrelevant. I think what Professor Miller is trying to say is that we have to begin to at least rethink the matter and begin to examine whether or not it is worthwhile to ensure that people have a judicial platform in which to attempt constitutionally to stem the tide of nuclear weapons growth. I sometimes wonder if the promise is more important, cosmetically, if nothing else, than the ultimate goal that they are seeking to achieve. So it would seem, at least initially, that if our Court is to continue or at least begin to serve what some authors used to call the republican schoolmaster role, it must open up the doors. It must at least allow persons the opportunity to express their creative positions in favor of what Professor Ball has called the constitutionality of this nuclear weapons issue.[2]

It is important for the nuclear weapons issue to be raised in all branches of government, whether Article I, Article II, or Article III. At present it is being raised in the Article I and Article II branches, leaving the Article III branch—the courts—completely isolated and completely free from any consideration of nuclear annihilation or holocaust. It seems to me that if the Court can help bring down a President or give people the right to have their vote counted or eliminate fifty-one years of legislative veto practice it can surely consider the "right to survive" as a due process or penumbra guarantee in the Constitution.

Historically, constitutional law has been viewed by commentators and certainly by some members of the Court itself as a dynamic function of creativity in this country. Constitutional law is the dynamic process by which we create constitutional rights. This Court, like every previous Court, at least beginning with that of the fourth Chief Justice, John Marshall, has always taken the position, whether intended or not, that it will deal with constitutional issues in a creative manner. I frankly believe most of the creative decisions coming out of the present Court, especially in the realm of the first, fourth, fifth, and sixth amendment rights, with some notable exceptions such as *Swann v. Charlotte-Mecklenburg Board of Education,*[3] the school busing case, are negative creative decisions. But there are many decisions, going back to 1803, in which the Court has been rather creative because the language of our six thousand-odd word Constitution is, to say the least, nebulous. *Marbury v. Madison,*[4] a case to which all those discussing nuclear weapons and the Constitution must in effect allude, is certainly one of the more creative decisions of the Court, but, then again, so was *Plessy v. Ferguson,*[5] the case that in effect segregated parts of our citizenry. *Brown v. Board of Education*[6] was attacked as a creative decision by persons who merely wanted their own people on the Court so that they could articulate creative decisions in their own way. *Miranda,*[7] I think, was a creative decision, a response to a real need. There are a lot of creative decisions that the Court has decided, *Roe v. Wade,*[8] for example, the abortion case; the list is endless.

In the foreign affairs field there are also decisions that the Court has rendered, whether creative or not, that certainly have developed at least the Court's theme for our role as a nation in foreign affairs. In this regard, I point to the concurring opinion of Justice Jackson in *Youngstown Sheet & Tube*[9] and to *Curtiss-Wright Export Corp.*[10] In the latter case, Justice Sutherland said that as far as foreign affairs are concerned, we should leave it to the executive branch of government. We don't want the courts stepping in and embarrassing the nation. Let the Congress and the Executive fight it out; it's a political battle.

Nevertheless, the Court has always been careful to point out that where the foreign affairs doctrine impacts upon domestic constitutional rights of persons, the Court and the Constitution are quite capable of analyzing and dealing with those foreign affairs—at least to the point that they affect individual rights. See, for example, *Reid v. Covert.*[11] There are indeed cases in which the Court does delve into foreign affairs. There are cases in which the Court does deal with the powers of the President or the powers of Congress where those powers affect people as the Court interprets the rights of those people under the Constitution.

Since *Marbury v. Madison* and Chief Justice Marshall it would seem that the Court has been the primary agency responsible for keeping the Constitution abreast of the times. Up to the present Chief Justice the Court has given life to the Constitution. Any time an issue is based upon observable facts and the issue also develops a constitutional principle, whether that constitutional principle is outlined in the Constitution itself, the Court can, and indeed does, at times, consider the matter. The Court does have the power constitutionally to engage in creative implementation of rights. As long as one develops the creative thought, the Court at times is willing to listen. *Roe v. Wade,* some commentators tell us, was a creative amendment to the Bill of Rights. *Dombrowski v. Pfister,*[12] and *Baker v. Carr,*[13] both chilling effects cases in a sense, involved the Court as a court of final resort. The parties had in reality nowhere else to turn.

So it would seem to me that all Professor Miller is trying to say is that Article III indeed does permit review of matters moral, social, or political in nature and there is precedent for such a role for the Court. The Court considers moral matters all the time: the abortion case one might suggest is a moral matter; prostitution; the death penalty. As long as the issues that are presented to the Court come within a theory that is fairly inferrable from the Constitution in general, or from the Bill of Rights in particular, there is a fair chance that the Court has the capability to consider the matter. So what we come down to, if I read Professor Miller's paper correctly, is simply trying to find the proper constitutional machinery. I don't think this involves the power of the President or the power of Congress, but the power of people to say:

> Hey, wait a minute. We have certain rights in the Bill of Rights or maybe in the first three words of the Preamble to the Constitution which says "We the People," and we would like them analyzed in this Court. We'd like the Court to consider the issue based upon our perception and our founders' perception of the purpose behind this Constitution, unique though it was when it was first drafted and put before the various states. Certainly one of the main purposes was that people contract to live together in peace without fear of their government destroying them.

The Court under due process of law has directed itself historically, substantially, and procedurally to assess whether or not governmental acts, either legislative or executive, affect individuals in a way that comports with domestic freedoms as we understand them. The freedom to live is certainly one of them. Whatever those domestic freedoms may be, it seems to me that the due process clause is big enough and strong enough and has sufficient foundations substantially and procedurally to at least give persons a platform to develop whatever rights they think might be implicated in a nuclear holocaust or a threatened nuclear holocaust. Domestic freedoms and the freedom to live free from fear of annihilation perhaps predate the Constitution, as do some other aspects of constitutional rights. If, indeed, certain natural rights do predate the Constitution, then it is self-evident that they are much more important than the Constitution itself. If they don't predate, if the right to life (or the right not to be annihilated) doesn't predate the Constitution, then it is surely a penumbral right, flowing throughout the Constitution itself. I would certainly not suggest or be foolish enough to suggest that it is found directly in the Constitution, because indeed it is not. I think, however, that had the framers thought it necessary they certainly would have placed it in.

The problem is whether or not we will have the platform available to use, that is, whether we have standing to get into the Court. I think there is sufficient theory at least that would support that type of standing. One could suggest that *Bivens v. Six Unknown Named Agents*,[14] the case that gave people standing directly under the fourth amendment to challenge activities of federal officers, might be a starting point to safeguard these other guarantees that we would like to develop or add to our Constitution.

So a decision on the constitutionality of nuclear proliferation is a decision worthy of judicial consideration. It is a matter for judicial consideration if for no other reason than it would be the people who will be primarily affected by a presidential act of pushing the wrong button, a button given to him by a generous and unthinking Congress.

We must have a platform in which to raise and question these governmental decisions that affect us all. I do not by any means suggest that having developed a platform the Court will decide that it is unconstitutional for the government to continue its rush toward universal annihilation. For indeed, if the Court does, I would suggest, no one would pay any attention. Certainly the other two branches of the government wouldn't pay any attention to the Court—they rarely do. But at least the constitutional debate would be renewed. It seems to me that having the debate in so heady a forum is all Professor Miller is suggesting: that there be a platform available so that people will have their views expressed. Perhaps then governments might come to their senses. I would suggest that the civil rights movement created that platform and resulted in governmental sanity. No matter what the Court did in the civil rights cases—which really was very little—at least Congress in 1964 got busy—finally—and put together a Civil Rights Act,[15] an act that was an attempt to implement what was happening or about to happen in our court system. So I think at least Professor Miller's call to begin to think about the issue is one that we cannot dismiss and indeed should make a serious effort to implement regardless of the predicted results.

NOTES

1. *See* Miller, Nuclear Weapons and Constitutional Law, 7 Nova L.J. 21 (1982), *reprinted in* Nuclear Weapons and Law (A. S. Miller & M. Feinrider eds. 1984).

2. *See* Ball, Nuclear War: The End of Law, 7 Nova L.J. 53 (1982), *reprinted in* Nuclear Weapons and Law (A. S. Miller & M. Feinrider eds. 1984).

3. 402 U.S. 1 (1971).

4. 1 U.S. (1 Cranch) 137 (1803).

5. 163 U.S. 537 (1896).

6. 347 U.S. 483 (1954).

7. Miranda v. Arizona, 384 U.S. 436 (1966).

8. 410 U.S. 113 (1973).

9. Youngstown Sheet & Tube Co. v. Sawyer, 343 U.S. 579 (1952).

10. United States v. Curtiss-Wright Export Corp., 299 U.S. 304 (1936).

11. 354 U.S. 1 (1957).

12. 380 U.S. 479 (1965).

13. 369 U.S. 186 (1962).

14. 403 U.S. 388 (1971).

15. Civil Rights Act of 1964, Pub. L. No. 88-352, 78 Stat. 241 (*codified at* 42 U.S.C. § 1971 (1964)).

25.
In Brief Rejoinder*

Arthur Selwyn Miller

The editors of the *Nova Law Journal* have invited me to comment upon the responses that were received to my preliminary foray into the applicability of constitutional norms to nuclear weapons. I am happy to do so.[1] At the outset, I should like to express my deep appreciation to those who took time from their busy schedules to write responses, as well as the editors of this *Journal* for making the symposium possible. It is, I believe, the first attempt by a legal periodical to tackle from a constitutional standpoint what by all odds is the overriding moral and political (and thus constitutional) question of the day.

Lawyers of whatever specialty have until quite recent times ignored the problems attendant to the manufacture, storage, deployment and possible—even probable—use of weapons that threaten the very fabric of civilization as we know it. Now, however, two groups of lawyers have been formed—one with Boston headquarters and the other centered in New York City; members of the American Bar Association, as well as other bar associations, are beginning to focus upon the growing peril. That is all to the good: lawyers, as Professor Levinson suggests, can play an important role in the developing dialogue. They exemplify in modern version what Samuel Johnson said long ago: "Depend upon it, Sir, when any man knows he is to be hanged in a fortnight, it concentrates his mind wonderfully."[2] For the first time since Hiroshima and Nagasaki were all but obliterated in August, 1945, the minds of lawyers—some but far from all of them—are beginning to concentrate upon what Jonathan Schell has called "the fate of the earth."[3]

---

* Reprinted, with permission, from *Nova Law Journal*, Volume 7, Number 1 (1982).

1. Although mention will be made of several responses, this rejoinder is general in nature. It seeks to extend the argument, rather than to comment upon each of the responses in detail.

2. 6 J. BOSWELL, THE LIFE OF SAMUEL JOHNSON 309 (W. Crocker ed. 1846) (1st ed. London 1791).

3. J. SCHELL, THE FATE OF THE EARTH (1982).

The need, as Professor Dunne adumbrates, is for a "mutational change"[4] in our modes of thinking about constitutions and constitutionalism. If, as Paul Freund once observed, the Supreme Court is a theme that forces lawyers to become philosophers,[5] the very existence of nuclear weapons forces everyone, including lawyers, to think deeply about the nature of American constitutionalism. Professor Ball tells us that when Congress was delegated the "power to declare war," it did not include "the power to declare Armageddon."[6] Indeed, it does not. Nor does the President have such a power, now that he, because of long-standing Congressional ineptitude and pusillanimity, has become the person who can precipitate a nuclear holocaust. True enough, the President has the *ability* to engage in nuclear war, either by responding to external attack or by use of a first strike, but if constitutionalism means anything it must be taken to mean that such an ability cannot be equated with constitutional propriety. As Professor Jenkins reminds us, the central concept of *raison d'état* becomes irrelevant and inapplicable with nuclear weaponry, simply because the survival of the nation—the fundamental purpose of that silent constitutional principle—cannot be guaranteed.[7]

When the deep-thinkers of the national security establishment speak about nuclear war, they mention sooner or later what would be an "acceptable" number of Americans killed in such a war. The figure usually runs into tens of millions. Of course, the nuclear planners are making provision for the safety of key figures in government. A command center has been hollowed out of a hillside in Virginia, furnished with equipment and supplies and suitably protected. For ordinary Americans a "civil defense" program is envisaged (some $4.3 billion is allocated to it in the current budget). Cities will be evacuated, but no one quite seems to know how, say, the residents of New York or any other major city will survive. An official in the Pentagon has suggested that everyone should get a shovel, dig a hole, cover it with a couple of doors and throw three feet of dirt on top of it—after which a person or a family presumably will huddle in the hole until danger ceases. The

---

4. Dunne, *A Grenville Clark Hypothetical,* 7 Nova L.J. 167, 171 (1982).
5. P. Freund, On Understanding the Supreme Court 1 (1949).
6. Ball, *Nuclear War: The End of Law,* 7 Nova L.J. 53, 61 (1982).
7. Jenkins, *Admirable Ends — Ineffective Means,* 7 Nova L.J. 127 (1982).

absurdity of such a view requires no comment: It bespeaks a mind so dulled by computerized war games and thinking about the unthinkable that the person wallows in a swamp of consummate nonsense. Let no one fail to see the point: there is *no* escape for most Americans should nuclear war break out.

That does not mean, of course, that those who sit in positions of political power do not today and did not in the past toy with the use of nuclear weapons. To take the latter first, recently revealed documents tell us how very close the United States was to using atomic bombs in Indo-China as long ago as 1954—at the time when the French were being defeated at Dienbienphu.[8] That they were not used, either by American forces or by the French (who had obtained them from the United States), came from a decision taken not on humanitarian grounds but because of a fear of a worldwide public uproar. As for today, in August, 1982, Secretary of Defense Caspar Weinberger was busily engaged in trying to stifle—through representations to the media—the fact that the Reagan administration was prepared to fight a "protracted nuclear war."[9] Small wonder, therefore, that the "doomsday clock" on the cover of the *Bulletin of the Atomic Scientists* has moved from seven to four minutes to midnight.

Professor McDowell believes that the idea of a living Constitution "is ultimately at odds with the logic of the Contitution itself."[10] He of course has a full first amendment right to such a view. The fact that it runs contrary to the vast majority of constitutional scholars will not, and perhaps should not, deter him. How he can square his position with the development of constitutional law in the almost two centuries since 1789 remains completely mysterious. He misreads *McCulloch v. Maryland*,[11] and seems to think that Chief Justice Marshall's allusion to popular sovereignty in *Marbury v. Madison*[12] is the *ne plus ultra* of

---

8. *See* Marder, *When Ike Was Asked to Nuke Vietnam,* Wash. Post, Aug. 22, 1982, at Cl, col. 1.

9. *See* Halloran, *Weinberger Angered by Reports on War Strategy,* N.Y. Times, Aug. 24, 1982, at B8, col. 3; Wilson, *Weinberger Lobbies Editors on War Policy,* Wash. Post, Aug. 25, 1982, at A9, col. 1.

10. McDowell, *Nuclear Weapons: Unconstitutional or Just Unjust?,* 7 NOVA. L.J. 145, 146 (1982).

11. 17 U.S. (4 Wheat.) 316 (1819).

12. 5 U.S. (1 Cranch) 137 (1803).

understanding about "the" Constitution.[13] That just ain't so. The inescapable point, it seems to me, is that the *meaning* of the Constitution alters with the exigencies faced by succeeding generations of Americans—but the *words* remain the same. Each generation of Americans must undertake the task of writing its own constitution; that, at least, is the clear and unmistakable teaching of history. Professor McDowell does not like that; but he cannot gainsay it. The Constitution has always been relative to circumstances. To repeat Franz Neumann's point:

> No society in recorded history has even been able to dispense with political power. This is as true of liberalism as of absolutism, as true of laissez-faire as of an interventionist state. No greater disservice has been rendered to political science than the statement that the liberal state was a "weak" state. *It was precisely as strong as it needed to be in the circumstances.* It acquired substantial colonial empires, waged wars, held down internal disorders, and stablilzed itself over long periods of time.[14]

The relevant "circumstance" today is the imminence of nuclear holocaust. Those circumstances call, not for an expansion of governmental power but for the development of means by which government, in Madison's words, can be obliged "to control itself."[15] Professor Morris suggests that a constitutional judgment should be made that nuclear weapons "unreasonably jeopardize American well-being."[16] That is the language of due process, and opens still another argument for the applicability of constitutional norms to the circumstances that confront us.

Professor Alfange asserts that the *Duke Power*[17] case is relevant to the nuclear weapon issue.[18] I cannot agree with his conclusion; but

---

13.   McDowell, *supra* note 10, at 147. For a preliminary inquiry into the meaning of what the Constitution is, see Miller, *Toward a Definition of "The" Constitution,* ___ U. DAYTON L. REV. ___ (1983).

14.   F. NEUMANN, THE DEMOCRATIC AND THE AUTHORITARIAN STATE 8 (1957) (emphasis added).

15.   THE FEDERALIST No. 51, at 349 (J. Madison) (J. Cooke ed. 1961).

16.   Morris, *The Constitution and Nuclear Defense,* 7 NOVA L.J. 151, 164 (1982).

17.   Duke Power Co. v. Carolina Envtl. Study Group, 438 U.S. 59 (1978).

18.   Alfange, *Wisdom, Constitutionality, and Nuclear Weapons Policy,* 7 NOVA

would like to draw upon that Supreme Court decision, and particularly the opinion of Judge McMillan in *Carolina Environmental Study Group v. United States Atomic Energy Commission*[19] which was reversed by the Court. Environmentalists in North Carolina challenged the constitutionality of the Price-Anderson Act, setting monetary limits on the liability for damage resulting from a nuclear power plant. Judge McMillan ruled the statute unconstitutional, stating that "the destruction of the property or the lives of those affected by nuclear catastrophe without reasonable certainty that the victims will be justly compensated"[20] violated the fifth amendment.

The Supreme Court reversed—unanimously. Where, then, does that leave us? I maintain that we are left exactly where the plaintiffs were on March 31, 1977 when Judge McMillan issued his opinion. The two situations are not analogous. Chief Justice Warren Burger, speaking for the Court, employed a limited standard of review in what he perceived to be an economic regulation. He found that the Act was neither arbitrary nor irrational; thus it "passe[d] constitutional muster."[21] Burger also relied upon "an explicit congressional commitment to take further action to aid victims of a nuclear accident in the event that the $560 million ceiling on liability is exceeded."[22] Surely Burger's alleged "reasoning" is inapplicable to nuclear weapons. The point, as Professor Morris tells us, is that the danger created by nuclear weaponry is of such enormity that Americans are being deprived of their right to personal and psychic well-being.[23]

Nuclear weapons, accordingly, constitute an "anticipatory taking" contrary to the fifth amendment and an "anticipatory" deprivation of life, liberty and property without due process of law. Due process, Justice Felix Frankfurter stated in 1950, "is that which comports with the

---

L.J. 75 (1982).

19. 431 F. Supp. 203 (1977). For further discussion of "anticipatory" deprivation of life, liberty and property see Miller, *The Constitutional Challenge of Nuclear Weapons: A Note on the Obligation to Ward off Extinction*, ___ Brooklyn Int'l L. J. ___ (1983).

20. *Carolina Envtl. Study Group*, 431 F. Supp. at 222.

21. *Duke Power Co.*, 438 U.S. at 84.

22. *Id.* at 93.

23. Morris, *supra* note 16.

deepest notions of what is fair and right and just."[24] It means, in current context and to adopt Judge McMillan's classification, that Americans have a right to be free from both the *immediate* and the the *potential* effects of nuclear weaponry.[25]

The immediate effects are bad enough. Storage of bombs and nuclear waste present as yet insoluble problems of safety. Furthermore, as Ruth Leger Sivard has concluded, increasingly vast sums are being spent to purchase what may be an illusory sense of security at the price of economic stagnation, repression, and poverty.[26] I have elsewhere sought to draw attention to the emergence of a new "constitution of control";[27] surely, nuclear weapons contribute to that development.

The potential effects are far worse. Drawing upon Judge McMillan's opinion, the following conclusions seem to be beyond argument.

First, there is a high probability of nuclear war, coming either by design or by accident.

Second, there is no escape from the impact of nuclear war.

Third, civil defense measures cannot possibly protect the residents of any city in the United States.

Fourth, the risks involved in nuclear weaponry are not the types that a responsible government places upon its citizens.

Fifth, there is no way that Americans can be compensated for losses of life, liberty, or property.

Sixth, nuclear war will be the "last epidemic." There is no way that the health services of the nation could take care of the casualties of such a war.

Given those effects, the conclusion of an anticipatory violation of the fifth amendment is unanswerable.

I do not, it is emphasized, wish to be placed in the position of one who uses constitutional argumentation as "desperate legal acrobat-

---

24. Solesbee v. Balkcom, 339 U.S. 9, 16 (1950) (Frankfurter, J., dissenting). As was his practice, Frankfurter did not divulge how he determined those "deepest notions of what is fair and right and just." *Id.* Compare his concurring opinion in Louisiana *ex rel.* Francis v. Resweber, 329 U.S. 459, 466 (1947).

25. *Carolina Envtl. Study Group,* 431 F. Supp. at 209.

26. R. SIVARD, WORLD MILITARY AND SOCIAL EXPENDITURES, 1981 (1982).

27. *See* A. MILLER, DEMOCRATIC DICTATORSHIP: THE EMERGENT CONSTITUTION OF CONTROL (1981).

ics."[28] The ideas presented may be new, but I do not think they are foolish. If our modes of thinking about constitutions and constitutionalism are to be changed, the basic requirement, in the words of Alexander Pekelis, is to have

> the will to discover the will to enlarge the tiny segment of the world we know, the will to learn and to do better, the firm and deepseated conviction that men may, again and again, in everyone's lifetime, see "thin with distance, thin but dead ahead, the line of unimaginable coasts."[29]

There may well be an "arrogance of humanism"[30]—the belief that humankind through the exercise of reason can control the future. Surely, however, we have to act as if what humans do can make a difference, as if they have the intelligence, the will, and the stamina to ward off extinction.

A final note: calling nuclear weapons a constitutional problem does not, of course, mean that they are *ipso facto* not a political problem. As Professors Alfange and McDowell note, those weapons should be dealt with by the political process.[31] My belief is that the courts, and specifically the Supreme Court, are deeply immersed in politics and, indeed, would be quite meaningless unless seen as part of the political process. Judges are important political actors—now, in the past, and certainly in the future. Professor Judith Shklar has observed that the prevailing ideology of lawyers is "legalism"—the notion that law is somthing separate and apart from the remainder of society.[32] But, as any sociologist of law knows, law and the state are closely intertwined. To call for a political solution to the nuclear threat does not foreclose action by courts. Quite the contrary. The Supreme Court sits as an authoritative faculty of political theory and of social ethics. It can, should the Justices so wish, set standards toward which all Americans can aspire.[33]

---

28. Levinson, Book Review, *Self-Evident Truths in the Declaration of Independence,* 57 TEX. L. REV. 847, 858 (1979).

29. Pekelis, *The Case for a Jurisprudence of Welfare,* in LAW AND SOCIAL ACTION 1 (M. Konvitz ed. 1950).

30. *See* D. EHRENFELD, THE ARROGANCE OF HUMANISM (1978).

31. *See* Alfange, *supra* note 18; McDowell, *supra* note 10.

32. J. SHKLAR, LEGALISM (1964).

33. It is worth special mention that the General Counsel of the Department of

On the other hand, as Professor Gerhard Casper has cogently observed, "constitutional rules are authoritative regardless of whether courts are able to interpret and enforce them.[34] Congress and the President, Casper continues, "must be ready to reconsider fundamental constitutional policies and basic propositions of political theory."[35] So they do. The Constitution is not a mere lawyers' document, not a plaything (or workthing) of lawyers only. It is the vehicle of the nation's life. And government officers, including the President, swear to "preserve, protect and defend the Constitution of the United States."[36] If that means anything, and surely it is not mere *brutum fulmen,* it means cognizance of and adherence to a constitutional duty to insure the preservation of the nation and the values that they are embedded in the Constitution. In the age of thermonuclear bombs, that can only mean the total elimination of such weapons wherever they may be. In sum, no useful purpose is served by calling nuclear weaponry a "policy" question or a problem of "politics," for all branches of government deal with policy and politics.[37]

Defense, William H. Taft, IV, acknowledges "the existence of the constitutional duty to reduce and, if possible, eliminate the threat that nuclear weapons pose to the individual freedom and rights of Americans set out in the Constitutions." Taft, *Letter from the Government,* 7 Nova. L.J. 141, 143 (1982). One hopes that Mr. Taft's recognition of such a constitutional *duty* is communicated to the Secretary of Defense, the Joint Chiefs of Staff, and the President — and that they agree that such a duty rests upon their shoulders. I am, of course pleased to learn that my view on the existence of a constitutional duty has drawn the approbation of a high government officer — who, indeed, advances even more constitutional arguments than do I in support of such a position. Mr. Taft's letter merits wide circulation.

34. Casper, *Constitutional Constraints on the Conduct of Foreign and Defense Policy; A Nonjudicial Model,* 43 U. Chi. L. Rev. 463, 473 (1976).

35. *Id.*

36. U.S. Const. art. II, § 1, cl. 7.

37. For discussion, *see* A. Miller, Toward Increased Judicial Activism: The Political Role of the Supreme Court (1982); M. Shapiro, Courts: A Comparative and Political Analysis, (1981); J. Griffith, The Politics of the Judiciary (1977); Griffith, *The Political Constitution,* 42 Mod. L. Rev. 1 (1979); Miller, *Dames & Moore v. Regan: A Political Decision by a Political Court,* 29 U.C.L.A. L. Rev. 1104 (1982).

PART III
AN ENVIRO-MEDICAL CONTEXT

26.
Consequences of Nuclear Weapons Use as Viewed by an Environmental Lawyer*

Frank P. Grad**

There is a risk that environmental or ecological concerns about nuclear weapons use may be trivialized and treated as a kind of sick joke. Does anyone really care whether the Abrams tank violates automotive emissions standards? Does anyone really care whether the snail darter or the peregrine falcon survives another nuclear attack? Viewed in this narrow fashion, environmental concerns are minor indeed. The environmental consequences I have in mind are of a greater, not to say central nature in the consideration of the consequences of a nuclear attack, because the environmental consequences are so closely connected with the immediate destruction and injury of human beings and with the future of the life of man on our planet. Moreover, the ecological consequences of nuclear weapons use compel us to face up to difficult legal and moral issues.

The sequence of events following the use of twenty kiloton nuclear bombs in Hiroshima and Nagasaki has been described in some detail.[1] The vast number of persons killed and maimed has been documented, as has the extent of the physical destruction, and the destruction of the capacity of governments and other institutions to respond appropriately. Yet the use of nuclear weapons at Nagasaki and Hiroshima (directed at a non-combatant civilian population as other nuclear weapons are likely to be in the future) was a "limited" use of small bombs by current measures. One megaton bombs are now regarded as mere tactical weapons. Nonetheless, even such a "limited" nuclear attack produces long-range and substantial ecological consequences—in terms of impact on human genetics, plant and animal life, and in terms of the impact on increases in background radiation.

Our good and serviceable planet is capable of withstanding even some severe ecological insults, and the scars on the landscape from such insults

---

* This essay is based on remarks delivered at the Conference on Nuclear Weapons and Law held at Nova University Center for the Study of Law on February 5, 1983.

** Chamberlain Professor of Legislation, Columbia University Law School.

are local and, superficially, seem to be transitory. That's because we bury the dead if there are any to be found, and we bury the severely injured after they die. We also clear the rubble and rebuild the cities, with a fitting memorial here and there. But the increase in background radiation from weapons use and testing will be there for a long time, as will the genetic damage to man and other living things, with increased incidence of carcinomas and of premature aging.

Because the scars from limited uses of smaller nuclear devices can be played down, the notion of limited nuclear war has achieved some plausibility. In *The Third World War, August 1985*, for instance, General Sir John Hackett and his NATO colleagues[2] project a Soviet first-strike nuclear attack on the city of Birmingham, England (leaving some 300,000 dead within minutes, and 250,000 seriously and 500,000 less seriously injured), followed by a retaliatory U.S. strike against the city of Minsk, with similar results. Again, it is clear that the General's novel aimed its nuclear missiles at civilian populations.

Cumulatively, many limited, relatively low-level nuclear attacks will have devastating and long-lasting effects, though not of the cataclysmic kind produced by a massive nuclear war.

Ecological consequences—and health consequences flowing from changed environmental conditions—are of significance only to survivors. The greater the confrontation, the fewer survivors, and the fewer ecological concerns after the event. Thus, we must consider the survival of man's habitat, of his natural environment, in advance of its destruction, because it is unlikely that there will be too many people around to consider it, let alone do anything about it, after the habitat has been severely damaged or destroyed. In *The Fate of the Earth* Jonathan Schell notes that "what happened at Hiroshima was less than a millionth part of a holocaust at present levels of world nuclear armament,"[3] and he relies on sources that project the use of ten thousand weapons of one megaton each, a total yield of 10,000 megatons.[4] An attack of this nature would reduce tens of millions of people to ashes, and would destroy most of the physical plant of the country, turning vast areas into "immense infernal regions, literally tens of thousands of square miles in area, from which escape is impossible."[5] In the process, the natural basis of life for the future would also be destroyed for the few persons who might somehow manage to survive. Aside from an irradiated environment, with gamma rays and beta particles doing their work of destruction, livestock and most useful plant life would be killed off, and there would be practically irreversible impact on the ozone layer, and on biota in the oceans. Injury to the ozone layer, which provides a shield against the sun's radiation, would give rise to deadly skin cancers, and the destruction of life in the oceans would kill off our main source of oxygen, already depleted by firestorms.

There would also be vast changes in climate, caused by the firestorms and by the masses of particulate matter, resulting in cutting off of sunlight and in reducing the temperature. The full extent of these impacts can only be surmised. But we have reason to know that these impacts would be major, persistent, and world-wide. The use of nuclear weapons boomerangs because the fallout and the ecological impact cannot be restricted to the target area.

I shall leave to others the international legal issue of the use, by any nation, of nuclear weapons against civilian populations, and I shall also leave to others the discussion of the rationality of the nuclear arms race and of its self-defeating aspects discussed by George F. Kennan in his recent book on *The Nuclear Delusion*.[6] But I will mention some general principles that underlie much of our environmental law, and our law relating to the protection of man's habitat. Some of this is stated, rather grandiloquently, in our National Environmental Policy Act that seeks to protect our natural heritage against other, lesser invasions and insults. Most significantly, Congress declares that it is the national policy,

> to create and maintain conditions under which man and nature can exist in productive harmony, and fulfill the social, economic, and other requirements of present and future generations of Americans.[7]

Perhaps deeper, more philosophically grounded approaches are called for, but in considering the law of environmental protection, the thought occurs that we may well be the only planet that has produced advanced forms of life, and that has been hospitable to the advanced biological development represented by man. It would be a great shame to destroy such a long and interesting development. It seems wrong to destroy the environment in which such a development can thrive and produce not only the means for physical survival, but which has also made it possible to produce the cultural, artistic, and intellectual attainments of mankind.

Those of us who enjoy life on earth also have an interest in affording similar opportunities to our children and grandchildren—and, if possible, to generations to follow.

It is probably useless to debate whether the earth and its resources are here for us to exploit, but it is clear that there is no justification for the wanton destruction of our habitat, or for the wanton and unreasonable infliction of persistent, irreversible damage on our ecological resources. It has sometimes been suggested that we are trustees for future generations, or at least mere life tenants who must not commit waste. The characterization of our hold on earth, or the terms of our lease, matter little as long as we retain our sense of responsibility and avoid the infliction of unnecessary harm in nuclear confrontations which cannot be won.[8]

In short, with all our problems on this rather serviceable planet, we have a chance. Let's not damage it beyond repair.

NOTES

1. J. Hersey, Hiroshima (1946); J. Schell, The Fate of the Earth 36-43 (1982).

2. J. Hackett, The Third World War, August 1985 (1980).

3. Schell, *supra* note 1, at 45,

4. *Id.* at 55.

5. *Id.* at 57.

6. G. Kennan, The Nuclear Delusion: Soviet-American Relations in the Atomic Age (1982).

7. Pub. L. 91-190, 42 U.S.C. 4321-4347, Jan. 1, 1970, as amended by Pub. L. 94-83, Aug. 9, 1975. This portion of Title I of the National Environmental Policy Act reads as follows:

Sec. 101. (a) The Congress, recognizing the profound impact of man's activity on the interrelations of all components of the natural environment, particularly the profound influences of population growth, high density urbanization, industrial expansion, resource exploitation, and new and expanding technological advances and recognizing further the critical importance of restoring and maintaining environmental quality to the overall welfare and development of man, declares that it is the continuing policy of the Federal Government, in cooperation with state and local governments, and other concerned public and private organizations, to use all practical means and measures, including financial and technical assistance, in a manner calculated to foster and promote the general welfare, to create and maintain conditions under which man and nature can exist in productive harmony, and fulfill the social, economic, and other requirements of present and future generations of Americans.

(b) In order to carry out the policy set forth in this Act, it is the continuing responsibility of the Federal Government to use all practicable means, consistent with other essential considerations of national policy, to improve and coordinate Federal plans, functions, programs, and resources to the end that the Nation may—

(1) Fulfill the responsibilities of each generation as trustee of the environment for succeeding generations;

(2) Assure for all Americans safe, healthful, productive, and esthetically and culturally pleasing surroundings;

(3) Attain the widest range of beneficial uses of the environment without degradation, risk to health or safety, or other undesirable and unintended consequences;

(4) Preserve important historic, cultural, and natural aspects of our national heritage, and maintain, wherever possible, an environment which supports diversity, and variety of individual choice;

(5) Achieve a balance between population and resource use which will permit high standards of living and a wide sharing of life's amenities; and

(6) Enhance the quality of renewable resources and approach the maximum attainable recycling of depletable resources.

8. "We, for the most part, are under no illusions about the dangers of a nuclear war between the major powers," Mr. Weinberger [Secretary of Defense] said in his annual report to Congress. "We believe that neither side could win such a war." New York Times, Feb. 1, 1983, p. 1 col. 5.

27.
Medical Consequences of Nuclear War*

Jay Kerzner, M.D.**

One may ask: "Why should a doctor be talking about nuclear war? Isn't that out of his realm of expertise? Shouldn't that just be a subject for military and defense people, or government leaders?" The answer is that what is at issue in the nuclear arms race is *human life and survival.* And, while this means that the threat of nuclear war is everyone's concern, it means also that doctors have a particular contribution to make.

The nuclear weapons of today are capable of causing death and casualties of a magnitude unprecedented in history. The cost in human life is often obscured by jargon such as "counterforce exchange" and "surgical strike." We read of generals and political leaders "playing out" scenarios of nuclear war on computers, which sounds like our kids playing "Space Invaders" or "Star Wars" on TV computer games. (One TV ad says "you can wipe out a planet with just the press of a button.") And, most frightening of all, members of the present administration talk of fighting a limited, protracted, but winnable nuclear war—that is, actually using nuclear weapons; they talk of the so-called nuclear war fighting scenarios or Nuclear Utilization Theories (NUTS)—a prospect that since Hiroshima and Nagasaki has been regarded as unthinkable. Physicians in the anti-nuclear war movement, on the other hand, have been suggesting that we look at what these weapons actually do to people, that we move away from the abstractions and the jargon and the euphemisms and the computer scenarios, and look at the cost in human death and suffering. Since survival is inherent in "winning" or, to use the currently preferred term, "prevailing," in a nuclear war, we must take a hard look at the concept of survival in a nuclear war.

---

* This essay is based on remarks delivered at the Conference on Nuclear Weapons and Law held at Nova University Center for the Study of Law on February 5, 1983.

** Associate Professor of Cardiology, University of Miami School of Medicine; Member, National Board of Directors, Physicians for Social Responsibility.

In discussing the medical consequences of nuclear war, we need to consider two categories: (1) the direct, primary, or immediate effect of a nuclear explosion, and (2) the delayed, secondary, long-term effect. It is well to keep in mind that today's nuclear weapons, often measured in megatons, are far more powerful than the bombs used on Hiroshima and Nagasaki.

The direct, immediate destructive effect of nuclear weapons occurs principally by three mechanisms—blast, heat, and radiation. Blast does two things: (1) it causes static overpressure, which is like a giant sledgehammer out of the sky, and (2) it causes dynamic pressure, or high winds which may be up to five hundred miles per hour. The blast will level everything in the area around its point of impact—ground zero—and will cause heavy structural damage to the surrounding area. Deaths and all manner of traumatic injuries due to blast result from the collapse of occupied buildings, from people being blown by the high winds into objects, from buildings falling on people or objects blowing into people. Glass windows will be turned into thousands of tiny, sharp missiles traveling at high speed.

The heat generated by a nuclear explosion at its center is equivalent to the heat of the sun. It causes, even before the blast wave, an intense thermal pulse—like a two-second flash from an enormous sunlamp. This intense heat will vaporize everything in the immediate area of ground zero. It will cause extensive fires and tens of thousands of burn injuries. The fires could coalesce into a firestorm, turned in on itself by inrushing high winds, which would then cause people trapped in shelters to be burned or asphyxiated (as happened in Dresden and Hamburg during World War II) and this would extend the lethal area five-fold.

Radiation is the most insidious effect of nuclear weapons because it isn't anything you can touch or feel. It can, nevertheless, cause acute radiation sickness which can be fatal (assuming you haven't been killed by blast or fire), radioactive fallout which may remain at dangerous levels for two to four weeks and cover an area of almost a thousand square miles, and, as was learned from the long-term follow-up study of Hiroshima survivors, an increased incidence in future years of all types of cancer.

If a one megaton bomb were dropped in the downtown of Miami, a city with a total area population of two million three hundred thousand, there would be approximately four hundred sixty-nine thousand deaths and five hundred thousand seriously injured, yielding a total casualty rate of forty-two percent of the population. If a nuclear attack were directed not at a civilian population but at military targets, which are concentrated most heavily in the midwest—that is, a so-called counterforce exchange or "limited" nuclear war—then it is estimated that there would be about twenty million deaths plus the radioactive fallout that would be carried by winds to the east coast. To many defense strategists, twenty million deaths is somehow an "acceptable" figure, one that is still consistent with the notion of "prevailing" in a nuclear exchange. If we consider an all-out nuclear war between the United States and the Soviet Union, and there is no guarantee that a so-called "limited" counterforce strike against military targets could in fact be limited so as not to escalate into an all-out nuclear war, then it is estimated that the United States would sustain about one hundred forty-five million deaths and the Soviet Union one hundred fifteen million. This would be, in other words, mutual genocide; it is hard to see how issues such as communism or capitalism, our political system or their system, right or wrong, or good or evil would matter very much.

In terms of medical response to a nuclear attack, the bottom line is that *there is no effective medical response*. I emphasize this because this is a major point physicians have been making, lest it be felt that the health care system can respond effectively as it does to conventional military casualities or natural disasters. During a nuclear attack, doctors and nurses are killed and injured along with everyone else, and hospitals, equipment, drugs, and medical supplies are destroyed. And with the likelihood of multiple weapons exploding in surrounding areas, there would be no help available from outside as there was for Hiroshima and Nagasaki. There would be no way of transporting injured people to a health care facility, and with destruction to the terrain, collapsed buildings and rubble in the streets, it would be difficult for health care workers to reach the sick and injured. In fact, most people would die without even the administration of narcotics for their pain, and, as it has been said, the survivors would truly envy the dead.

The case of burn treatment brings home the ineffectuality of medical care. To treat one serious burn victim requires a special intensive care facility, teams of doctors and nurses, and vast amounts of medical supplies. In the entire United States there are about two hundred burn intensive care unit beds. As I mentioned before, a nuclear explosion would cause tens of thousands of such injuries in one locality.

Let us turn now from the immediate destructive effects to the delayed or long-term effects of nuclear explosions. It is in this realm that we see how nuclear weapons threaten human survival way beyond the numbers of people killed directly by the explosion, extraordinary though these numbers may be. We begin to see how the entire complex biological, social, and economic fabric of society can be disrupted, why physicians have called nuclear war "the last epidemic," and why, as Jonathan Schell discussed in his book *The Fate of the Earth,* there is the potential for destroying all of human civilization, present and future.

Let's take a look at what a post-attack world would be like. There would be vast destruction of buildings and structures, making the environment almost unrecognizable and making shelter from the elements a problem. There would be no transportation, no electric power or other sources of energy, and no effective communications. There would be widespread radioactive contamination of the food and water supply, and massive shortages as stockpiles are depleted. Thus, people would die of starvation, dehydration, and exposure to the elements.

Infectious diseases would be rampant in epidemic proportion. Exposure to radiation would lead to stillbirths and fetal malformations, genetic defects, and an increased incidence of cancer in later years.

In a broader dimension, the whole ecosystem—the complex interlinking chain of environment and plant and animal life that sustains human existence —would be threatened. Animals and plants would be destroyed in large numbers and the survivors would undergo genetic mutation. There would be climatic changes and temperature changes which would affect future ability to grow food, and could cause either another ice age or, alternatively, melting of the polar ice cap and massive flooding. The ozone layer of the stratosphere would be depleted causing everything—people, animals, plants, the soil—to be exposed to ultra-violet rays of the sun which can cause retinal damage and blindness. Beyond these effects on the environment that we have some knowledge of, there are many about which we don't yet know, and others whose severity we can't estimate. We need to be concerned just as much about what we don't know as about what we do know.

Existence or survival in such a post-attack world would be harsh. It would be like living in medieval times or an even more primitive era where there was no technology, no complex economic or social structure, and where a premium would be placed on the ability to obtain the rudiments of living—food, water, clothing, and shelter. People's psychological will to continue to struggle for existence and their desire to procreate in this post-attack world might well be eroded. This scenario is to be contrasted with the glib picture of prevailing and surviving a nuclear war presented by those who talk about dusting themselves off, getting our industry rolling again, and getting back to normal, although they say it might take two to four years.

Central to the notion of fighting and winning a nuclear war is the belief that civil defense measures can be effective in saving large numbers of lives during a nuclear attack. To follow this line of thinking, neither side would launch an attack unless it felt it could protect a significant amount of its population (whatever that means) from a retaliatory strike. The Federal Emergency Management Agency (FEMA), which is in charge of United States civil defense, has proposed a 4.3 billion dollar project over a seven-year period which it thinks will prevent 80 to 90 percent of the estimated deaths from any type of nuclear attack.

How do they propose to do this? They would rely on mass evacuation (called crisis relocation) and hastily built fallout shelters. This is based on a scenario in which nuclear war would occur in a time of increasing global tensions. The Russians, either in planning themselves for a nuclear strike or in anticipation of a possible U.S. strike, would begin evacuating the cities. This mass movement of people would be detected by our satellites, and then we could begin to evacuate our cities—a process which it is said would take three to five days. After relocating to designated host areas, people would begin to construct fallout shelters in a manner suggested by T. K. Jones of our Defense Department: "You dig a hole, cover it with a couple of doors, and then throw three feet of dirt on top. It's the dirt that does it. Everybody is going to make it if there are enough shovels to go around."[1]

The question from a public health standpoint is, given what we know about the consequences of nuclear war, how effective is this civil defense program likely to be? The prospect of evacuating the populations of large metropolitan areas and relocating them to small rural areas raises many problems. To begin with, how do we know we would have the three to five days warning necessary to begin the process in time? We may only have fifteen or twenty minutes—the time it takes between detection of the launch of an intercontinental missile and the time it lands. The FEMA plan presumes that people would proceed in an orderly fashion out of the cities according to some prescribed mode, even though faced with the possibility of nuclear extinction. Can you imagine this plan in New York City, or even in Miami (where several of the main exit routes are two-lane highways)? Then there are the problems for the host areas attempting to accommodate the huge influx of people. And what is the certainty that the host areas won't also be targeted for attack?

The protection offered by shelters also needs to be critically examined. If one were in an area of direct attack, shelters would afford no effective protection against blast, and with regard to fire, they might even worsen one's chance of survival.

What about life in a shelter for up to thirty days? What about oxygen supply, food and water supply, ventilation, elimination of wastes, treating the sick and injured, and removing the dead? There are a myriad of health hazards—physical and mental—that would result from shelter life after a nuclear attack has devastated the surroundings. And what about the long-term problems after emerging from the shelters? What about the social fabric of life and the long-term problems of the environment?

For all these reasons, the civil defense program proposed by FEMA would be ineffective in dealing with the effects of nuclear war, just as we said the response of the health care system would be ineffective. To pretend otherwise with cheerful, glib booklets making evacuation and shelter-building look like a family picnic in the park is to perpetrate a cruel hoax. And, worse than that, instituting mass evacuation of the cities because of the perception, real or mistaken, of imminent attack, might itself bring on an attack. It can feed into the mutual fear and paranoia bred by the nuclear arms race. If a strategy of actually using nuclear weapons—the so-called nuclear war-fighting strategy as outlined by the Defense Department—rests on the notion that civil defense will effectively protect the survival of a majority of the population, then the facts and the logic of this strategy ought to be re-examined.

A most frightening aspect of the nuclear arms race is the potential for human error and/or computer malfunction to lead to accidental nuclear war. We have had several false alarms—one caused by the failure of a computer micro-chip which cost forty-five cents, one when someone inadvertently inserted into the system a training tape of a Russian launch, and, others when the rising of the moon and the flight of a flock of geese have been mistaken for a missile launch. The danger of newer weapons systems such as the MX and the Pershing II, which have greater accuracy and can hit their target in a shorter time, is that they could force a strategy of *launch on warning,* that is, relying completely on computer and radar systems not only to detect a presumed launch, but to start a retaliatory launch. We have all had experiences with computer errors: in medicine the computers foul up laboratory tests, and, in everyday life, we get mistakes in bank statements or department store bills due to errors of the computer or its operator.

What about human error? What about the people with their fingers on the button or key? A recent report revealed that about five thousand persons per year in the United States missile system are removed because of alcohol or drug abuse, emotional instability, criminal behavior, or negligence. What about the Soviet Union where alcoholism is rampant? The possibility of accidental nuclear war should cause us to examine trends in the nuclear arms race and ask whether newer weapons systems increase our security or decrease it.

The arms race itself costs society huge amounts of money that might otherwise be used for health and social needs. For example, in 1982 the MX missile program, which has caused a great deal of controversy and may never be deployed, cost 2.9 billion dollars. In contrast, cuts totaling less than the cost of the MX missile program were made in such federally funded health and social programs as maternal and child health, medicaid, alcohol, drug abuse and mental health, and food stamps. The cost of one Trident ballistic missile submarine (1.6 billion dollars) is equal to the amount cut from the child nutrition program.

Worldwide, the cost of obtaining a sanitary water supply, the lack of which causes 80 percent of the world's illnesses, would be the equivalent of the cost of three weeks of the arms race. The World Health Organization was able a decade ago to eliminate smallpox for the cost of five hours of the arms race. Thus it would appear that even without the explosion of a single weapon, the arms race is destructive of human life.

Lastly, we ought to examine briefly the psychological aspects of the nuclear arms race. At the heart of the nuclear weapons problem is the way people think—government leaders, military people, ordinary citizens. It is not the weapons themselves that cause nuclear war, or the threat of nuclear war, but the people who build them and use them. In particular it is the way we think about nuclear weapons, national security, and the Russians.

For example, there is the attitude among many to regard nuclear weapons in the same way as conventional weapons, except that they are just larger and more powerful. This gives rise to the notion that one can gain some destructive advantage in the way that over the centuries if you had more bows and arrows, or more tanks and battleships than your adversary, you had a military edge over him. Psychiatrist John Mack calls attention to the mindsets that operate here, and divides people into what he calls *"think-ables"* and *"unthinkables."* The "thinkables" believe that nuclear war would be terrible, but that it is still survivable in a meaningful sense, and that one should plan in terms of a nuclear war actually occurring and even for its aftermath. This of course gives rise to war-fighting scenarios, civil defense, and weapons superiority strategies to increase our security. The "unthinkables," on the other hand, in Mack's paradigm, have different assumptions and different conclusions. They believe that a nuclear war once begun would create a disaster of such magnitude that it is not meaningful to plan in terms of its actual occurrence. They believe that building newer weapons merely escalates the arms race, increases the threat of nuclear war, and decreases our security.

The concept of mindsets is particularly applicable to people's view of the Russians. There is a point of view, a mindset, that the Russians are the source of all evil in the world, that they are bent on world domination and will use any means including nuclear war to achieve this end. They are a godless society without the same regard for human life that we have. Their experiences in World War II with twenty million deaths, and with the millions who died in the civil war and the purges have inured them to the idea of mass death. Therefore, it is believed, they are prepared to accept massive numbers of casualties in a nuclear war.

A different mindset, on the other hand, can take the same fact—twenty million deaths in World War II—and draw a different conclusion—that because of this experience the Russians are especially sensitive to the prospect of mass deaths in a nuclear war and are deeply desirous of preventing it. In this mindset we and the Russians have a common interest in survival that transcends all differences between us. Therefore it is in our interest as well as their interest to prevent nuclear war.

Modes of thinking are the central, focal point in the nuclear arms race. As Albert Einstein said, "The splitting of the atom has changed everything except our way of thinking, and thus we drift toward unparallelled catastrophe."

In summary, the main issue in the nuclear arms race is the threat to human life and survival. When we look at the effects of today's nuclear weapons, we readily see that they can cause death and destruction of unprecedented, almost incomprehensible magnitude. Nuclear war could easily be "the last epidemic." *There is no effective medical response.* Civil defense measures not only would be ineffective, but they promote an illusion of survivability that supports a dangerous strategy of actually using nuclear weapons with the feeling that in some areas someone can prevail. The ways that people think—about nuclear weapons, about security, and about each other on a global scale—are a central feature of the nuclear arms race.

What is needed is *preventive medicine.* The only way to deal with a disease you can't cure or treat is to prevent it.

NOTE

1. *Quoted in* R. Scheer, With Enough Shovels: Reagan, Bush, and Nuclear War (1982).

Index

ABOUT THE CONTRIBUTORS

DEAN ALFANGE, JR., is Professor of Political Science and Acting Chancellor at the University of Massachusetts. He has an A.B. from Hamilton College, an M.A. from Colorado, and a Ph. D from Cornell. A frequent contributor to political science and legal journals, in 1977-78 he was Visiting Scholar at Yale Law School.

HARRY H. ALMOND, JR., is Professor on the faculty of the National War College in Washington, D.C. A graduate of Yale University and Cornell University, he has his law degree from Harvard and also holds a Ph.D. in International Law from the London School of Economics and Political Science. Professor Almond has served as a member of the Executive Council of the American Society of International Law, as a Senior Attorney-Advisor for International Affairs in the Office of the Secretary of Defense of the United States and is a member of the London-based International Institute of Strategic Studies. He teaches as an Adjunct Professor at Georgetown University and is an expert on the law of war.

FLETCHER N. BALDWIN, JR., is Professor of Law at the Spessard L. Holland Law Center of the University of Florida. He has an A.B. and J.D. from the University of Georgia, and an LL.M. from Yale University. He has been a Fulbright Professor at Makerere University in Uganda, and has served as the Principal Investigator for the Center for Governmental Responsibility since 1973. He is an expert in constitutional law.

MILNER S. BALL is Professor of Law on the faculty of the University of Georgia School of Law. He has an A.B. from Princeton, an S.T.B. from Harvard, and a J.D. from the University of Georgia. He was a Fulbright Fellow at Tubingen and served on the staff of the Secretary of State's Advisory Committee on the United Nations Conference on the Human Environment. He teaches both constitutional and international law subjects.

RICHARD B. BILDER is Professor of Law at the University of Wisconsin Law School. He has a B.A. from Williams College and a J.D. from Harvard. He is a Vice-President of the American Society of International Law and serves on the Board of Editors of the American Journal of International Law. He has been a

Fulbright Scholar at Cambridge University in England, and an attorney in the Office of the Legal Advisor of the United States State Department. Professor Bilder is a member of the Consultative Council of the New York-based Lawyers' Committee on Nuclear Policy.

STANLEY C. BRUBAKER is Assistant Professor of Political Science at Colgate University. He has a B.A. from Miami University, and an M.A. and Ph. D. from the University of Virginia. A member of the American Political Science Association, he contributes to political and legal journals.

RICHARD FALK is Albert G. Milbank Professor of International Law and Practice at Princeton University. He has a B.S. from the University of Pennsylvania, an LL.B. from Yale, and a S.J.D. from Harvard Law School. He has been a member of the Executive Board and a Vice-President of the American Society of International Law, and currently serves on the Editorial Board of the American Journal of International Law. He is the author of many books, including *A Study of Future Worlds* and *Human Rights and State Sovereignty,* and editor of the four-volume series entitled *The Vietnam War and International Law.* Along with Burns Weston and Anthony D'Amato he authored *International Law and World Order,* one of the international law textbooks widely used in American law schools. Professor Falk is a member of the Consultative Council of the Lawyers' Committee on Nuclear Policy.

MARTIN FEINRIDER is Associate Professor of Law at Nova University Center for the Study of Law. He has a B.A., M.A., and J.D. from the State University of New York at Buffalo and an LL.M. in International Legal Studies from New York University School of Law. Additionally, he holds the Diploma, *cum laude,* of the Hague Academy of International Law and the Diploma of the International Institute of Human Rights in Strasbourg, France. Professor Feinrider is a member of the Consultative Council of the Lawyers' Committee on Nuclear Policy and organized the Conference on Nuclear Weapons and Law held at Nova Law Center on February 5, 1983.

THOMAS M. FRANCK is Professor of Law at the New York University School of Law. He has a B.A. and LL.B. from the University of British Columbia and an LL.M. and S.J.D. from Harvard Law School. He's been the Director of the Center for International Studies of New York University since 1965 and served as Director of the International Legal Program of the Carnegie Endowment for International Peace between 1973 and 1979. Professor Franck was Director of Research for the United Nations Institute for Training and Research during 1980-82. The author of many books, including *Foreign Policy by Congress* (with Edward Weisband), he is currently writing a book on the United States and the United Nations. He is Vice-President of the American Branch of the International Law Association, a member of the Executive Council of the American Society of International Law, and Editor-in-Chief of the American Journal of International Law.

JACK M. GOLDKLANG is Attorney-Advisor with the Office of Legal Counsel of the United States Department of Justice. He has his B.A. from Cornell University and his LL.B. from Harvard Law School. Mr. Goldklang has been a member of the

United States delegations to the United Nations Human Rights Commission and to the United Nations' Third Committee of the General Assembly. He was also a member of the U.S. delegation to the conference at which the American Convention on Human Rights was drafted, and appeared on behalf of the United States before the International Court of Justice in the U.S. v. Iran (Hostages Case).

FRANK P. GRAD is Joseph P. Chamberlain Professor of Legislation on the faculty of Columbia University Law School. He has an A.B. from Brooklyn College and an LL.B. from Columbia University Law School. He was a member of the Legal Advisory Committee of the U.S. Council on Environmental Quality and has authored, among other books, *Treatise on Environmental Law* and *Environmental Law: Sources and Problems.*

IREDELL JENKINS is Professor Emeritus of Philosophy at the University of Alabama. He has a B.A., M.A., and Ph. D. from the University of Virginia and is the author of *Social Order and the Limits of Law.*

JAY KERZNER is a practicing cardiologist and Clinical Associate Professor of Cardiology at the University of Miami School of Medicine. He has his B.A. from Swarthmore College and his M.D. from the University of Pennsylvania. He served as Chief of Cardiology at Hollywood Memorial Hospital from 1977 to 1979. He is on the National Board of Directors of Physicians for Social Responsibility and is Vice-President of the Miami Chapter. He has done extensive writing and speaking on the subject of medical consequences of nuclear weapons use.

DINESH KHOSLA is Associate Professor of Law on the faculty of the City University of New York Law School at Queens College. He has a B.Com., LL.B., and LL.M. from Delhi University, an M. Phil. from Nehru University, and an LL.M. and J.S.D. from Yale Law School. He has been a Lecturer in Law at Delhi University in India and a Law Fellow at Yale University. He is a member of the Law and Society Research Board of the International Sociology Association, and teaches comparative and international law subjects.

OVID C. LEWIS is Dean and Professor of Law at Nova University Center for the Study of Law. He has an A.B. from Duke University, an A.B. and J.D. from Rutgers University, and an LL.M. and J.S.D. from Columbia University. Before joining the Nova faculty, he was Professor of Law at Case Western Reserve University and the Dean of Salmon P. Chase College of Law in Kentucky. During 1977-78 he was Special Counsel to the Governor of Kentucky. He is an expert in constitutional law.

SAUL MENDLOVITZ is Professor of Law at the Rutgers (Newark) S.I. Newhouse Center for Law and Justice. He has a B.A. from Syracuse University and an M.A. and J.D. from the University of Chicago. He has served on the Executive Council of the American Society of International Law, and, since 1968, serves as Director of the World Order Models Project. Professor Mendlovitz is a member of the Consultative Council of the Lawyers' Committee on Nuclear Policy.

ELLIOTT L. MEYROWITZ is Vice-Chairperson of the New York-based Lawyers' Committee on Nuclear Policy and Adjunct Professor of Law at the Benjamin N. Cardozo School of Law of Yeshiva University. He has a B.A. from the University of North Carolina, an M.A. from the University of Pennsylvania, a J.D. from Rutgers University, and is currently a Ph. D. candidate in history at the University of Pennsylvania. He has served as a consultant to the Institute for World Order, as Executive Director of the Lawyers' Committee on Nuclear Policy and is currently an attorney in the Legal Department of Banker's Trust Company in New York City. He has done extensive writing and speaking on the subject of the illegality of nuclear weapons.

ARTHUR SELWYN MILLER is Professor Emeritus at the George Washington University National Law Center in Washington, D.C. and was the 1982-83 Distinguished Visiting Professor at Nova University Law Center. He has an A.B. from Willamette University, an LL.B. from Stanford, and a J.S.D. from Yale. He has been a Fellow of the Guggenheim Foundation, a Law Faculty Fellow with the Ford Foundation, a Consultant to the United States Senate Sub-Committee on Separation of Powers and Chief Consultant to the U.S. Senate Select Committee on Presidential Campaign Activities. An expert in constitutional law, Professor Miller has written a number of books, the most recent of which are *Democratic Dictatorship: The Emergent Constitution of Control* and *Toward Increased Judicial Activism: The Political Role of the Supreme Court.* He is a member of the Consultative Council of the Lawyers' Committee on Nuclear Policy.

JOHN NORTON MOORE is Walter L. Brown Professor and Director of the Center for Law and National Security and the Center for Oceans Law and Policy at the University of Virginia School of Law. He has a B.A. from Drew, an LL.B from Duke, and an LL.M. from University of Illinois College of Law. He has been Counselor on International Law to the U.S. Department of State, a member of the U.S. delegation to the U.N. General Assembly, U.S. Ambassador to the Third U.N. Conference on the Law of The Sea, and a Fellow at the Woodrow Wilson Center. He is a member of the Board of Editors of the American Journal of International Law.

ARVAL A. MORRIS is Professor of Law at the University of Washington School of Law. He has a B.A. from Colorado College, an M.A. and a J.D. from the University of Colorado, an LL.M. from Yale Law School, and an LL.D. from Colorado College. He has been a Fellow of the American Council of Learned Societies at Oxford University, and Senior Fulbright Lecturer at Freiburg.

W. MICHAEL REISMAN is Hohfeld Professor of Jurisprudence at Yale Law School. He has his LL.B. from Hebrew University and an LL.M. and J.S.D. from Yale. He has been a Fulbright Fellow in the Netherlands, is a member of the Board of Editors of the American Journal of International Law, and in 1981 gave the Harold D. Lasswell Memorial Lecture at the American Society of International Law 75th Anniversary Convocation. Professor Reisman has published widely in the field of international law and, along with Professor Myres McDougal, wrote *International Law in Contemporary Perspective,* one of the international law textbooks widely used in American law schools.

CAROL A. ROEHRENBECK is Associate Professor of Law and Director of the Law Library at Nova University Center for the Study of Law. She has a B.A. from Delaware and an M.L.S. and J.D. from Rutgers (Newark). She serves on the Law Library Advisory Committee to the Inter-American Court on Human Rights.

B.V.A. RÖLING is Professor Emeritus of International Law and Polemology (peace research) at the University of Groningen in the Netherlands. He was Netherlands Judge on the International Military Tribunal for the Far East after World War II, and later served his country as Justice on the Special Court of Cassation and as a member of the Dutch delegation to the United Nations General Assembly. He founded and was Director of the Polemological Institute at Groningen, and has authored a number of books, including *International Law in an Expanded World, The Science of War and Peace,* and *The Law of War and Dubious Weapons.*

AVIAM SOIFER is Professor of Law at Boston University School of Law. He has a B.A., M.U.S., and J.D. from Yale, and was 1976-77 Law and Humanities Fellow at Harvard.

WILLIAM HOWARD TAFT, IV is General Counsel of the Department of Defense. He has an A.B. from Yale and a J.D. from Harvard Law School, and has had a distinguished career in government.

BURNS H. WESTON is the Bessie Dutton Murray Professor of Law at the University of Iowa College of Law. He has a B.A. from Oberlin College, and an LL.B. and J.S.D. from Yale. He has been Director of the Center for World Order Studies, Senior Fellow and Director of the Transnational Academic Program of the Institute for World Order, and Chairperson of the Executive Committee of the Consortium on Peace Research, Education, and Development. He currently serves as a member of the Board of Editors of the American Journal of International Law and as a member of the Editorial Committee of the Bulletin of Peace Proposals published by the International Peace Research Institute of Oslo, Norway. An expert in international law, Professor Weston has authored several books including *International Law and World Order* (with Richard Falk and Anthony D'Amato), one of the international law textbooks widely used in American law schools. He is a member of the Consultative Council of the Lawyers' Committee on Nuclear Policy.

About the Editors

ARTHUR SELWYN MILLER is Leo Goodwin, Sr. Distinguished Professor of Law at Nova University Center for the Study of Law and Professor Emeritus of Law at George Washington University. His previously published books include *The Modern Corporate State: Private Governments and the American Constitution* (1976), *The Supreme Court: Myth and Reality* (1978), *Social Change and Fundamental Law: America's Evolving Constitution* (1979), *Democratic Dictatorship: The Emergent Constitution of Control* (1981), *Toward Increased Judicial Activism: The Political Role of the Supreme Court* (1982), *A "Capacity for Outrage": The Judicial Odyssey of J. Skelly Wright* (1984), and *On Courts and Democracy: Selected Nonjudicial Writings of J. Skelly Wright* (1984).

MARTIN FEINRIDER is Associate Professor of Law at Nova University Center for the Study of Law, where he specializes in international law and the protection of human rights. He is a member of the Consultative Council of the Lawyers' Committee on Nuclear Policy, and has written on international law subjects for a variety of publications, including the *Encyclopedia of Public International Law.*